Th

3 | D1339017

**This book is due for return not later than the last
date stamped below, unless recalled sooner.**

VERSITY
ERVICES

WITHDRAWN
FROM STOCK

7 DAY LOAN

The Economics of Taxation: Principles, Policy and Practice

Twelfth Edition

2012/13

Simon James

Christopher Nobes

FISCAL

PUBLICATIONS

The Economics of Taxation Twelfth Edition 2012/13

First Published Phillip Allen Publishers 1978
Second edition 1983
Third edition 1988
First published under the Prentice Hall Imprint, fourth edition 1992
Fifth edition 1996
Sixth edition 1998
Seventh edition 2000
Seventh edition revised 2001/2002
Seventh edition revised 2002/2003
Seventh edition revised 2003/2004
Seventh edition revised 2004/2005
Seventh edition revised 2005/2006
Seventh edition revised 2006/2007
Seventh edition revised 2007/2008
Eighth edition 2008
Ninth edition 2009
Tenth edition 2010
Eleventh edition 2011
Twelfth edition 2012

Copyright © 2008, 2009, 2010, 2011, 2012 Simon James and Christopher Nobes

The rights of Simon James and Christopher Nobes to be identified as authors of this work have been asserted by them in accordance with the Copyright, Designs, and Patents Act 1988.

For more information, contact Fiscal Publications, Unit 100, The Guildhall Edgbaston Park Road, Birmingham, B15 2TU, UK or visit: http://www.fiscalpublications.com

All rights reserved by AccountingEducation.com Ltd 2012. The text of this publication, or any part thereof, may not be reproduced or transmitted in any form or by any means, electronic or mechanical, including photocopying, recording, storage in an information retrieval system, or otherwise, without prior permission of the publisher.

While the Publisher has taken all reasonable care in the preparation of this book the publishers make no representation, express or implied, with regard to the accuracy of the information contained in this book and cannot accept any legal responsibility or liability for any errors or omissions from the book or the consequences thereof.

Products and services that are referred to in this book may be either trademarks and/or registered trademarks of their respective owners. The publishers and authors make no claim to these trade-marks.

British Library Cataloguing-in-Publication Data
A catalogue record for this book is available from the British Library

ISBN 978 1906201 19 7

Cover design by Filter Design
Printed and bound by CPI Group (UK) Ltd, Croydon, CR0 4YY
Typesetting by macbride.org.uk

Contents

List of tables and figures

Tables

Figures

Preface

Purpose

This book sets out to provide an introduction to the economic theory of taxation, together with an account and discussion of the tax system operating in the United Kingdom, with some overseas comparisons.

In the field of taxation, generalisations are always subject to qualification (including, no doubt, this one!). Some of the analysis in this volume is subject to detailed qualifications that are the proper province of the theoretical economist. We have not tried to include all these qualifications and special cases since this would have resulted in a much more theoretical and lengthy book than we thought appropriate. We have, however, tried to indicate where these finer points exist, and to provide sufficient references for those interested in pursuing them.

Timeliness

The book assumes that the reader has some background in economics, but not necessarily a great deal; perhaps a first year university course or equivalent. It is intended, therefore, that it will be suitable for all undergraduates studying taxation, whether their main discipline is economics, accountancy, business management, law, politics or social administration.

This book has been updated for changes to taxation announced in the Budget of 2012. These changes relate mainly to the tax year 2012/13, although some relate to subsequent years, as is pointed out in the appropriate places in the text. One notable recent development was that after a separate existence which can be traced back over centuries, the Inland Revenue and HM Customs and Excise were finally merged in April 2005. The new department is HM Revenue and Customs and is responsible for collecting over 80 per cent of net taxes and social security contributions in the UK.

Acknowledgements

Our first debt in writing this book must be to the many students whose interest in the subject has encouraged us tremendously. Their differing approaches have presented many stimulating challenges. We are also very grateful to many colleagues who made helpful comments and suggestions on various drafts, and to the numerous anonymous questionnaire respondents who participated in the market survey. Needless to say, remaining errors and obscurities are our own.

Simon James, *University of Exeter*
Christopher Nobes, *Royal Holloway, University of London*

CHAPTER ONE

General introduction

1.1 Background

'And it came to pass in those days, that there went out a decree from Caesar Augustus, that all the world should be taxed' (Luke ii 1). And it was. In fact, the world has been 'rendering unto Caesar' ever since!

Taxation has been associated with many historical developments other than the Christmas story. A very early example is reported by Dowell (1884). It appears that taxes were one of the causes of the revolt of the Iceni, and were referred to as oppressive in the harangue of Boadicea to her forces before the battle with Suetonius. Taxation has also played a part in many other revolts. The demands of King John for 'scutage' (an early form of taxation) advanced the crisis of 1215 which led to John's submission and the issue of Magna Carta. In the seventeenth century, the King's need for money from taxation resulted in the recall of Parliament and was a factor leading to the Civil War and the execution of Charles I. The importance of taxation as one of the causes of the French and American Revolutions is also well known.

In addition, taxation has contributed to major administrative developments. As we shall see in Chapter 10, the census in ancient Rome was used to record the property of each citizen for the purposes of taxation. The Domesday Book was compiled to meet the necessities of a new government in difficult times, and formed the basis of taxation for several centuries. Taxation also had an immense influence on the development of Parliament in the United Kingdom.

In modern Britain, the importance of taxation is clear from its sheer volume alone. Some idea of the magnitude of modern tax revenues may be gained by comparing it with gross domestic product. In 2010, GDP at market prices in the United Kingdom amounted to around £1,395 billion. In the tax year 2010/11, UK residents paid about £529 billion in taxes to governments in the UK and the European Union. Looked at in a different way, the average level of taxation in 2010 was nearly £8,500 per head of population.

As we shall see, the effects of taxation percolate throughout the economy via changes in prices, output and incomes. In this way, even individuals who are not direct taxpayers are affected by the tax system. The authors tried very hard to imagine circumstances in which an individual would be immune from the effects of taxation, but without success.

1.2 Structure and outline of the book

In examining the subject of taxation, it appeared logical to divide the book into two parts. The first part is concerned almost entirely with analysis. It begins with a chapter on the need for taxation, and the classification of taxes. The effects of taxation on different aspects of economic life are then dealt with in turn. Chapter 3 examines the effects of taxation on the efficient (or inefficient) operation of a market economy. Chapter 4 deals with the effects on incentives, in particular incentives to work; and Chapter 5 with equity considerations. The final chapter in Part I discusses fiscal policy and the aggregate level of economic activity, together with the rate of inflation.

There is, without doubt, some overlap in the subject matter in each of these chapters. Any tax will almost certainly have effects in each of the four areas described. Furthermore, a tax designed to meet the requirements of one area may well conflict with the requirements of another. A tax designed to provide incentives to work and save, for example, may be considered for other reasons to be an inequitable tax. Alternatively, a tax system designed to be equitable may impede the efficient operation of the economy.

It follows that the first six chapters have very little to say overall about the sort of tax system society should have. Society may, perfectly rationally, prefer an equitable tax system to an efficient one, or vice versa. The first part of the book simply sets out to show some of the effects of such decisions.

Part I is also concerned with the general principles of taxation, without close reference to institutional arrangements. It is to be hoped, therefore, that many of the results will be applicable to the actual tax system operating at any particular time in any particular country.

Part II, on the other hand, is much more closely concerned with the operation of the tax system in the United Kingdom. Attempts are made to assess the advantages and disadvantages of particular institutional arrangements in the light of the principles discussed in the first part of the book and, in some cases, in the light of overseas tax systems.

Part II begins with a chapter on general tax policy questions. This includes an indication of the complexity of the process of tax policy and reform. There are also sections on tax compliance, tax ethics, a comparison of different taxes within the United Kingdom and a comparison of taxation in different countries. Chapter 8 closely scrutinises income tax and its administration and includes capital gains tax and National Insurance contributions. The process is taken further in Chapter 9, where some possible reforms are presented. Chapter 10 turns to the taxation of wealth, including inheritance tax and the arguments for and against a personal wealth tax. Chapter 11 is concerned with indirect taxation, such as value added tax, and includes local authority taxation. Chapters 12 and 13 deal with corporation tax systems in general and with UK corporation tax in particular. Finally, Chapter 14 turns to international aspects of corporate income taxation.

Reference

Dowell, S. (1884), *A History of Taxation and Taxes in England*, Longmans, Vol. 1, p. 6.

PART ONE

Principles of taxation

Taxes, after all, are the due that we pay for the privileges of membership in an organised society.
FRANKLIN D. ROOSEVELT, in a speech at Worcester, Mass., 21 October 1936.

The art of taxation consists in so plucking the goose as to obtain the largest possible amount of feathers with the smallest possible amount of hissing.
JEAN BAPTISTE COLBERT (attributed), c.1665

CHAPTER TWO

Introduction to taxation

LEARNING OBJECTIVES

After reading this chapter, you should be able to:

- Describe the main economic functions of government.
- Understand the circumstances in which markets may not operate efficiently.
- Give a definition of a tax.
- Explain the meaning of average and marginal tax rates and how they can be used to define the progressivity of a tax.
- Describe the main economic criteria which can be used to assess a particular tax or proposed tax reform.

2.1 The need for taxation

Before dealing with the theory of taxation in detail, there are two areas which should be discussed. The first of these concerns the purpose of taxation, and the second covers the definition and classification of taxes.

It has been said that 'what the government gives it must first take away'. The economic resources available to society are limited, and so an increase in government expenditure normally means a reduction in private spending. Taxation is one method of transferring resources from the private to the public sector, but there are others. One of these alternative methods is the debasement of the currency through the production of too much money. The government simply creates more money and uses it to purchase goods and services. This technique has been tried many times over the centuries and was, for example, vehemently condemned in the fourteenth century by Nicholas Oresme (c. 1360). The main problem is that it leads to inflation. As the value of money falls, purchasing power is transferred from the holders of money to the government. This process has therefore been described as an 'inflation tax' by Johnson (1971), Friedman and Friedman (1980) and others.

Another possibility is for the government to charge for the goods and services it provides. This is quite straightforward where the government operates like a commercial business. However, it would be very difficult, or even impossible, to charge individuals directly on the basis of the use they make of many government services. Particular examples include defence and law enforcement. A further method of raising money is to borrow it. Governments can borrow either from their own citizens or from overseas, but there are limits to the amounts that people are prepared to lend, even to governments.

Taxation has its limits as well, but they considerably exceed the amounts that can be raised by resorting to the printing press, charging consumers directly, or borrowing. So while governments often use all four methods of raising resources, taxation is usually by far the most important source of government revenue.

According to Musgrave (1959), the economic functions of government may be divided into three main categories. The first is to overcome the inefficiencies of the market system in the allocation of economic resources. The second is the redistribution of income and wealth in order to move towards the distribution that society considers to be 'just' or 'equitable'. Third, there may be a role for government in smoothing out cyclical fluctuations in the economy and ensuring a high level of employment and price stability. As we shall see in Part I, taxation has an important role to play in each of these functions of government.

Market failure

Under certain circumstances, the market mechanism is able to supply goods and services efficiently. The concept of efficiency is discussed in Section 3.2 so there is no need for duplication here. Suffice it to say that market efficiency requires the following:

> Individuals can be excluded from consuming goods if they do not
> pay for them. There are no external effects.
> The market is perfectly competitive.

Under these conditions, the market will tend to conform to consumer preferences. If, for example, consumers suddenly wanted more of a particular good, its price would rise and more would be produced. The market would also tend to use the methods of production which cost least.

In other circumstances, however, the market may operate inefficiently. It may be worth looking briefly at four of these circumstances: public goods, merit goods, externalities and imperfect competition.

The existence of public goods was described early on by Adam Smith (1776). He acknowledged that the government has the:

> duty of erecting and maintaining certain public works and certain public
> institutions, which it can never be for the interest of any individual or
> small number of individuals, to erect and maintain; because the profit

could never repay the expense to any individual or small number of individuals, though it may frequently do much more than repay it to a great society. (Book IV, Ch. IX, p. 185)

The characteristics of a public good are found in varying degrees in a wide range of goods and services. It is possible to isolate these characteristics by looking at a 'pure' public good which has two important features. First of all, individuals cannot be excluded from consuming a pure public good, even if they do not pay for it. This means that firms would have great difficulty in charging individuals for any public goods they produced. The market, if left to itself, would therefore tend to under-produce public goods. For example, suppose a firm set up in business to provide national defence. It would find it very difficult to charge individuals, because they could benefit from the firm's activities whether they paid or not.

The second feature of a pure public good is that consumption by one individual does not prevent anyone else from consuming the good. For example, if one more person is born and benefits from national defence, this does not stop anyone else from benefiting. This is quite different from a private good, for example, a meal, when, if one person consumes the good, no one else can.

If extra individuals can benefit from a public good at no cost to anyone else, it is inefficient to exclude them (if this can be done) just because they do not pay. For example, up to capacity, extra individuals can use a particular bridge without preventing anyone else from crossing. To exclude them from doing so would therefore be wasteful.

So, for two reasons, the market may be an inefficient method of providing public goods. There is scope, therefore, for a non-market method of provision in which the government provides the good, and finds the money by raising taxes.

In addition, the government often supplies, or encourages the supply of, goods and services which have little in common with public goods, but are perhaps considered to have some 'merit' in their own right. Examples of these 'merit goods' include performances of opera and free school meals. By the same token, the government also discourages goods that are considered to be undesirable. These 'de-merit' goods include alcohol, tobacco and other drugs.

Such policies may be considered by some to be paternalistic. Indeed, in order to justify such action on purely economic grounds, one might want to show that the government acts more in the consumer's interest than the consumer himself does. However, we do not need to concern ourselves too much here with whether or not governments are *justified* in encouraging consumption of some goods and discouraging others (this is discussed further, for example, in Musgrave and Musgrave (1989), pp. 57-8). We simply need to acknowledge that they do. It can then be seen that taxation is a useful source of finance for merit goods; it is also a handy method of discouraging the consumption of de-merit goods.

External effects can also provide a role for government. There are two possibilities here – external benefits and external costs. Where there are external benefits associated with the production of a particular good, the private sector is likely to produce too little because firms do not take into account the benefit to individuals other than their customers. With external costs, the same line of reasoning suggests over-production. There are several possible policy solutions for external effects. For instance, the production of goods with external benefits could be subsidised so that production increases. Again, this may be paid for out of tax revenue. With external costs, one solution might be to impose a tax – as we shall see in Section 3.6.

Imperfect competition provides a different set of implications for the tax system. For example, basic economic theory suggests that an industry which becomes monopolised may supply its product in smaller quantities and at a higher price than when the industry was competitive. This may imply the need for a regulating body, such as the Monopolies Commission, which would require public funds for its support.

Distribution

A distribution of income and wealth that is solely determined by the market is unlikely to be the distribution most desired by society. In the market system, an individual's income is determined by the factors of production he or she owns and the price which those factors will fetch in the market. Society may not consider this to be a proper way of distributing its resources among its members. In an extreme case, for example, where an individual did not own any factors of production (that is, he had no capital or land and was unable to work), the individual would receive no income. If the community decides to influence the distribution of income and wealth, it is likely that the tax system will be one of the main methods employed.

Stabilisation

The third function of government is that of stabilising the economy at a high level of employment while simultaneously stabilising prices. As Chapter 6 shows, there has been some debate on the role of government in this area. What is not in dispute, however, is that the tax system is a powerful method of influencing the level of activity, should the government wish to use it.

2.2 Definitions and classification

A tax is a compulsory levy made by public authorities for which nothing is received *directly* in return. We have seen that the levy is partly used to provide public goods in return, but that its size is also determined by many other factors. Taxes are, therefore, transfers of money to the public sector, but they exclude loan transactions and direct payments for publicly produced goods and services.

Some problems are encountered when trying to draw the line between those payments which are taxes and those which are not. For example, it might be argued that National Insurance contributions are directly paid in order to receive subsequent benefits, and that, therefore, they do not constitute a tax. However, they have other characteristics which are sufficiently like those of taxes that they are reasonably considered to be a tax - the payments are compulsory and are charged on a basis which does not take into account factors which a normal insurance scheme would include, but which does consider an individual's income. In addition, the payments do not cover the whole cost of the system, and increases in contributions are often for macroeconomic fiscal reasons, irrespective of whether the National Insurance Fund requires more revenue.

Other borderline cases are such payments as those for passports or television licences, which exhibit some features which are like taxes and some which are not. Our main concern in this book will be with payments which are very obviously taxes, such as income tax and value added tax. These are compulsory and are not directly related to benefits received by taxpayers. However, although both these payments are taxes, they are clearly different types of taxes. This realisation leads us into a discussion of classification or taxonomy (pun gently intended).

It is possible to classify taxes in many different ways. A fairly straightforward, though detailed, classification is that used by the Organisation for Economic Cooperation and Development (OECD, 1976). Taxes are grouped into those on goods and services, those on income, profits and capital gains, those on net wealth, and so on, and each group is further sub-divided (Table 2.1). When comparing taxes from one country to another, such a classification is very useful, but it avoids a number of important problems about the real economic nature of different taxes. As a means of understanding taxes, the following ways of classifying them by their characteristics may be more illuminating.

Direct or indirect

This split depends upon the nature of the past and present administrative arrangements for assessment and collection of the tax. If the tax is actually assessed on and collected from the individuals who are intended to bear it, it is called a *direct* tax. For example, capital gains tax is assessed on an individual who realises a capital gain. The tax is paid by personal cheque from the individual to the HM Revenue and Customs. On the other hand, value added tax is collected from all the businesses involved in the production and distribution of a good for a final consumer. To an extent, the tax will cause the price to the consumer to rise (see Chapter 5). Therefore, this tax on consumers is collected from businesses: it is an *indirect* tax. The way in which the burden of taxes is distributed throughout the economy is examined in Chapter 5. Taxes were originally classified as direct or indirect at a time when it was thought that direct taxes were not shifted at all (i.e. the taxpayer bore the tax fully), and indirect taxes were shifted completely.

Table 2.1 The OECD classification

1 000 Taxes on goods and services
1100 Taxes on the production, sale, transfer, leasing and delivery of goods and
      rendering of services
      11 10 General taxes
      1120 Taxes on specific goods and services
            1121 Excises
            1122 Fiscal monopolies
            1123 Customs and import duties
            1124 Taxes on exports
            1125 Taxes on specific services
            11 26 Other taxes

1200 Taxes in respect of ownership and use of, or permission to use, goods or to
      perform activities
      1210 Recurrent taxes
      121 1 Paid by households in respect of motor vehicles
      1212 Paid by others in respect of motor vehicles
      1213 Paid in respect of other goods
      1220 Other taxes
2000 Taxes on income, profits and capital gains
      2100 Paid by households and institutions
            2110 On income and profits
            2120 On capital gains
      2200 Paid by corporate enterprises
            2210 On income and profits
            2220 On capital gains

3000 Social security contributions
      3100 Paid by employees
      3200 Paid by employers
      3300 Paid by self-employed or non-employed persons

4000 Taxes on employers based payroll or manpower

5000 Taxes on net wealth and immovable property
      5100 Recurrent taxes on net wealth
            5110 Paid by households
            5120 Paid by corporate enterprises
      5200 Recurrent taxes on immovable property
            5210 Paid by households
            5220 Paid by enterprises
            5230 Paid by institutions, etc.
      5300 Non-recurrent taxes on net wealth and immovable property
            5310 On net wealth
            5320 On immovable property

Table 2.1 (cont)

6000 Taxes and stamp duties on gifts, inheritances and on capital and financial
      transactions
      6100 On gifts and inheritances
            6110 Gifts
            6120 Inheritances
      6200 On capital and financial transactions

7000 Other taxes
            7100 Paid solely by enterprises
            7200 Other

Modern opinion is rather more sophisticated, but the original labels are still used.

Income tax on earned income is, in most cases, deducted from the wages or salaries of employees by their employers. The employer then pays the income tax to the Revenue authorities (see Chapter 8). However, the individual deals with the Revenue personally on any matters that are not straightforward, and there are many other sources of income on which the assessment and payment of income tax is completely direct. Therefore, income tax is said to be a direct tax.

A feature that direct taxes share is that the amount of tax can be related to individual circumstances, for example, the taxpayer's commitments or family size. Indirect taxes cannot take individual circumstances into account. Manipulation of the average rate of tax borne by different individuals is also possible with direct taxation, as mentioned below. Direct taxes include income tax, corporation tax, capital gains tax, inheritance tax and any future wealth tax. Indirect taxes include value added tax and excise duties.

Tax base

Taxes may also be classified by tax base. Taxes may be based on a stock of something (capital taxes), or on a flow of something (current taxes). However, here there is ample room for definitional problems. Income tax and corporation tax are current taxes on income. In principle, capital gains tax is also a form of tax on current income, despite the confusion that its name might lead to. The tax base of capital gains tax is the increase in value which accrues to an investment over time. This 'income' is not taxed until it is realised, at the time of the sale of the investment. Therefore, it might be called a postponed current tax.

Value added tax and excise duties are current taxes on expenditure. Inheritance tax is really a tax on capital, although it has a facet which reminds one of a tax on income, in that the tax is only borne when the capital moves. Wealth taxes are purer examples of capital taxes.

It would be possible to divide current taxes further, into those on sources of income and those on uses of it. Income tax and capital gains tax are examples of the former, value added tax is an example of the latter.

Specific and ad valorem taxes

Taxes may be divided up on the basis of the relationship of the amount of tax to the size of the tax base. A tax whose size bore no relationship to any tax base except the existence of the taxpayer would be a poll tax, for example a tax of £200 per head throughout the population. Taxes which are based on the weight or size of the tax base are called 'specific' or 'unit' taxes: for example, an excise duty of £1 per bottle of whisky or £200 per ton of tobacco. Taxes which are based on values are called ad *valorem* taxes. Value added tax and all the direct taxes we have met are examples of these.

Rate structure

Since direct taxes are assessed on individuals, it is possible to arrange for the marginal and average rates of a tax to change according to the size of an individual's tax base. Taxes can be classified according to the way the rate varies with income. Taxes which take an increasing proportion of an income as the income rises are called *progressive*. Those which continue to take the same proportion (though an increasing absolute amount, of course) are called *proportional*. Those which take a decreasing proportion of income are called *regressive*.

As an example, suppose that there is a system of income tax which taxes individuals on the following basis. Income up to £1,000 per year is exempt from tax, extra income between £1,000 and £2,000 per year is taxed at 30 per cent, and income above £2,000 per year is taxed at 50 per cent. Let us look at the tax paid by four individuals on incomes of £1,200, £1,800, £2,200 and £2,800 respectively. These results are shown in Table 2.2.

We can see that the proportion taken in tax (the average tax rate) is rising as income rises. Another identifying feature of progressive systems is that the marginal rate of tax will always be above the average rate of tax. It is this fact which causes the average rate to rise.

Inheritance tax and wealth taxes have increasing average rates. If these taxes are to be called 'progressive', we must be clear that they are progressive to increasing wealth rather than, necessarily, to increasing income. Value added tax and excise duties, being indirect, cannot operate on the basis of a changing rate for those who spend different amounts. However, they can be progressive or regressive, as income changes, by applying different rates of tax to different goods. If the goods that tend to be bought by those with higher incomes bear a higher rate of tax, the indirect tax may be progressive: on average, a higher proportion of higher incomes would be paid in tax.

Table 2.2 A progressive system

	£	£	£	£
Income	1,200	1,800	2,200	2,800
Exempt income	1,000	1,000	1,000	1,000
Remainder	200	800	1,200	1,800
Tax at 30%	60	240	300	300
Tax at 50%	–	–	100	400
Total tax	60	240	400	700
Average tax rate				
total tax%	5.0	13.3	18.2	25.0
income				
Marginal rate %:	30.0	30.0	50.0	50.0

These classifications and definitions will be used and developed throughout this book, particularly in Part I. The important taxes that will be met are shown in Figure 2.1. Since there are several ways of classifying taxes, as we have seen, a large number of alternative tables would be possible.

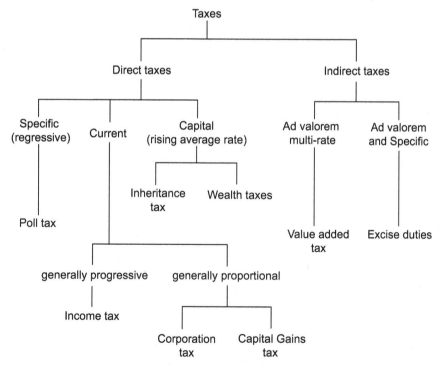

Figure 2.1 Classification of some important taxes

Evasion, avoidance and tax planning

At their simplest, the above three terms might be defined as follows:
- Evasion is the illegal manipulation of one's affairs so as to reduce tax.
- Avoidance is the manipulation of one's affairs within the law in order to reduce tax.
- Tax planning is arranging one's affairs to take advantage of the obvious and often intended effects of tax rules in order to maximise one's after-tax returns.

In principle, British tax law allows a taxpayer to use the letter of the law to his or her best advantage, although there are some 'legal' arrangements which are so artificial that they might be seen as evasion. Indeed, the courts are prepared in some cases to seek the reality behind arrangements, for example in the case of *W.T. Ramsey Ltd v. CIR* (54 TC 101, 1 All ER 865). The relationships between equity and evasion and avoidance are discussed in Section 5.9.

Just as the borderline between evasion and avoidance is fuzzy, so is that between avoidance and tax planning. Perhaps tax planning is just a polite way of referring to avoidance. Tax planning is examined in various places in this book. For example, in some tax systems, some taxpayers may choose investments yielding capital gains instead of income, because the two forms of 'income' may be taxed differently. This is looked at in Chapters 5 and 8. Businesses may be able to choose whether to operate as partnerships or as companies, and the tax results of this will be relevant (see Chapter 13). Businesses can also plan to be tax efficient with respect to their capital raising decisions and their investment decisions (see Chapter 12). The location of oneself or one's company will also be a matter for tax planning in some cases.

When tax planning, it is important to remember that one should try to take account of possible future changes in one's own circumstances and in taxes. Also, the objective is of course to maximise one's after-tax returns, not to minimise taxes. For example, certain investments may yield tax-exempt interest, but that does not necessarily mean that they are the best use for one's money.

Good or bad?

It is also possible to analyse taxes as to whether they are good or bad according to certain criteria. The question is how to appraise existing tax systems and how to distinguish potentially worthwhile reforms from inappropriate ones. For example, Adam Smith (1776) proposed four canons of taxation:
(i)   equity, i.e. fairness with respect to the tax contributions of different individuals;
(ii)   certainty, i.e. a lack of arbitrariness or uncertainty about tax liabilities;
(iii)   convenience, with respect to the timing and manner of payment;

(iv)   efficiency, i.e. a small cost of collection as a proportion of revenue raised, and the avoidance of distortionary effects on the behaviour of taxpayers (i.e. the principle of neutrality).

In Chapter 1 it was stated that taxes would be looked at from different economic aspects and, with some relatively minor changes to Adam Smith's analysis, the suggestion here is that each tax and proposed tax reform may be scrutinised in the light of four main criteria. Of course, not all of these criteria are relevant in all cases. There may also be other matters of importance in particular areas. Nevertheless, these criteria do provide a framework within which various proposals can be considered and they can also be used as a checklist for important aspects that might otherwise be overlooked. The four criteria are efficiency, incentives, equity, and macroeconomic considerations. Before examining them in detail in the following chapters it seems worthwhile to provide a summary here:

1. *Efficiency*. How might a particular proposal affect the efficiency of the economy? Would it create or increase distortions in the price mechanism which would affect the behaviour of consumers and producers? A tax imposed on some goods but not on others might push consumers towards the untaxed sector which might or might not be desirable. Moreover, a tax may offset an existing distortion, and the traditional example of this is a tax designed to discourage pollution. Also to be considered on grounds of efficiency are:
(i)   Administrative costs - will the proposal be expensive to administer?
(ii)   Compliance cost - will the proposal be difficult or expensive, or both, for taxpayers to comply with?

2. *Incentives*. This is really a special case of efficiency but is sufficiently important to be considered separately. The question is, how are taxes likely to affect the willingness of individuals to:
(i) work or to accept certain types of work,
(ii) save and invest,
(iii) accept the risks associated with economic enterprise?

3. *Equity*. There are two aspects to this criterion:
(i)   Is the tax 'fair'? Naturally this is largely a matter of opinion. However, some progress can usually be made. For example, a proposal may conflict with the principle of horizontal equity, which says that similar people in similar circumstances should be treated similarly.
(ii)   Tax incidence. Since in economics 'everything depends on everything else', taxes will affect prices, rates of interest and so on. The question is, who will actually end up being affected by a tax, either directly or indirectly? For instance, an increase in the tax on scotch will be partly suffered by scotch drinkers, but it might also be suffered by people involved in the production of scotch. Also, there is tax capitalisation. This occurs when the taxation of income or expenditure affects the capital value of assets. For example, the

tax treatment of mortgage interest almost certainly influences the price of housing.

In many cases mortgage interest relief simply makes houses more expensive to buy.

4. *Macroeconomic considerations*. Does a proposal have any implications for the level of unemployment and so on?

An additional important area involves administrative concerns. This is an aspect which is often overlooked but, particularly given the nature of the British tax system, is often the ugly rock that sinks the most beautiful ideas. One important point is not to overlook how a proposal might fit in with existing taxes/benefits and other administrative arrangements. Although there is no separate chapter on administration these issues are considered in the relevant areas of the book. However, we now turn to a more detailed discussion of the first criterion, which is taxation and efficiency.

Further reading

For those interested in the need for taxation and the economics of the public sector there is no shortage of reading. For example, Lindert (2004) examines the links between tax financed social spending and economic growth.

Many issues are raised by Musgrave and Musgrave (1989). Musgrave (1959) and Hockley (1992). There is also plenty of controversy. Seldon (1987), for instance, argues that a large amount of taxation should be replaced by a system of charges.

For an introduction to the UK's tax system, see Lymer and Oats (2009) or for a general discussion of our tax system design issues, see Sandford (2000).

References

Friedman, M. and Friedman, R. (1980), *Free to Choose*, Seeker and Warburg, pp. 267-70.

Hockley, G.C. (1992), *Fiscal Policy*, 2nd edn, Routledge.

Johnson, H.G. (1971), *Macroeconomics and Monetary Theory*, Gray-Mills, p. 152.

Lindert, P.H. (2004). *Growing Public: Social Spending and Economic Growth Since the Eighteenth Century*, Vols I and II. Cambridge University Press.

Lymer, A. and Oats, L. (2009) *Taxation: Policy and Practice*, (16th ed. 2009/10), Fiscal Publications.

Musgrave, R.A. (1959) , *The Theory of Public Finance*, McGraw-Hill.

Musgrave, R.A. and Musgrave, P.B. (1989), *Public Finance in Theory and Practice*, 5th edn, McGraw-Hill International edn.

OECD (1976), *Revenue Statistics*, OECD, Paris, Part II.

Oresme, N. (c.1360), *De Origine, Natura, Jure et Mutationibus Monetarum*.

Seldon, A. (1987), *Charge*, Temple Smith.

Sandford, C. (2000), *Why Tax Systems Differ: A comparative study of the political economy of taxation*, Fiscal Publications.

Smith, A. (1776), *The Wealth of Nations*, Cannan edn, Methuen, 1950.

Self assessment questions

Suggested answers to self-assessment questions are given at the back of the book.

2.1   What are the main economic functions of government?

2.2   Under which circumstances might markets operate inefficiently?

2.3   What is a tax?

2.4   Is corporation tax a direct or an indirect tax?

2.5   What is an average rate of tax?

2.6   What is a marginal rate of tax?

2.7   If a tax takes more from a richer person than it does from a poorer person, is it necessarily a progressive tax?

2.8   What are the main economic criteria which can be used to judge a tax or potential tax reform?

Discussion questions

1.   Why is taxation necessary?

2.   Are there any viable alternatives to taxation?

3.   What are the main economic criteria for judging a particular tax or proposed tax reform?

CHAPTER THREE

Taxation and efficiency

LEARNING OBJECTIVES

After reading this chapter, you should be able to:

- Define economic efficiency.
- Explain the concept of the excess burden of taxation.
- Identify circumstances in which taxes can distort economic behaviour.
- Demonstrate how tax might sometimes be used to increase economic efficiency.
- Describe administrative and compliance costs and their main features.
- Understand the meaning of tax expenditure and the implications it has for the tax system.

3.1 Introduction

Adam Smith's fourth canon of taxation was that 'every tax ought to be so contrived as both to take out and keep out of the pockets of the people as little as possible, over and above what it brings into the public treasury of the state'. He then went on to describe four ways by which taxes could fail to meet this requirement (Smith, 1776, Book V, Ch. II). A 'great number of officers' may be needed to levy the tax; it may 'obstruct the industry of the people'; penalties may be inflicted on individuals attempting to evade the tax; and finally, taxpayers may be subject to 'frequent visits and the odious examination of the tax-gatherers'. And so, he concluded 'it is in some one or other of these four different ways that taxes are frequently so much more burdensome to the people than they are beneficial to the sovereign'.

For the purposes of this and the following chapters we shall reclassify these burdens of taxation into three groups. The first category, known in modern literature as the excess burden of taxation, develops Smith's point about the impediment of taxation to production, but extends it to include the distortion of consumer choice between goods that are actually produced. The second, administrative costs, covers the burden to the public sector of administering taxes. It corresponds to Smith's 'great number of officers' required to levy the tax. The third group covers those costs incurred by the private sector in complying (or not complying) with the requirements of the tax system; that is, compliance costs. It includes both Smith's frequent visitations from tax-gatherers and his penalties for evasion, but in this modern age we can also add in the 'great number of officers' employed by firms and individuals in the private sector to look after their tax affairs.

In this chapter, we shall look first at the concept of economic efficiency and examine the excess burden of various taxes in the light of efficiency criteria. Then we shall consider administrative and compliance costs, and finally describe and comment on the phenomenon of 'tax expenditure'.

Throughout the chapter we shall concentrate on the use of existing resources within an economic system. We shall proceed therefore on the assumption that there is a given supply of resources: that is, a given total amount of labour looking for employment, and a given amount of capital and enterprise. Questions concerning the effects of taxation on the supply of these factors will be postponed to Chapter 4.

3.2 Economic efficiency

The first task is to describe the meaning of economic efficiency. It is occasionally suggested that the conditions required for efficiency are unlikely to be found in what is referred to as 'the real world'. Yet, in order to make any significant analytical progress, it is necessary to have a clear idea of efficiency and how an 'optimal allocation of resources' may be defined. It is then possible to use such criteria to judge how taxes might interfere with the efficient functioning of an economy. It is also possible to recognise those circumstances in which different taxes may be used to encourage an economy to move towards a more 'desirable' allocation of resources than that currently prevailing.

The simplest form of economic efficiency can be seen by imagining an economy with a single consumer: a Robinson Crusoe society. This one individual has a given supply of resources which he or she can use to produce various goods. He or she also has a set of preferences regarding the products he would like to consume. It may be said that in such a one-person economy, the consumer behaves efficiently if he or she uses these resources to produce that combination of goods which maximises the benefit he can derive from the resources available to him.

In a society with many consumers, the issue becomes more complicated as the output of the economy can be distributed between individuals in many different ways. To keep our discussion reasonably straightforward, we shall defer our treatment of the more controversial issue of the distribution of income to Chapter 5 and confine ourselves here to the narrower issue of resource allocation.

Pareto efficiency

To examine the issue of resource allocation the concept of 'Pareto efficiency' is especially useful. A particular allocation of resources is said to be Pareto-efficient if no rearrangement of resources could make one person better off without making someone else worse off. Or, to put it the other way round, if it is possible to change the methods of production, or the type of goods produced, so that one person can be made better off without others being made worse off, then the existing allocation of resources is sub-optimal and the efficiency of the economy can be increased by making the change.

In practice, of course, because most economic changes make some people better off and some people worse off, the concept of efficiency may be modified so that the requirement is that the gainers gain more than the losers lose. In other words, efficiency would be enhanced if, as a result of a change, the gainers were able to compensate the losers by the amount of their loss, and still be better off. Whether or not the losers are actually compensated is a question of distribution, and so again will be left for Chapter 5.

Ideal output

The private sector may achieve a Pareto-optimal output through the market mechanism if two conditions prevail: the presence of perfect competition and the absence of economic effects external to the market. The conditions of perfect competition imply that each firm faces a perfectly elastic demand curve for its output and a perfectly elastic supply curve for its inputs. In other words, no firm is large enough to be able to influence the market prices at which it sells its produce or purchases its inputs. If firms wish to maximise their profits under these circumstances they will attempt to supply the level of output where the price (marginal revenue) of the good is just equal to the marginal cost of producing it. The owners of factors of production would be at an optimum position if they provided the services of their factors up to the point where the price equals the marginal cost of provision. Consumers would also be at an optimum position if they allocated their expenditure to maximise the benefits they received from it. In this situation, no one (consumers, owners of factor services, or owners of firms) could be made better off without someone else being made worse off. It can be seen from this brief description of perfect competition that the private sector can achieve an efficient level and pattern of output through the market, provided there are no effects external to the market.

The essential characteristic of external effects is that private costs and benefits differ from social costs and benefits. For example, an external cost would exist where an industrial firm imposed costs on the surrounding community in the form of noise, pollution and congestion for which the firm did not have to pay. As the firm is not facing all of its costs, over-production will result if the market is left to itself.

An example of an external benefit is refuse collection in an urban area. The benefits of refuse collection to the community as a whole are normally greater than the benefits accruing to the individuals whose refuse is actually collected. Where the production of a particular good confers external benefits on the community, the market would tend to supply a level of output below the optimum since the external benefits would not be taken into account.

So, for the unregulated private sector to be able to produce an optimum output, the conditions of perfect competition must prevail and there must be no external effects. The concepts of efficiency and optimality may now be used to illustrate the concept of excess burden.

3.3 The excess burden of taxation

Clearly, taxes transfer spending power from the taxpayer to the government. In addition to this transfer of resources, taxes may distort consumers' choices between goods, or producers' choices between factors, and so impose an additional burden on the taxpaying community. This point can be made more explicit by distinguishing between the income effects of a tax and the substitution effects. These effects are discussed further in Section 4.2, but it is also worth introducing them here.

The income effects arise because, when a tax is imposed or increased, the taxpayer's spending power is reduced. Income effects do not in themselves result in economic inefficiency. They simply represent the transfer of resources from the taxpayer to the government.

Substitution effects arise when a tax affects relative prices and so leads individuals to substitute one form of consumption or activity for another. For example, suppose that a tax were placed on margarine, but not on butter. Consumers might then substitute butter for margarine even when, in the absence of the tax, they would have preferred the latter. The substitution effects of taxes can, therefore, lead to economic inefficiency because they interfere with consumer choice.

As a second example, it may be noted that after 1747 many taxpayers decided to avoid the window tax by bricking up their windows. (Before stricter powers were introduced in 1747, the normal method of avoiding the tax was by stopping up the windows before the assessor arrived, and re-opening them after he had left!) The lack of amenity arising from the blocking of windows was clearly a cost of the window tax; but although it was a cost to the taxpayer, it was of no benefit to the government. This type of cost may be described as the excess burden of taxation.

Excess burden may be analysed further by looking at the effects of imposing a specific tax on a single commodity, X. Suppose that the conditions of supply and demand for X are as described in Figure 3.1. If there are no external effects and the market is working perfectly, the supply schedule SS will reflect the social opportunity cost of producing X. On the other side of the market, DD indicates the benefits received by individuals from consuming X (as demonstrated by the amount they are

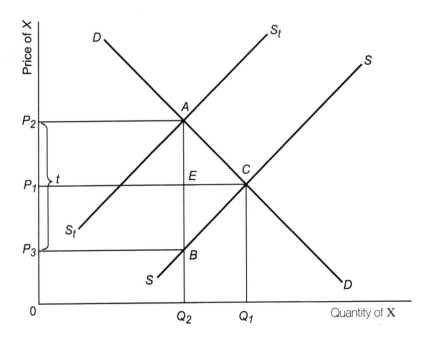

Figure 3.1 Imposition of a tax *t* on good *X*

willing to pay for it). If the market is working perfectly, the level of output will move towards an equilibrium point of Q_1 At this point the marginal cost of producing X is just equal to the marginal benefit of consuming it. By the above definition, the ideal level of output is Q_1 and any other level of output must be inferior. If more X were produced, the cost of the extra units would exceed the benefit; if less were produced, the lost units would reduce consumer benefit by more than they reduced producer cost.

Clearly, at the margin, the last unit of X produced confers little or no net benefit on the community, as the cost of production is just equal to the benefit of consumption. Equally clearly, all the other units produced confer a greater benefit than their cost. This extra benefit may be divided into two parts. First of all, there is the consumer surplus which is the benefit (as shown by the demand curve DD) received from the consumption of units of X, minus the price the consumer has to pay (P_1). In other words, it is the benefit the consumer gets but does not have to pay for. (Strictly speaking, it is an approximation to net consumer benefit: for further discussion see, for example, Hicks (1939), Note to Chapter 2.) Secondly, there is the concept of producer surplus which is the price (P_1) that the producer receives less the cost of production. The concept is not quite as straightforward as consumer surplus, but it remains useful for our purposes and so it will be retained.

Now suppose that a tax of value t is imposed on every unit of X produced. In this example it may be assumed that it is the supplier rather than the consumer who is responsible for paying the tax to the authorities. As a result, the tax increases the cost of producing X by an amount t, and so the supply curve shifts upwards to S_tS_t. The market price consequently rises to P_2. However, the supplier, who hands over the tax, only keeps an amount P_3 per unit, which is the market price P_2 minus the tax t. Following the rise in the market price to P_2, the equilibrium level of output falls from Q_1 to Q_2.

The revenue paid by the taxpayers and received by the government is t times the number of units sold, and is shown in Figure 3.1 as the area $P_3P_2 AB$. As a result of the price rise the consumers are worse off by an amount $P_3P_2 AC$. Yet the government receives only $P_3P_2 AE$ of this, leaving a net loss of consumer surplus of AEC. Similarly there is a net loss of producer surplus of ECB. The excess burden of the tax is therefore shown by the area ABC.

A slightly different way of looking at this loss of economic welfare is to notice that the tax has resulted in a drop in production from Q_1 to Q_2. It is clear that these lost units of X would confer greater benefit (shown by DD) on the community than their cost (shown by SS). The tax has obstructed opportunities for profitable trade, and the loss is again described by the triangle ABC. The way in which the costs of the tax are distributed between the producers and consumers is left for Chapter 5, but it is fairly easy to see from Figure 3.1 that it depends on the price elasticities of supply and demand.

We shall see that, in nearly all circumstances, all taxes have some effect on the allocation of resources. The only tax which it could be claimed was neutral with respect to the working of the price mechanism is a lump sum tax on each person - that is, a poll tax. Because such a tax does not vary with different forms of economic behaviour, it might be said that it is unlikely to affect that behaviour and so to impose an excess burden. Yet even with a poll tax it is possible to visualise an excess burden. A poll tax imposed on all heads, including children, may have some effect on taxpayers' plans regarding family size. Certainly, tax systems have been used to influence family size; a particular example is the French quotient familial system (see Barr *et al.* (1977), p. 123). Even a poll tax, therefore, would only be completely neutral in the unlikely event that it came as a complete surprise.

Nevertheless, the concept of a lump sum tax will be useful in order to isolate certain characteristics of the other taxes. To avoid distraction by issues such as changes in government expenditure, our main method of analysis will be to compare taxes of equal yield, supposing that government expenditure remains the same, both in size and in allocation. One of the best 'dummy' taxes for this purpose is the poll tax.

Some of the implications of excess burden for fiscal policy may now be explored. A useful illustration is the time-honoured debate over the relative merits of income and excise taxes.

3.4 Income taxes versus excise taxes

An early proposition put forward by Hicks (1939) and by Joseph (1939) held that income taxes impose a lower excess burden than taxes on specific goods, as income taxes do not distort consumers' choices between goods. We shall first examine this argument, and then go on to consider the circumstances in which income taxes also impose an excess burden on taxpayers.

To isolate the basic proposition, it will be assumed that several other variables remain constant. These assumptions will be withdrawn later to see how the argument is likely to be modified in practice. It will be supposed to begin with that perfect competition prevails, that there are no external effects and that a Pareto-efficient allocation of resources exists before either tax is imposed. We will assume that the supply of factors of production is fixed, and that these factors are fully employed both before and after either the income tax or the excise tax is imposed. To abstract the analysis from distributional considerations, each individual will be assumed to be the same that is to have the same income, tastes and so on. At this stage we shall also suppose that neither tax involves any administrative or compliance costs. We further suppose that the same amount of revenue has to be raised by whichever tax is used, and that the pattern of government spending is the same in both cases. The taxes will be applied to a simple two-good (X and Y) model. Finally, let us suppose that the choice of tax is between a commodity tax, which is levied on good X but not on good Y, and a proportional income tax, which is levied on all incomes. We begin with a 'partial' approach to the problem, that is an approach confining itself to the effects of the taxes on the choice which a typical consumer makes between the two goods, and then proceed to a more general analysis of a simple economic system.

Partial approach

Figure 3.2 represents the position of a typical individual with a choice of consuming different combinations of X and Y. Before either tax is imposed, and with a given money income, the individual faces a budget constraint of AB, which shows that he could consume a maximum of B of X, or A of Y, or some combination of X and Y. The slope of AB reveals the relative prices of X and Y. Next, our consumer's preferences are represented by a set of indifference curves, each of which is a locus of the combinations of X and Y between which the individual is indifferent. If the consumer wishes to maximise the benefits he derives from consumption, he will choose that combination of X and Y which enables him to reach his highest possible indifference curve is, given his budget constraint. Without either tax the highest attainable indifference curve is I_1 and so our individual will consume at point P_1.

A specific excise tax levied on commodity X has the effect of shifting the consumer's budget constraint from AB to AC. It must swivel in this way because, if our individual consumed only Y, he would be able to buy the same amount as

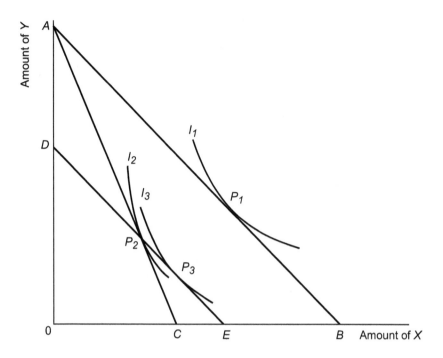

Figure 3.2 Income tax versus a specific excise tax

before. The increase in the slope of the budget constraint signifies an increase in the relative price of X. Given a budget constraint of AC, the highest attainable indifference curve is now I_2. The difference between the levels of benefit derived at P_1 on indifference curve I_1 and at P_2 on indifference curve I_2 represents the amount the consumer is worse off as a result of the tax.

If an income tax is imposed instead, the effect is also to shift the budget constraint inwards. The income tax does not distort the consumer's choice between X and Y, and so their relative prices must remain the same. Therefore, the new budget constraint DE must be parallel to AB. The tax simply reduces his income so that he can afford less of both. As the income tax is required to raise the same revenue as the excise tax, DE will pass through P_2, so that the individual is left with sufficient income to be able to buy the same combination of goods, irrespective of the tax to which he is subjected. However, with a budget constraint of DE he can attain the higher indifference curve of I_3. Clearly he is better off on I_3 than on I_2. On the assumptions listed above, therefore, an income tax inflicts less excess burden on the taxpayer than does a specific tax of equal yield. It does so simply because it interferes less with consumer choice and the allocation of resources.

Note that the argument depends on the indirect tax being imposed on X but not on Y. If the tax were levied on both goods, the analysis would be the same as that for an income tax. The crucial point is that the excess burden of a tax depends on the extent to which that tax distorts the price mechanism. This result suggests that a tax system with a broad tax base is likely to impose less excess burden than one with a narrow base. If the collection of tax is spread over a large number of goods and activities, then generally it will interfere less with consumer choice than if taxes were concentrated on a smaller area of the economy. This simple model, however, is not the end of the story because it cannot be used to examine the total effects on the economy as a whole. We shall, therefore, now turn to a more general approach.

The general approach

The general approach is not (as the partial approach is) limited to the consumption side of the economy: it also includes the production of goods. Again, we keep to a simple two-commodity model with goods X and Y. We continue to assume that each individual is the same and has the same income, expenditure patterns and so on. The position of the community can then be described, on a much smaller scale, by the position of anyone of its individual members.

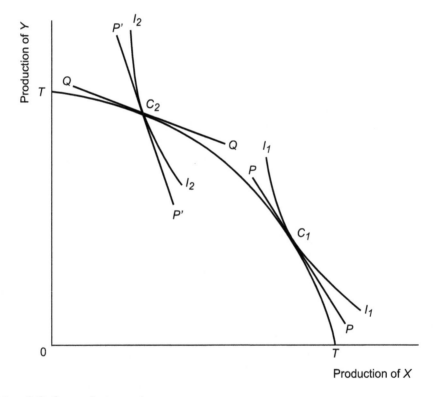

Figure 3.3 General approach

This is done in Figure 3.3. TT represents a microcosm of the production possibility frontier and shows the combinations of X and Y which can be produced. It is concave to the origin because the production of X and Y is subject to diminishing returns. The slope of TT at any point represents the social opportunity cost of producing each good in terms of the other. The highest indifference curve attainable by our representative individual is $I_1 I_1$ which means that his most preferred combination of X and Y is the point C_1 This is also the point which maximises profit for producers and is economically efficient in the way described earlier in this chapter. At C_1 the tangent to both TT and $I_1 I_1$ is the line PP, the slope of which represents the initial relative price of X and Y in terms of each other. This same price ratio initially faces both producers and consumers. Finally, as an additional simplifying assumption, suppose that the tax revenue raised is shared out equally among the taxpayers.

If a specific tax is imposed on X, its price will rise, and the relative price ratio will become steeper as shown, for example, by $P'P'$. As a result, consumers buy less X but more Y. Because the tax revenue is redistributed among consumers, our representative individual is not forced inside the production frontier. However, given the new relative price ratio, the highest attainable indifference curve is now $I_2 I_2$. Producers still face the real opportunity cost of producing Y in terms of X. This is shown by the price ratio represented by the slope of QQ. It is only the prices between producers and consumers that have been distorted. However, in a similar fashion to the situation described in Figure 3.1, a wedge has been driven between the price paid by the consumer for X and that received by the producer. Again, consumers have substituted away from consuming X as though the higher price were the result of a higher social opportunity cost of production, whereas it is only a result of the tax. Because the tax revenue is redistributed to taxpayers, the difference in benefit between $I_1 I_1$ and $I_2 I_2$ is the excess burden of the specific tax.

Contrast this result with that of an income tax. Under the previous assumptions such a tax would not affect the relative prices facing consumers. Also, because the tax is returned to taxpayers, our representative individual could continue to attain $I_1 I_1$, It follows, therefore, that in these circumstances the income tax imposes no excess burden.

So from both the partial and general approaches it is possible to examine the proposition that a specific indirect tax has a greater excess burden than an income tax. The time has now come to withdraw some of the assumptions and see if the proposition still holds in other circumstances. We begin by withdrawing the assumption that a state of Pareto-optimality existed before either tax was imposed.

A sub-optimal economy

The question now is whether a Pareto-optimal allocation of resources (C_1 in Figure 3.3) is the most appropriate starting point for the analysis. If either of our earlier assumptions of perfect competition or no external effects does not hold, then private marginal costs will diverge from price and the economy will tend to move away from an efficient allocation of resources. For example, if competition were restricted in an industry, from the extreme case of a monopoly to situations with a large number of sellers, we should expect the price of the goods produced by that industry to exceed the marginal cost of production. The greater the difference between price and marginal cost, the more encouragement there is for resources to be pushed away from the non-competitive industry. Hence in Figure 3.3, if the X industry were to be monopolised, the output of X would tend to fall, the production of Y to rise and the economy to move from C_1 to C_2.

With an economy starting at a sub-optimal position, it can easily be seen that the relative merits of an income tax and a specific tax might be reversed. If our economy is at C_2, an income tax will not alter this misallocation of resources for the reasons described above. On the other hand, an excise tax on Y will tend to readjust the relative price ratio of X and Y and push the economy back towards C_1 Despite the surprising implication that the output of the more competitive industry should be taxed in such circumstances, we can see that an indirect tax may have superior allocative effects over a direct tax. It could be said that an indirect tax may even have a 'negative excess burden' in such a situation, in that the value of the revenue received is greater than the costs imposed on taxpayers. A similar result occurs where there are external effects. Discussion of these circumstances, however, will be saved for Section 3.6 on indirect taxes.

Supply of labour

Although detailed consideration of the effects of taxation on the supply of resources is reserved for Chapter 4, we should show here how the withdrawal of the assumption of a fixed supply of labour affects the preceding analysis. In these circumstances, it is clear that income tax can also be a distorting factor. Rather than distorting the choice between different goods, it can distort the choice between goods and leisure. This was shown convincingly by Little (1951).

Suppose we have a simple three-good model consisting of food, clothing and leisure. Suppose also that labour is the only factor of production. If an excise tax were introduced on clothing, but not on food, it would distort the choice between food and clothing and also the choice between clothing and leisure. It would, however, leave the choice between food and leisure as before. A similar analysis applies for an excise tax on food, but not on clothing.

If an income tax were introduced it would also create distortions. It would distort the choice between food and leisure, and the choice between clothing and leisure. It would not, however, distort the choice between food and clothing. The two excise taxes and the income tax each distort two choices, but not the third. The relative merits of income and excise taxes depend, therefore, on how far each would actually distort particular choices. This in turn depends on a number of practical considerations, and we come now to the first of these, which is how direct taxes are actually operated in practice.

3.5 Direct taxes

There is no income tax in the world which taxes all incomes in the same way, as assumed above. An income tax which discriminates between incomes is likely to influence the allocation of resources and, as a result, may impose an excess burden on the community. One of the best ways of examining these influences is to compare the effects of an income tax with those of a poll tax of equal yield.

Income in kind

The first type of income that is difficult to tax is income in kind. This is income in the form of goods and services rather than cash, for example fringe benefits given by employers. This type of income is often not taxed adequately, or even not taxed at all, mainly because it is simply too difficult to measure or administer. The result is that there is a tendency for income to be taken in kind rather than in cash. It is not hard to show that this is economically inefficient. If an individual is paid for his services partly by the provision of, say, a new company car, he has to keep it unless he is allowed to sell it. If he were paid the cash equivalent he could buy the car if that were his first choice, but if he preferred anything else, he could use the cash to obtain it and so be better off. A likely preference might be to buy an older and cheaper car and use the rest of the money for other purposes. Ashworth and Dilnot (1987) estimated that overall tax revenue is some £1.1 billion less than if income in kind in the form of company cars were taxed in full.

Clearly, the greater the difference in tax liability between income paid in cash and income paid in kind, the greater the incentive for employees to demand (and employers to make) payment in kind rather than in cash. It is a curious effect of modern income tax that it may be encouraging the economy back towards a system of barter from which it took our impoverished ancestors an age to escape.

Examples of income in kind are abundant and the system appears to be thriving. For instance, nearly all forms of 'do-it-yourself' work fall into this category. If a man paints his own home, he does not pay income tax on his own services. In contrast, if he paid someone else to paint his house (or if he painted someone else's for cash) income tax is imposed on the transaction. The result is an incentive towards do-it-yourself work, even where it may be more efficient for individuals to specialise in the occupations at which they have a comparative advantage. Another example is the exemption from tax of the implicit income which individuals who own their homes receive from living in them. In contrast, the rent a tenant pays his landlord is taxed. The result may be an incentive to buy one's own home, even when it might otherwise be economically more efficient to rent, especially for the many people who have to move house from time to time.

It is interesting to speculate about how far income tax is responsible for the modern trend towards self-sufficiency simply because it fails to tax income in kind. Picture a modern income tax payer. Not only does he (or she) own and maintain his house, but he is his own chauffeur, mechanic, handyman, electrician, plumber and window-cleaner. Sundays are devoted to washing the car and gardening. He produces his own wine and serves himself at the local supermarket. Without pushing speculation too far, it is clear than an income tax which exempts most income in kind will encourage individuals towards self-sufficiency and trade by barter more than an equi-yield poll tax would. Some evidence on the extent of the distortion towards 'household labour' was provided by Boskin (1975) using US data for 1972. Boskin estimated that the annual cost of this distortion to the US economy was of the order of $20-$40 billion. For taxes in general, Ballard, Shoven and Whalley (1985) estimated that the gain from replacing the distortionary tax system in the USA with certain lump sum taxes would be between 13 and 24 per cent of revenue. The incremental deadweight cost is also high. Feldstein (2008, p. 137) estimated that the deadweight loss of an increase in all tax rates was 76 per cent and thus the costs of an additional $1 billion in taxes might be $1.76 billion.

Evasion

Apart from the lack of tax on income in kind, some incomes escape tax by evasion, even though they are received in cash. Although by the very nature of the subject very little is (officially) known about it, 'casual empiricism' suggests that evasion is fairly widespread, particularly in categories such as landlords, small businessmen and shopkeepers, and certain forms of casual employment. The factors determining tax evasion have been examined by Tanzi and Shome (1993), and there have been various estimates. For example, in 1979 Sir William Pile, then Chairman of the Board of Inland Revenue, stated that it was 'not implausible' that incomes not declared for tax purposes could amount to 7.5 per cent of gross domestic product: a view endorsed in 1980 by his successor as Chairman (Inland Revenue, 1981). Slemrod (2007) concluded that the net noncompliance rate overall for US federal taxes and the individual income tax appears to be around 14 per cent. Further evidence on the 'black' economy is provided by Smith (1986) and Pyle (1989) and research in a number of disciplines on tax evasion is reviewed by Spicer (1986). The importance of tax evasion is due to the likely effects on the allocation of labour, since occupations which afford opportunities to evade tax are likely to be more attractive than those which do not. There are, of course, also administrative and non-compliance costs, both in the efforts of individuals to evade tax, and in the efforts of the tax authorities to prevent such evasion. There may be further economic distortion in product markets where traders who evade taxes have a price advantage over traders who pay their full tax liability. Another form of excess burden caused by evasion is an increase in uncertainty because, of course, those intending to evade taxes do not know whether or not they will be caught (Jung et al. 1994).

Administration

Administrative considerations may result effectively in tax being levied at different rates on different incomes. For instance, in practice more deductions are available to the self-employed than to employees (see Section 8.6 for the UK arrangements). In effect, this can mean that self-employment income is taxed at lower rates. The result again may be a reallocation of resources. In this case, individuals may seek to become self-employed, even though from an economic viewpoint it might be more efficient for them to work as employees.

Spending patterns are almost certain to be affected when particular items of expenditure are allowable against income for particular political purposes. The tax treatment of mortgage interest payments has been one example. It may well be that society considers itself to be better off by encouraging particular forms of expenditure in this way, but it should be realised that it may involve a loss of economic efficiency. We shall have more to say about these tax deductions in Section 3.8 below.

Allocation of factors of production

Income taxes (as opposed to, say, a poll tax) may also affect the allocation of factors of production between different industries. Again, to allow us to concentrate on the allocation of resources, discussion of the overall supply of factors will be deferred to the following chapter. We can begin here with the allocation of labour.

One of the reasons why different occupations are associated with different wage rates is that some jobs are more demanding than others. A particular job may involve more effort, risk, discomfort, or training than other occupations. The less attractive aspects of the job have therefore to be compensated for in money, so that a sufficient number of individuals are prepared to undertake it. North Sea diving is a good example. Other jobs may be more pleasant, even enjoyable, and so require less pecuniary compensation: teaching, for instance. In the development of economic thought these divergences in wages were known as 'equalising differences', because they tended to equalise the net benefit (pecuniary and non-pecuniary) of different occupations for similar individuals.

A proportional income tax, as opposed to a poll tax, can influence these 'equalising differences' where different jobs require different levels of pecuniary remuneration. Imagine, for instance, a simple economy where workers are exactly the same in the sense that they have the same abilities, attitudes, preferences and so on, and that there are two types of job.

The first job, which is rather a pleasant occupation, can attract the required number of workers with a wage of £6,000 per year. The second job is less pleasant and, to persuade enough workers to come forward, requires a further premium of £4,000 per annum, making £10,000 in all. Suppose now that a certain level of government revenue has to be raised, either by a proportional income tax, or by a poll tax. Suppose that the required level of the poll tax would be £4,000 per person, and that to raise the same revenue (after allowing for any effects resulting from the imposition of the tax) the proportional income tax rate would have to be set at 50 per cent of income. Finally, suppose for simplicity that neither tax affects gross wages.

It can be seen at once that the poll tax would not change the wage differential between the two jobs:

	No tax wage £	Net wage with a £4,000 poll tax £	Net wage with a 50% income tax £
Pleasant job	6,000	2,000	3,000
Unpleasant job	10,000	6,000	5,000
Differential	4,000	4,000	2,000

A proportional income tax, however, may have such a result, as it reduces the differential between the two jobs, in this case by half. We may, therefore, expect a flow of labour away from those jobs which require pecuniary compensation for their unpopular characteristics, and towards jobs that are more congenial. A progressive income tax will have even more pronounced effects.

Progressive income taxes may also discriminate against occupations with fluctuating earnings, because each tax year is usually considered separately from every other tax year. For example, take two occupations which yield the same income over the lifetime of the worker. The first job yields the same amount of income each year, and consequently incurs the same tax liability each year. The second job has a lower income in some years and a higher income in others. Over a lifetime, the job with the fluctuating income will incur a higher tax liability because the progressive tax structure pushes the worker into higher tax brackets in the high income years. Examples of jobs like this include authors and actors. Also, this applies to those occupations where incomes rise over a person's working life.

In principle, the adverse treatment of incomes that rise or fall (or both) could be avoided by appropriate averaging provisions. In other words, an individual's tax liability in anyone year could be determined with reference to his income in other years. There are some such provisions in a number of countries, but their potential complexity prevents their widespread adoption. For instance, in the United Kingdom authors are permitted to spread their income, but this concession is not extended to most occupations. So we may conclude, therefore, that a progressive income tax is likely to discriminate against those occupations where the remuneration changes from year to year.

In a similar fashion, it can be shown that a progressive income tax may affect the allocation of capital between different industries more than a proportional income tax or a poll tax would. The important features in this case are the risk involved in different types of investments and how individuals react to this risk. A further influence is the extent to which individuals are permitted to offset their losses against their gains for tax purposes. These will not, however, be examined closely in this chapter, though a parallel discussion appears in Chapter 4, concerning the overall supply of capital.

3.6 Indirect taxes

In Section 3.4 it was suggested that, in certain circumstances, indirect taxes could improve economic welfare. This section will explore these circumstances in more detail, and then go on to examine the welfare losses associated with indirect taxes in other circumstances.

Possible welfare gains

In looking at the effects of indirect taxes on the efficient operation of an economy, let us first consider the case where a tax might actually increase economic welfare. As we have seen in Section 3.4, this may occur where there are external effects.

The traditional example of an external cost is a factory polluting the surrounding environment. If the owners of this factory do not remove the effects of the pollution, a cost is clearly imposed on the community. Another example concerns congestion costs. If a large firm moves into a crowded city it will increase the congestion suffered by the inhabitants, yet only a small part of the increase in inconvenience will apply to the firm itself. This point is explored by Mishan (1967). Like many other ideas in economics, this one finally gained wider attention, in this case as a result of growing concern for 'the environment'. There has, therefore, been increasing discussion of the potential benefits of 'pollution charges' and other forms of corrective taxation, for example by Cordes *et al.* (1990), Nicolaisen *et al.* (1991), Summers (1991), Smith (1992), Symons *et al.* (1994) and Oates (1995).

Turning to an illustration, suppose an industry in the process of producing a good X inflicts external costs on the community at large. In Figure 3.4 the demand for X is represented by the demand curve DD. The total cost to society of producing X is shown by S_SS_S. However, because there are external costs, the private costs of production (that is, those costs borne by the industry itself) are less than S_SS_S and are represented by S_pS_p.' If the market is competitive, the industry will tend to produce an amount Q_1 which is the level at which private costs are just equal to the price. Yet by the definition in Section 3.2, the optimum level of production is the lower amount Q_2. At levels of output in excess of Q_2, the total costs to society of the extra production exceed the benefits.

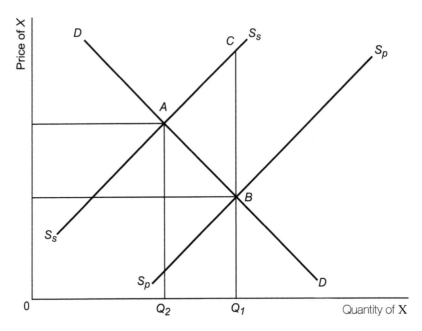

Figure 3.4 An excise tax and external effects

Clearly, there are a number of ways by which the industry could be encouraged to cut back production, for example by regulation. However, it may be possible to retain the benefits of the market mechanism by imposing an excise tax on X to represent the external costs inflicted by the industry on the community. If the tax accurately reflected the external costs, the industry's supply curve would become SsSs' and production would tend to fall back to Q2' Such a tax would therefore have a beneficial effect on economic welfare, that is a negative excess burden. By similar reasoning to that in Section 3.4, this welfare gain is given by the triangle ABG.

A similar result may occur where a consumer does not act in his own best interest. For instance, it is possible (nay, all too easy) to imagine an individual who does not take full account of the future results of some of his actions, and who smokes or drinks (or both) to excess. In the words of Pigou (1932), 'it follows that the aggregate amount of economic satisfaction which people in fact enjoy is much less than it would be if their telescopic faculty were not perverted'. If it is true in some instances that the government knows better than individuals what is in their best interests (and is prepared to act in those interests), then there is an economic case for public sector intervention to discourage excess consumption of certain goods. One way of doing this is to impose an excise tax on such goods. Such arguments have therefore been used to support the taxation of alcohol (Cook and Moore, 1994; Irvine and Sims, 1993) and the taxation of tobacco (Viscusi, 1994) with some form of sin tax.

Minimising welfare losses

If more revenue is needed after having used all the taxes which have beneficial effects on economic welfare, we must· turn to those taxes which impose least excess burden. These are the taxes which distort economic activity the least. The size of the excess burden varies directly with substitutability in supply and demand (Georgakopoulos, 1991). This can be illustrated by examining the price elasticities of demand and supply for various commodities. To begin with, let us suppose that the elasticities of supply of different commodities are the same. It is then possible to show that, for any given level of indirect taxation, excess burden will be minimised if the tax is imposed on the goods with the lowest elasticities of demand.

In Figure 3.5 it is assumed for simplicity that there is a perfectly elastic supply schedule (S_1S_1) for good G. It is also supposed that there are two possible demand curves for G; the first is D_1D_1 and the second a more elastic schedule, D_2D_2. A specific tax on G will result in the supply schedule rising to S_tS_t. The tax will raise the same amount of revenue whichever demand schedule applies. However, it can be seen that, if the relevant demand curve were D_2D_2 the loss of the consumer surplus as a result of the tax would be the area ABC. However, if the demand curve were the less elastic D_1D_1, the welfare loss would be the smaller triangle ADC.

The moral of this story is that if a tax is imposed on a good and if all other things are equal, then the lower the price elasticity of demand is for a particular good, the lower will be the welfare loss. This point may also be seen intuitively from Figure 3.5, by noticing that the output of G would be less affected by the tax if D_1D_1 (the less elastic schedule) applied. For example, the demand for alcohol is relatively price

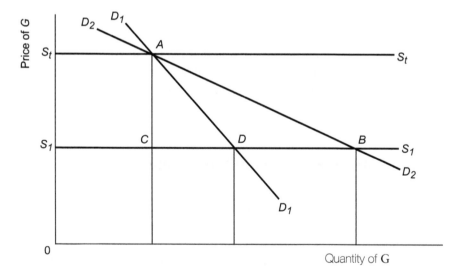

Figure 3.5 Excess burden and price elasticity

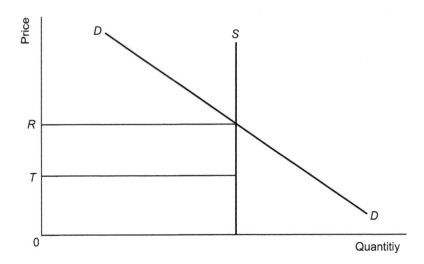

Figure 3.6 Zero elasticity of supply

inelastic and, despite the external costs associated with drinking, revenue raising appears to be the main rationale for alcohol taxes (O'Hagan, 1983).

It can also be shown that, if all other things are equal (including the elasticity of demand), then with the imposition of a tax, lower welfare losses will be associated with lower elasticities of supply. An extreme case would be a zero elasticity of supply, as shown in Figure 3.6. Here an excise tax lower than an amount OR (for example, a tax of RT) would affect neither the amount produced nor the price at which it was sold. As we shall see in Chapter 5, the entire burden in such cases will be borne by the supplier. It is interesting to note that this is one of the traditional arguments in favour of taxing land; on the assumption that land is in fixed supply, taxing the rent will not reduce the amount of land available for production. In the words of Henry George (1882), 'it is not necessary to confiscate the land; it is only necessary to confiscate rent'. It should be added that, in a number of senses, the supply of land as a factor of production is not inelastic in supply – see for example Prest (1981).

3.7 Administrative and compliance costs

Excess burden is not the only characteristic which should be considered in judging the relative merits of various taxes. There are also the direct costs of actually running a tax system. Earlier, we described the costs to the public sector as administrative costs, and those to the private sector as compliance costs.

Some costs can be imposed on either the private or the public sectors. The process of assessment, for example, may be undertaken by the revenue service, or taxpayers can be made to assess themselves; see Barr *et al.* (1977). More generally, however, those features of a tax that impose costs on one sector also tend to impose costs on the other. The most important of these features, the degree of complexity, clearly influences administrative and compliance costs in the same direction.

It is relatively easy to isolate some of the more detailed factors that determine the costs of a tax to both sectors. These include the amount of work required to determine liability, the frequency of payment, and the number of 'tax points' or taxpayers from whom the revenue has to be collected. Attempts at avoidance and evasion involve both compliance (or 'non-compliance') costs to the private sector in taking advantage of these opportunities, and administrative costs to the public sector in trying to hinder the process.

Change is also expensive. When the administration of an existing tax is changed, or a new tax is introduced, both the taxpayers and the authorities face costs of adaptation to the new system. Yet, although administrative and compliance costs have many things in common, it is worthwhile taking a look at each in turn.

Administrative costs

In comparison with the excess burden of taxes and with compliance costs, administrative costs are easy to measure. Administrative costs should, of course, include the full resource cost to the public sector of operating each tax. They should therefore include not only the wages and salaries of staff, and the full cost of the accommodation and materials used by the staff, but also the services received but not paid for from other departments.

The most useful way of presenting these costs is as a percentage of the revenue collected. It is then possible to compare the costs of collecting different taxes, and to see how these costs have been changing over time. For example, Table 3.1 indicates that the percentage cost of collecting VAT is high relative to the administrative costs of collecting excise duties. It also indicates that the cost of collecting customs duties is unusually high, though that figure also includes the costs of activities such as the prevention of drug smuggling and enforcing a variety of other prohibitions and restrictions. Presenting these costs as a percentage of revenue is also a very useful way of comparing the costs of revenue authorities in different countries.

Table 3.1 Examples of administrative costs of collecting taxes in 2000/01

	Revenue	Cost	Cost as a percentage of revenue
	£m	£m	%
VAT	58,622	406.1	0.69
Excise duties	38.444	53.4	0.14
Customs duties	2,099	110.3	5.26

Source: House of commons, Hansard, Written Answers for 25 April 2002.

Compliance costs

Compliance costs are very much more difficult to calculate. The costs of complying with the requirements of a tax include not only money spent on accountants and tax guides, but also taxpayers' time spent in completing returns. The mental costs to taxpayers of any anxiety suffered as a result of the operation of the tax must also be included. Although this is not a direct pecuniary expense, it is 'certainly equivalent to the expense at which every man would be willing to redeem himself from it' (Smith, 1776, Book V, Ch. II). Then there are the costs to third parties, such as friends and relatives who are asked to assist taxpayers with their returns, and the costs to firms and other institutions of acting as tax collectors, for example in withholding their employees' tax and accounting for it to the Revenue.

Clearly, compliance costs, or the 'hidden costs of taxation' in the words of Sandford, are very much harder to calculate than administrative costs. Such estimates as there are of compliance costs suggest that they can be substantial. For example, Sandford (1973, p. 44) estimated that the measurable compliance costs of direct personal taxes in England and Wales in 1970 were somewhere between 2.5 and 4.4 per cent of the revenue collected. Sandford's initial work has been followed by a series of studies which have thrown considerably more light on compliance costs. These include four main surveys, the first of which was a survey of the compliance costs associated with value added tax in 1977/78. The second was a study of employers' costs of administering the Pay-As-You-Earn (PAYE) system of withholding income tax and National Insurance contributions from salaries and wages paid in 1981/82. The next was an investigation of the compliance costs of personal taxpayers in relation to their personal income tax and capital gains liabilities for 1983/84, and the fourth main survey was concerned with value added tax once more, this time for the year 1986/87. These surveys are notable, among other things, for the full co-operation given by the tax authorities.

This work has been summarised in Sandford *et al.* (1989) and up-dated and extended so that estimates may be made of the total operating costs (that is administrative plus compliance costs) of the United Kingdom tax system for the year 1986/87. It was estimated that for 1986/87 total operating costs amounted to over £5 billion, or some 4 per cent of total tax revenue. Looked at a different way, compliance costs appear to exceed 1 per cent of the United Kingdom Gross Domestic Product at factor cost and, together with administrative costs, add up to about 1.5 per cent of GDP. As the authors suggest, figures of 1 or 1.5 per cent might seem small, but they represent the activities of a very large industry and compare, for example, with the 1.8 per cent of GDP accounted for by agriculture, fishing and forestry combined.

Apart from the sheer size of the sums involved, there are several important policy implications. One is the distribution of compliance costs. In the personal sector they have fallen disproportionately on certain sectors of the population, in particular poorer pensioners and, at least before the introduction of independent taxation in 1990, widows and divorced or separated women. Under the pre-1990 arrangements, married women were often left out of the tax assessment process so that bereavement or separation often imposed something of a tax culture shock. The distribution of compliance costs among businesses is such that they fall disproportionately on small firms, which can put them at a significant disadvantage in competition with larger firms.

Comparisons with other countries are not always easy, but high compliance costs have also been reported elsewhere. For example, on the basis of a survey of taxpayers in Minnesota, Slemrod and Sorum (1984) estimated US income tax compliance costs to be between 5 and 7 per cent of revenue. The survey covered state as well as federal income taxes and the ratio would be affected by the lower yield of US income tax per capita. Slemrod (1989) has also attempted to estimate possible savings in compliance costs from simplification of the US tax system, and clearly this area provides considerable scope for increasing the efficiency of tax systems. So, in considering the costs of various taxes, one has to include not only the excess burden of the taxes and public sector administrative costs, but also the private sector's costs of compliance.

The allocation of costs

Where administrative functions can be carried out either by the private sector or by the public sector, the question arises as to which should perform these tasks. It has been suggested by Sandford (1973, p. 160) that, all other things being equal, there are three reasons for preferring public administrative costs to private compliance costs.

First, administrative costs are met out of general tax revenue which is extracted from the taxpaying community in line with the government's concept of equity and general tax policy. Compliance costs, on the other hand, fall unevenly on private taxpayers (and some non-taxpayers) and can be surprisingly regressive in their incidence; see Sandford (1973). Second, compliance costs may lead to more taxpayer resentment and reluctance to comply with the tax system than would equivalent administration costs. Third, we have seen that compliance costs are very much harder to calculate than administrative costs. This may lead to a tendency for tax policy-makers to be less concerned about rising compliance costs than about rising administrative costs.

However, in some cases it might be cheaper for particular tasks to be done in the private sector. For example, the Pay-As-You-Earn scheme uses employers as tax collectors and is almost certainly cheaper than any method by which the tax authorities could undertake equivalent work. In addition, it could be argued that a competitive private market sector is more likely than the public sector to find and develop the most efficient methods of carrying out such work.

3.8 Tax expenditure

A separate topic, but nevertheless one relevant to discussion of taxation and efficiency, is the subject of *tax expenditure*. This occurs when some fiscal advantage is conferred on a group of individuals, or a particular activity, by reducing tax liability rather than by direct cash subsidy. This area was first seriously considered by Surrey (1973) who reported a tax expenditure budget for the USA of between $60 billion and $65 billion, a sum equal to a quarter of the regular budget at that time. More recently, Weinberg (1987) estimated that the annual revenue loss arising from tax expenditure in the USA was approximately $250 billion, and Davie (1994) found some 244 tax expenditure provisions in US Federal excise taxes. In the UK tax expenditure includes contributions to registered pension schemes, personal tax credits, individual savings accounts, and further examples, as shown in Table 3.2.

Table 3.2 Examples of estimated tax expenditures in the UK 2011/12

Income tax	£ million
Registered pension schemes	18,900
Personal tax credits	4,800
Individual savings accounts	2,100
Income of charities	1,550
Redundancy payments	900
Employer supported childcare exemption	380
Corporation tax	
R & D tax credits	880
National Insurance Contributions	
Relief for employer contributions to registered pension schemes	8,200
Capital gains tax	
Disposal of a person's only or main residence	11,500
Value added tax - zero rating	
Food	15,700
Construction of new dwellings and DIY builders	6,250
Domestic passenger transport	3,200
Water and sewerage services	1,900
Books, newspapers and magazines	1,700
Children's clothing	1,550
Reduced rate - Domestic fuel and power	5,450

Source: http://www.hmrc.gov.uk/stats/tax_expenditures/table1-5.pdf

The case of UK occupational pensions is analysed by Dilnot and Johnson (1993). Clearly, both tax concessions and cash subsidies have much in common. They allow the government to favour certain groups of activities, and they both require the level of taxation on others to be higher, or public expenditure on alternative projects to be lower, than would otherwise be the case. But the use of tax expenditure to achieve these aims may be less efficient than an equivalent system of cash payments.

The first difficulty is that subsidies through a tax expenditure programme are relatively hidden. When the government provides cash aid, the figures are widely known, and are scrutinised carefully by the executive and by Parliament both in debate and in committees such as the Treasury and Civil Service Committee. Direct subsidies are therefore open to review, debate and possible alteration at regular intervals. This is not so for tax concessions. Although deductions against tax liabilities are costs to government in the same way as cash payments or provisions in kind, they remain comparatively hidden and secure from scrutiny. Hence, it is even more likely than with outright subsidies that tax deductions may remain even when the case for them has diminished or even disappeared.

There are difficulties in calculating the level of tax expenditure. The net revenue loss of anyone allowance depends on the marginal tax rates of the taxpayers concerned. This in turn depends on what other allowances are received by the relevant taxpayers. It also, of course, depends on their incomes. A list of direct tax allowances and relief's now appears each year in official statistics, but it is clear that tax expenditure still receives far less attention than cash expenditure does.

A second and related difficulty is that the 'tax expenditure budget', being relatively hidden, is not methodically co-ordinated with the regular government Budget. The results can be quite curious. The 1972 Green Paper, Proposals for a Tax-Credit System, for example, looked at the interaction of the then current tax allowances and cash payments for children. It found that the overlap formed 'a serious problem. The combination of the full tax allowances and family allowances alone resulted in nine different rates. Nor can it really be said that the differing amounts have a logical connection with one another' (para. 3).

A third problem is that allowances against tax are not worth the same amounts to different people. The most obvious example is that people who do not receive a sufficiently high income to render them liable to tax do not gain any benefit from deductions against tax. Furthermore, the benefit in tax saved is greater for individuals subject to higher rates of tax.

A fourth difficulty is that tax expenditures complicate the tax system itself.

Increased complexity inevitably increases administrative and compliance costs and, given the other problems, it seems reasonable to suggest that a convincing case ought to be made before aid for a particular cause is given through tax expenditure rather than by explicit subsidy.

The question why tax expenditure rather than direct subsidy is used to dispense aid is interesting. Apart from any historical reasons, it might be that politicians would prefer not to be seen spending public money, and so they hide behind the veil of taxation. For the same sorts of reasons, those in receipt of benefits from the state may well prefer a tax concession to a cash handout. It might be that the pervasiveness of the modern tax system is such that tax expenditure is a convenient tool for those wishing to manipulate the economy. Whatever the reasons, it is clear that the subject of tax expenditure deserves more attention than it has received to date.

3.9 Summary

Apart from the revenue actually raised, taxation imposes economic costs on society. These costs may be classified into three groups: the excess burden of taxat ion, compliance costs, and administrative costs.

The excess burden of a particular tax depends on its effects on the working of the price mechanism. In practice, the actual burden is determined by a large number of factors, such as the rates and coverage of particular taxes. In some circumstances, where the market is not working efficiently, it is possible that some taxes can be used to improve economic welfare.

Administrative and compliance costs are the costs of operating a tax system imposed on the public and private sectors respectively. The evidence suggests that these costs can be considerable, and vary significantly between different taxes.

'Tax expenditure' is used to provide assistance to particular groups, or for particular causes, through reductions in tax liability rather than by the more direct method of cash payments. There are a number of possible disadvantages associated with the use of tax expenditure.

Further reading

The relative merits of direct and indirect taxes are considered further in Little (1951), Friedman (1952), Walker (1955), Harberger (1974) and Atkinson (1977). Cnossen (2005) has edited a collection of essays on excise taxation including the taxation of tobacco, alcohol, gambling, pollution, solid waste and road use and Muller and Sterner (2006) present 28 papers on environmental taxation. Tax evasion is examined by Slemrod (2007) and administrative and compliance costs by Sandford *et al.* (1989). Tax expenditure is covered by Surrey (1973), Willis and Hardwick (1978) and Aaron and Boskin (1980), Part II. Much of the material in this and the following three chapters is treated in greater detail by Prest and Barr (1985) and Musgrave and Musgrave (1989).

References

Aaron, H.J. and Boskin, M.J. (1980), *The Economics of Taxation*, Brookings Institution.

Ashworth, M. and Dilnot, A. (1987), 'Company cars taxation', *Fiscal Studies*, Vol. 8, No. 4, pp. 24-38.

Atkinson, A.B. (1977), 'Optimal taxation and the direct versus indirect tax controversy', *Canadian Journal of Economics*, Vol. 10, pp. 590-606.

Ballard, C.C., Shoven, J.B. and Whalley, J. (1985), 'The total welfare cost of the United States tax system: a general equilibrium approach', *National Tax Journal*, Vol. 38, No. 2, pp. 125-40.

Barr, N.A., James, S.R and Prest, A.R (1977), *Self-Assessment for Income Tax*, Heinemann Educational Books.

Boskin, M.J. (1975), 'Efficiency aspects of the differential tax treatment of market and household economic activity', *Journal of Public Economics*, Vol. 4, pp. 1-25.

Cnossen, S. (ed.) (2005), *Theory and Practice of Excise Taxation: Smoking, Drinking, Gambling, Polluting and Driving*, Oxford University Press.

Cook, P.J. and Moore, M.J. (1994), 'This tax's for you: the case for higher beer taxes', *National Tax Journal*, Vol. XLVII, pp. 559-73.

Cordes, J.J., Nicholson, KM. and Sammartino, EJ. (1990), 'Raising revenue by taxing activities with social costs', *National Tax Journal*, Vol. XLIII, No. 3.

Davie, B.F. (1994), 'Tax expenditures in the federal excise tax system, *National Tax Journal*, Vol. XLVII, pp. 39-62.

Dilnot, A. and Johnson, P. (1993), 'Tax expenditures: the case of occupational pensions', *Fiscal Studies*, Vol. 14, No. 1, pp. 42-56.

Feldstein, M. (2008), 'Effects of taxes on economic behavior', *National Tax Journal*, Vol. LXI, No. 1, pp. 131-139.

Friedman, M. (1952), 'The "welfare" effects of an income tax and an excise tax', *Journal of Political Economy*, pp. 25-33, plus a revision in pp. 332-6.

Georgakopoulos, T.A. (1991), 'Substitutability and the size of the excess burden of taxation: a general equilibrium presentation', *Public Finance*, Vol. XXXXVI, No. 3, pp. 415-23.

George, H. (1882), *Progress and Poverty*, Kegan Paul, Trench & Co., p. 364.

Harberger, A.C. (1974), *Taxation and Welfare*, Little Brown.

Hicks, J.R. (1939), *Value and Capital*, Oxford University Press.

Inland Revenue (1981), *123rd Report* (for the year ended 31st March 1980), HMSO

Irvine, I. J. and Sims, W.A. (1993), 'The welfare effects of alcohol taxation', *Journal of Public Economics*, Vol. 52, pp. 83-100.

Joseph, M.F.W. (1939), 'The excess burden of indirect taxation', *Review of Economic Studies*, Vol. 6, No. 3, pp. 226-31.

Jung, Y.H., Snow, A. and Trandel, G.A. (1994), 'Tax evasion and the size of the underground economy', *Journal of Public Economics*, Vol. 54, pp. 391-402.

Little, I.M.D. (1951), 'Direct versus indirect taxes', *Economic Journal*, Vol. 61, pp. 577-84.

Mishan, E. J. (1967), *The Costs of Economic Growth*, Penguin Books.

Muller, A. and Sterner, T. (eds) (2006), *Environmental Taxation in Practice*, Ashgate Publishing.

Musgrave, R.A. and Musgrave, P.B. (1989), *Public Finance in Theory and Practice*, 5th edn, McGraw-Hill.

Nicolaisen, J., Dean, A. and Hoeller, P. (1991), 'Economics and the environment: a survey of issues and policy options', *OECD Economics Studies*, No. 16, Spring.

Oates, W.E. (1995), 'Green Taxes, Can we protect the environment and improve the tax system at the same time?', *Southern Economic Journal*, Vol. 61, pp. 915-22.

O'Hagan, J.W. (1983), 'The rationale for special taxes on alcohol: a critique', *British Tax Review*, pp. 370-80.

Pigou, A.C. (1932), *The Economics of Welfare*, 4th edn, Macmillan, p. 26.

Prest, A.R (1981), *The Taxation of Urban Land*, Manchester University Press.

Prest, A.R and Barr, N.A. (1985), *Public Finance in Theory and Practice*, 7th edn, Weidenfeld and Nicolson.

Proposals for a Tax-Credit System, Cmnd. 5116, HMSO, 1972.

Pyle, D. (1989), *Tax Evasion and the Black Economy*, Macmillan.

Sandford, C.T. (1973), *Hidden Costs of Taxation*, Institute for Fiscal Studies.

Sandford, C.T., Godwin, M. and Hardwick, P. (1989), *Administrative and Compliance Costs of Taxation*, Fiscal Publications.

Slemrod, J. (1989), 'The return to tax simplification: an econometric analysis', *Public Finance Quarterly*, January.

Slemrod, J. (2007), 'Cheating ourselves: The economics of tax evasion', *Journal of Economic Perspectives*, Vol. 21, No. 1, pp. 25-48.

Slemrod, J. and Sorum, N. (1984), 'The compliance cost of the US individual tax system', *National Tax Journal*, Vol. XXXVII, No. 4, pp. 461-74.

Smith, A. (1776), *The Wealth of Nations*, Cannan edn, Methuen, 1950.

Smith, S. (1992), 'Taxation and the environment', *Fiscal Studies*, Vol. 13, No. 4, pp. 1-57.

Smith, S.R. (1986), *Britain's Shadow Economy*, Oxford University Press.

Spicer, M.W. (1986), 'Civilization at a discount: the problem of tax evasion', *National Tax Journal*, Vol. XXXIX, No. 1, pp. 13-20.

Summers, L.H. (1991), 'The case for corrective taxation', *National Tax Journal*, Vol. XLIV, No. 3, September.

Surrey, S.S. (1973), *Pathways to Tax Reform*, Harvard University Press.

Symons, E., Proops, J. and Gay, P. (1994), 'Carbon taxes, consumer demand and carbon dioxide emissions: a simulation analysis for the UK', *Fiscal Studies*, Vol. 15, No. 2, pp. 19-43.

Tanzi, V. and Shome, P. (1993), 'A primer on tax evasion', *IMF Staff Papers*, Vol. 40, No. 4, pp. 807-28.

Viscusi, W.K. (1994), 'Promoting smokers' welfare with responsible taxation', *National Tax Journal*, Vol. XLVII, pp. 547-58.

Walker, D. (1995), 'The direct and indirect tax problem: fifteen years of controversy', *Public Finance*, Vol. 10, pp. 153-76.

Weinberg, D. (1987), 'The distributional implications of tax expenditures and comprehensive income taxation', *National Tax Journal*, Vol. XL, June.

Willis, J.R.M. and Hardwick, P.J.W. (1978), *Tax Expenditures in the United Kingdom*, Institute for Fiscal Studies.

Self assessment questions

Suggested answers to self-assessment questions are given at the back of the book.

3.1   What is the 'excess burden' of a tax?

3.2   List some factors which might affect the size of the 'excess burden' of a tax.

3.3   Under an existing progressive income tax system, an individual is indifferent between a low paid but pleasant job and a higher paid but unpleasant job. Suppose the income tax were now made proportional. Would the individual be more likely to favour the pleasant or the unpleasant job?

3.4   How might a tax be used to increase economic efficiency?

3.5   What excess burden of a tax is imposed on a good which has a zero price elasticity of supply?

3.6   What excess burden of a tax is imposed on a good which has a zero price elasticity of demand?

3.7   Apart from an excess burden, what other economic costs might be associated with a tax?

3.8   What is tax expenditure?

Discussion questions

1.   Why is the efficiency of a tax system important?

2.   What economic costs can taxation impose on society?

3.   What factors might cause a tax to be inefficient?

4.   Under what circumstances might the excess burden of an income tax exceed the excess burden of an indirect tax of equal yield?

5.   For any particular tax with which you are familiar, analyse the main features in terms of economic efficiency or inefficiency.

6.   How would you reform the tax system if you wished to increase the level of economic efficiency?

7.   Suppose that the government had to choose between two taxes which were identical in every way, except that one increased administrative costs and the other increased compliance costs by the same amount. Which tax would you recommend and why?

8.   Assess the advantages and disadvantages of using tax expenditure as a method of influencing economic activity

CHAPTER FOUR

Taxation and incentives

After reading this chapter, you should be able to:

- Define economic efficiency.
- Identify the income and substitution effects of a tax.
- Use the income and substitution effects to analyse the effect of change in tax rates on a person's work effort.
- Understand the effect that changing the degree of progressivity of a tax system might have on the supply of labour.
- Summarise the empirical evidence of the effects of taxation on labour supply.
- Describe the effects that taxation might have on saving and capital formation.
- Explain the effects that taxation might have on risk-taking and enterprise.

4.1 Introduction

It is regularly asserted that taxation provides a disincentive to people to undertake economic activity. The frequency and vigour of these statements is perhaps understandable. As a popular political issue, the subject is capable of generating a fair amount of heat but, it seems, very little light. Certainly it has long been known by economists that, in some circumstances, taxation can provide positive incentives. For example McCulloch (1864) took the view that an increase in taxation 'so long as it is confined within moderate limits ... acts as a powerful stimulus to industry and economy, and most commonly occasions the production of more wealth than it abstracts'. John Stuart Mill (1871) suggested that 'experience has shown that a large proportion of the results of labour and abstinence [saving] may be taken away by fixed taxation, without impairing, and sometimes even with the effect of stimulating, the qualities from which a great production and an abundant capital rise'. The purpose of this chapter, therefore, is to examine the theory of the effects of taxation on incentives, and to look briefly at some of the empirical work that has been carried out. We shall deal in turn with the effects of taxation on work effort, on saving and on enterprise.

4.2 Effects of income tax on work effort

The question that should be tackled first is why one should wish to examine the effects of taxation on work effort. Economic welfare consists of not only the material income from work, but also the psychic benefit individuals receive from leisure. Man does not live by GNP alone! Individuals will maximise their welfare in this respect if they work up to the point where the benefit from a small amount of extra work is just equal to the benefit of taking the same amount of time as leisure. Below that level the marginal benefits from work exceed those from leisure, and above that level the reverse is true.

Therefore, the problem is not simply maximising the number of hours people spend at work. The role of economics here is to see if the effects of various taxes on work effort can be predicted and, if they can, whether or not they are likely to influence adversely individuals' choices between work and leisure. For example, individuals may work less than the ideal amount because part of the benefit from working is taxed away.

One other preliminary point should be made at this stage. The total supply of labour is determined by both the average amount that individuals work, and the overall size of the population. However, for three reasons, we shall not concern ourselves here with the effect of taxes on population growth. First, it is not clear what the optimum population for any given area is. Second, it seems unlikely that any normal tax system would have a major effect on the birth rate (though this is possible: see the end of Section 3.3); and such effect as there is on work effort would clearly occur only in the very long run. Third, even if the total supply of labour were increasing as a result of population growth, there would still be concern about the per capita level of income, and therefore concern about the work effort of existing individuals. So we shall confine ourselves here to the examination of the work effort of the existing population.

Initially we shall look at the effects of taxation in the context of the supply curve of labour, and then go on to analyse these effects in more detail.

Supply curve of labour

Examining the supply curve of labour is perhaps the simplest way of tackling this issue. To concentrate on the essential points, we shall make some simplifying assumptions which will be relaxed towards the end of this section. We shall assume that individuals can vary their hours of work; that there are no non-pecuniary benefits

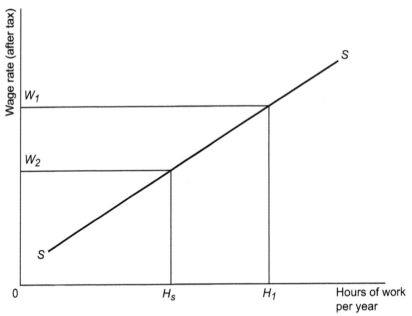

Figure 4.1 The supply curve of labour

from work; and that all earnings are taxable. Let us further suppose that each hour of work is equally productive that there is only one wage rate and that the demand for labour is perfectly elastic. The tax imposed is a proportional income tax, and the revenue raised by it is spent on something that does not affect the workforce.

If the supply curve of labour is upward sloping (like SS in Figure 4.1), it follows that an increase in income tax will reduce the number of hours worked. This can be seen by imagining the pre-increase wage rate to be W_1 and the hours worked to be H_1. An increase in income tax would reduce the net wage rate to, say, W_2 and the hours of work to H_2. However, while it is true that in these circumstances an income tax is a disincentive to work effort, in other circumstances it may result in more work.

Suppose now that the supply curve of labour bends back on itself, as in Figure 4.2. This simply means that if wage rates rise beyond a certain point people will choose to work less. This may be interpreted as individuals choosing to enjoy part of their increased prosperity in the form of more leisure. Historically, in industrialised countries hours of work have fallen as wage rates have risen, and some further evidence for the existence of a backward-bending supply curve is discussed in Section 4.3.

In these circumstances, a similar increase in income tax will result in more hours worked. In Figure 4.2, a drop in the after-tax wage rate from W_3 to W_4 will result in an increase in hours worked from H_3 to H_4. So it can be seen that the effects of taxation are not as straightforward as might appear at first sight. We shall now take the analysis a little but further.

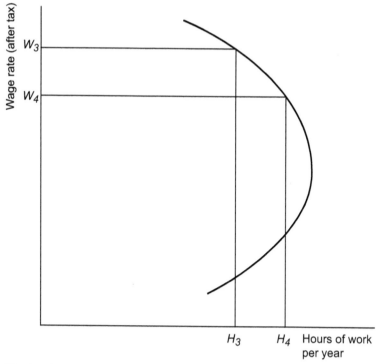

Figure 4.2 The backward-bending supply curve of labour

Income and substitution effects

We can distinguish between two quite separate influences on work effort when a tax is imposed or increased. The first is the income effect, which results from the taxpayer being made worse off than he or she would be without the extra tax. Normally, when a tax is imposed we should expect the *income effect* to encourage the taxpayer to work harder. The reason is that, as the tax makes him poorer, he can afford less of all things, including leisure. The extent of the income effect is determined by the proportion of an individual's gross income which goes in tax, that is the average rate of tax.

The second influence is the *substitution effect*. In economic theory the substitution effect describes the relationship between a change in relative prices and any resulting change in a person's expenditure pattern. In other words, it describes the extent to which an individual substitutes goods for each other as their prices rise or fall. In the context of taxation, the substitution effect describes the effect on a person's choice between work and leisure as the marginal benefit from either or both alters. For example, if the rate of income tax rises so that the marginal benefit from work falls, a person may choose to substitute some leisure for some of his working time. A tax which reduces the marginal benefit from work will normally have a substitution effect which discourages work effort. In the case of an income tax, the extent of the substitution effect is determined by the marginal rate of tax.

The theory, therefore, leaves us unable to predict the overall effect of a tax change on the supply of labour, as the income and substitution effects usually work in opposite directions. The two effects can also be shown by using indifference curve analysis and this method has the advantage of enabling us to compare the work effects of different taxes. It will still not be possible to predict the overall effects of the taxes, but it can be shown how different taxes are likely to have different effects on work incentives.

The analysis is similar to that used in the partial approach in Section 3.4, except that instead of two goods X and Y, the individual is faced in Figure 4.3 with a choice between work (represented by earnings) on the vertical axis, and leisure on the horizontal axis. To avoid unnecessary complexity the assumptions made for the analysis of the supply curve of labour will be retained for the time being. In addition, it will be assumed that both leisure and consumption are superior goods; in other words that the demand for both rises as income rises. On the supposition that the

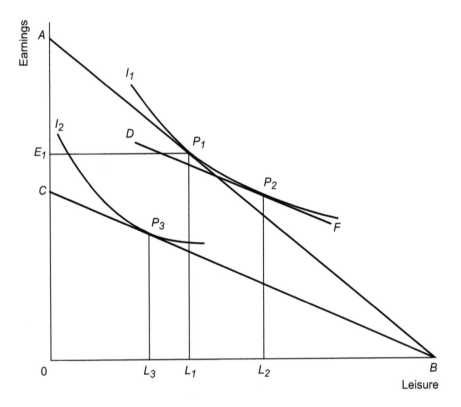

Figure 4.3 The choice between work and leisure

individual can vary his hours of work, his choice between work and leisure is represented by AB in Figure 4.3. Given some set of individual preferences, his highest attainable indifference curve before any taxes are imposed is I_1 and he will choose to spend OL_1 hours of leisure, leaving time to earn OE_1.

If a proportional income tax is now imposed on all earnings, the individual's 'budget constraint' will swivel inwards to CB. The line still terminates at point B, as an individual choosing no income in these circumstances would still not pay any tax. The flatter slope of CB shows that the individual's earnings/leisure trade-off has altered; that is, to earn the same amount of income after tax, the individual has now to give up more leisure. We shall look first at the situation where the individual works harder as a result of the tax. Suppose, therefore, that he moves to point P_3 and takes a reduced amount of leisure OL_3.

The income and substitution effects may be observed separately as follows. The income effect can be removed by compensating the individual with an amount just sufficient to make him as well off as he would have been without the tax. In other words, his income would have to be increased so that he could just attain his former indifference curve I_1, This can be done by shifting the new budget constraint BC outwards until it is at a tangent to I_1, This is shown by DF. The line DF must be parallel to CB because we wish to retain the post-tax trade-off between earnings and leisure and so preserve the substitution effect.

The substitution effect alone can now be seen as the movement from P_1 to P_2, round the indifference curve, as the individual substitutes more leisure for less work. In the diagram, the individual (if the income effect were zero) would take an amount OL_2 of leisure after the tax was imposed, rather than OL_1.

The income effect can be seen as the remaining effect of the tax. This effect is operating in the opposite direction and encourages the individual to work harder. The combination of the two effects results in the taxpayer taking OL_3 of leisure rather than OL_2. It should be pointed out that this result depends on the assumption that leisure is a superior good. If it were an inferior good, then the demand for leisure would be inversely related to the level of income, and the income effect would work in the same direction as the substitution effect. This seems to be an unlikely possibility. It would imply, for example, that when an individual's investment income rose (his marginal wage rate remaining the same), he would spend more time at work. We shall continue, therefore, to assume that leisure is a superior good, and that the income effect of a tax increase encourages people to work harder.

In the case described in Figure 4.3, the income effect outweighs the substitution effect with the overall result that the individual works harder. This is not the only possible result. The two effects could cancel out, or the substitution effect could predominate, in which case the tax would lead to less work. This is the same result as before, but we now have the tools to compare the effects on work of different taxes. The first comparison presented will be between a proportional income tax and a poll tax, followed by a comparison of considerable importance to a modern British fiscal policy, that is between proportional and progressive taxes.

Poll tax versus proportional income tax

The basic proposition here is that although the overall effect of either tax cannot be predicted by theory alone, it can be shown that a poll tax will have a more favourable (or less unfavourable) effect on work effort than a proportional income tax of equal yield. This is shown in Figure 4.4. The line AB represents the individual's budget constraint when neither tax is imposed, and CB represents the constraint when the proportional income tax has been imposed. Confronted with the income tax, our individual chooses point P_2 and takes OL hours of leisure.

When the poll tax is imposed, the budget constraint is represented by DE. This line is parallel to AB because a poll tax does not vary with the amount of income earned and so does not distort the trade-off between earnings and leisure (that is, the slope of the budget constraint). As the two taxes yield the same amount of revenue, DE must pass through point P_2.

It can now be seen that, faced with a poll tax, the individual can attain the higher indifference curve I_3, which leads him to take less leisure than he would if faced with the income tax. This result occurs because the income effect is the same for the two taxes as they absorb the same amount of income. The income tax, however, has a substitution effect adverse to work effort because it distorts the trade-off between earnings and leisure. The poll tax does not have this effect and so provides less of a disincentive to work.

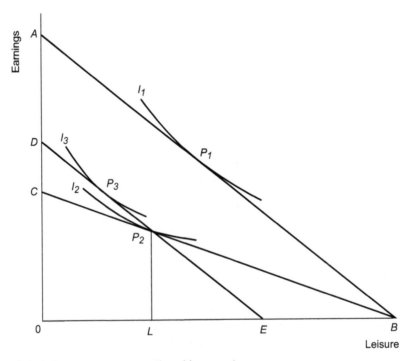

Figure 4.4 Poll tax versus proportional income tax

Proportional versus progressive income taxes

This type of analysis can be extended to show that a proportional income tax has a more favourable (or less unfavourable) effect on individual work effort than does a progressive income tax of equal yield. This may be explained as follows. The definition of a proportional income tax is that the marginal and average rates are equal. With progressive income tax, the marginal rate exceeds the average rate of tax. Since the comparison is between taxes of equal yield, we should expect the income effect to be the same in both cases. However, the progressive tax involves a higher *marginal* rate. This means that the progressive tax has a stronger substitution effect and therefore is likely to be more adverse to work effort than a proportional tax. (An exception is where the substitution effect is zero: that is, the individual will work the same number of hours regardless of his after-tax wage rate.)

The same analysis can also be applied in the opposite direction to show that a regressive tax is more likely to be favourable to work effort than a proportional tax. The income effect of a regressive tax will be much the same as the income effect of a proportional tax of equal yield. But the regressive tax will have a lower marginal rate and therefore a weaker substitution effect than the progressive tax.

Progressive taxation and the community

The comparison between the effects of proportional and progressive taxes on the community as a whole is a little more complex. Clearly, as the income tax becomes more progressive, people on lower incomes pay less, and people on higher incomes pay more. For convenience we will divide the community into five groups according to their level of income and the comparative effects of a proportional and a progressive tax. The groups range from group I with the lowest incomes up to group V with the highest incomes, though the actual division is based more on analytical convenience than on any attempt to reflect the distribution of income precisely. Using these groups, we shall compare a proportional and a progressive tax which each extract the same revenue yield from the community as a whole, but not from each group or individual.

As we have seen, a proportional income tax is one that is levied at the same rate on all income, so that the marginal rate is always equal to the average rate of tax. Each income group, therefore, will be subject to the same rates. This is illustrated in Figure 4.5. Under an alternative progressive tax each group is treated differently. We might arrange that the first income group would be exempt from tax altogether. The second group would be subject to lower marginal and average rates than in the proportional case. The third group would face the same marginal rate with both types of tax, but a lower average rate under a progressive system. For the fourth group the marginal rate would be higher but the average rate lower with the progressive tax. The fifth group would suffer both higher marginal and higher average rates under

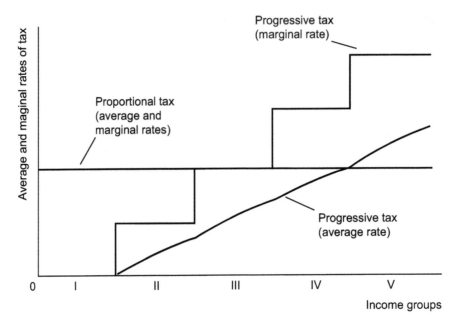

Figure 4.5 Progressive and proportional taxes

the progressive tax. The position of each of these groups can be seen from Table 4.1 (although the table itself is designed to illustrate the more general case of any increase in the progressivity of income tax).

We have already examined the effects of changes in the marginal and average rates of tax, but it is useful to summarise the argument at this stage:

(a) An increase in the marginal rate of tax results in a substitution effect which normally provides a disincentive to work.

(b)   A decrease in the marginal rate produces the opposite result – an incentive to work.

Table 4.1 Work effects of an increase in the progressivity of income tax

Income group	Change in average rate of tax	Change in marginal rate of tax	Work effects		
			Income effect	Substitution effect	Net effect
I	-	-	D	I	=	?
II	-	-	D	I	=	?
III	-	0	D	0	=	D
IV	-	+	D	D	=	D
V	+	+	I	D	=	?

Key: + Increase in the rate of tax; - decrease in the rate of tax; I incentive effect;
D disincentive effect; ? uncertain effect; O no effect.

(c) An increase in the average rate of tax results in an income effect which is usually associated with an incentive to greater work effort.

(d) A decrease in the average rate of tax produces the opposite result.

Referring to Table 4.1, the comparative effects of a proportional and a progressive tax on each of the five groups can now be traced through. Beginning with the first and second income groups, it can be seen that an increase in the progressivity of income taxes has two opposing effects. The lower average rates of the more progressive tax imply income effects that are unfavourable to work effort. However, the lower marginal tax rates imply offsetting substitution effects which are favourable to increased work effort. We cannot say, therefore, a priori, what the net effect of increasing progressivity would be on low income groups.

Nevertheless, it may be noted that a particular area of disincentive effects exists at and just beyond the threshold of the progressive tax. At this point, the marginal rate of tax is significant (and unfavourable to work), but the average rate and its associated income effect are very small.

The outcome for the next two groups is more certain - a net disincentive effect. For the third group, the marginal rate of tax is the same in both cases, but under a more progressive tax the average rate is lower, suggesting an income effect with an adverse effect on work. The fourth group also faces greater disincentive with the progressive tax, but this time from both income and substitution effects. This arises from the higher marginal but lower average rate of tax under the progressive tax. The net effect on the fifth group is uncertain.

So it is not possible to predict on purely theoretical grounds what the overall effects of a more progressive tax would be on the work effort of groups I, II and V. It cannot be predicted, therefore, what the fiscal effect on the total supply of labour would be. It would depend on the strength of the opposing income and substitution effects, and the number of people, in each group. However, under the assumptions made above, it can be said that the effects of groups III and IV are unambiguously adverse to work effort.

Complications

The analysis so far has ignored many of the practical considerations which influence the amount of work done under different taxes. Our conclusions may be modified, for example, if there are non-pecuniary benefits from work which are not taxed, or not taxed as heavily as money income. One particular consideration which should be dealt with here is whether or not individuals have any choice over the number of hours they work. It might be argued that individuals must either work the standard week or not work at all.

At first sight, this line of argument appears quite convincing, especially in the short term. Yet there must be considerable doubt about its importance in the longer term. The first response is that, if the labour market is at all competitive, employers have an incentive to conform to the wishes of the workers. If for example, workers suddenly decide they want a shorter working week, employers who offer it will gain an advantage over employers who do not. Those employers who provide popular working conditions are likely to find it easier to attract suitable employees than those employers who provide unpopular working arrangements. Even if the labour market is not competitive, working conditions may be altered as a result of workers' preferences being expressed through union pressure, or government activity, or both.

In addition, there is often scope for absenteeism, overtime working, or 'moonlighting' on a second job. Furthermore, some individuals can choose to leave the job market through early retirement, or to delay joining it by remaining in further education. Housewives are often in a position where they can choose whether or not to work. On top of this, the standard working week is very different in different occupations, so workers can usually choose the job that comes closest to satisfying their preferred working arrangements. It seems safe to conclude, therefore, that the existence of a standard working week is unlikely to prevent changes in taxation from influencing the supply of labour.

A second practical consideration is the quality of the work done. The discussion so far has assumed that each hour of work is equally productive. It is quite possible that adjustment in the labour market comes through changes in the quality of the labour supplied, rather than the quantity. In other words, if the tax system provided a disincentive to work, people might still work the same number of hours, but choose more congenial or easier jobs, even though those jobs involved relatively low wages.

There are several ways by which taxation can influence the level of productivity.

Taxation might affect the willingness of individuals to go to the trouble and expense of acquiring more productive skills, or of moving to a more productive job. It might also affect their willingness to work in more difficult jobs, or to strive for promotion. In addition, it is conceivable that taxation might influence the amount of encouragement parents give to their children to acquire skills, and so on.

As a final complication in this context, Brown and Dawson (1969, p. 90) have pointed out that misconceptions of the tax system may also influence incentives. If people think that tax rates are higher or lower than they really are, then this in itself can affect their work effort. Enlightening them may also affect it.

Income taxes versus excise taxes

The question here is whether an income tax has the same effects on work effort as a system of excise taxes covering all goods and services. Clearly, a fair comparison requires the excise taxes to be arranged so that they are equally progressive and raise the same revenue as the alternative income tax. The requirement of an equal degree of progressivity raises difficulties, because the only feasible method of increasing the progressivity of excise taxes is by taxing goods consumed by the rich more heavily than the goods consumed by the poor. But this is a very rough and ready way of influencing progressivity, since individuals' tastes differ. Some of the rich may purchase large amounts of goods normally consumed by the poor. Some of the poor may consume goods normally considered the province of the rich. Furthermore, as will be demonstrated in the following chapter, heavier taxes on goods consumed by the rich may also adversely affect those employed in producing these goods, whether they are rich or poor. Income taxes, on the other hand, can (evasion apart) be levied precisely in accordance with each individual's income.

Nevertheless, in order to carry our reasoning a little further, let us suppose it is possible to compare an income tax with a system of excise taxes of equal yield and progressivity. Under these circumstances, it might be thought that the two tax systems would have the same effects on the supply of labour. However, this may not be true for two reasons.

The first is that many goods and services may be complementary to (or substitutes for) work or leisure. An increase in tax on goods or services consumed during leisure time may reduce the incentives to take time off work. Relevant examples include midweek sports activities such as cricket, tennis and football; holiday accommodation; and 'leisure goods' such as sailing boats, camping equipment and alcohol. Similarly, more work may be encouraged by a reduction in taxes on items complementary to work, for example tools and transport for commuters.

The second reason is that excise taxes may be more 'hidden' than income taxes. Indirect taxes which increase prices also reduce the real net wage rate. However, excise taxes may not be shown separately in the prices of goods and services on which they are imposed, whereas income taxes may appear more obvious and direct, especially on weekly or monthly payslips. But it is not possible to predict whether income taxes have more of a disincentive effect than excise taxes. It would depend on whether a more 'hidden' tax has different substitution and income effects than a more obvious tax.

There is a further point here in relation to Musgrave's 'spite effect' (Musgrave, 1959, p. 240). Individuals may work less as a result of a tax increase in order to satisfy some need for revenge on the government, or perhaps to strengthen the case for tax cuts. The effect may be strengthened if the taxes are considered to be unfair. If such a spite effect is significant, it seems reasonable to suppose that it will be stronger the more obvious the tax.

It is clear from the discussion so far that economic theory cannot predict the actual effects of a change in taxation on work effort. It depends on the relative strengths of the income and substitution effects. It also depends on a number of practical considerations. We turn now, therefore, to look at some of the empirical work that has been undertaken in this area.

4.3 Empirical evidence

Many attempts have been made to assess the effects of taxation on the supply of labour. There are two main sources of empirical evidence: econometric studies of observed labour market behaviour, and a large number of surveys into taxpayers' attitudes and their perceived behaviour. There is also some experimental evidence which is discussed under negative income tax in Chapter 9.

Econometric evidence

Following a pioneering study by Douglas (1934), there has been a large number of attempts to estimate the relationship between the supply of labour and real wage rates. Many of these studies have been summarised by Break (1953; 1974), Godfrey (1975), Cain and Watts (1973), Brown (1983), Killingsworth and Heckman (1986), Pencavel (1986) and Blundell (1992).

It should be pointed out that the econometric evidence has to be interpreted carefully for a variety of reasons, as shown, for example, by Atkinson and Stiglitz (1980, Ch. 2) and Brown (1981; 1983). One reason is that inferences about taxation are only drawn indirectly from evidence relating labour supply to net wages. If individuals do not react to changes in taxation in the same way as they react to other changes in their net wages, such inferences may not be valid. Another limitation is that time series evidence may not take account of changes in the conditions of supply such as tastes, cultural values and the level of education over time. Furthermore, a bias may arise if those who are not currently in the labour force are not included in the data, and problems have also been encountered in estimating the variation in the net wage and other variables. In recent years several investigators have tackled an increasing number of these difficulties but, while they have had some success, it is clear that much remains to be done.

Despite such limitations, the overwhelming weight of econometric evidence paints a fairly clear picture and cannot be ignored. It appears that, for many individuals, taxation has little influence on labour market activity, but the behaviour of married women appears to be quite different. Taking a wide range of studies from both the USA and the UK (a summary of many of these is to be found in Pencavel (1986)) it is clear that taxation does not have much effect on the labour supply of men. To the extent that there are some small effects, they are consistent with the hypothesis of a backward-bending supply curve of labour of men.

Examples of studies in the UK include those by Ashworth and Ulph (1981) based on 335 married men, and Blundell and Walker (1982) based on 103 working couples. Another UK study with similar results, by Metcalfe *et al.* (1976), analysed the structure of hours of work and hourly earnings from 96 manufacturing industries. The authors of this study also pointed out an interesting implication of a backward-bending labour supply curve. Such a curve provides one of the few examples of a policy for greater equality which may be consistent with a policy encouraging work effort. In the authors' own words:

> A compression of the wage structure, if desired on equity grounds, would *not* have the kind of work disincentive effects popularly associated with such a move. If anything it would actually *raise* hours supplied. (p. 300)

The econometric results for married women, perhaps not surprisingly, are rather different from the results for men. Generally, it appears that a change in wage rates has a large and positive effect on the number of hours of paid employment which married women undertake. This has been reported in a wide range of studies, many of which are reviewed in Killingsworth and Heckman (1986). In addition, Ashenfelter and Heckman (1974) and Greenhalgh (1977) found that the effect of a change in the husband's wage rate on the wife's labour supply was large and negative. In other words, it seems that an increase in the *wife's* net wage rate is likely to encourage her to work more, but that an increase in her husband's wage may have the opposite effect.

Therefore, and perhaps unfortunately for husbands, a tax policy designed only to increase labour market activity implies taxing husbands more (both to exploit the backward-bending supply curves of labour of men and to encourage the wives to increase their paid employment) and taxing the wives themselves less.

The labour market decisions of married women may, of course, be heavily influenced by family considerations. Despite many years of discussion about changes to gender roles, there is evidence that women with children still see themselves primarily as care-givers, while their male partners still perceive themselves as the 'breadwinners' (James et al., 1992; James, 1995). Women, therefore, may face difficulties in fitting their paid employment around their family commitments, and this may affect econometric estimates of their labour market behaviour.

Early studies of female participation assumed that women who did not have paid employment were not prepared to accept any. However, as pointed out by Blundell *et al.* (1987), it is more realistic to suppose that at least some such women were willing to work but unable to find suitable employment. To ignore this possibility can result in overestimates of women's responsiveness to changes in net wages.

The age of children is also significant. For example, as Blundell and Walker (1988) point out, women with children aged under 5 are less likely to have paid employment, but women with the youngest child between 11 and 18 are as likely to be in the labour market as are women without children, though more likely to work part-time. This would seem to reflect children's needs for unpaid care when they are small, and increasing material demands as they get older. Again, ignoring such factors can bias estimates of female labour supply.

Other evidence

The other main source of evidence of the effects of taxation o n work effort are the many surveys which have been carried out. Once more there are methodological difficulties, many of which are discussed, for example, in Moser and Kalton (1971).

The essential problem is, of course, how to extract information which is both accurate and relevant. Individuals may not give accurate replies in response to a survey for a number of reasons. The respondents may not be aware of the real answers, or there may be other reasons why they wish to give an impression of their behaviour which is not wholly consistent with the facts. A traditional example here is surveys of alcohol consumption! It is also possible that respondents may be influenced by the interviewer, or by the layout of the questionnaire.

The questions themselves are also important. Vague questions are likely to lead to vague answers. However, more detailed questions may put ideas into respondents' minds and so affect their replies. Finally, sample surveys present a number of well-known difficulties in terms of obtaining respondents who are representative of the population as a whole.

While the problems of survey methodology can be serious and should be kept in mind, they do not mean that the evidence unearthed by various surveys can be ignored. There is not, however, sufficient space here to present the full results of all the surveys and how they coped with the various methodological problems. All that will be attempted is a description of some of the main results.

Break (1957) undertook a survey of 306 self-employed solicitors and accountants in England in 1956. Considerable care was taken to avoid influencing the respondents. For example, the subject of taxation was not raised by the interviewer until the person interviewed had had a full opportunity to describe the reasons for doing the amount of work he was doing. On the basis of his findings Break concluded that:

> The chorus of complaints, vehement and eloquent, against 'penal' taxation, echoed by the great majority of respondents interviewed for the present study, was surprisingly infrequently translated into action. It was almost a commonplace for respondents to state categorically that taxes were removing all their incentives; but when the facts were assembled, about as many actually were working harder as were working less.

Barlow et al. (1966) undertook personal interviews in the United States in 1964 with 957 individuals whose incomes in 1961 were $10,000 or higher. Only one eighth of the sample reported that they had reduced their work effort as a result of progressive income tax, though many of these respondents still continued to work 60 or more hours a week. Barlow et al. concluded that:

> It is clear that there are many more powerful motives affecting the working behaviour of high-income people than the marginal income tax rates. People are aware of taxes and do not enjoy paying them, but other considerations are far more important to them in deciding how long to work.

Chatterjee and Robinson (1969) surveyed a sample of 103 'professionals' (accountants, lawyers and insurance agents) and 266 'non-professionals' from the Kitchener-Waterloo metropolitan area in Canada. Their results appear to indicate that taxation had more effect on the work effort of the non-professionals than that of the professionals. Although Chatterjee and Robinson gave no estimate of the quantitative effects of taxation, they did conclude that 'generally ... taxation influences in the aggregate supply of effort seem to be relatively negligible'.

In a survey of low income recipients, Brown and Levin (1974) studied the effects of tax on overtime undertaken by weekly paid workers in 1971. Over 2,000 individuals were interviewed. They were first asked a large number of questions about their work, and at this stage tax was not mentioned by the interviewer. They were then asked if tax made any difference to the amount of overtime they worked. Brown and Levin were then able to eliminate those replies which were inconsistent with earlier statements. They also deleted those who claimed that tax had no effect on their overtime, either because they were not regular taxpayers, or because they could not vary their hours of work. The conclusion was that:

> The evidence clearly suggests ... that the aggregate effect of tax on overtime is small; it may perhaps add about 1 per cent to the total hours worked, since on balance tax has made people work more, rather than less overtime. The only evidence which is not consistent with this is that the number of women claiming to work less is greater than the number claiming to work more.

Fields and Stanbury (1970; 1971) repeated the earlier study undertaken by Break (1957). They did this to see if the effects of taxation had varied over time, and also to provide an additional test of the various hypotheses regarding work incentives. The results appear to show that there had been little change in the effects of taxation on incentives, except that there had been some increase in the number of respondents experiencing disincentives.

The studies carried out have covered many different groups of taxpayers in different countries and at different times. Yet the results do give a general impression of the effects of taxation on work incentives. An important result is that there appears to be no substantial disincentive effect from taxation. Instead, it appears that there are both small incentive and small disincentive effects which tend, of course, to offset each other, so that the net effect of taxation on the supply of labour is likely to be small. So far as males are concerned, this is consistent with the econometric evidence described briefly above. However, the econometric studies also suggest more clearly that there is a greater effect on the work effort of married women.

4.4 Effects of taxation on saving and capital formation

Saving is important for a number of reasons. When people save part of their income, economic resources are released which may be invested in various projects. In the long run, therefore, the level of saving may influence the rate of economic growth.

Changes in the level of savings can also affect the level of economic activity in the short term. However, discussion of the problems of stabilisation policy is reserved for Chapter 6. What will be attempted here is a brief comparison between the likely effects of different taxes on the level of saving. The traditional comparison is between taxes on income and taxes on expenditure. The taxes on expenditure could take the form of the indirect taxes we have already come across. Alternatively, the comparison is often between an income tax and a personal expenditure tax. The latter is discussed in greater detail in Chapter 9.

There are two main areas of interest here, which again may be classified into income and substitution effects. The substitution effects operate on the rates of return to saving under different taxes. The income effects mainly involve the relative burden of different taxes on different sections of the community.

The substitution effect

The substitution effect has often been discussed in terms of the 'double taxation of savings' by an income tax. The argument is that an income tax is imposed on both the income when it is first received, and any interest paid when the income is saved. A tax on expenditure, on the other hand, only taxes the savings once when they are spent. An expenditure tax, therefore, allows a more favourable return to saving, as interest can be received on the gross amount of any income saved.

This may be illustrated with an example. Suppose that an individual receives £1,000 which he intends to save for one year and then spend, together with the interest received. Suppose also that the current rate of interest is 10 per cent and that the individual can either be subject to an income tax or to an expenditure tax. To keep things straightforward, it will be assumed that both taxes are levied on a 'gross' basis; that is, on the amount inclusive of tax itself. (In practice, of course, taxes on expenditure are normally applied to the value net of tax, though the Swedish value added tax is levied on the gross amount.)

The differential effects of the two taxes are shown in Table 4.2. With the 50 per cent income tax, £500 is extracted in tax, leaving £500 to be saved. The interest after one year amounts to £50, but half of this is taxed as well, leaving a total of £525 to be spent.

Table 4.2   An income tax, an expenditure tax and saving

	Income Tax			Expenditure Tax		
	Gross amount	Tax	Net amount saved	Gross amount	Tax	Net amount saved
Money received	1,000	500	500	1,000	0	1,000
Interest after one year	50	25	25	100	0	100
Money spent	525	0	525	1,100	550	550

With the expenditure tax there is no liability when the money is received. This means that the entire £1,000 can be saved, and that a higher amount (£100) is received in interest after a year. As the interest is not taxed when it is paid out, this makes a total amount of £1,100. When this is spent, the 50 per cent expenditure tax on the gross figure accounts for £550, leaving a spending power of £550.

The benefit to saving under an expenditure tax arises because the tax liability on income that is saved is deferred until the savings are spent. It follows that the comparative gain to saving under an expenditure tax will be equal to the after-tax yield on the postponed tax. In our example, £500 of tax is deferred with the expenditure tax and the post-tax interest on the £500 is £25. It can therefore be seen that an expenditure tax results in a higher return to saving than an income tax. If the higher return encourages a higher level of saving, then an expenditure tax is likely to be more favourable to saving than an income tax imposed at the same rate.

It follows that, all other things being equal, a tax on expenditure will favour those who save rather than those who spend. If the rich save a larger proportion of their incomes than the poor, then taxes on expenditure may attract criticism on equity grounds.

One particular qualification should be made to the example. The revenue of the expenditure tax is usually worth less than the revenue from the income tax. This may sound surprising as it can be seen from Table 4.2 that the income tax raises £525 in revenue, whereas the expenditure tax raises £550. The reason is that the effect of an expenditure tax (as opposed to an income tax) is to delay the actual payment of tax when saving is undertaken. Provided society discounts the future, receipts from the expenditure tax will tend to be worth less than receipts from income tax.

This can be easily demonstrated using the example in Table 4.2. Suppose that society discounts the future at a rate of 10 per cent per annum. In the first year, the present value of the income tax yield would be £523 [£500 plus £25/(1 + 0.1)]. The present value of the expenditure tax, on the other hand, would be only £500 [£550/(1 + 0.1)]. It is true that, in this example, a substantially lower discount rate would reverse this result. However, in practice this would be unlikely, since a lower discount rate would also imply a lower real rate of interest. It is fairly safe to conclude, therefore, that the real value of the expenditure tax will usually be lower than that of an income tax levied at the same 'gross' rate. The same result holds during inflationary periods. Because the expenditure tax results in payment being postponed, the tax can be paid in depreciated currency.

A second qualification to this comparison arises with the possibility that the community as a whole could run down the level of its savings. In other words, the community might spend more than it received for a period. In this case, the yield of a tax on spending (expenditure tax) would exceed that of an income tax. This possibility, however, is unlikely to be important for any lengthy period.

The next point concerns how to make a fair comparison between an income tax and an expenditure tax. We could, as before, compare taxes of equal yield. This would mean that the expenditure tax would normally have to be levied at a higher gross rate to raise the same amount of revenue as an income tax. Nevertheless, even a higher rate expenditure tax would still be more likely to favour saving than an equal yield income tax.

However, it might be argued in this particular case that the right comparison is not between taxes of equal yield, but between taxes which reduce private expenditure equally. If the introduction of an expenditure tax actually led to an increase in private saving, then this in itself would release resources which could be used to support a higher level of government expenditure. This means that it is not necessarily true that an expenditure tax would have to be levied at a higher rate than an equivalent income tax.

Substitution effects may influence not only the overall level of savings but also the way in which savings are made. Hence, savings may tend to be diverted through those channels which attract tax relief rather than through those which do not. For example, it can be considerably more profitable to save by contributing to a pension fund or buying one's own home with a mortgage than by investing more directly, say, in shares.

One of the features of the UK tax system that the Meade Committee (1978) revealed most clearly was the wide range of after-tax yields on different forms of saving and investment. This was caused by different aspects of income tax, capital gains tax and corporation tax, and also by such factors as whether the company using the savings was incorporated or not, whether the savings were used as equity capital or fixed interest loans, and whether the profits arising were reinvested in the company or distributed to shareholders.

It is not clear that such differentials are the result of some carefully thought out overall strategy. As Leape (1990, p. 39) put it: 'This mosaic of different regimes is not the result of a coherent policy towards saving, but rather the lasting by-product of a wide variety of ad hoc responses to changing circumstances over the years'. All this suggests that probably the main tax disincentives to saving are to particular forms of saving, rather than to the total level of saving.

Income effects

The income effects of taxation with respect to saving should also be examined. A comparison between taxes will be affected if different taxes fall more heavily on different sections of the community. The 'double taxation' of saving feature of the income tax also has income effects in that the income tax will have a greater impact than an equivalent expenditure tax on those who save.

A separate and more important factor with income effects is the degree of progressivity of different taxes. A progressive tax will fall more heavily than a less progressive tax on prosperous members of society. As the rich save a larger proportion of their incomes than the poor, a more progressive tax may be considered as falling more heavily on savings.

The crucial factor is the marginal propensity to consume, rather than the average propensity to consume - see Lubell (1947). If the marginal propensity to consume is the same for each income group, then an extra £1 of tax will have the same effect on saving wherever the burden falls. For example, suppose that the marginal propensity to consume is 0.75 throughout the income scale; suppose also that an extra £1 in tax is imposed on the rich and the proceeds redistributed to the poor. The aggregate levels of consumption and saving will remain the same. All that happens is that 25p of saving by the rich is replaced by 25p of saving by the poor.

If, however, the marginal propensity to consume falls as income rises, the degree of progressivity of a tax will influence the level of saving. Suppose, by way of example, that the rich all have a marginal propensity to consume of 0.5, and the poor a propensity of 0.9. If £1 is now redistributed from the rich to the poor, the aggregate level of saving will fall. The rich would save 50p less, but the poor would save only 10p more.

So if the marginal propensity to consume declines as income rises, savings will generally be discouraged more by a highly progressive tax than by a less progressive tax of equal yield. On this basis, it could be said that the income tax, which is levied at progressive rates, falls more heavily on savings than indirect taxes do. As we shall see in Section 11.6, indirect taxes are slightly regressive overall.

For two reasons, therefore, savings are more likely to be adversely affected by income taxes than by taxes on expenditure. The substitution effect means that there is a lower rate of return to saving under an income tax. Secondly, the income tax is generally more progressive than taxes on expenditure are. The result is that the income tax is more often paid out of income that would otherwise be saved.

Qualifications

The first qualification is that income taxes can be designed to favour saving. An income tax that exempted investment income would avoid the 'double taxation of savings' characteristic discussed above. As already indicated, the income tax in the United Kingdom favours some forms of saving. Particularly important is the tax treatment of contributions to pension schemes but there are also concessions to specific forms of saving and investment, such as individual savings accounts (ISAs). Also, investment income is not subject. A second qualification is that, in some cases, the level of saving may be determined by some target rather than by the rate of return. For example, some individuals may wish to achieve a certain capital sum for their retirement or some other purpose. In these cases, factors such as the 'double taxation' of saving under an income tax will not necessarily reduce the amount saved.

ASTON UNIVERSITY
LIBRARY & INFORMATION SERVICES

Empirical evidence

As perhaps might be expected, there are difficulties involved in isolating the effects of taxation on saving. Many other factors, such as demographic and other social changes and the existence of state pension schemes, are likely to affect personal savings. For instance, it has often been claimed by foreigners that the high savings rate in Japan has been caused by large tax concessions to personal savings. However, such assertions neglect other relevant factors, such as rapid income growth, the socio-cultural background of the savers, a limited social security system and so on. On the basis of the best knowledge available, Japanese tax incentives seem to have only a minor influence on personal savings (Ishi, 1989).

Corporations and government also undertake saving, and the extent to which they do so can be influenced by other factors again. Furthermore, personal, corporate and, quite probably, government savings are related. On the question of the relationship between the rate of return and the level of saving, different investigators have found different results: see, for instance, the paper by Howrey and Hymans (1980) and the discussion in Pechman (1980). To take a few examples, a study by Blinder (1975) implied a very low savings elasticity. Wright (1969) found that there was a relationship between saving and the rate of interest, but that the relationship was not very strong. Boskin (1978) found a much stronger relationship, and inconsistencies in some of the empirical evidence were surveyed by Carlino (1982). Friend and Hasbrouck (1983) reviewed a number of previous studies which had found a substantial positive interest elasticity of saving, but their empirical evidence failed to support the view that higher after-tax rates of return increased saving. As with the empirical research on labour supply, a great deal remains to be done and further research will, one hopes, add considerably to our knowledge of this topic.

With regard to the marginal propensity to consume, the empirical evidence has also sometimes led to conflicting conclusions. Nevertheless, there is evidence suggesting that the marginal propensity to consume declines as income rises. Husby (1971), for example, using both cross-sectional and time series data, obtained results which implied that, 'in the short run, the marginal propensity to consume of high income families is lower than that of low income families'. Further empirical studies on the effects of taxation on saving are given in Break (1974).

4.5 Effects of taxation on enterprise and risk-taking

It was pointed out in the previous section that saving releases economic resources for investment. In this context, investment refers to individuals and companies investing both directly in capital goods and other inputs, and indirectly by buying shares or bonds issued by enterprises. Both types of investment are normally expected to yield a return. However both also carry a risk that losses rather than profits will be made. The question here, then, concerns the effects of taxation on the willingness of individuals to make investments involving an element of risk.

Why do people take risks? It is quite plausible that some people enjoy taking risks. This would provide one possible explanation for gambling. Nevertheless, more generally, there is evidence to suppose that individuals would prefer to avoid risk, all other things being equal. This preference helps to account for the popularity of insurance, which is a method of pooling risks, thereby reducing the amount of risk faced by each individual. In the investment field itself, unit and investment trusts are popular methods of investing in a large number of companies, thereby spreading the risk of loss.

If people are generally averse to taking risks, it is reasonable to suppose that they will only be induced to do so if they expect to receive some sort of return. Clearly, taxation will affect these returns and therefore the level of investment.

To examine these effects, one may begin with a proportional income tax that does not allow losses to be offset against gains in the calculation of taxable income. In other words, the government shares in the profits of enterprise, but not the losses. The result is that the tax lowers the expected return to risky investments by more than it would reduce the return to a 'safe' investment such as National Savings Certificates. It also reduces the expected return of investments with a high level of risk by more than it does for investments associated with lower levels of risk. It follows that such a tax provides more of a disincentive to undertake risk than, for example, a poll tax of equal expected yield would.

What happens if losses are allowed to be set off against profits? In these circumstances, the government would share in the losses as well as the profits, in that when losses are incurred, tax revenue falls. In a sense, the government then becomes a sleeping partner in enterprises. When enterprises make profit, the government, through taxation, takes a share, but it also shares in the risk through loss-offsets. For individual investors, a loss-offset system which works perfectly would remove the disincentive effect mentioned in the previous case. It is true that the income tax would still reduce the expected return to investment, but with loss-offsets it would also reduce the risks associated with that return.

In this situation it was shown by Domar and Musgrave (1944) that the overall amount of risk-taking could actually increase following an increase in income tax. When an income tax is imposed or increased, the individual finds that both his expected (after-tax) return and the level of risk he faces diminish. As a result, he may decide to increase his income from investment. He can do this either by increasing his investment, or by transferring his investment to projects or shares which offer a higher return but are more risky. As the individual increases the amount of risk he faces, the government as well has to accept more risk through the tax system. The combined effect on society as a whole, therefore, may be to increase the amount of risk-taking.

Qualifications

There are, as usual, some qualifications to the analysis. The most important is that even with loss-offsets, the expected rate of return on risky investment may still be reduced by taxation. The main reasons for this are as follows.

First, there may be nothing to set the losses against. This may occur where a firm goes out of business before it has time to make a profit.

Second, the losses may have to be carried forward to be set against future profits. This may happen either because no profits were made previously, or because the tax system limits the extent to which losses may be carried backwards. For example, in the United Kingdom losses can usually be carried forward, but normally cannot be carried back further than the previous three years. As people discount the future, it can be seen that losses carried forward to be set against future income are worth less than the amount actually lost. Inflation will normally increase the difference.

Third, personal income tax (unlike corporation tax) is levied at progressive rates. As the income tax does not have adequate provisions to average out income over the years, loss-offsets cannot be fully effective. The reason is that losses may be set off against income in years when an individual's marginal rate of tax is relatively low. So, loss-offsets may not work fully, and income tax may still lower the rate of return on high risk as opposed to low risk assets.

Finally Peck (1989) has also shown that the effects of a tax on profits with full loss-offsets also depend on economies of scale.

We have seen in this section that it is not necessarily true that income tax decreases risk. It is possible that the effect of an income tax may be to increase the amount of risky investment undertaken by society as a whole. However, if losses are not fully set off against income, the rate of return on risky investments will be lowered.

4.6 Optimal taxation

Although a great deal of the work that has been undertaken on 'optimal taxation' is beyond the scope of this book, it seems worthwhile to provide a (very) brief summary of such work and to indicate to those interested where a start could be made on the literature.

Using the criterion of economic efficiency, a good tax system is one which minimises the excess burden (including the effects on the supply of factors of production) at a given level of tax revenue. A more complete approach from the efficient viewpoint would also take account of administrative and compliance costs. However, a tax system can also be evaluated in terms of how fair or equitable it is perceived to be (and this topic is discussed in the following chapter). The literature on optimal taxation has been concerned with the integration of both efficiency and equity criteria. The main difficulty is the trade-off which often exists between efficiency and incentives on the one hand, and equity on the other. For example, it may be that society considers a highly progressive tax to be equitable, but that such a tax might damage incentives to work. The problem in this case is therefore to find the tax rates which give the best trade-off between incentives and equity.

While almost all the literature on optimal taxation tends to be highly mathematical, a brief non-technical account of optimal income taxation appears in the Meade Committee (1978, Chapter 14). The committee concluded (on p. 316) that:

> as a general principle (i) *average* rates of tax should be high on high incomes and low on low incomes, but at the same time (ii) *marginal* rates of tax should be exceptionally low at both the bottom and the top ends of the income scale.

For example, the argument for low marginal (but not average) rates of tax at the top end of the scale may be summarised as follows. There are relatively few taxpayers at the top end, so a reduction in marginal rates would not cost very much in forgone tax revenue, even if no extra work were forthcoming. However, it is the substitution effect associated with the marginal rate which provides the disincentive, so a reduction may increase work effort and therefore possibly also increase tax revenue.

Although the optimal tax literature is now voluminous, there are several useful surveys, such as that by Bradford and Rozen (1976). Sandmo (1976) provides an introductory survey of optimal commodity taxation, and Atkinson (1977) reviews the issue with respect to the direct versus indirect tax controversy. A more general, but also more technical, discussion appears in Atkinson and Stiglitz (1980). An interesting early paper written in 1951 by Samuelson for the US Treasury was finally published 35 years later (Samuelson, 1986).

The work undertaken to date on optimal taxation has attracted some criticism. For instance, Brennan and Buchanan (1977, p. 255) went so far as to describe it as institutionally vacuous, and Ricketts (1981, p. 44) concluded that, 'the literature on tax policy ... is almost exclusively concerned with factors which are entirely missing from models of optimal taxation'. There is also an amusing article by Broome (1975). The criticism that the analysis has neglected several important aspects such as horizontal equity, evasion, administration and taxpayer preferences between different taxes is largely accurate. However, this does not, of course, prevent such aspects from being incorporated into future work.

A second criticism has been that the conclusions of optimal tax analysis could have been reached by intuitive argument, without the need for extensive mathematical analysis. While this is true of a number of results, it does not apply to some others. A third point, acknowledged by Atkinson and Stiglitz, is that the analysis does not lead to unambiguous policy conclusions and that the results depend on economic relationships about which there is little empirical evidence. Nevertheless, the analysis of optimal taxation has yielded a substantial amount of insight into various arguments and some of these have been presented by Heady (1993). At the risk of some apparent repetition, it can safely be asserted that this is a third area in this chapter in which we can expect future work to extend knowledge of taxation considerably.

4.7 Summary

This chapter has examined the effects of taxation on work effort, saving and risk-taking. It has shown that an increase in income tax does not necessarily provide a disincentive to work. On the contrary, it is quite possible that an increase in taxation could spur the working population to greater efforts.

Even though we cannot say on theoretical grounds alone whether or not taxes influence the amount of work done, we can compare the effects of different taxes. Thus, for example, we would expect a poll tax to have a more favourable (or less unfavourable) effect on work effort than a proportional tax of equal yield. Similarly, we would expect a proportional income tax to provide more of an incentive (or less of a disincentive) to work than a progressive income tax of equal yield.

It is also possible to compare the effects of different taxes on the level of saving. Generally, it is likely that income taxes will provide more of a disincentive to saving than expenditure taxes of equal yield. This is for two reasons. First, the 'double taxation of savings' feature of an income tax lowers the rate of return to saving by more than a tax on expenditure would. Second, if income taxes are more progressive than indirect taxes, it is more likely that they will be paid out of income that would otherwise have been saved.

Taxation may also affect the level of enterprise in the community. However, the effect of a tax system which allows losses to be offset against gains in the computation of taxable income is that the government shares in both the return and the risk involved in investment. In these circumstances, the amount of risk undertaken within the community may rise when a tax is imposed or increased.

Further reading

A more theoretical treatment of the material in this chapter appears in Musgrave (1959) and Atkinson and Stiglitz (1980). Taxation and the labour supply is dealt with in Brown (1981; 1983), Blundell (1992) and Feldstein (2008), the labour supply of men is surveyed by Pencavel (1986) and that of women by Killingsworth and Heckman (1986). Savings are examined further by Gapinski (1993) and by Boadway and Wildasin (1994). The argument with respect to risk-taking is examined further by Kaplow (1994).

References

Ashenfelter, O. and Heckman, J. (1974), 'The estimation of income and substitution effects in a model of family labour supply', *Econometrica*, Vol. 42, pp. 73-85.

Ashworth, J.S. and Ulph, D.T. (1981), 'Endogeneity I: estimating labour supply with piecewise linear budget constraints' in C.V. Brown (ed.), *Taxation and Labour Supply*, Allen & Unwin.

Atkinson, A.B. (1977), 'Optimal taxation and the direct versus indirect tax controversy', *Canadian Journal of Economics*, Vol. 10, pp. 590-606.

Atkinson, A.B. and Stiglitz, J.E. (1980), *Lectures on Public Economics*, McGraw-Hill.

Barlow, R., Brazer, H.E. and Morgan, J.N. (1966), *Economic Behavior of the Affluent*, Brookings Institution.

Blinder, A.S. (1975), 'Distribution effects and the aggregate consumption function', *Journal of Political Economy*, Vol. 83, pp. 447-75.

Blundell, R. (1992), 'Labour supply and taxation: a survey', *Fiscal Studies*, Vol. 13, No. 3, pp. 15-40.

Blundell, R., Ham. J. and Meghir, C. (1987), 'Unemployment and female labour supply', *Economic Journal*, Vol. 97, conference supplement.

Blundell, R. and Walker, I. (1982), 'Modelling the joint determination of household labour supplies and commodity demands', *Economic Journal*, Vol. 92.

Blundell, R. and Walker, I. (1988), 'Taxing family income', *Economic Policy*, 6, April.

Boadway, R. and Wildasin, D. (1994), 'Taxation and savings: a survey', *Fiscal Studies*, Vol. 15, No. 3, pp. 19-63.

Boskin, M.J. (1978), 'Taxation, saving and the rate of interest', *Journal of Political Economy*, Vol. 86, pp. S3-S27.

Bradford, D.F. and Rozen, H.S. (1976), 'The optimal taxation of commodities and income', *American Economic Review*, Papers and Proceedings, Vol. 66, pp. 94-101.

Break, G.F. (1953), 'Income taxes, wages rates and the incentive to supply labour services', *National Tax Journal*, Vol. 6.

Break, G.F. (1957), 'Income taxes and the incentive to work: an empirical study', *American Economic Review*, Vol. 47, pp. 529-49.

Break, G.F. (1974), 'The evidence and economic effects of taxation', in A. Blinder *et al.*, *The Economics of Public Finance*, Brookings Institution.

Brennan, G. and Buchanan, J.M. (1977), 'Towards a tax constitution for Leviathan', *Journal of Public Economics*, Vol. 8, pp. 255-74.

Broome, J. (1975), 'An important theorem on income tax', *Review of Economic Studies*, Vol. 42, pp. 649-52.

Brown, C.V. (ed.) (1981), *Taxation and Labour Supply*, Allen & Unwin.

Brown, C.V. (1983), *Taxation and the Incentive to Work*, 2nd edn, Oxford University Press.

Brown, C.V. and Dawson, D.A. (1969), *Personal Taxation Incentives and Tax Reform*, PEP Broadsheet, No. 506, London.

Brown, C.V. and Levin, E. (1974), 'The effects of income taxation on overtime: the results of a national survey', *Economic Journal*, Vol. 84, pp. 833-48.

Cain, G.G. and Watts, H.W. (1973), *Income Maintenance and Labour Supply*, Rand McNally.

Carlino, G.A. (1982), 'Interest rate effects and intertemporal consumption', *Journal of Monetary Economics*, Vol. 9, pp. 223-34.

Chatterjee, A. and Robinson, J. (1969), 'Effects of personal income tax on work effort: a sample survey', *Canadian Tax Journal*, May/June.

Domar, E.D. and Musgrave, R.A. (1944), 'Proportional income tax and risk-taking', *Quarterly Journal of Economics*, Vol. 58, pp. 388–422.

Douglas, P.H. (1934), *The Theory of Wages*, Macmillan.

Feldstein, M. (2008), 'Effects of taxes on economic behavior', *National Tax Journal*, Vol. LXI, No. 1, pp. 131-139.

Fields, D.B. and Stanbury, W.T. (1970), 'Incentives, disincentives and the income tax: further empirical evidence', *Public Finance*, Vol. 25, pp. 381-415.

Fields, D.B. and Stanbury. W.T. (1971), 'Income taxes and incentives to work: some additional empirical evidence', *American Economic Review*, Vol. 61, pp. 435-43.

Friend, I. and Hasbrouck, J. (1983). 'Saving and after-tax rates of return', *Review of Economics and Statistics*, Vol. LXV, November.

Gapinski, J. (ed.) (1993), *The Economics of Saving*, Kluwer Academic.

Godfrey, L. (1975), *Theoretical and Empirical Aspects of the Effects of Taxation on the Supply of Labour*, OECD.

Greenhalgh, C. (1977), 'A labour supply function for married women in Great Britain', *Economica*, Vol. 44, pp. 249-65.

Heady, C. (1993), 'Optimal taxation as a guide to tax policy: a survey', *Fiscal Studies*, Vol. 14, No. 1, pp. 15-41.

Howrey, E.P. and Hymans, S.H. (1980), 'The measurement and determination of loanable-funds saving', in J.A. Pechman (ed.), *What Should Be Taxed: Income or Expenditure?*, Brookings Institution.

Husby, RD. (1971), 'A nonlinear consumption function estimated from time-series and cross-section data', *Review of Economics and Statistics*, Vol. 53, pp. 76-9.

Ishi, H. (1989), *The Japanese Tax System*, Oxford University Press.

James, S. (1995), 'Female labour supply and the division of labour in families', *Journal of Interdisciplinary Economics*, Vol. 5, pp. 273-91.

James, S., Jordan, B. and Redley, M. (1992), 'The wife's employment family fit', in S. Lea, P. Webley and B. Young (eds), *New Directions in Economic Psychology*, Edward Elgar.

Kaplow, L. (1994), 'Taxation and risk taking: a general equilibrium perspective', *National Tax Journal*, Vol. XLVII, pp. 789-98.

Killingsworth, M.R and Heckman, J.J. (1986), 'Female labor supply: a survey', in Ashenfelter, O. and Layard, R (eds), *Handbook of Labor Economics*, pp. 103-204, North-Holland.

Leape, J. (1990), 'The impossibility of perfect neutrality: fundamental issues in tax reform', *Fiscal Studies*, Vol. 11, No. 2, May.

Lubell, H. (1947), 'Effects of redistribution of income on consumers' expenditure', *American Economic Review*, Vol. 37, pp. 157-70.

McCulloch, J.R. (1864), *Principles of Political Economy*, A. & C. Black.

Meade Committee (1978), *The Structure and Reform of Direct Taxation*, Institute for Fiscal Studies.

Metcalfe, D., Nickell, S. and Richardson, R (1976), 'The structure of hours and earnings in British manufacturing industry', *Oxford Economic Papers*, Vol. 28, pp. 284-303.

Mill, J.S. (1871), *Principles of Political Economy*, 7th edn, Longmans.

Moser, C.A. and Kalton, G. (1971), *Survey Methods in Social Investigation*, 2nd edn, Heinemann Educational Books.

Musgrave, R.A. (1959), *The Theory of Public Finance*, McGraw-Hill.

Pechman, J.A. (ed.) (1980), *What Should Be Taxed: Income or Expenditure?*, Brookings Institution.

Peck, R.M. (1989), 'Taxation, risk and returns to scale', *Journal of Public Economics*, Vol. 40, No. 3.

Pencavel, J. (1986), 'Labor supply of men: a survey', in Ashenfelter, O. and Layard, R. (eds), *Handbook of Labor Economics*, pp. 3–102, North-Holland.

Ricketts, M. (1981), 'Tax theory and tax policy', in A. Peacock and F. Forte, *The Political Economy of Taxation*, Basil Blackwell.

Samuelson, P.A. (1986), 'Theory of optimal taxation', *Journal of Public Economics*, Vol. 30, No. 2.

Sandmo, A. (1976), 'Optimal taxation: An introduction to the literature', *Journal of Public Economics*, Vol. 6, pp. 37–54.

Wright, C. (1969), 'Saving and the rate of interest', in A.C. Harberger and M. J. Bailey (eds), *The Taxation of Income from Capital*, Brookings Institution.

Self assessment questions

Suggested answers to self-assessment questions are given at the back of the book.

4.1   What is the income effect of a tax?

4.2   Is the income effect of a tax determined by the average or the marginal rate of tax?

4.3   What is the substitution effect of a tax?

4.4   What determines the substitution effect of a tax?

4.5   If taxes were increased, would the income effect be likely to encourage taxpayers to work more or to work less?

4.6   If the marginal rate of income tax were increased, would the substitution effect be likely to encourage taxpayers to work more or to work less?

4.7   If the supply curve of labour bends backwards, which of the income and substitution effects dominates?

4.8   Suppose that the first £3,000 of income is tax free and the rest subject to a rate of 25 per cent. Analyse the likely effects on work effort of increasing the tax threshold to £4,000.

4.9 What is the 'double taxation of savings'?

4.10 Why might a tax system with provision for loss-offsets actually increase enterprise?

Discussion Questions

1. Is taxation a disincentive to work effort?

2. Explain carefully the circumstances in which taxation might *increase* the amount of work done.

3. Is it possible to assess the likely effects on work effort of increasing the *progressivity* (but not the overall yield) of income tax?

4. Suppose that the government wishes to reduce income tax while maintaining the real value of its tax receipts. Assess the likely effects on work effort of each of the following possible methods of achieving this result:

   (a) introducing a flat-rate National Insurance contribution of £x per worker per week,

   (b) increasing the tax on alcohol,

   (c) increasing the tax on petrol,

   (d) increasing value added tax.

5. Do income taxes and excise taxes have different effects on work incentives?

6. How would you reform the tax system if you wished to increase labour supply?

7. Is it necessarily true that an income tax is more likely to discourage saving than an expenditure tax of equal yield would?

8. Do income taxes discourage enterprise and risk-taking?

CHAPTER FIVE

Taxation and equity

After reading this chapter, you should be able to:

- Understand the meaning and importance of fairness in taxation.
- Appreciate the judgement necessary in choosing and using criteria for fairness.
- Identify the effects of various taxes on distribution of income and wealth in theory and in practice.
- Explain the effects on inflation of the above issues.
- Distinguish between avoidance and evasion.

5.1 Introduction

This chapter attempts to introduce and to summarise some of the facts and theories relating to a very broad subject. The reader should be aware that here we can only scratch the skin of this fascinating corpus of knowledge.

In the first section we will look briefly at the importance of being fair and at some definitional matters. Then, in the next two sections, equity criteria are examined in greater detail and the ability-to-pay approach in particular is explored further. Sections 5.5 and 5.6 look at the distributional effects of different taxes, and redistribution in the UK since 1938. Then, there are sections on the effects of inflation on equity, and the importance of administrative fairness. Finally, there is a section on avoidance and evasion.

5.2 The importance of being fair

Among the considerations which Adam Smith thought that a tax should include was that 'the subjects of every state ought to contribute towards the support of the government as nearly as possible in proportion to their respective abilities; that is in proportion to the revenue which they respectively enjoy under the protection of the state' (Smith, 1776, Book V, Ch. II, Part II, p. 310) or, possibly, for the rich: 'something more than in proportion' (p. 327). This first canon of taxation is concerned with equity among taxpayers.

The importance of fairness in taxation rests particularly in the natural desire of governors and governed for justice. This may seem a somewhat circular argument. However, this is not the place for a rigorous philosophical analysis of the concept of justice. What is clear is that practical problems arise if the taxation system is perceived to be unjust. At the extremes, such cataclysmic events as the French and American Revolutions were partly due to perceived inequity in taxation. Less dramatic, but nevertheless important, is the tendency for evasion and other forms of taxpayer resistance to increase under systems which are perceived to be seriously unfair (see Section 5.9).

The most obvious requirement of equity or fairness is to treat equal people in equal circumstances in an equal way. This is called preserving 'horizontal equity'. If there is a reason for not discriminating between equals, then this suggests that there should be discrimination between those who are not equal. Such different treatment of people in different circumstances would be used to preserve 'vertical equity'.

There are, of course, great problems in deciding who is equal to whom. Does equality mean equality of income, expenditure, wealth, total utility, benefit gained from the expenditure of the tax-raising authority, or some combination of these and other factors? We will look at this question in the next two sections.

Economists are trained from an early age to steer clear of normative arguments, and consequently are inclined to leave the definition of equity to others. In practice, decisions about the redistribution of income via progressive taxation and transfer payments to the poor, for example, are based on widely held feelings that this is equitable. We will try to get as far as we can in examining the reasonableness of these feelings within the limitations of our knowledge, the space available here and the desire to remain 'positive'.

It is important, also, to recognise that it is not enough to ask whether a tax is equitable *in vacuo*. It is necessary to know whether the pre-tax distribution of income, and other benefits which might be considered to have a bearing on equity, is satisfactory in the context of our criteria of fairness. If it is, then an equitable tax would have to raise money without altering the balance among the members of the population. If it is not, and if redistribution is to be an aim of the tax, a quite different tax structure will be necessary.

We will wait until Section 5.5 to look at the distributional effects of taxes. As an introduction to this and to the sections immediately following, we must now consider alternative criteria for judging whether a distribution is fair.

One possibility is to use endowment-based criteria. These assume that an individual has an innate right to the fruits of his own labour. The inequalities in ability between individuals are recognised and allowed for. The resulting 'natural' distribution of income is deemed to be fair. Clearly, this basis has a long history in our civilisation and we do not have to look further than nineteenth-century Britain to find an approximate example. Reliance on endowment-based criteria will lead to laissez-faire government. It is possible to modify this approach by allowing for adjustments to the distribution to take account of the 'unfair' benefits of monopoly power, or of inherited, married or gifted wealth, or of superior education or status.

A second basis for criteria about the fairness of distribution is that which seeks the greatest utility or the greatest happiness for the greatest number. This does not necessarily mean that all men must be made equal; this only becomes an inevitable result if everyone's marginal utility curves are the same, as we shall see in Section 5.4.

A third set of criteria are those which are equity-based. At one extreme this means that, since all individuals are of equal worth, they must be allowed equal welfare. However, there are more moderate interpretations, as we will see soon. From now on, this chapter concerns itself with these equity-based criteria.

A good example of the use of equity arguments for the introduction of a tax arose in 1964 when the then Chancellor, James Callaghan, was introducing capital gains tax in the Commons. He said that 'Capital gains confer much the same kind of benefit on the recipient as taxed *earnings* more hardly won. Yet earnings pay full tax while capital gains go free. This is unfair to the wage and salary earner' (Hansard, vol. 710, col. 245). We will investigate this particular case further in Section 5.7 on equity and inflation.

5.3 Equity criteria

The benefit approach

One idea for equity which was discussed by early thinkers and political economists such as Smith, Locke, Rousseau, Bentham and Mill was that the tax burden should be split up according to the benefits gained from the government expenditures which are funded by the taxation. These benefits are not directly traceable to individual recipients because of the nature of government expenditures. It is partly true today, and was largely true in the days of the above philosophers, that government expenditure consisted of the provision of public goods such as defence, justice, and law and order. Although the benefits of these goods cannot be traced, it is possible to theorise about which groups in society receive the most 'protection'. Some theorists said that the rich benefited most from this protection and would clearly be prepared to pay most for it, whereas others said that the weak and poor benefited more. This latter argument would require a fair tax to take a larger proportion of low incomes than of high incomes, that is to be regressive.

This problem, about who benefits most, makes it very difficult to use the benefit approach to equity. There are other problems too, which contribute to its lack of applicability. For example, there are types of government expenditure which are designed to be straightforward redistributions of income towards those in need. Income Support and old age pensions are examples of such 'transfer payments'. It would be absurd to try to operate the benefit principle when it came to deciding who should bear the taxes that pay for these.

The benefit approach is clearly seen in action only in several special cases such as television licences and motor taxation, although the move in the 1980s towards a 'community charge' or poll tax involved the argument that all benefit so all should pay (see Section 11.5). The main attraction of the benefit approach is that it can include both the taxation and the resulting government expenditure. If it were considered equitable that a tax should be distributionally neutral then, under the benefit approach, an equitable tax should leave everyone with the same net benefit, which takes account of both the tax and the benefits.

Other approaches to equity, which we are about to examine, are less satisfactory in this respect for they consider only the effects of raising the tax. However, it is possible to solve this problem of estimating the effects of a new tax by supposing that there is a distributionally neutral equal reduction in another tax or equal increase in government expenditure.

The ability-to-pay approach

Before examining whether the ability-to-pay approach requires that taxpayers should be taxed until they are left equal, or until they have made an equal sacrifice, or until some other criterion is met, we will discuss what attributes give a taxpayer any ability to pay, that is in what his taxable capacity rests.

Possible candidates include income, expenditure and wealth. At first sight, an increase in any of these suggests an increase in ability to pay. Income is perhaps the most obvious, but considerable problems of definition exist. One is whether income includes capital gains, gifts received and gambling wins. If it does, ways must be found to include these in the tax base if equity is to be maintained between earners with different mixes of income. A further problem is to decide the extent to which a person's ability to pay is altered by his circumstances. Has a single person an ability to pay equal to a person with an equal income who is married and who maintains his mother-in-law? It seems clear that the latter has a lower ability to pay and, on this reasoning, income taxation is based on a net income after the deduction of a formalised series of allowances for expenditure.

Criticisms are made against using income as the basis, on the grounds that expenditure would be a more satisfactory basis. First, expenditure out of income from capital gains, gifts, gambling winnings and even the cashing-in of wealth is automatically included. Second, it has been suggested that income tax represents a double taxation on saving: once by reducing the amount that can be saved and then by taxing the returns to saving. On the other hand, it might be argued that the income from savings constitutes extra ability to pay and that a sales tax would lead to under-taxation of savings by postponing tax temporarily or indefinitely, depending on expenditure plans. This was discussed in Section 4.4.

A further criticism of income as a basis can be traced back to the *Leviathan* of Hobbes in which saving and investment are regarded as beneficial, whereas consumption is anti-social. Therefore, taxation should be based on consumption (what people take out of the common pool), not income (what people put in). This is really another argument for the lighter treatment of saving, which is the difference between income and consumption. However, it does not recognise that saving is just a decision to postpone consumption on economic grounds (such as the ruling rate of interest) and that benefits of status, economic power and security are gained by building up capital, in addition to the return on it.

An additional practical advantage which might be claimed for the income basis is that it is much easier to build progressiveness into income taxation than into sales taxation, because only the former is a direct tax based on the individual. However, this need not be the case if an expenditure tax is used as proposed particularly by Professor Kaldor (1955) and the Meade Committee (1978).

An expenditure tax would involve personal assessment based on an individual's expenditure. This could be deduced from his income of all kinds, his saving and his dis-saving. Certain types of expenditure could be exempted if necessary, and adjustments could be made for the extent to which expenditure on durable goods was seen to be other than current expenditure. This form of taxation is looked at in more detail in Chapter 9.

In practice, despite very considerable arguments in favour of an expenditure tax, the net income concept has remained the prime basis for taxation based on ability to pay.

There remains the question whether wealth represents a separate ability to pay. This is examined in some detail in Chapter 10, but will be briefly discussed here. There are really two cases. One concerns wealth which arises from an individual's savings out of income, the other concerns wealth arising in other ways, such as inheritance, marriage, gifts and gambling.

Leaving aside for the moment the opportunity to dis-save in order to spend more than one's income allows, it is clear that the possession of wealth provides advantages such as security and status in both the above cases. This suggests that, just on these grounds, there may be a case for the taxation of wealth. The further fact that an individual with wealth can dis-save to increase his expenditure suggests, for example, that an individual with a certain income and two Rembrandt paintings has a greater ability to pay than another with an equal income and no Rembrandts. The former may at worst sell one Rembrandt to pay a wealth tax on them both, and he is still left with one Rembrandt more than his fellow.

However, on grounds of equity, we need to look separately at the two different cases mentioned above, relating to the source of the wealth. In the former case, in which the individual's wealth comes from his own saving, if we hold to the *income basis* for ability to pay, it will be inequitable to tax first the income out of which savings were made, then the return to the savings and then the accumulated savings themselves.

A wealth tax of 2 per cent each year is equivalent to an income tax of 20 per cent when the return on capital is 10 percent each year. To tax both capital and the income from the capital is inequitable when the capital has been accumulated out of taxed income which would otherwise have been spent without further direct taxation. Any expenditure taxes will merely be postponed by building up the capital, assuming that the intention in saving is to postpone consumption. If the intention is to build up security, status and economic power, we are back to the argument previously raised, which may provide an equitable basis for the taxation of wealth even when it has been accumulated by an individual from taxed income.

The second case, that of wealth from other sources, much more obviously suggests an extra taxable capacity. It seems fair to regard the wealth as representing a separate ability to pay. However, assuming that the taxation on inheritance and gifts had been set at an appropriate level (see Section 10.5), wealth tax would seem to be a double taxation even in this case.

We have argued, then, that income is the most usual basis for the ability-to-pay approach, and that the ability-to-pay approach is the most useful basis for a consideration of equity. In practice, decisions about how to raise taxes are usually taken out of the context of the effects of the resultant expenditures, because there is seldom the possibility of tracing a tax to a type of expenditure. Consequently, although there are theoretical reservations about the one-sidedness of the ability to-pay approach, at least these reservations are not problems for the analysis of real taxes.

5.4 Income and utility

If equity considerations are to be based mainly on ability to pay which is measured by income, we next need to establish the quantitative relationship between ability to pay and income. It should be noted that a similar analysis to that below could be applied for a 'direct' lifetime expenditure tax. It has already been mentioned that some form of net income will be used so as to take account of the individual's circumstances. Does twice as much net income mean twice the ability to pay? In order to answer this question, we will first make a recourse to the traditional theory of sacrifice of utility as discussed by such economists as Mill, Sidgwick, Edgeworth and Pigou.

The assumptions of the sacrifice approach are that it is possible to correlate units of income with unit of utility, that everyone has the same utility function which slopes downwards, and that the expenditure effects of the taxation can be ignored by making other distributionally neutral adjustments, as mentioned before. The assumption of a downward-sloping utility curve is another way of saying that there is diminishing marginal utility for money and the goods that it can buy. These assumptions will be challenged later, but can first be maintained while we look at three suggestions as to what an equitable split of the total sacrifice due to taxation would be.

The first suggestion is that it would be equitable if all income earners were to make an equal sacrifice of utility. The assumption has been made that the marginal utility curve slopes downwards. In other words, each extra unit of money brings with it less utility than the last, or the loss of a unit of money is less of a sacrifice of utility for the individual with a higher income. Clearly, then, to achieve an equal sacrifice of utility on these assumptions, a higher income must yield a higher amount of tax. However, depending on the slope of the marginal utility curve, the proportion of income paid in tax may not rise. It is possible for the appropriate tax system to be regressive, proportional or progressive.

An alternative suggestion is that each income earner should make an equi-proportional sacrifice of utility. On our present assumptions, since marginal utility declines with extra income, the greater an individual's income the larger the proportion of it he would have to give up in order to lose a certain proportion of his total utility. This means that income taxation needs to be progressive in this case.

A third suggestion is that there should be the least aggregate sacrifice of total utility. This would maximise the total utility throughout the population. It means that having paid the taxation, each member's marginal utility for money would be the same. There would be no way of taking a unit of money from any taxpayer and giving it to another that would increase total utility. On our assumption of identical utility schedules, this means that everyone must end up with the same post-tax income. This needs a taxation system which would involve 100 per cent marginal rates.

At this point it may be useful to refer to Figure 5.1, which gives a diagrammatic representation of the various approaches to equity. There have been more complex suggestions about equity in this context. For example, society might give priority to improving the position of the least advantaged (Rawls, 1972). Such matters must be left to more specialised books.

On the above assumptions, each of these utility sacrifice suggestions satisfies the simplest of criteria for equity: that people with the same income will pay the same amount of tax. It is also clear that people with different incomes will pay different amounts in tax. In each case a higher income will bear a higher amount of tax. The second suggestion, of equiproportional sacrifice, may seem particularly reasonable and a useful justification for a progressive system of income tax. It was important in early arguments in favour of progression (Pigou, 1932). Unfortunately, the assumptions we have used are rather difficult to substantiate.

Let us reconsider the assumption that everyone has the same downward-sloping marginal utility curve. This would mean that one person's utility curve would remain the same as his income increased, and that two people with different incomes would needs of life (such as food, clothing and shelter) will gain more utility from an extra unit of money than someone who has. However, it is certainly possible to produce

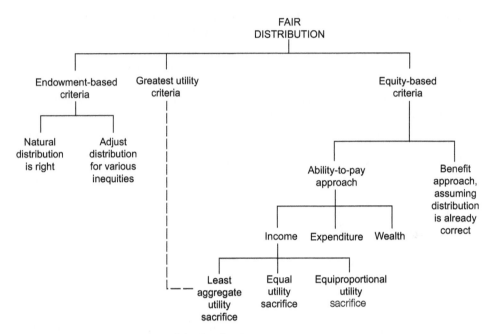

Figure 5.1 Approaches for a fair distribution

reasons that might lead to *upward*-sloping parts of the marginal; utility curve. For example, it may be that appetites for some goods are stimulated by consumption. Also, some types of consumption which yield great utility may only be possible once a certain threshold has been reached.

This inconclusiveness is confirmed when one adds in the importance of individual personality, background and expectations. These must affect individual relationships between income and utility. It may be that different people are not on different parts of the same utility curve. Consider C who has been used to drinking cider, living in a bed-sitter and taking holidays in Skegness; and D who drinks claret, lives in a substantial villa and takes holidays in the Caribbean in the winter and at St Tropez in the summer. Both individuals are reasonably content, although C would like to be able to afford D's life-style. However, D would similarly like to afford the much grander ways of E. These would seem to C like wealth beyond the wildest dreams of avarice.

It appears implausible to suggest that we would hurt D much less by causing him to sacrifice some part of his accustomed way of life than we would hurt C. Consequently, it appears unreasonable to suggest that D is on the same utility curve as C (though further along it). The other requirement of the initial assumption, that as C's income moved towards D's, his marginal utility would continue to fall, is only slightly more plausible. This topic is dealt with in much greater depth by other writers (Musgrave, 1959; Simons, 1970).

Difficulties like these which are met when dealing with the treatment of people in different circumstances make it impossible to construct a sound theoretical case for progressive taxation based on such manifestly reasonable propositions as equiproportional sacrifice of utility. However, we observe that decisions are made about tax rates, poverty definitions and welfare programmes, and they seem to be based in the long run on what society considers to be equitable. We find the Royal Commission on Taxation (1954) saying that 'not merely progressive taxation, but a steep gradient of taxation, is needed in order to conform with the notions of equitable distribution that are widely, almost universally accepted'.

This is, of course, a highly unsatisfactory, begging-the-question basis for progression (Blum and Kalven, 1953). However, as we shall see in Section 5.6, the British income tax system, and especially the total taxation system, is much less progressive than we are sometimes led to believe. Before this, let us look at the redistributional effects of direct and indirect taxes.

5.5 Distribution effects of taxes

If it can be decided what a fair distribution of income, wealth and so on would be, and if plans for particular types of taxes to achieve this are to be made, we must know in greater detail what the effects of such taxes as a progressive income tax will be. Despite our theoretical rejection of an expenditure base for the ability-to-pay approach, would it be more effective to institute a high rate of VAT on luxury goods than to have a progressive income tax, if we wished to take money from high income earners and not from low income earners?

The effects of progressive income taxes on individuals have been examined in the previous chapter. The direct and immediate effects on the distribution of income will clearly be towards reducing the disparity of income. However, there are many indirect effects. For example, the total amount to be distributed may fall as a result of efficiency costs and extra leisure taken by high earners (see Chapter 4). The resulting reduced hours of work may lead to a rise in the return of labour which will raise prices for consumers. The way in which the burden of tax eventually falls is called the 'effective' or 'economic' incidence. In this example we can see that it is the *consumers* who would suffer part of the economic incidence of the progressive income tax which had statutory incidence on the high income earners.

Expenditure taxes also have this difference in incidence which is called 'shifting'. The taxes are levied on producers, but borne to some extent by consumers. This is why such taxation is called indirect. In the long run, of course, the incidence of all taxes is on individuals. The reactions between individuals and companies to taxation will include the adjustment of sales and purchases in such a way that prices or wages or profits may suffer most, but eventually each is felt fully by individuals. The distributional effects are due to the fact that the various prices, wages, profits and so on are of different relative importance to different people.

Let us look at the distributional effects of indirect taxes in a little more detail, assuming a general sales tax on all consumption goods. The tax enters as a wedge between net and gross prices. Assuming that there are no effects on money wages or costs of production, this will mean that there is a real income effect. As there is no tax on saving or on capital goods, the burden on a particular household will depend upon the split of its income between consumption and saving. If it is true that the ratio of consumption expenditure to incomes falls as income increases, then the proposed sales tax will be regressive.

In the long run, however, it is not so clear that there is a diminishing average propensity to consume as suggested above. Over a person's lifetime, income may be saved in order to be spent later, in which case the general sales tax is merely being postponed. Traditionally, this has been said to be an advantage, because paying now is worse than paying later. However, during times when inflation rates were higher than interest rates, this would no longer be so. Nevertheless, the administrative difficulties of running a lifetime sales tax would be enormous. We should at least realise that, over a lifetime, the regressiveness of a general sales tax would be much less than a cross-sectional study at one point in time would suggest.

A *selective* sales tax on good Y only would lead to a rise in the price of Y. The size of this price rise depends on the price elasticities of demand and supply for Y. This was illustrated in Chapter 3 using a diagram similar to Figure 5.2, which shows that, under certain elasticities of supply and demand, both the supplier and the consumer bear some of the tax. The price rises from P_1 to P_2, but the suppliers' receipts fall from P_1 to P_3 for each unit.

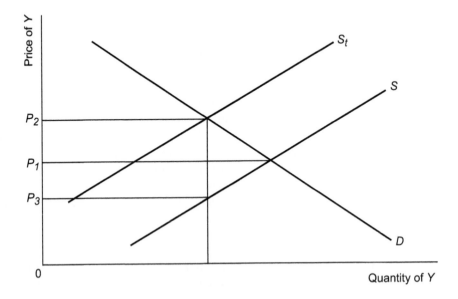

Figure 5.2 The imposition of sales tax

On the other hand, if demand is perfectly elastic, the suppliers suffer all the price fall and hence the whole burden of the tax. If the demand is perfectly inelastic, the consumers suffer fully. These cases are illustrated in Figure 5.3.

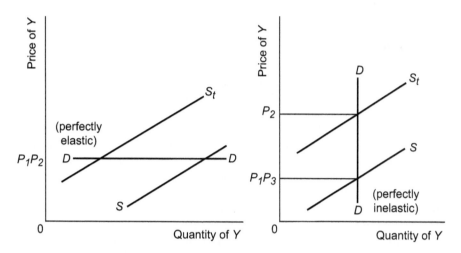

Figure 5.3 Sales tax with polar demand conditions

Similarly, it could be shown that a tax on goods in perfectly elastic supply will borne by consumers, and a tax on goods in perfectly inelastic supply will be borne by producers.

We may expect that most goods will not be in perfectly inelastic supply or perfectly elastic demand, therefore some immediate burden will be borne by consumers. Depending upon the nature of good Y, and therefore upon what categories of households tend to buy it, the imposition of a selective sales tax may be regressive, proportional, or progressive. If the goods bearing high rates of sales tax constitute a higher proportion of the budgets of low income households than they do of high income households, the tax will be regressive. This is examined in more detail using real taxes in Section 11.6. As an indication of the lengths to which it may be necessary to take this analysis, the effects on employment should be noted. If the goods consumed by the rich are produced by particularly labour-intensive industries which employ the poor, then a sales tax designed to affect consumption by the rich would also affect the incomes of the poor if employment or wages were lower than they would otherwise have been.

A further indirect tax should be mentioned and that is a payroll tax. In competitive markets with a fairly inelastic total labour supply, a general payroll tax cannot be avoided by moving to tax-free employment, and it should be borne by wage earners whether the employer or the employee actually pays it (Musgrave and Musgrave, 1989). However, many markets are not competitive, and unions may not accept a reduction in wages when an employer has to pay increased contributions for national insurance, for example. Therefore, either prices must go up, in which case the wage earner shares the burden with others, or prices cannot be raised, in which case the employer bears the tax.

Tax capitalisation

Taxes can also affect the capital value of assets. This happens because the value of an asset reflects the income (both pecuniary and non-pecuniary) that the asset is expected to yield. As an illustration of this relationship it can be mentioned that the prices of securities usually fluctuate so that their expected yields stay (roughly) in line with interest rates generally. If a tax changes the expected yield of an asset, then it will also change its market price. In other words, the tax has been capitalised.

As a simple example, consider the value of an undated government bond which yields £10 per year. Suppose also that to begin with there is no taxation on income from investments. If interest rates generally were, say, 10 per cent, the market price of the bond would tend towards £100. The reason is that at £100 the higher yield on the bond would also be 10 per cent and therefore in line with interest rates elsewhere. If the price of the bond were higher, then its yield would be lower than that of alternative investments. Its price would tend to fall since investors could gain by selling their stock and investing elsewhere. The opposite tendency would occur if the price were lower than £100.

Suppose now that a tax of 50 per cent were imposed on the income from this particular bond only. Suppose also that this new tax was expected to be permanent. If interest rates generally remained at 10 per cent, the price of the bond would fall to £50. This would restore the net yield to 10 per cent, again in line with that available from other assets. Even though the tax was imposed on the income from the asset, the burden, in the form of a *capital* loss, would have been suffered by the holders of the bond at the time the tax was introduced. Anyone who invested in the bond later would avoid this capital loss and yet still receive a 10 per cent return.

In practice, of course, the effects of tax capitalisation may be less dramatic. For instance, the prices of redeemable bonds will tend to move slowly towards their repayment price.

Nevertheless, tax capitalisation remains an important part of tax incidence and adds complexity to tax policy generally and equity in particular. One of the number of possible cases is mortgage interest relief. It is sometimes suggested that this relief should be retained in order to help individuals buy their own homes. However, the concession has increased the demand and therefore the price of housing. In other words, the concession has been capitalised, and the beneficiaries were those who already owned houses when the relief was introduced, rather than those who sought to purchase them. This example also illustrates the point that, once a certain tax has been introduced and capitalised, removing it can have further inequitable effects. If the tax relief on mortgage interest were withdrawn, those who had bought at the relief-inflated price would suffer a capital loss. Indeed, this happened in 1974 when the relief was restricted to that on a loan of £25,000. Following this restriction the prices of more expensive houses generally fell (Kay and King, 1990, Ch. 5).

Conclusion

In order to operate an effective redistributional package of taxes, the economic incidence of each tax must be known. As we have seen, the variety of taxes that may be used is considerable. There may be taxes on labour income or capital income or both, and there is the opportunity to be selective by geographical area or type of industry. In addition, there can be expenditure taxes on all goods, or certain types of goods.

Having identified the types of individuals that we wish to bear most tax and those who should bear the least, a suitable package may be assembled. Equal attention must be paid to the sources of income and to the uses. As long as we are content with a fairly broad approach to equity rather than one which identifies individuals, we can rely on the general relationships between the level of income and the types of sources and uses of it. For example, the contribution to income made by capital sources, and the proportion of income spent on champagne, both rise as income rises. Making sure that the economic incidence has been taken into account, these may be areas towards which to aim taxation if we wish the tax system to be progressive. For further detail, see Keller (1980).

5.6 Redistribution and the British tax system

An immense amount of ink has flowed on the subject of the distribution of wealth and income. Some of these writings are referred to in this section and in suggestions for further reading at the end of this chapter. There is space here for an introduction only.

Measures of distribution and redistribution

Distribution of income is often examined by measuring the proportion of the total income that is received by the top percentile of recipients, the next percentile down, and so on. This approach can then be repeated over many years to see how distribution is changing. If such information is arranged cumulatively, that is showing the top percentile, then the top two percentiles together and so on (see Table 5.1), Lorenz curves can be drawn to compare different years. An example is shown in Figure 5.4.

Table 5.1 Percentage distribution of incomes after income tax and surtax

Group of income recipients	1949	1957	1960	1963	1967	1970/71	1976/77
Top 1%	6.4	5.0	5.1	5.2	4.9	4.5	3.5
2%-5%	11.3	9.9	10.5	10.5	9.9	10.0	9.4
6%-10%	9.4	9.1	9.4	9.5	9.5	9.4	9.5
11%-40%	37.0	38.5	39.8	39.5	39.2	40.4	40.6
41'%-70%	21.3	24.0	23.5	23.5	24.5	23.8	24.1
Bottom 30%	14.6	13.4	11.7	1 1.8	12.0	1 1.8	12.9

Source: Diamond Commission (1979), Table 2.3.

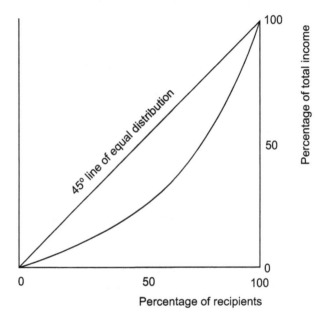

Figure 5.4 A Lorenz curve

A statistical measure of the inequality that this information reveals can be calculated. This is called the Gini coefficient. It relies on the fact that an equal distribution
would produce a straight line and that the greater the area between the straight line
and the Lorenz curve, the greater the inequality. The Gini coefficient measures this
area graphically (from a Lorenz curve) or statistically. There are some problems
with Gini coefficients, but these need not concern us here (Cowell, 1977). A more
sophisticated coefficient is suggested by Atkinson (1980, p. 41).

These techniques can be used to compare distributions of pre-tax or post-tax
income over different years (or different countries, for other purposes), or of pre-tax
income with post-tax income. This latter comparison will provide a measure of the
redistributional effectiveness of the tax system. The distribution of wealth can be
examined in a similar way.

An alternative measure of redistribution looks at the way in which the excess of traceable taxes over traceable benefits is split up by type of household. This is a measure of what should be causing redistribution, whereas the previous measures are of how much redistribution has been caused.

All these measures, which are used in the following pages, take the 'household' as the unit of comparison because of the great difficulties of separating the population into individuals for these purposes. One important problem concerns the 'income' of dependent children who would nearly all appear to be at the bottom of the table for the distribution of income using normal definitions. Clearly, such a result would be highly misleading when income is being used, at least partly, as a proxy for welfare. The majority of children do not have standards of living which can be sensibly related to their measurable incomes. For a discussion on measures of tax progression, see Formby *et al.* (1981).

The distribution of income from 1938

There have been several surveys of the distribution of income. Those of F.W. Paish from 1938 to 1955 (Paish, 1957) and H.F. Lydall from 1938 to 1957 (Lydall, 1959) show that the concentration of income in the hands of the top 5 per cent of income earners was reduced and was reducing at an accelerating rate from 1938 to the mid-1950s.

A later survey by R.J. Nicholson from 1949 to 1957 (Nicholson, 1973) shows that the growth rate of pre-tax incomes was faster in the lower income bands than in the higher bands. During this period there were rising prices and increasing employment, and earned income was rising faster than other types of income. For these reasons, the distribution moved towards equality in those years.

From 1957 onwards these effects were counteracted by an increase in the number of salaried employments, the rewards of which were larger and were growing faster than wages; by an increase in the levels of professional self-employed incomes; and by a large increase in the values of rents, dividends and interest. These counter-influences meant that the distribution of pre-tax incomes remained fairly stable for the decade to the mid-1960s. In the 1970s, the slight trend towards equality continued. The early 1970s saw large pay rises and then limits on rises, especially for the better paid.

There were considerable changes in the proportions of personal income that went in income taxation and National Insurance contributions: for example, from 14.9 per cent of personal income in 1963 to 23.4 per cent in 1975. There was, however, a fall in taxes on expenditure from 13.2 per cent to 11.3 per cent in this period (Table 3 of Diamond Commission, 1976).

In 1973 and 1979 there were substantial changes to the income tax system that benefited those on moderately high incomes, and indirect taxation was increased. After 1979, greater attention was paid to lowering the basic rate of tax than to reducing higher levels of taxation, so progressivity appeared to increase.

Table 5.2 Distribution of income 1949-77

	1949	1959	1964	1967	1972/73	1976/77
Pre-tax income of top 10%	33.2	29.4	29.1	28.0	26.9	25.8
Post-tax income of top 10%	27.1	25.2	25.9	24.3	23.6	22.4
Pre-tax Gini	41.1	39.8	39.9	38.2	37.4	36.5
Post-tax Gini	35.5	36.0	36.6	33.5	33.1	31.5

Source: Diamond Commission (1976), Table 3 and (1979), pp. 16 and 24.

Table 5.3 Distribution of income 1968-83

	1968	1977	1983
Pre-tax income of top 10%	24.8	25.0	28.6
Post-tax income of top 10%	21.6	21.2	23.7
Pre-tax Gini	0.361	0.395	0.459
Post-tax Gini	0.267	0.277	0.308

Source: Morris and Preston (1986).

Table 5.4 Distribution of income 1978/79 to 1984/85

	1978/79	1981/82	1984/85
Pre-tax income of top 10%	26.1	28.3	29.5
Post-tax income of top 10%	23.4	25.6	26.5
Pre-tax Gini	37	40	41
Post-tax Gini	34	36	36

Source: Economic Trends, HMSO, November 1987, p. 94

The distributional effects of all these changes can be seen in Tables 5.2 and 5.3, which are calculations by different researchers. The tables show the changes in the shares of income of the top 10 per cent of earners and the Gini coefficients for the whole distributions. There was a gradual movement towards equality of pre-tax incomes until the late 1970s, which appeared to reverse after that. Equality was enhanced throughout the period by the effects of taxation. Other data also show a slight move away from equality. Table 5.4 shows distributional measures from 1978/79 to 1984/85.

Even by 1985 it was still very clearly the case that the income tax system was progressive, that is, tax became a successively higher proportion of pre-tax income at successively higher levels of income. This is partially illustrated in Table 5.5, although there are only two levels of income, and indirect taxes are included.

From 1985 to 1995, there were further switches from direct to indirect taxation, which reduces progressivity. Table 5.6 shows the Gini coefficients for pre-tax equivalent income and post-tax equivalent income under the 1985 and 1995 tax regimes. Clearly, the tax system still redistributed in 1995, but not as much as it had done in 1985.

Table 5.5 Progressiveness of UK taxation since 1951

	Average tax rate* on £5,000 p.a. * (1985/86 prices)	Average tax rate on £10,000 p.a. (1985/86 prices)	Average of marginal tax rates
1951	45.4	54.2	62.9`
1964	46.1	50.1	54.1
1970	50.3	54.0	57.6
1774	42.1	48.5	55.0
1985	44.1	53.2	62.4

As faced by a couple where the wife does not work and the husband is a basic rate taxpayer contracted into SERPS (State Earnings Related Pension Scheme) and earning between the NI floor and the NI ceiling.

Source: Kay (1985).

Table 5.6 Gini coefficients pre-tax and after 1985 and 1995 tax system

	Gini
Pre-tax	0.3700
After 1985 system	0.3232
After 1995 system	0.3362

Source: Giles and Johnson

An alternative way of measuring the direction and comparative size of distribu-tional effects of taxation was mentioned at the beginning of this section. This relies on measuring the excess of taxes over transfer benefits by types of household. A study of this showed that the excess was greater for rich families and small families; thus this method suggests that redistribution of income towards poor and large families should have occurred (Nicholson and Britton, 1976). Similar information is also available in Diamond Commission (1979, Chapter 3) and in CSO (1994).

Criticisms

Partly due to the impact of inflation, some serious effects became particularly notice-able in the late 1970s. First, there were large numbers of people at the bottom end of the income scale whose implicit marginal rates of taxation were in excess of 100 per cent (Field et al., 1977). This was due to the interaction of the systems of income tax, National Insurance, Family Credit and Income Support. The poverty levels as defined for these latter two are above the level at which income tax begins to operate.

Table 5.7 Marginal tax rates 1995/96

Income (£)[a]	Marginal rate (tax and NI) %
0-3,015[b]	0
3,015-3,525[c]	10
3,525-6,725[d]	30
6,725-22,880[e]	35
22,880-27,825[f]	25
27,825+	40

[a] This represents income before allowances, on which National Insurance works. The rates of income tax used here have assumed a single person's allowance, and it is assumed that the employee is 'contracted in'.

[b] The level above which National Insurance becomes payable.

[c] the single person's allowance.

[d] The level above which the basic rate applies (i.e. £3,525 + £3,200).

[e] The level above which National Insurance is not levied.

[f] The level above which the higher marginal rate of income tax is levied.

Even at higher levels, if one includes National Insurance contributions (which in 1995/96 were not levied on slices of income above £440 per week), the system is not seriously progressive except at the bottom end, as shown in Table 5.7. In 1995/96 a very large majority of taxpayers had income before allowances of less than £27,825. The only substantial change in marginal rates as income rises within these bands was a fall from 35 per cent to 25 per cent, when the ceiling for employees' National Insurance contributions was exceeded.

Further, the allowances, which are supposed to benefit low earners by removing them from the tax net, turn out to be of proportionally greater benefit to higher rate taxpayers. This can be seen from Table 15 of Diamond Commission (1976).

Despite these detailed criticisms (that certain aspects of the system are not at all progressive), we have seen that there was a slight but continuous movement towards equality of income from 1938, although this appears to have been reversed since 1977. In the 1980s, inequality increased, but by 1991 this had been arrested (Goodman and Webb, 1994). Movement towards equality has been assisted by the total effect of the taxation system. Nevertheless, the progressive nature of the tax system is much less severe than a simple look at income tax rates would suggest. Clark and Leicester (2004) found that, from 1979 to 1999, income tax cuts of the late 1970s and late 1980s increased inequality but direct tax rises of the early 1980s and 1990s decreased it. Ramos and Roca-Sagales (2008) also study the UK over the long term. They find that an increase in public spending reduces inequality but a rise in indirect taxes increases it.

As a postscript, it should be noted that such analysis is of course also carried out in other countries. In the USA a long-term research project (Pechman, 1985) suggested that progressiveness declined between 1966 and 1985.

Distribution of wealth

There are very great difficulties in defining and measuring personal wealth. The Diamond Commission Report (1976, Table 29; 1979, Table 4.4) contains considerable information on the subject, including a Gini coefficient calculation suggesting a gradual move towards greater equality, in the years from 1960 to 1976. The distribution of wealth is very susceptible to high rates of wage inflation, stock market falls and other factors unconnected with tax, some of which may be reversible; therefore measures from year to year are rather less reliable than long-term trends, which certainly suggest a movement towards equality. We discuss this topic further in Chapter 10. The current methods of measuring the distribution of wealth are discussed by Good (1990).

5.7 The effects of inflation on equity

This section examines the different effects that inflation has on different taxes. Because of these different effects, if the mix of taxes had been equitable in the mid-1960s when inflation was low, it could not have been equitable by the mid-1970s and afterwards when inflation was much higher.

If there is a general price inflation during which all prices rise to the same extent, the equity of ad valorem taxes on expenditure will not be directly affected, even if there are several rates of tax. However, if there are relative price changes and the goods concerned bear atypical tax rates, there will be equity effects. For example, if luxury goods rise more in price than other goods and if they bear a higher tax, the expenditure tax system will become more progressive than it was intended to be. Nevertheless, in practice, the major problems arise with direct taxation. We will look at the effects of inflation on earned income, and on two types of unearned income: capital gains and interest.

Earned income

Under inflation, the equity aspects of the taxation of earned income will be affected, unless either the income tax system is proportional or adjustments are made to it to counter the effects of inflation. Without such adjustments to a progressive rate structure, inflation pushes earners into higher rate bands without increasing their real gross incomes. Let us postulate a progressive system which exempts the first

£1,000 of income each year, taxes the next £4,000 at 30 per cent and any extra income at 50 per cent. Let us now suppose that F starts with an income of £1,500 and G with £6,000. Their taxation will appear thus:

	F	G
Income	1,500	6,000
Allowances	1,000	1,000
Taxable income	500	5,000
Tax at 30%, 50%	150	1,700
Average tax rate	10.0%	28.3%

Suppose that, after a few years, inflation has run to a cumulative total of 100 per cent and has affected incomes and prices identically. The position now becomes:

	F	G
Income	3,000	12,000
Allowances	1,000	1,000
Taxable income	2,000	11,000
Tax at 30%, 50%	600	4,700
Average tax rate	20.0%	39.2%

If the previous system is thought to have been equitable, there will now be an inequity between high and low earners and between income taxpayers and expenditure taxpayers, whose average rate will have stayed the same. As usual, it has been assumed that the extra tax would result only in distributionally neutral adjustments in either government expenditures or other taxes. For an application of this to UK income tax, see Nobes (1977).

Fortunately for income taxpayers, the allowances are raised and the taxable income levels at which higher marginal rates apply are also occasionally raised. Indeed in 1977, rather against the will of the Chancellor and the Treasury, Parliament decided that there would in future be a presumption in favour of automatic indexation of allowances to the rate of inflation at each yearly Budget. (This was called the Rooker-Wise Amendment after the two MPs who proposed it.) Despite this, governments have since persuaded Parliament to vote for some Finance Bills which do not fully adjust allowances. Nevertheless, the UK income tax system is partially indexed, and the disturbing effects on average rates (referred to above) have not come to pass.

For a general review of the problem of indexation, see Brinner (1976).

Capital gains

Capital gains tax is a rather more complex case because, whereas income tax is a tax on the current returns to current toil, capital gains tax works on gains which accrue over time. This is because capital gains tax, which is now charged at income tax rates, only becomes due when an asset is sold and the gain is realised (see Section 7.4 for more details). It means that both the real gain and an inflationary or monetary gain are brought in to charge to tax. In inflationary times it is clear that, since gains evolve over a long period, the comparison of purchase money with sales money is not performed in sensibly comparable units. Consequently, real tax rates are much higher than nominal tax rates. If, for example, one adjusted purchase money of 1986 to a date for sale in 1996, after 10 per cent per annum inflation, the calculation below would occur. £1 in 1986 is equivalent to £2.5937 in 1996, making the simplifying assumption that the factor $(1 + \text{rate})^{10}$ can be used.

	1986 pounds	1996 pounds
Original purchase	10,000	25,937
5% real growth over 10 years	6,289	16,312
Final value	16,289	42,249
Less Original purchase price	-10,000	
Tax based on		32,249
Tax at 30% (for example)		9,675
Effective rate (9.675 ÷ 16,312)		59.3%

Further similar calculations produce the following table of real rates under different inflation and growth assumptions:

Rates of inflation	0%	10%	20%
5% real growth	30%	59%	70%
10% real growth	30%	42%	46%

These rates apply to the whole ten years' gain. The fact that they are deferred is not relevant for our analysis of the effects of inflation, because they are deferred whether or not there is inflation. These very high real rates of taxation which are caused by the taxation of money gains have unfortunate effects. First, they may involve a disincentive to save. Secondly, since taxation only comes into effect when an asset is realised, there is a 'locked-in' effect. That is, there is an incentive to leave one's investment where it is despite more attractive pre-tax opportunities. This is economically inefficient. The 'locked-in' effect would exist even without inflation, but is worsened by it.

Thus, there seem to be arguments for the indexation of capital gains tax. These include an equity argument based on a comparison with income tax which is approximately indexed. However, despite the fact, mentioned in Section 5.2, that capital gains tax was introduced by the Commons as a necessity for equity when compared with the taxation of earned income, a more relevant and closer comparison would be with other types of unearned income, such as interest. Therefore, before firmly accepting the above conclusion about the indexation of capital gains tax, we must examine the effects of inflation on other unearned income.

Fixed-interest securities

The effects of inflation on the returns of fixed-interest securities are very severe. Not only does the interest get less valuable year by year in real terms, but also the original investment loses value cumulatively. Both effects are included in the formula:

$$(1 + r) \; = \; \frac{(1 + n)}{(1 + i)}$$

where r equals real rate of interest, n is the quoted nominal rate of interest, and i is the rate of inflation. When the rate of inflation exceeds the nominal rate of interest, the real rate of interest on capital can be seen to be negative.

The effects of this can be seen in Table 5.8, in which the post-tax returns over ten years on debentures and such assets as paintings are expressed as percentages of the returns under no inflation. This is taken from Nobes (1977), which assumed tax rates ruling at the time. However, later tax rates would give broadly similar results; it is assumed that there is no indexation of capital gains tax, but that marginal rates of income tax are adjusted.

The figures in Table 5.8 suggest that real post-tax returns on fixed-interest securities suffer much more seriously than those on investment to which capital gains accrue, even if there was no indexation of capital gains tax.

In the Finance Act 1982 a form of indexation of capital gains tax was introduced and there have been further changes in this area since then (see Section 8.4).

Corporate tax

The effects of inflation on corporation tax will be considered in section 13.6

Table 5.8 An example of real post-tax returns over a 10-year period

Rates of inflation	0%	10%	20%
8% debentures after basic tax	100	(-57)	(-119)
8% debentures after higher tax	100	(-131)	(-220)
5% growth paintings after basic tax	100	79	72
5% growth paintings after higher tax	100	58	43

5.8 Administrative fairness

It is of great assistance to the smooth running of the tax system and to the reduction of evasion if the government and revenue authorities can build administrative fairness into the system. Taking a broad view of what might be included under this heading, this section discusses several examples.

The general attitude of HM Revenue and Customs in its dealings with the public by letter, telephone and face to face is important. In the experience of the authors (and there seems to be no more objective evidence available at present), although written contact is extremely formal, contact by telephone or face to face seems to be pleasant and helpful. In general, the Revenue operates a walk-in enquiry service in decentralised tax offices throughout the country. If a person's tax is not dealt with locally, the local office is prepared to send for the file and deal with the case locally. Indeed, in London, where these problems occur most frequently, PAYE enquiry bureaux have been set up.

A further example of the willingness of the Revenue and Customs to answer questions in a helpful way is the extensive enquiry service at the East Kilbride Computer Centre. This service was greatly expanded to deal with the unexpectedly large flow of personal enquiries. Although it seems unrealistic to expect that the Revenue will ever be popular, this willingness to discuss and explain the rules and individual assessments is gratifying.

Also, there is a very large number of explanatory leaflets available. In general, they are fairly easy to understand. An analysis of the complexity of such information has been carried out, using a 'fog index' which relies on the length of words and sentences. Many of the leaflets were found to be easier to read than 'quality' daily newspapers (James and Lewis, 1977); and the whole issue of the comprehensibility of taxation is tackled in James *et al.* (1987).

The existence of an appeals system is a further example of administrative fairness. This is reinforced by the involvement of independent Commissioners (see Chapter 8). There is also some provision for postponement or cancellation of assessments when this would reduce trivial transactions or allow the process of appeal to relieve hardship. Such a detail as rounding in favour of the taxpayer when performing calculations is also an endearing trait.

These examples of practical administrative fairness work within a system which has some properties which are generally regarded as equitable, at least in theory. Many of these have already been discussed ,like progressiveness. This has the side effect that, since it implies a system based on marginal rates, it is usually the case that the absurd situation of receiving an increase in income but suffering an even larger increase in tax is avoided.

Another factor which would be perceived to be equitable is the favourable treatment of earned income as opposed to unearned income. This idea that those who toil should be more lightly taxed than those who sit back and count the takings is called 'differentiation' (see Chapter 7). It was given practical effect by a Liberal administration in 1907. However, differentiation was reversed to some extent in

1995 (see section 8.3). A further example of equity is the use of net income which takes account of family and other commitments.

Although a theoretical argument was put forward for the use of income as a basis for an ability-to-pay approach to equity, we saw that, because of the problems of economic incidence and because of practical difficulties of bringing all income into tax, a package of taxes of various sorts which operated on both sources and uses of income might be the best way to work towards an equitable distribution. When one looks at the mix of taxes in use in the UK at present, it is clear that they have no main and consistent purpose of accomplishing an equitable distribution. Nevertheless, it is a tenable opinion that, given a lack of consistent and sound theory, it is fairer to tax everything relatively lightly than to tax one thing very heavily, be it unearned income, luxury goods, inherited wealth, or whatever. This is a rare illustration of the compatibility of equity and efficiency, as it was mentioned in Section 3.4 that a tax with a broad base is likely to impose less excess burden than one with a narrow base. As will be seen in the next section, the perception by taxpayers of general fairness in the whole tax system is important in the control of avoidance and evasion.

5.9 Avoidance and evasion

Definitions

As we have seen, avoidance is an individual's manipulation of his affairs within the law so as to reduce his tax liability. Evasion is illegal manipulation to reduce tax. Accountants refer to avoidance as 'tax planning' or 'tax mitigation', which emphasises its legality. In order to enable a more precise discussion of avoidance in this section we need to look a little more closely at its definition.

It could be said using the above definition that, if an individual reduced his consumption of gin and increased his consumption of tonic water when a tax on spirits was imposed, he was avoiding tax. Similarly, if an individual gets married, he could be said to be avoiding tax (but at what cost!). Clearly, the usefulness of the term 'avoidance' is reduced if these examples are included within it.

Following Professor Sandford's suggestion (Sandford, 1973), avoidance will be used to mean something which is contrary to the spirit of the law and which accomplishes the pre-tax objective. For example, if an individual splits up his estate in various ways and into various sorts of property solely in order to pass on as much wealth as possible to his heirs, he is attempting to accomplish the objective he had before inheritance tax was introduced, and he is operating against the spirit of the law. On the other hand, in the previous examples the intention of the law may have been to discourage drinking and to encourage owner-occupation, and at least to have been neutral about marriage.

Prevalence

Not surprisingly, information about avoidance and evasion is sparse. There are no accurate quantitative estimates of their importance. It is clear, however, that the Inland Revenue is continually worried by the problem and has produced high estimates of the level of evasion (see Section 3.5). Also, a survey of accountants (Sandford, 1973) has shown that they are keen that their clients should take advantage of the possibilities for avoidance, though many of them draw the line at complex artificial schemes. Their clients also dislike complex means of avoidance. However, the search for loopholes continues and if there has been any reduction in avoidance it is probably due to the closing of loopholes rather than restraint by taxpayers. The replacement of estate duty by capital transfer tax and then by inheritance tax has removed the most fruitful source of avoidance schemes (see Chapter 10).

The survey was not informative about evasion, except to reveal that some clients of accountants did not know the difference between avoidance and evasion, and to record the feeling of accountants that evasion may be on the increase and is particularly popular with the self-employed.

Causes

The causes of avoidance and evasion include high tax rates, imprecise laws, insufficient penalties, and inequity.

Avoidance and evasion become more rewarding as rates of tax become higher. Therefore, it is worth spending more money on advice, performing more complex manoeuvres and taking greater risks.

Imprecise laws make neither the letter of the law tight, nor the spirit of the law clear. It is obviously very difficult to legislate with great precision and foresight for the steadily more complex taxes which we now face. However, the speed with which the professional accountants and others find loopholes is alarming. Another improvement would be gained if it became clear that loopholes would be speedily closed once discovered. This would reduce both the incentive for expending effort in finding them and the number of cases that got through them. Adam Smith's canon on 'certainty' relates to this. He wrote that the 'tax which each individual is bound to pay ought to be certain and not arbitrary' (Smith, 1776). The increasing legal complexity which is necessary to maintain equity and to reduce avoidance has the unfortunate side effect of reducing comprehensibility. A survey of the length of Income Tax Acts has shown that, if this is any proxy for complexity, there has been a great increase in complexity over the last century (Grout and Sabine, 1976).

If the penalties available to the Revenue and the courts were unimportant compared to the benefits, evasion would increase. In the UK it is more the case that the penalties imposed may be inadequate, and that the Revenue may err too much towards giving hints that evasion has been detected, rather than treating it more seriously. It is often the case now that minor forms of evasion are 'punished' merely by charging interest on the tax that should have been paid earlier. This interest may even be less than the benefit the taxpayer has gained from the use of the unpaid money.

In the UK, the social penalties of evasion are probably greater than in the USA, for example, where evasion is regarded as a national sport, or in Italy where it is regarded as a moral duty! If an atmosphere could be created to the effect that evasion was not only illegal but also morally wrong and socially inequitable, this might be very effective in controlling it. A survey of taxpayers in European countries (including Britain) indicates that a positive attitude by taxpayers towards the tax system, and a negative attitude towards offenders, can contribute to the control of evasion (Strümpel, 1969).

If the system is commonly regarded as being inequitable, this will lead to an increased desire to avoid or evade tax, and these activities will become increasingly socially acceptable. We have looked at equity in some detail in this chapter. One other obvious inequity would be the ease of avoidance and evasion. In addition to the suggestion that one could get away with paying less tax there would be the feeling that one did not want to pay more tax just because other people were allowed to be successful at avoidance and evasion.

One commentator on the ease of avoidance of the old estate duty writes that 'where those with good tax advisers - and perhaps fewer scruples - can pay little tax while others pay tax at rates of up to 75 per cent, there can be little respect for the equity of taxation' (Atkinson, 1974). A survey in the United States has provided evidence that there is a relationship between inequity and evasion (Spicer, 1975).

Effects

Finally, let us look at the costs and other disadvantages of avoidance and evasion. Both forms of reducing taxation involve the taxpayer's time and the consequent adjustment to his affairs which may run counter to commercial or economic logic except for the tax advantages. Avoidance, and sometimes evasion, also involves the time and resources of expert advisers. The costs in terms of reduced economic welfare of all this effort and re-arrangement must be considerable. In addition, there are rather more subtle mental costs created by having to draw up complex wills early in life, or by having to pass property before one would most like to, or by general anxiety. At the extremes, there are the mental and physical costs of leaving one's country for tax reasons.

The disadvantageous effects on distribution are of the most obvious concern in this chapter. Some forms of avoidance and evasion may render particular redistributional plans completely ineffective. Clearly, the old estate duty was intended to redistribute wealth, but was much less effective than it might have been because of the ease of avoidance through lifetime gifts. When planning such a tax, estimates need to be made of the possible re-arrangements that might follow its introduction, and the sort of people who would thereby avoid the redistributional effects.

Income and wealth are redistributed towards those who successfully commit avoidance and evasion, and away from those who do not. This comes about not only because the avoiders and evaders pay less than they otherwise would, but also because the rates of taxation have to be increased in order to raise a predetermined amount of revenue from other taxpayers. This is clearly inequitable and, as has already been mentioned, the perception of this will lead to further avoidance and evasion. All these costs and disadvantages suggest that the effective effort put into the reduction of avoidance and evasion would be well worthwhile. This will be so up to the point at which the extra policing, complexity and other costs outweigh the benefit to society as a whole of the reduction in avoidance and evasion.

5.10 Summary

This chapter began by looking at the philosophical and practical benefits of fairness in taxation. Equal treatment of equals must be the most basic of requirements, but even this involves a series of assumptions and definitional problems. These problems are as nothing compared with those of satisfactorily treating those who are not equal.

The benefit approach to equity turns out to be of little practical value because it is difficult to trace benefits to individuals or groups; because it breaks down when considering transfer payments, for example; and because taxes and expenditure are not usually directly linked. The ability-to-pay approach usually relies upon an income basis. Its assumptions are not strong enough for us to rely upon the argument for progressiveness that it appears to provide.

Turning to the distributional effects of taxes, we see that the incidence of taxes is usually shifted to some extent from the point of assessment. The indirect effects of an income tax may involve hours worked and prices charged. The degree to which consumers suffer directly from sales taxes depends on elasticities of demand and supply. Studies of distributional effects need to include the effective incidence of taxes and the dispersal of benefits of government expenditure. This is likely to be very complicated.

The British income tax system has been mildly re distributive since 1938. However, it is less progressive than a simple look at income tax rates might suggest.

The effects of inflation on equity are important and unintentional. Earned income fares reasonably well because of its current nature and because effort is put into correcting for inflation. Capital gains suffer increasingly high real rates in inflationary conditions. However, indexation of capital gains taxation seems inappropriate unless there is also indexation of fixed interest securities which suffer even more under inflation.

The chapter concluded with consideration of the various elements of the tax system that may contribute to equity, and a discussion of the causes and costs of avoidance and evasion.

Further reading

General reading on the subject matter of this chapter might include Atkinson (1980), Musgrave and Musgrave (1989, Chapters 5, 11, 12 and 13), Kay and King (1990), Prest and Barr (1985, Chapter 5), Kincaid (1973, Chapters 5 and 6), Brown and Jackson (1990, Chapters 15 and 17) and Lambert (1989). For measures of equality, refer to Cowell (1977) and Sen (1973). The effects of inflation are dealt with by Brinner (1976) and OECD (1976).

References

Atkinson, A.B. (1974), *Unequal Shares*, Penguin, p. 128.

Atkinson, A.B. (1980), *Wealth, Income and Inequality*, Oxford University Press.

Blum, W.J. and Kalven, H. (1953), The Uneasy Case for Progressive Taxation, University of Chicago Press.

Brinner, A.B. (1976), 'Inflation and the definition of taxable personal income', in H.J. Aaron (ed.), *Inflation and the Income Tax*, Brookings Institution.

Brown, C.V. and Jackson, P.M. (1990), *Public Sector Economics*, Blackwell.

Cowell, F. (1977), *Measuring Inequality*, Philip Allan, Chapt er 2.

Clark, T. and Leicester, A. (2004), 'Inequality and two decades of British tax and benefit reforms', *Fiscal Studies*, Vol. 25, No.2.

CSO (1994), 'The effects of taxes and benefits on household income, 1992', *Economic Trends*, January.

Diamond Commission (1976), *The Royal Commission on the Distribution of Income and Wealth*, Report No. 4, Cmnd. 6626, HMSO.

Diamond Commission (1979), Report No. 7, Cmnd. 7595, HMSO.

Field, F., Meacher, M. and Pond, C. (1977), *To Him Who Hath*, Penguin, Chapter 3.

Formby, J.P., Seaks, T.G. and Smith, W.J. (1981), 'A comparison of two measures of progressivity', *The Economic Journal*, December.

Giles, C. and Johnson, P. (1994), 'Tax reform in the UK and changes in the progressivity of the tax system, 1985-95', *Fiscal Studies*, August.

Good, F.J. (1990), 'Estimates of the distribution of personal wealth', *Economic Trends*, October.

Goodman, A. and Webb, S. (1994), 'For richer, for poorer: the changing distribution of income in the UK, 1961-91', *Fiscal Studies*, November.

Grout, V. and Sabine, B. (1976), 'The first hundred years of tax cases', *British Tax Review*, No. 2.

James, S.R. and Lewis, A. (1977), 'Fiscal fog', *British Tax Review*, No. 6.

James, S.R., Lewis, A. and Allison, E (1987), *The Comprehensibility of Taxation: A Study of Taxation and Communications*, Gower.

Johnson, P. and Stark, G. (1989), 'Ten years of Mrs. Thatcher: the distributional consequences', *Fiscal Studies*, May.

Kaldor, N. (1955), *An Expenditure Tax*, Unwin University Books.

Kay, J.A. (1985), 'Changes in tax progressivity, 1951-1985', *Fiscal Studies*, May.

Kay, J.A. and King, M.A. (1990), *The British Tax System*, Oxford University Press.

Keller, W.J. (1980), *Tax Incidence: A General Equilibrium Approach*, North-Holland.

Kincaid, J.C. (1973), *Poverty and Equality in Britain*, Penguin.

Lambert, P. (1989), *The Distribution and Redistribution of Income*, Blackwell.

Lydall, H.F. (1959), 'The long term trend in the size distribution of income', *Journal of the Royal Statistical Society*, Series A, 122, Part 1.

Meade Committee (1978), *The Structure and Reform of Direct Taxation*, Institute for Fiscal Studies (IFS), Allen & Unwin.

Morris, C.N. and Preston, I. (1986), 'Taxes, benefits and the distribution of income 1968-83', *Fiscal Studies*, November.

Musgrave, R.A. (1959), *The Theory of Public Finance*, McGraw-Hill, Chapter 5.

Musgrave, R.A. and Musgrave, P.B. (1989), *Public Finance in Theory and Practice*, 5th edn, McGraw-Hill.

Nicholson, J.L. and Britton, A.J.C. (1976), 'The redistribution of income', in A.B. Atkinson (ed.), *The Personal Distribution of Incomes*, Allen & Unwin.

Nicholson, R.J. (1973), 'The distribution of personal income', in AB. Atkinson (ed.), *Wealth, Income and Inequality*, Penguin.

Nobes, C.W. (1977), 'Capital gains tax and inflation', *British Tax Review*, No. 3.

OECD (1976), *The Adjustment of Personal Income Tax Systems for Inflation*, OECD.

Paish, F.W. (1957), 'The real incidence of personal taxation', *Lloyds Bank Review*, Vol. 43.

Pechman, J.A. (1985), *Who Paid the Taxes, 1966-85?*, Brookings Institution.

Pigou, A.C. (1932), *The Economics of Welfare*, 4th edn, Macmillan, Part 4, Chapter 9.

Prest, A.R and Barr, N.A. (1985), *Public Finance*, Weidenfeld and Nicolson.

Ramos, X. and Roca-Sigales, O. (2008), 'Long-term effects of fiscal policy on the size and distribution of the pie in the UK', *Fiscal Studies*, Vol. 29, No.3.

Rawls, J. (1972), *A Theory of Justice*, Oxford University Press.

Royal Commission on the Taxation of Profits and Income (1954), *Second Report*, Cmnd. 9105, HMSO, p. 33.

Sandford, C.T. (1973), *Hidden Costs of Taxation*, Institute for Fiscal Studies, Chapter 8.

Sen, A.K. (1973), *On Economic Inequality*, Clarendon Press.

Simons, H.C. (1970), 'The case for progressive taxation', in R.W. Houghton (ed.), *Public Finance*, Penguin.

Smith, A. (1776), *The Wealth of Nations*, edited by E. Cannan, Methuen, 1950.

Spicer, M. (1975), 'New approaches to the problem of tax evasion', *British Tax Review*, No. 3.

Strümpel, B. (1969), 'Contribution of survey research to public finance', in A. Peacock (ed.), *Quantitative Analysis in Public Finance*, Praeger, p. 26.

Self assessment questions

Suggested answers to self-assessment questions are given at the back of the book.

5.1   Compare 'horizontal equity' with 'vertical equity'.

5.2   Which criteria could be used to decide whether a tax is fair?

5.3   What characteristics of a taxpayer affect his/her ability to pay income tax?

5.4   Where does the effective incidence of expenditure taxes fall?

5.5   How can taxes affect the capital value of assets?

5.6   Does the UK tax system redistribute income?

5.7   What is the relationship between average and marginal tax rates in a progressive income tax system?

Discussion questions

1.   Is it fair to tax wealth as well as income?

2.   Is progression in taxation fair?

3.   Which taxes suffer the worst distortions under inflationary conditions?

CHAPTER SIX

Taxation and stabilisation

LEARNING OBJECTIVES

After reading this chapter, you should be able to:

- Explain the arguments for and against an active government policy of macro-economic stabilisation.
- Describe how fiscal policy works and what limitations it might have .
- Be able to judge the relative merits of different taxes as instruments of stabilisation policy.

6.1 Introduction

Unemployment and inflation are two of the major problems facing modern economies. They also present two interrelated issues. The first is that economies may, indeed have appeared to, develop secular trends towards higher levels of unemployment or inflation and, sometimes, both. In addition to any such trends, the level of economic activity has fluctuated over time. This has been described as the business cycle and consists of a continuing series of so-called 'booms' and 'slumps'. The practical implication of these problems is a policy (or policies) designed to smooth out the cyclical fluctuations and to minimise the levels of unemployment and inflation.

In this chapter we begin with the basic issue of the role of the state in achieving these aims. No doubt controversy over this issue will continue for ever, but most of the main points of current contention are described. This is followed by a discussion of fiscal policy, and the chapter ends on the relative merits of different taxes as instruments of stabilisation policy.

6.2 The role of the state

In the past few hundred years there has been an enormous range of views as to the extent to which the state ought to intervene in economic life. For instance, the 'mercantilist' theories generally held that the state had a major role to play in promoting economic welfare. In particular, it was considered that there should be intervention to build up and maintain a favourable balance of trade with other countries. This involved state regulation and protection in the form of tariffs and embargoes on imports. For example, the famous Navigation Acts (the first of which was passed in 1650) were designed to promote British shipping. Mercantilism also implied policies designed to encourage industries which exported goods and industries which could produce substitutes for imported goods. These views were widely held from the sixteenth to eighteenth centuries (and, it may be suggested, are still thriving in certain quarters!).

The succeeding doctrine of laissez-faire took the opposite view: that economic wealth was best produced by self-interested individuals directed by the 'invisible hand' of free markets, rather than by government. In the words of Adam Smith (1776):

> The uniform, constant and uninterrupted effort of every man to better his condition, the principle from which public and national, as well as private opulence is originally derived, is frequently powerful enough to maintain the natural progress of things toward improvement, in spite both of the extravagance of government, and of the greatest errors of administration. Like the unknown principle of animal life, it frequently restores health and vigour to the constitution, in spite, not only of the disease, but of the absurd prescriptions of the doctor.

The influence of laissez-faire was extensive in the nineteenth century.

In the twentieth century the arguments over the proper role of government have continued, of course, at least as vigorously. However, a new dimension of the debate has concentrated on the relative merits of the different methods by which any given level of government intervention should be conducted.

In particular, there are two major types of policy which the government can use to influence the level of economic activity: fiscal policy and monetary policy. Fiscal policy refers to changes in government spending or income including, of course, taxation. As its name suggests, monetary policy is mainly conducted through measures designed to influence the supply of money or the level of interest rates. There is a considerable overlap between fiscal and monetary policy. A change in fiscal policy will usually affect the monetary side of the economy, and thus in turn will affect the results of the original change in fiscal policy. For example, suppose that the government pursues an expansionary fiscal policy which results in an increase in the budget deficit. This increase in the deficit has to be financed one way or another. It can be done by borrowing, or it can be done by increasing the money supply. Either way, such changes will influence the effects of the expansionary fiscal policy.

Despite the interdependence of fiscal and monetary policies, there has been a vigorous controversy as to which of the two is the more effective. The debate has often been described as being between the 'Keynesians' on the one hand and the 'monetarists' on the other. This is very much a crude view of the discussion, but it does provide a useful way of presenting many of the issues involved in stabilisation policy.

The 'Keynesian' approach

The term 'Keynesian' is used here to indicate a range of views, rather than solely the work of John Maynard Keynes. Keynes was certainly one of the most prominent expounders of these views in the 1930s, but he was by no means the only economist to pursue them. It should be added that a number of propositions which are often included under the general heading of 'Keynesian' are quite different from the thinking of Keynes himself (see, for example, Leijonhufvud, 1968). Indeed, Sir Austin Robinson (1977) reports that Keynes himself, after dining with the Washington Keynesian economists in 1944, commented that 'I was the only non-Keynesian there'. Also, Colin Clark (1970) relates that, in 1946, Keynes explained in a letter to Abba Lerner: 'You see, I am not a Keynesian'. And, just to round it off, Samuelson (1970, p. 193) has quoted Milton Friedman, who is perhaps the most widely known prophet of monetarism, as saying 'we are all Keynesians now!'

Despite this daunting background, it is possible to present a stylised version of the 'Keynesian' approach. The initial contrast is with the preceding view of laissez-faire. As we have seen, that view suggested that markets were best left to themselves. In particular, involuntary unemployment was not seen as a fundamental problem. (Involuntary unemployment here refers to individuals who are willing to work at prevailing wage rates, or for less, but are unable to find employment.) In support of this proposition was 'Say's law' (Say, 1803) which held that supply creates its own demand. In other words, 'demand is only limited by production. No man produces, but with a view to consume or sell, and he never sells, but with an intention to purchase some other commodity' (Ricardo, 1821, Chapter XXI). Therefore, there cannot be a lack of aggregate demand and, so the argument runs, if there is unemployment, it is caused by obstacles to the efficient operation of the market, such as trade unions or custom or whatever, keeping wage rates at an artificially high level.

Although the mass unemployment and misery of the Great Depression concentrated minds wonderfully on the validity of this line of argument, it had encountered opposition much earlier. Malthus, perhaps best known for his views on population, expressed concern that 'effective demand' might be insufficient as he explained, for example, in a letter to Ricardo on 7 July 1821. It might be noted that Keynes's opinion was that, 'If only Malthus, instead of Ricardo, had been the parent stem from which nineteenth century economics proceeded, what a much wiser and richer place the world would be today!' (Keynes, 1933). It was also soon pointed out that whereas Say's law must be true for a barter economy (where buying and selling necessarily occur simultaneously), this does not have to happen in a monetary economy (Mill, 1844), though at the time this was not widely recognised as a major problem.

It was not until the 'Keynesian revolution' that the problem was placed firmly on the academic agenda. In particular, Keynes's General Theory of Employment Interest and Money (1936) provided a powerful focus for the following debate. Perhaps it is of interest to note that Keynes himself, in a letter dated 1 January 1935 to George Bernard Shaw, wrote: 'I believe myself to be writing a book on economic theory which will largely revolutionise - not, I suppose, at once but in the course of the next ten years - the way the world thinks about economic problems' (quoted in Harrod, 1951, Chapter 11).

In this book, Keynes provided a general theory for the economic system which suggested that the economy may move to a position involving involuntary unemployment, and would not then tend back towards full employment. For instance, a fall in investment would reduce aggregate demand, which in turn would reduce employment and national income. Furthermore, the drop in national income could be greater than the original fall in investment through the operation of the multiplier. This simply describes the process where a fall in the income of one group will cause them to spend less, which will reduce the income of others, who in turn will reduce their expenditure and so on. It might be possible to reduce the resulting unemployment through an expansionary monetary policy, but some Keynesians thought that it might not prove effective. For example, it may not be possible to reduce interest rates sufficiently to stimulate the required level of aggregate demand.

The answer then seemed to be an expansionary fiscal policy whereby the government increased spending or reduced taxation or both. Again, the multiplier may increase the changes in national income. The following unusual illustration from the *General Theory* (Keynes, 1936, Book III, Chapter 10) gives something of the flavour of the argument:

> If the Treasury were to fill old bottles with bank notes, bury them at suitable depths in disused coalmines which are then filled up to the surface with town rubbish, and leave it to private enterprise on well-tried principles of *laissez-faire* to dig the notes up again ... there need be no more unemployment and, with the help of the repercussions, the real income of the community, and its capital wealth also, would probably become a good deal greater than it actually is.

So the argument is that government is able to reduce unemployment, and can then maintain full employment by manipulating aggregate demand - a policy sometimes known as 'fine-tuning'. Beyond that, markets can be left to allocate resources more or less efficiently.

Such Keynesian principles exerted a very strong influence on UK macroeconomic policy in the 1950s and 1960s. However, increasingly, concern was aroused about whether full employment could be maintained at the same time as price stability. Both unemployment and inflation can be affected by the level of aggregate demand. This led to a further development in 'Keynesian' thought - the Phillips curve (Phillips, 1958; Lipsey, 1960). Phillips's view was that, as the pressure of aggregate demand rose, so the rate of increase of wages would rise. Also, the level of aggregate demand would be indicated by the level of unemployment. Phillips examined the wage and unemployment rates of nearly a century, and suggested that there was an inverse relationship between the two. As wages have a strong influence on prices, the analysis appeared to show that there was a trade-off between inflation and unemployment. It seemed that there was a whole range of possible combinations of these two variables, with high rates of inflation being compatible with low levels of unemployment, and lower rates of inflation being compatible with higher levels of unemployment. It was then only a small step to suggest that the government could 'choose' which combination it wished to aim at, by controlling the level of aggregate demand.

There is a further strand in 'Keynesian' thought which has become known as 'disequilibrium analysis'. This view also places considerable importance on the role of markets in the economy. However, it has stressed the possibility that prices may not always respond flexibly to economic pressures. Market adjustment may then occur through the *quantities* bought and sold, as well as, or instead of, through prices. This line of thought recognises the role of government intervention through fiscal and monetary policy, but perhaps with the assistance of some form of prices and incomes policy.

One other feature of the Keynesian approach contrasts with much of the pre-Keynesian thought and has been particularly evident in discussions of economic policy. In the nineteenth and early twentieth centuries a great emphasis was often placed on long-term considerations. Considerations such as involuntary unemployment sometimes received less attention, since it was supposed that in the longer term, markets were capable of dealing with them. Although a great deal of the 'Keynesian' stress on 'short-term' issues comes from Keynesians rather than Keynes, a clear lead in this came from Keynes himself. As Joan Robinson (1971) put it, Keynes 'brought the argument down from timeless stationary states into the present, here and now, when the past cannot be changed and the future cannot be known'. And as Keynes (1924) put it in an earlier work:

> This *long run* is a misleading guide to current affairs. *In the long run* we are all dead. Economists set themselves too easy, too useless a task if in tempestuous seasons they can only tell us that when the storm is long past the ocean is flat again.

It is difficult to summarise the 'Keynesian' approach in a short space. For our purposes, perhaps it is sufficient to say that it presumes that national income is determined by real, rather than monetary, magnitudes; and that government can intervene successfully, partly through fiscal policy, to reduce unemployment and inflation. Therefore, the government should do so.

The 'monetarist' approach

The Keynesian approach to macroeconomic policy has provoked criticism from various quarters, perhaps most noticeably from individuals belonging to the 'monetarist' school of thought. Like Keynesianism, monetarism means different things to different people. For instance, in the UK in political circles, it has been used to describe a belief in *laissez-faire* and as a term of abuse. Michael Foot (1983), as Leader of the Opposition, was quoted as saying that 'monetarism is a worldwide disease'.

On a less dramatic note, the term 'monetarism' covers a range of views which emphasise the role of money in the operation of the economic system. It therefore provides a considerable contrast to Keynesianism, which has tended to play down the importance of money and monetary policy, relative to fiscal policy. We shall not attempt a full account of monetarism here; descriptions can be found in Chrystal (1979) and Vane and Thompson (1979). Rather we shall summarise particular areas of debate and some of these will be discussed further, later in the chapter.

The first point is that monetarists have suggested that most of the instability in modern economics is monetary in origin. For example, from their study of the monetary history of the United States between 1867 and 1960, Friedman and Schwartz (1963) have argued that all major American recessions have been caused by a contraction of the money supply. Equally, Friedman (1970) has also argued that 'inflation is always and everywhere a monetary phenomenon', and this must be true for any sustained increase in the general price level.

Secondly, the effectiveness of fiscal policy on its own may in any case be very low. For example, suppose an expansionary fiscal policy were undertaken in order to increase national income. Suppose also that monetary policy were neglected and the money supply remained the same. The fiscal policy would put pressure on the money supply and interest rates would tend to rise. This in turn would tend to reduce private expenditure and so reduce the effectiveness of the original expansionary policy.

A third attack on the 'Keynesian' position is that attempts to 'fine-tune' the economy are unlikely to be accurate. In extreme cases, the results may even be perverse. The argument is that there are significant and variable time lags in the operation of both fiscal and monetary policy (see Section 6.3). By the time policy action actually influences the economy, circumstances may have changed, so that the action is inappropriate, or even working in the wrong direction.

Fourthly, there may be other reasons why fiscal policy is unsuitable for stabilisation policy, principally because of the efficiency costs of expanding and contracting public expenditure for this reason only. Instead, it has been argued, fiscal policy has a more appropriate role in other areas. Again, according to Friedman (1948), the level of government spending should be determined on the basis of the 'community's desire, need and willingness to pay for public services', and not by the cyclical fluctuations of the economy.

A fifth onslaught has centred around the possible trade-off between unemployment and inflation as illustrated by the Phillips curve. Whatever the accuracy of the Phillips curve in earlier years, by the end of the 1960s it was quite clear that both inflation and unemployment were rising to alarming heights simultaneously.

Several commentators, including Friedman (1968) and Phelps (1968) suggested that the trade-off disappears when people have adjusted to the new rates of inflation. In other words, the Phillips curve would appear to suggest only a short-run relationship between inflation and unemployment. In the long run, the 'curve' becomes vertical at the 'natural rate of unemployment'. This is an unfortunate term as there is nothing natural about it, it is just a possible equilibrium position. However, it is a rather more memorable term than the accurate title of 'non-accelerating inflation rate of unemployment' (NAIRU). Such a rate of unemployment can be changed by micro economic techniques, such as improving the efficiency of the labour market. The monetarist point is that macroeconomic policies designed to reduce unemployment below the NAIRU are unlikely to be successful in the long run.

Again, like Keynesianism, monetarism is difficult to summarise briefly. Perhaps it is sufficient here to say that it places far more importance on the influence of money on the economic system. However, given the various problems of stabilisation policy, such as lags, it also casts doubt on the effectiveness of attempts to fine-tune the economy. This has led to suggestions that perhaps the best the government can do is to stabilise its own activity in order to avoid increasing stability in the rest of the economy.

More recent developments

A more recent assault on the traditional Keynesian position developed from what has been referred to as the New Classical Macroeconomics (Artis, 1992) from the 1970s onwards. This approach is based more on a microeconomic analysis of the way in which individuals and firms adjust to changes in the economy. The main assumptions are that markets clear and that expectations of future changes are formed rationally in the light of all available information including, of course, anticipated government stabilisation policies. It can then be shown that such 'rational expectations' could frustrate such policies, though the extent to which this can happen is very much a matter of debate (for example, see Peel, 1981).

The response to this approach, the 'New Keynesianism', has been also to adopt the assumption of rational expectations but to cast doubt on the view that markets clear in the way that the New Classical approach assumes. For example, even if prices and wages are flexible there may be multiple points of equilibrium and markets may settle at a point well below a 'full employment' level (Howitt, 1990). However, the main attack is centred on the possibility that markets may not clear because prices and wages are insufficiently flexible. If prices and wages do not adjust to changes in the economy, these changes must be reflected in output and employment, and a potential role for government once again emerges.

Although, as has been pointed out by Fischer (1988), it has become increasingly realised that it is difficult to settle disputes of this nature with econometric evidence, work continues to shed further light on the debate. For example, McAleer and McKenzie (1991) re-evaluate a number of Keynesian and New Classical models, and an attempt to find the middle ground between the two approaches has been made by Farmer (1991).

A quite separate development, greater European integration, is having more immediate effects on the policy choices open to government in the UK, particularly with respect to monetary policy. In October 1990 the UK joined the European Exchange Rate Mechanism (ERM), so linking the value of sterling to the currencies of the other member countries of the European Union (EU). In joining the ERM, the UK was obliged to use monetary policy primarily to maintain parity with the other EU currencies rather than to support internal aims. It turned out that the UK was unable to maintain its position and left the ERM in September 1992.

However, the eventual aim of the EU is full monetary union, complete with a single European currency. If and when the UK joins such an arrangement, to all intents and purposes monetary policy could then be exercised only at the European level. It could not be operated separately by member states since they would no longer have any separate control of the money supply. In those circumstances fiscal policy would become relatively more important for individual countries since it would be their one remaining important policy instrument. The position could be thought of as rather like a UK local authority which, in principle at least, may increase or decrease local taxation and spending but obviously cannot alter the money supply, rates of interest or exchange rates.

What can we conclude from this brief account? Clearly, the role of the public sector will continue to be the subject of strenuous argument. It seems reasonable to conclude that fiscal policy is not an omnipotent instrument of economic policy. Yet it clearly has economic effects andtherefore it is unlikely that governments will refrain for long from using it as an instrument of macroeconomic policy. Indeed, they have used it extensively in the past. It is therefore important to look further at fiscal policy and some of its implications, and this is done in the rest of the chapter.

6.3 Fiscal policy

Although fiscal policy includes both the revenue and expenditure sides of government activity, we shall be concerned here almost exclusively with taxation. As in earlier chapters, we shall initially avoid a number of distracting complications by making certain assumptions. The sorts of problem these complications cause can then be discussed as the assumptions are withdrawn later.

It will be assumed that any tax change has an instantaneous effect on the economy, and does not affect the distribution of income; also, that the supply of money is sufficiently elastic to prevent any change in interest rates and that there is a certain level of unemployment. Furthermore, suppose the economy is closed, i.e. there are no exports or imports. In addition, it is assumed that the tax system does not affect the efficiency of the economy, or the supply of factors of production, and that it consists only of a lump sum tax of T.

We shall also make the 'Keynesian' assumption that the level of national income (Y) is determined by the amount which people wish to consume (C), invest (I) and the level of government expenditure (G). Hence:

$$Y = C + I + G \tag{1}$$

The amounts of investment and government expenditure are fixed. Another assumption is that there is a Keynesian consumption function which suggests that consumption consists of two elements. The first is a, which is the amount consumed regardless of the level of income. However, it is also suggested that as income rises, so consumption will rise, but not by as much. Thus, the second element is bYd, where b is the marginal propensity to consume and has a value between 0 and 1; and Yd is the level of disposable income. Hence:

$$C = a + bYd \tag{2}$$

Disposable income, Yd, is simply gross income Y minus the lump sum tax T:

$$Yd = Y - T \tag{3}$$

The term Yd in equation (2) can now be replaced by $Y - T$ and the new equation (2) substituted into (1), giving:

$$Y = a - b(Y - T) + I + G$$

This can be simplified by grouping the Y terms on the left-hand side and factoring out the Ys so that:

$$(1 - b)\, Y = a - bT + I + G$$

The next stage is to divide through by $1 - b$. This gives:

$$Y = \frac{a - bT + I + G}{1 - b}$$

from which the familiar multiplier is derived. From this we can also derive a tax multiplier:

$$\frac{-b}{1 - b}$$

which shows, in this simple model, the relationship between changes in taxation and changes in national income. If we now pick some plausible, but hypothetical, value for the marginal propensity to consume, say 0.8, the value of the tax multiplier becomes –4. This means that an increase or decrease in taxation would change national income by four times the original change – which is quite impressive!

Qualifications

The reason why the tax multiplier is so powerful in this model is, of course, that the only alternative to spending on domestic goods and services is saving. If some of the assumptions are relaxed, other alternatives become available and so the value of the multiplier is drastically reduced. In an open economy, such as that of the UK, a large amount of any change in expenditure will be absorbed by changes in imports. Also, the tax system does not consist of lump sum taxes. Not only do different taxes have different and usually more complex tax multipliers, but most taxes are related to income or expenditure, which further reduces the value of tax multipliers as a whole. The effect is further reinforced by the existence of many income-related benefits, which are discussed in Section 9.2.

The government budget

A further assumption was that government expenditure remained the same. Suppose now that the government wished, say, to increase taxation and its expenditure by the same amount. What then would be the value of this 'balanced budget' multiplier? Referring back to the simple model embodied in equations (1) to (3), it can be seen that the value depends on the type of additional government expenditure. If it consists of goods and services, then the normal multiplier applies, which added to the tax multiplier gives a value of 1:

$$\frac{1}{1-b} + \frac{-b}{1-b} = \frac{1-b}{1-b} = 1$$

In other words, if an increase of £1 in tax revenue were accompanied by an increase in government expenditure of £1, the result would be a final increase of £1 in national income. The reason for the rise is that in this case the government has a 'higher marginal propensity to consume' than the taxpayers. However, if the government expenditure consisted of an increase in transfer payments, there would be no increase in national income. The reason is that the taxpayers will reduce their consumption in line with the marginal propensity to consume and the recipients of the transfer payments will do the opposite, which might well leave no net result. An example of this is given in Section 4.4 under 'income effects'.

Crowding-out

'Crowding-out' refers to the possibility that an expansion of the public sector may result in a lower increase in national income because it displaces some private expenditure. If the economy were operating at full capacity (including full employment), then any increase in public expenditure must necessarily crowd out at least the same amount of private expenditure.

However, that situation is not the real concern in this context. The problem is that, if the government is trying to reduce unemployment (of all factors of production) by expanding public expenditure, any gains made will be offset by any resulting losses of employment in the private sector. This can be shown if the earlier assumption, that the money supply is sufficiently elastic to prevent any change in interest rates, is relaxed. We can also introduce the likely possibilities that private consumption and investment expenditure are influenced by interest rates. An expansionary fiscal policy will increase the demand for money for transactions purposes and, other things being equal, increase interest rates and so reduce private expenditure. A similar effect might occur if the expansionary policy led to increased prices.

As far as taxation is concerned, this is meant to crowd out private expenditure.

However, there are still some implications. For example, in certain circumstances described above, the balanced budget multiplier was shown to be equal to 1. Crowding-out will result in a value of less than 1.

Lags

One of the major assumptions made above was that any tax change had an instantaneous effect on the economy. Clearly, in practice, fiscal policy, and for that matter monetary policy, usually encounter a number of delays in their operation. The importance of lags in stabilisation has been stressed by Friedman (1947; 1948). Since 1948 the nature of these delays has been much explored, but the basic classification still remains useful. This classification recognises three types of lag: the recognition lag, the implementation lag, and the response lag.

The *recognition lag* is the delay from the time the need for action arises until that need is actually recognised by the government. Or, as Prest (1975, p. 102) put it: 'It may be that the authorities are too slow to recognise the onset of slump or boom, either because no storm signals are flying or else because their vision is defective.' It may also take time to come to a decision.

Much of the recognition lag exists because of the time taken to collect and analyse economic data. The delay could be very small or even negative if it were possible to forecast future levels of economic activity. However, economic forecasting has its limitations, perhaps best summarised by Denis Healey (1974) when Chancellor of the Exchequer:

> The numbers contained in the forecasts - specific to 1/2 per cent in every case - give a spurious impression of certainty. But their origin lies in the extrapolation from a partially known past, through an unknown present, to an unknowable future according to theories about the causal relationships between certain economic variables which are hotly disputed by academic economists, and may well in fact change from country to country or from decade to decade.

The *implementation lag* is the delay between the decision to take action and the implementation of that action. The delay occurs because, naturally, it takes time to carry out policy changes. It may be wise for the Chancellor to wait for the next Budget, or the most appropriate time to hold a 'mini-Budget'. It then takes time for the tax authorities to put the changes into operation.

The *response lag* (sometimes known as the 'outside lag') refers to the time between the implementation of a policy measure and the time it finally influences the economy. For example, when income tax rates are increased, it may take many months for taxpayers to adjust the level of their expenditure.

Clearly, the existence of lags limits the effectiveness of stabilisation policy and, in some circumstances, can result in greater instability. For instance, suppose that without any government intervention, the economy would follow the path AB shown in Figure 6.1. Suppose also that the government intends to pursue a policy of stabilisation. As the economy approaches point D this would imply an expansionary policy.

However, depending on the length of the lags, the expansionary policy would not take effect until conditions had changed. If it took effect around, say, point E, then it would add to existing inflationary pressures. At this point, the government may be tempted to pursue a contractionary policy which, because of lags, may serve only to worsen the following recession. So it can be seen that lags, together with an inability to forecast the future level of economic activity accurately, can lead to a 'stabilisation' policy which actually contributes to instability. In these circumstances, the economy may follow a path such as AC in Figure 6.1.

The second major argument against discretionary change is that its very existence might contribute to economic instability. In using its discretionary powers, it is conceivable that the government may be influenced more by the proximity of the next election than by the interests of long-term economic stability. It might be possible for a government to increase its electoral popularity by inflating the economy a year or so before the election.

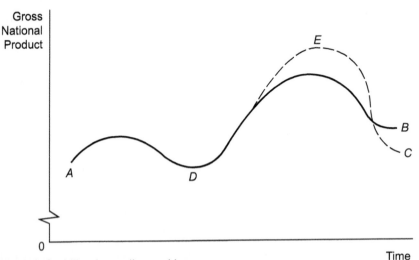

Figure 6.1 Stabilisation policy and lags

Following the election, the effects of the inflationary policy could be seen by the government to be undesirable, with the result that the pre-election policy could be reversed. If voters do not realise what is going on, or discount the future, the 'political business cycle' could continue indefinitely to provide a destabilising influence on the economy.

An early theory of the political business cycle was put forward by Kalecki (1943). He argued that, if the government were faced with a slump, it would expand the economy to avoid large-scale unemployment. However, in the subsequent boom, political pressure for a cutback would develop. Particular pressure would come from 'big business' because it would be more difficult to control the workforce when there was full employment. This pressure would cause the government to reduce its budget deficit and a 'slump would follow in which government spending policy would come again into its own' (p. 330).

The subject was later examined by Nordhaus (1975). He looked at the implications of the short-run Phillips curve trade-off between inflation and unemployment within a political framework. Some of the historical evidence was also considered. One of Nordhaus's conclusions was that 'within an incumbent's term of office there is a predictable pattern of policy, starting with relative austerity in early years and ending with the potlatch right before elections' (p. 187). (A potlatch is an occasion when members of some Indian tribes of the American North-West consume large quantities of food and present generous gifts to each other. They also destroy valuable goods as a sort of conspicuous consumption.)

Further work along these lines has also been done by, for example, Lindbeck (1976), Frey (1978), Frey and Schneider (1978) and Ellis and Thomas (1993). Swank and Swank (1993) found evidence that different political parties have different targets in this respect; that the US Republican administrations try to reduce tax rates when elections approach, whereas Democratic administrations appear to be more concerned about unemployment and inflation. Although UK evidence does not appear to support the conclusion that governments systematically manipulate the economy for electoral purposes, it is possible that they may sometimes be tempted to do so.

One possible reason for the lack of evidence of systematic manipulation is that in the UK, unlike some other countries, the timing of general elections is determined by the prime minister, who takes account of prevailing circumstances. It is, therefore, less important to manipulate the economy for political purposes when the date of the election need not be fixed until a few weeks in advance. Although it has been suggested that fixed-term parliaments would lead to greater stability, in fact they may have the opposite result by increasing the temptation for governments to try to arrange the economic cycle to coincide with the predetermined political one.

A further line of investigation has been concerned with voters' perceptions of such political manipulation. The 'rational expectations' approach mentioned in Section 6.2 might not provide a full explanation. For example, Smyth et al. (1994) found evidence that voters may be more influenced by recent actual events than by possible future ones. However, electorates clearly learn. For instance, Suzuki (1994) suggested that Japanese voting behaviour became more sophisticated in the early 1970s, following political manipulation in the 1969 and 1972 parliamentary elections.

Automatic versus discretionary intervention

A possible method of reducing such temptations to governments, and also some of the lags in policy effects, is to design a system of government finance which responds automatically to changes in the level of economic activity. This is in contrast to a more 'discretionary' policy which refers to deliberate adjustments made by the government as part of its day-to-day management of the economy. An increase in tax rates is therefore an example of discretionary policy. Automatic change, on the other hand, refers to potential changes which are built in to the system in some way - either into the tax structure itself, or as a set of rules determining the action to be taken in various situations.

For the tax system, this implies that tax revenue should rise and fall as national income rises and falls. So, for example, as an economy moves into a recession, the fall in national income should be partially offset by a fall in tax receipts. This feature of the tax system is sometimes referred to as 'built-in flexibility'.

The most important example of built-in flexibility is the progressivity of the income tax system. Progressivity means that income tax receipts change proportionately more than any original change in national income. For example, if all wages and prices in the economy doubled, then, all other things being equal, income tax revenue would more than double. Clearly this effect will be greater, the greater the progressivity of the tax. With the introduction of provisions indexing the income tax to changes in the price level (see Chapter 8), tax revenue no longer changes as a result of inflationary changes. However, it still responds to changes in real incomes, so that for example, in a recession, income tax receipts in real terms can still be expected to fall proportionately more than the original fall in real national income. Also, of course, some elements of public expenditure automatically help to stabilise the economy, the most obvious one being unemployment benefit. There has been some dispute about the strength of the built-in flexibility of taxation and expenditure in the UK, and it is difficult to estimate the full effects satisfactorily. However, further has suggested that the overall effects are stronger than had previously been thought (Davies, 1991).

One of the main advantages of built-in flexibility is that it avoids the recognition lag altogether. It might also avoid at least part of the implementation lag, though this depends on the type of tax. For instance, delays in the collection of a particular tax will postpone changes in the level of tax receipts.

Nevertheless, built-in flexibility has its limitations as a stabilising device. First of all, it cannot cope with large exogenous changes. The fourfold increase in the price of oil in 1974, for instance, created a deflationary effect in Western countries that could not possibly be offset by built-in flexibility alone.

Secondly, built-in flexibility cannot eliminate cycles; it can only reduce them. This is because it requires an initial change in the level of national income before tax receipts can change. Unless the rates of tax were set at 100 per cent (or more!) one would not expect the initial change to be completely offset.

The third limitation is that, while built-in flexibility undoubtedly cushions the effects of economic depression, it also impedes recovery. As the economy picks up, part of the additional national income is siphoned off in taxes. Clearly, the greater the degree of built-in flexibility, the more such economic recovery will be impeded.

Fiscal drag

'Fiscal drag' refers to the effect that, as nominal incomes rise over time, a progressive tax system will take an increasing proportion of national income. It occurs whether the rise in nominal income results from inflation (in the absence of indexation), or from an increase in real output per head, or both. The element of fiscal drag arising from real changes could also be roughly offset by using an index of average earnings (though changes in the proportion of national income which accrue as a profit, interest or rent would modify the process).

Fiscal drag becomes a less important phenomenon after the indexation of income tax. However, the problem with indexation is that it greatly reduces the effectiveness of the tax system in automatically stabilising the economy. Yet there is still likely to be some small element of built-in flexibility. For example, suppose that (in the case of income tax) the tax threshold and rate bands were linked to average earnings. Suppose also that when the economy moves into recession, most of the fall in national income is reflected in a decrease in the number employed rather than a decrease in the average wage of those still at work. Under these circumstances, one may still expect a drop in national income to be partially offset by a fall in tax receipts. As a second example, if the index-linked adjustment took place once a year, there would still be a small stabilising effect within the tax year, though not from one year to the next.

Nevertheless, despite these examples, indexation tends to neutralise the built-in flexibility of a progressive tax system. It seems reasonable to conclude, therefore, that however attractive a system of automatic stabilisers may appear, discretionary policy is almost certain to remain an essential element of macroeconomic policy.

6.4 The relative merits of different taxes

Taxes differ considerably in their suitability as instruments of stabilisation policy. Some taxes have only indirect effects on the level of national income, other taxes affect income directly, but sometimes only after a considerable delay; and the revenue from some taxes is too small to make much impact on the overall economy. We shall deal with each of these points in turn.

Appropriate and inappropriate taxes

Given that the intention is to influence aggregate demand, taxes on various forms of expenditure play a useful part in fiscal policy. An increase in value added tax, for example, has a direct effect on spending in the economy. It is also useful for stabilisation purposes if the indirect taxes with the highest rates are imposed on goods for which the demand fluctuates considerably over the trade cycle. In other words, for this purpose tax should be imposed on the goods with the highest income elasticities of demand.

Income tax is also appropriate in this respect as changes in after-tax income must influence the level of expenditure. This should be qualified, however, as spending habits may not adjust quickly to changes in income. Friedman's permanent income hypothesis (Friedman, 1957), for example, suggests that consumers ignore short-run fluctuations in income when planning their consumption. Instead, consumers take into account their 'normal' or 'permanent' level of income. One implication of this is that a tax change which is regarded only as a short-term measure is unlikely to influence consumption significantly.

Taxes on corporate income (corporation tax) could also be useful stabilisers. A particular advantage is that company profits are likely to fluctuate more than the average form of income over the business cycle, though, as suggested below, there may be a disadvantage where these taxes are collected in arrears.

Taxes on wealth, or the movement of wealth, are very much less appropriate than either indirect taxes or income taxes. Levies such as inheritance tax or a wealth tax will obviously have some effect on individuals' spending plans, but only indirect effects. They are therefore unsuitable for use as instruments of stabilisation policy.

A different point arises when the government's primary aim is to reduce unemployment or to reduce inflation, but not both equally. Some taxes are more appropriate for the first of these two targets than for the second. For example, suppose that the main aim is the reduction of inflation. It is true that an increase in, say, value added tax would have a deflationary effect. Yet it is possible for the price increases resulting from an increase in VAT to impede a policy of reducing inflation. The VAT-induced price increases may be interpreted as inflationary and so support expectations of future inflation. The increases may trigger wage and further price increases elsewhere in the economy.

Although the VAT may have limitations where inflation is the main problem, there is more confidence in its usefulness regarding the level of output. For that reason, for example, the standard rate of VAT was temporarily reduced from 17.5 to 15 per cent between 1 December 2008 and 31 December 2009 as part of a fiscal stimulus package to counter an economic downturn. The use of VAT in this way has been discussed by Blundell (2009).

Speed of adjustment

The next consideration is the time it takes for the stabilising influence of a particular tax to take effect. We saw in the previous section that lags can easily reduce the effectiveness of an adjustment in taxation. We also saw that the first lag (the recognition lag) could be avoided if the revenue of a particular tax reacted automatically to a change in national income. The income tax has an advantage in this respect because of its progressivity.

It should be remembered that the UK income tax is progressive despite its long basic rate band (see Sections 2.2 and 8.3). The reason is that, for the majority of taxpayers, the first part of their income is exempt from tax. The proportion of their income going in tax therefore rises as their income rises. In addition, of course, if a person becomes unemployed he or she will usually cease to pay tax (and National Insurance contributions, but not indirect taxes).

Indirect taxes and corporation tax are less advantageous in this respect because they are not generally progressive, as Section 11.6 shows. Some indirect taxes are also based on quantity rather than value: for example, the excise duties on alcoholic drinks which are charged at fixed rates per litre. The result is that the yield of these taxes does not respond automatically to changes in prices.

Indirect taxes are better with respect to the second category of lag (the implementation lag), as changes in tax rates can be put into force fairly quickly. For VAT the Treasury has the power to vary the rate by up to 25 per cent during the year for the purposes of economic management. This has the considerable advantage of avoiding the need to wait for the annual Budget or having to arrange an extra one. In some ways, income tax can also be adjusted quickly. For example, it is possible to increase personal allowances during the tax year and the Pay-As-You-Earn system will automatically adjust the amount of tax withheld from employees' pay. However, as we shall see in Chapter 8, it is not quite so easy to reduce the value of allowances in the middle of the tax year, because of the cumulative feature of PAYE.

On the third type of lag (the response lag), income tax scores highly because the PAYE system ensures that tax payments are kept up to date with tax liability. Corporation tax as a whole suffers more from delay because much of the revenue is collected in arrears. But the amount of revenue from mainstream corporation tax is unimportant compared to that from income tax.

The size of the tax base

If the yield of a tax is very small, it can have only a small effect on aggregate demand, regardless of its advantages in other respects. No doubt every little helps, but the main instruments of stabilisation policy must raise substantial amounts of tax in order to be effective.

Under this criterion, income tax must emerge as the most important single tax. In 2010/11 some £153 billion was raised in income tax. VAT also scores well in this respect – in 2010/11 it raised £86 billion.

A related aspect is the width of the tax base. If a tax has a reasonably broad coverage, such as income tax or value added tax, its stabilising effects are likely to be felt fairly evenly throughout the economy. In contrast, a tax on a narrow range of goods, such as fuel duties, is likely to have a concentrated effect on a small part of the economy. If such a tax were used to stabilise the economy as a whole, it might decrease stability in the sector of the economy to which it was applied. In addition, as we have seen in earlier chapters, such a tax may also have undesirable implications for efficiency and equity.

So what can we conclude regarding the relative merits of different taxes as potential stabilising devices? The only tax which scores well on each of the three criteria put forward in this chapter is income tax. Some other taxes may also be useful. Value added tax, for example, has a relatively wide base.

6.5 Summary

In this chapter we have discussed some of the arguments for and against government intervention to stabilise the level of economic activity. Whether or not the government should intervene, it has been tempted to do so in the past and no doubt will do so in the future. It therefore becomes necessary to examine the implications of stabilisation policy. Using a simple model, it was shown that fiscal policy can have powerful effects, but these effects will vary considerably under different circumstances. In considering the relative merits of different taxes it soon becomes clear that the income tax is the major weapon in the stabilisation armoury.

Further reading

Issues of stabilisation are discussed further in Musgrave and Musgrave (1989), Peacock and Shaw (1976) and Stevenson et al. (1988). An analysis of fiscal models is given by Dornbusch et al. (2004). Johnson (1991) presents a series of valuable papers first published in the 1970s and 1980s concerned with monetary policy and its contrasts with Keynesianism. An account of the New Classical economics is given by Hoover (1988). Developments in macroeconomic forecasting are surveyed in Wallis (1989), and Layard et al. (2005) analyse macroeconomic policy in relation to unemployment. For evidence on the stability or otherwise of British fiscal policy, a useful start can be made with Boltho (1981). An account of reforms to the UK's macroeconomic policy framework appears in Balls and O'Donnell (2001). Lee and Sung (2007) empirically investigated the effectiveness of fiscal policy using data from 22 OECD and 72 non-OECD countries and Alesina and Ardagna (2010) compared changes in taxes and spending in fiscal policy. The use of VAT as a tool of stabilisation policy is examined by Barrell and Weale (2009), Crossley et al. (2009) and Blundell (2009). The empirical literature regarding the cyclical response of fiscal policies in the euro area is survey by Golinelli and Momigliano (2009).

References

Alesina, A. and Ardagna, S. (2010), 'Large changes in fiscal policy: taxes versus spending', *Tax Policy and the Economy*, Vol. 24, No.1, pp. 35-68.

Artis, M. (1992), 'Macroeconomic theory', in J. Maloney (ed.), *What's New in Economics?*, Manchester University Press.

Balls, E., and O'Donnell, G. (eds.) (2001), *Reforming Britain's Economic and Financial Policy*, HM Treasury.

Barrell, R. and Weale, M. (2009), 'The economics of a reduction in VAT', *Fiscal Studies*, Vol. 30, No. 1, pp. 17-30.

Blundell, R. (2009), 'Assessing the temporary VAT cut policy in the UK', *Fiscal Studies*, Vol. 30, No. 1, pp. 31-38.

Boltho, A. (1981), 'British fiscal policy 1955-71 – stabilising or destabilising?' *Oxford Bulletin of Economics and Statistics*, Vol. 43, pp. 357-62.

Chrystal, K.A. (1979), *Controversies in British Macroeconomics*, Philip Allan

Clark, C. (1970), *Taxmanship*, Institute of Economic Affairs.

Crossley, T.F., Low, H. and Wakefield, M. (2009), 'The economics of a temporary VAT cut', *Fiscal Studies*, Vol. 30, No. 1, pp. 3-16.

Davies, S. (1991), 'Fiscal developments and the role of the cycle', *Treasury Bulletin*, Vol. 2, No. 1.

Dornbusch, R. , Fischer, S. and Startz, R. (2004), *Macroeconomics*, 9th edn, McGraw-Hill.

Ellis, C.J. and Thomas, M.A. (1993), 'Credibility and the business cycle', *Journal of Macroeconomics*, Vol. 15 , No. 1, pp. 69-89.

Farmer, R.E.A. (1991), 'Sticky prices', *Economic Journal*, Vol. 101, November.

Fischer, S. (1988), 'Recent developments in macroeconomics', *Economic Journal*, Vol. 98, June.

Foot, M. (1983), 'Sayings of the week', *The Observer*, 13 February.

Frey, B.S. (1978), *Modern Political Economy*, Martin Robertson.

Frey, B.S. and Schneider, F. (1978), 'A politico-economic model of the United Kingdom', *Economic Journal*, Vol. 88, pp. 243-53.

Friedman, M. (1947), 'Lerner on the economics of control', *Journal of Political Economy*, Vol. 55, pp. 405-16.

Friedman, M. (1948), 'A monetary and fiscal framework for economic stability', *American Economic Review*, Vol. 38, pp. 245-64.

Friedman, M. (1957), *A Theory of the Consumption Function*, National Bureau of Economic Research.

Friedman, M. (1968), 'The role of monetary policy', *American Economic Review*, Vol. 58, pp. 1-17.

Friedman, M. (1970), *The Counter-Revolution in Monetary Theory*, Institute of Economic Affairs.

Friedman, M. and Schwartz. A.J. (1963), *A Monetary History of the United States, 1867-1960*, Princeton University Press.

Golinelli, R. and Momigliano, S. (2009), 'The cyclical reaction of fiscal policies in the euro area: The role of modelling choices and data vintages', *Fiscal Studies*, Vol. 30, No. 1, pp. 39-72.

Harrod, R.F. (1951), *The Life of John Maynard Keynes,* Macmillan.

Healey, D. (1974), Budget Statement, 12 November, *Hansard,* Vol. 881, Cols 252, 253.

Hoover, K.D. (1988), *The New Classical Macroeconomics,* Basil Blackwell.

Howitt, P. (1990), *The Keynesian Recovery,* Philip Allan.

Johnson, C. (ed.) (1991), *Monetarism and the Keynesians,* Pinter.

Kalecki, M. (1943), 'Political aspects of full employment', *Political Quarterly,* Vol. 14, pp. 322-31.

Keynes, J.M. (1924), *A Tract* on *Monetary Reform,* Macmillan, p. 80.

Keynes, J.M. (1933), 'Thomas Robert Malthus', *Essays in Biography,* Macmillan.

Keynes, J.M. (1936), *The General Theory of Employment, Interest and Money,* Macmillan.

Layard, R., Nickell, S. and Jackman, R. (1991), *Unemployment: Macroeconomic Performance and the Labour Market,* Oxford University Press.

Lee, Y. and Sung, T. (2007), 'Fiscal policy, business cycles and economic stabilisation: Evidence from industrialised and developing countries', *Fiscal Studies.* Vol. 28, No. 4, pp. 437-462.

Leijonhufvud, A. (1968), *On Keynesian Economics and the Economics of Keynes,* Oxford University Press.

Lindbeck, A. (1976), 'Stabilisation policy in small open economies with endogenous politicians', *American Economic Review: Papers and Proceedings,* Vol. 66, pp. 1-19.

Lipsey, R.G. (1960), 'The relationship between unemployment and the rate of change of money wage rates in the United Kingdom, 1862-1957', *Economica,* Vol. 27, pp. 1-31

McAleer, M. and McKenzie, C.R. (1991), 'Keynesian and New Classical models of un employment revisited', *Economic Journal,* Vol. 101, May.

Mill, J.S. (1844), *Essays on Some Unsettled Questions of Political Economy,* Longman.

Musgrave, R.A. and Musgrave, P.B. (1989), *Public Finance in Theory and Practice,* 5th edn, McGraw-Hill.

Nordhaus, W.D. (1975), 'The political business cycle', *Review of Economic Studies,* Vol. 42, pp. 169-90

Peacock, A. and Shaw, G.K. (1976), *The Economic Theory of Fiscal Policy,* revised edition, Allen & Unwin.

Peel, D.A. (1981), 'On fiscal and monetary stabilisation policy under rational expectations', *Public Finance,* Vol. 26, pp. 290-6.

Phelps, E.S. (1968), 'Money wage dynamics and labour market equilibrium', *Journal of Political Economy,* July/August.

Phillips, A.W. (1958), 'The relation between unemployment and the rate of change of money wage rates, 1861-1957', *Economica,* Vol. 25, pp. 283-99.

Prest, A.R. (1975), *Public Finance in Theory and Practice,* 5th edn, Weidenfeld and Nicolson.

Ricardo, D. (1821), *The Principles of Political Economy and Taxation,* Everyman edition, 1969.

Robinson, Sir Austin (1977), 'Comment', in T.W. Hutchison, *Keynes v. the 'Keynesians'* ... ?, Institute of Economic Affairs.

Robinson, J. (1971), *Economic Heresies,* Macmillan.

Samuelson, P.A. (1970), *Economics,* 8th edn, McGraw-Hill.

Say, Jean Baptiste (1803), *Traite d'economie politique.*

Smith, A. (1776), *The Wealth of Nations,* Cannon edn, Methuen, 1950.

Smyth, D.J., Dua, P. and Taylor, S.W. (1994), 'Voters and macroeconomics: are they forward looking or backward looking?', *Public Choice,* Vol. 78, pp. 283-93.

Stevenson, A., Muscatelli, V. and Gregory, M. (1988), *Macroeconomic Theory and Stabilisation Policy,* Philip Allan.

Suzuki, M. (1994), 'Evolutionary voter sophistication and political business cycles', *Public Choice,* Vol. 81, pp. 241-61.

Swank, O.H. and Swank, J. (1993), 'In search of the motives behind US fiscal macroeconomic policy', *Applied Economics,* Vol. 25, pp. 1013-22.

Vane, H.R. and Thompson, J.L. (1979), *Monetarism: Theory, Evidence and Policy,* Martin Robertson.

Wallis, K.F. (1989) 'Macroeconomic forecasting: a survey', *Economic Journal,* Vol. 99, March.

SELF ASSESSMENT QUESTIONS

Suggested answers to self-assessment questions are given at the back of the book.

6.1   What is fiscal policy?

6.2   Describe the tax multiplier.

6.3   How might 'crowding-out' reduce the effectiveness of fiscal policy?

6.4   What types of lag might exist before an adjustment to fiscal policy can take effect?

6.5   Which criteria might be used to assess the suitability of individual taxes as instruments of stabilisation policy?

DISCUSSION QUESTIONS

1.   Should the government try to stabilise the level of economic activity?

2.   What difficulties might arise in using fiscal measures to combat unemployment and inflation?

3.   How useful might the following taxes be as instruments of stabilisation policy:

(a) income tax,

(b) inheritance tax,

(c) value added tax,

(d) tax on alcohol,

(e) corporation tax?

PART TWO

Taxation policy and practice

'The schoolboy whips his taxed top; the beardless youth manages his taxed horse, with a taxed bridle, on a taxed road; and the dying Englishman, pouring his medicine, which has paid seven per cent, into a spoon that has paid fifteen per cent – flings himself back upon his chintz bed, which has paid twenty-two per cent – and expires in the arms of an apothecary who has paid a licence of a hundred pounds for the privilege of putting him to death.'

REV. SIDNEY SMITH, *Words* (1859) vol i, 'Review of Seybert's Statistical Annals of the United States'

'The Income Tax has made more Liars out of the American people than golf has.'

WILL ROGERS, 'Helping the Girls with Their Income Taxes', *The Illiterate Digest* (1924)

CHAPTER SEVEN

Introduction to taxation policy and practice

LEARNING OBJECTIVES

After reading this chapter, you should be able to:

- Give an account of the difficulties of achieving a successful tax policy or particular tax reform.
- Explain the arguments for earmarked taxes.
- Explain what tax compliance is and what factors might affect it.
- Describe the basic structure of taxes in the United Kingdom.

7.1 Overview

In Part I there was an examination of various theoretical problems relating to taxation in general. Particular taxes were used as illustrations from time to time, but there was no systematic description and analysis of present taxes in the United Kingdom. Part II contains such a description of the present taxes, analysis of their strengths and weaknesses, and discussion of alternatives and possible reforms. There are three chapters on direct personal taxation, a chapter on indirect taxation and three chapters on corporation taxation. Many of the characteristics of the taxes are illustrated numerically in these chapters.

This chapter sets the scene for Part II by looking briefly at some general areas. The first is that of tax policy itself: how proposals for tax reform emerge and the process by which they are implemented. Section 7.3 deals with the question of tax compliance and Section 7.4 with tax ethics. Tax harmonisation is examined in Section 7.5. After that, the relative importance of various United Kingdom taxes is discussed in Section 7.6, and in Section 7.7 some broad international comparisons are drawn.

7.2 Tax policy and reform

'The nation should have a tax system which looks like someone designed it on purpose.' It is all too easy to agree with this comment of William E. Simon, a former

Secretary of the US Treasury (US Treasury, 1977), but a great deal harder to find a modern tax system that fits the description. It has been pointed out, for example by Hagemann et 01. (1988), that the tax systems in many OECD countries do not meet even the basic criteria of efficiency and equity against which a tax system may be judged. The main reason is that the conduct of successful tax policy is a very complex matter. The tax system is used to achieve a wide range of aims which are not always consistent and which vary from time to time. The tax system is also subject to continual pressure for change in particular areas. This sometimes succeeds but there is no guarantee that the outcome will be consistent with wider policy goals or with other parts of the tax system.

In principle, the characteristics of a 'good' tax system are fairly clear, at least in the economic terms described in Part I. The tax system should be efficient in that it does not distort economic decision-making and its administrative and compliance costs should not be excessive (Chapter 3). Nor should it unduly interfere with economic incentives to work, save and invest (Chapter 4). A tax should be considered fair (Chapter 5) and it should be consistent with macroeconomic policy (Chapter 6). A further issue in tax policy is that any tax change should take account of existing administrative arrangements, including existing taxes.

The fact that many taxes do not meet these criteria might be predicted from public choice analysis which examines the way individuals attempt to achieve their aims through the public sector (for example, see Mueller, 1979). Using this approach, it can be seen that the various interactions and conflicts in the political process, including the results of different voting systems, the behaviour of bureaucracies, special interest groups and so on, might frustrate attempts to achieve an 'optimum tax system'.

Bird and Oldman (1990, p. 3) gave a good indication of the complexity of successful tax reform as follows:

> The best approach to reforming taxes ... is one that takes into account taxation theory, empirical evidence, and political and administrative realities and blends them with a good dose of local knowledge and a sound appraisal of the current macroeconomic and international situation to produce a feasible set of proposals sufficiently attractive to be implemented and sufficiently robust to withstand changing times, within reason, and still produce beneficial results.

Even an analysis of an existing system and the development of coherent recommendations is a major undertaking. For example, it was originally envisaged that the prestigious Meade Committee (1978) should examine the UK tax system as a whole, produce a statement of the objectives of taxation and make recommendations for reform - all within a year. In the event this could not be done and the Committee restricted its scope to direct taxation only and took two years - a feat described as 'a remarkable achievement' by the Director of the sponsoring Institute for Fiscal Studies (Meade Committee, 1978, p. xi).

Piecemeal reform stands a greater chance of being carried through but may still fail to achieve the original aims. One example among many is the introduction and subsequent repeal of selective employment tax (Section 11.3). An even more spectacular failure was the community charge, more commonly known as the poll tax (Section 11.4).

The pressure of change

The impetus for change may come from a number of directions. The most obvious is that the government may need extra tax revenue. However, governments use taxation to achieve many goals other than simply raising revenue. These include the management of macroeconomic policy and the use of taxation to achieve other aspects of economic policy such as favouring one type of activity rather than another. The tax system is also used to implement aspects of social policy in terms of the distribution of income and to achieve specific social objectives. Examples here include the introduction of capital transfer tax by the Labour government in 1975 (subsequently replaced by inheritance tax by the Conservative government in 1986) and the proposals for a wealth tax (both described in Chapter 10).

Proposals for change also come from various representative bodies, interest groups, government departments and sometimes-interested individuals. A significant number of ideas originate in the revenue raising departments. Such proposals can range from the relatively minor and technical to more substantial reforms.

One of the difficulties of tax reform is to ensure that the proposed reform is likely to support the relevant policy goals in practice and to do so without unintended and undesirable side-effects. Unfortunately this is not always achieved. For instance, James and Edwards (2008) demonstrate how too narrow an approach to tax reform – one which takes insufficient account of wider considerations - may result in an undesirable outcome. One of the conclusions of Robinson and Sandford (1983, p. 221) from their study of tax policy-making in the UK was that political parties 'showed only limited capacity for rational consideration of their chosen objectives. They did not examine them in sufficient detail, nor did they fully explore the consequences of their chosen actions'.

Such a failing appears more likely where the original pressure for change comes from strong dissatisfaction with the current system. This happened, for instance, when UK income tax was extended very rapidly to millions of new taxpayers and the burden of tax increased substantially in the early years of the Second World War. The previous methods of collection proved to be inadequate and, following strong resistance to any change by the Revenue authorities, the peculiar British system of Pay-As-You-Earn was finally introduced (Section 8.5).

It has also happened where the pressure for the reform of a tax dominated the political agenda so much as to distract attention from the need to establish the best alternative. The most famous example in modern times was the replacement of domestic rates by the poll tax (Section 11.4), but similar results are to be found in the processes leading to the reform of purchase tax, selective employment tax, estate duty and capital transfer tax.

The process of implementation

Whatever the source of a particular proposal, the final decision on whether to proceed with a particular reform rests with ministers, most particularly the Chancellor of the Exchequer. Nevertheless, ministers may respond to advice and representations from a wide variety of sources.

One source, of course, is the advice of civil servants. For example, in the case of direct taxation, HM Revenue and Customs has a number of policy divisions which provide advice on personal taxes, business taxes, capital taxes and so on. Revenue staff in these divisions also liase with relevant policy staff in the Treasury and other departments as appropriate. The Revenue uses a range of considerations in evaluating proposals, and a list of the main ones appeared in the 1986 Public Expenditure White Paper (HM Treasury, 1986, Vol. 2, p. 314). They were:

(i)   the cost or yield to the Exchequer and the distribution of gainers and losers among different categories or taxpayer.

(ii)   the economic effects of the proposals and any behavioural changes they would be likely to induce;

(iii)   the consistency of the proposals with the general thrust of the Government's tax policy, and its broader economic financial and social policies;

(iv)   the implications for other parts of the tax system, for the social security system, or for other proposals which ministers may be considering;

(v)   the likely effect on the perceived fairness and general acceptability of the tax system;

(vi)   the effect of the proposals in increasing or reducing the complexity of the tax system;

(vii)   the administrative implications, including effects on public expenditure and the use of public service manpower;

(viii)   the compliance burden on employers, businesses and other taxpayers;

(ix)   any views bearing on the proposals expressed in Parliament, or by representative bodies or by individual taxpayers;

(x)   any relevant international obligations arising from, for example, double taxation agreements or European Community obligations.

Although some background papers and articles may be published, a great deal of such advice is not made public as it is bound up with advice to ministers (Beighton, 1987). The extent to which such advice is accepted by ministers depends, of course, on a range of political and other factors. Nevertheless, it has been argued that more such material should be made public in order to facilitate more informed public debate and, one hopes, increase the chances of a successful outcome.

To promote such a debate, the government may actively seek comments on tentative proposals. This may be done by the publication of a 'green paper' which is intended to form the basis for discussion and may be contrasted with 'white papers' which are normally used to present more fixed government intentions. Such a move can dramatically increase the input from interested parties. As an illustration, in the three months following the publication of the Green Paper on value added tax on Budget day in March'1971, comments were received from over 800 different trade and professional organisations.

As a proposed reform progresses through its parliamentary stages it may be subject to quite significant modification which mayor may not take account of wider issues. An example given by Robinson and Sandford (1983) is the public and parliamentary pressure which resulted in the zero-rating of children's clothing for the purposes of VAT. Although providing financial support for children is a noble aim, this was not an accurate way to do so since it does not benefit large children, and may benefit small adults. A more effective measure may have been to increase direct child support.

A similar process occurs in other countries, and in Section 9.3 the example is given of the implementation of the personal expenditure tax in India. In that case the tax which was finally implemented bore little resemblance to its original design and was later repealed.

The influence of pressure groups also continues after a change has been implemented. As indicated in Section 3.8, the benefits of tax concessions or 'tax expenditures' might be considered more advantageous than direct subsidies since they may be more hidden. Also, it might be seen as politically more attractive to receive a tax concession than a 'cash handout', even though the end result is often effectively the same. An example of apparently successful pressure over time is the relief to agriculture made by successive governments in respect of capital taxation (Robinson and Sandford, 1983).

To summarise this brief account of tax policy, it is clear that a tax reform which is likely to be successful must be carefully thought out and researched. Its effects must be clearly understood and the proposal sufficiently robust to survive the various pressures which will tend to frustrate the original intention of the reform.

The budget

The formal introduction of the most important proposed tax changes in the UK takes place in the Chancellor of the Exchequer's Budget which is then incorporated into a Finance Bill. After completing its various legislative stages the proposals become law in the form of a Finance Act.

The preparation for the Budget goes on throughout the year and, for those who wish to try to influence the Chancellor, making representations up to four months in advance 'is nowadays none too early for the following Budget' (Beighton, 1987).

The Budget itself has become something of a ritual. In the period before the presentation of the Budget itself, the final preparations take place in strict secrecy and the Chancellor and other Treasury ministers do not comment on matters related to possible changes. This secrecy is only ended when the Chancellor formally delivers his Budget speech to the House of Commons.

In his speech the Chancellor reviews the economic situation and gives a forecast of future economic prospects. He also outlines the state of the public finances and explains government monetary and fiscal policy. Finally, the Chancellor presents his specific proposals for changes to the tax system. A summary of much of this is published on Budget day in the Financial Statement and Budget Report. More detailed information is also published separately in the form of press releases and so on by the relevant government departments since there is far too much material each year to include in a single speech. Incidentally, the longest Budget speech on record was that of William Gladstone on 18 April 1853, which lasted for 4 hours and 45 minutes.

There have been criticisms of the UK system. As already indicated, secrecy is one. Clearly there are certain matters which need to be confidential to avoid excessive tax avoidance before changes are implemented. This does not apply so much to other matters and when, so it is argued, important tax proposals are produced like rabbits out of a hat on Budget day, they may be implemented before a full public discussion has exposed serious shortcomings. It has also been argued that taxing decisions should be more closely tied to spending decisions. It was suggested that ministers in spending departments might be more careful in proposing additional spending if they had also to suggest how these proposals might be paid for. There is not the space to present these issues in full here, but they are discussed, for example, by the Armstrong Committee (1980). As a response to these pressures, following the March 1992 Budget, the traditional Spring tax budget was merged with Government's expenditure plans, normally presented in the Autumn. A single unified Budget then took place in November each year until the new Labour Government announced that its first budget of July 1997 would be followed by a return to a Spring Budget in 1998.

Earmarked taxes

A more specific way of linking taxation to spending decisions is through 'earmarked taxes'. Tax earmarking or tax hypothecation involves assigning the revenue from a particular tax to a specific part of public expenditure. A major instance in the United Kingdom consists of National Insurance contributions, which are used to fund National Insurance benefits, but the principle could be applied in other areas as well. One possible example would be the use of revenue from taxing cigarettes to finance the health service (Gravelle and Zimmerman, 1994). An extension of the concept of tax earmarking has considered the possibility that taxpayers could assign their taxes to particular uses (Bilodeau, 1994).

An early view was that such earmarking would reduce government efficiency, since it would impose an unnecessary constraint on budgetary decisions. However, as stated earlier in this chapter, public choice analysis has raised doubts that public spending decisions always reflect the best interests of the electorate as a whole. In these circumstances, as one of the pioneers of public choice theory has pointed out (Buchanan, 1963), linking specific taxes with specific expenditure might improve budgetary decisions precisely because it does constrain government decision-making. An increased element of democracy might be achieved, since elections could involve choices over different public spending decisions and their associated taxes rather than a single decision on the aggregate level of public spending and taxation. Teja and Bracewell-Milnes (1991) presented a range of arguments about how tax earmarking might produce greater public sector efficiency than expenditure from general funds does. One suggestion in particular is that there would be a closer connection between the benefits received from specific public services and the contribution required from taxpayers. Another is that individuals might be more willing to pay their taxes if they knew more precisely how the taxes are being spent.

However, some reservations have been expressed about such arguments. One is that earmarked taxes could be raised for popular forms of expenditure, but that this might simply release existing spending for other less popular purposes. Instead of being a safeguard against excessive public spending, therefore, earmarking might actually facilitate its increase. In addition taxes originally raised for one purpose might later be diverted to another. For example, in principle the Road Fund was a mechanism by which vehicle and fuel taxes paid for spending on roads. However, those taxes came to be used for general purposes and the independent life of the Road Fund finished in 1937 (Hicks, 1968).

As Wilkinson (1994) has suggested, there would be considerable difficulties in applying earmarking across the whole complex range of public expenditure. For example, strict adherence to the principle might involve many tax changes to maintain revenues over the economic cycle. Less than strict adherence might permit the very manipulation that earmarking was supposed to constrain. While it may be concluded that tax earmarking might be a useful way of undertaking specific public expenditure programmes, there would be serious difficulties in introducing it generally to public expenditure and taxation.

7.3 Tax compliance

A topic which has attracted interest from a variety of commentators is the issue of tax compliance. No tax system can function effectively without the co-operation of the great majority of taxpayers, so the factors which affect compliance are important.

The definition of compliance is usually cast in terms of the degree to which taxpayers comply with tax law. It has then been said that the degree of non-compliance can be measured in terms of the 'tax gap'. This represents the difference between actual revenue and that which would be received if there were 100 per cent compliance. Such a definition and measure are too simplistic for practical policy purposes, since successful tax administration often requires taxpayers to co-operate willingly over and above the bare statutory minimum. It also requires taxpayers to comply without the need for official enquiries, reminders or the threat or application of legal or administrative sanctions. A more appropriate definition might therefore include the degree of compliance with tax law and administration without the need for enforcement activity.

The issue of timing is also important. A taxpayer might eventually pay his or her full liability but, if the payment is late, the taxpayer cannot be considered to have been compliant. In economic terms, money in the future is worth less than the same sum now. So although late payments will satisfy the 'tax gap' measure, they do not represent full compliance.

The distinction between tax avoidance and tax evasion has been made several times in Part I of the book. Tax avoidance has been used to describe the legal manipulation (unlike evasion) of an individual's affairs in order to reduce tax. However, if taxpayers go to inordinate lengths to reduce their tax liability, this could hardly be considered 'compliance', even if it were within the letter of the law. A better definition of compliance might therefore include actions which are consistent with the spirit as well as the letter of the law. A definition of non-compliance might be the failure of taxpayers to act in accordance with the statutory requirements or intentions of the tax law and administration without the application of enforcement activity.

The implications of non-compliance can be analysed using the concepts presented in Part 1. Decisions may be taken on tax grounds rather than for primarily economic or commercial reasons. There may be equity effects - that resources are transferred away from those who comply with the tax system and towards those who avoid or evade. This may also be inequitable, because the more income a person has, the greater the incentive not to comply. If it is perceived that only those who are wealthy or dishonest or both benefit from non-compliance, this might reduce 'tax morale' and the willingness of the rest of the population to comply.

The question, therefore, is how best to ensure compliance. It has been noted by Wallschutzky (1993) that most of the attention in this area has been devoted to why some taxpayers do not comply rather than why others do. It might well be argued the other way round. The norm is usually to comply rather than not to comply. As already pointed out, for a tax system to be effective the majority of taxpayers have to comply. It follows that there may be greater gains in assisting basically compliant taxpayers to meet their fiscal obligations than in spending more resources in pursuing the minority of non-compliers. Many taxpayers might be willing to comply in full, but are unable to do so because they are not aware of, or do not understand, their full obligations. Even if such taxpayers understand their obligations, they may not know how to meet them or may be unable to do so for other reasons. Additional expenditure devoted to assisting such taxpayers, for example by informing or educating them, might yield greater additional revenues than if it were spent on additional enforcement activities.

Clearly much depends on the motives of taxpayers. This is a complex area and different commentators have offered different analyses. The two main approaches are to concentrate on the probability of detection and on penalties for non-compliance (the 'carrot and stick' approach) or activities designed to promote voluntary compliance (the 'responsible citizen approach').

The carrot and stick approach

This view is based on a relatively narrow interpretation of economic rationality. According to this approach, totally amoral individuals maximise their utility by maximising their income and wealth. They will evade tax if they consider that by doing so they can expect to increase their spending power. Non-compliance can therefore be explained by factors such as the level of tax rates, the probability of being caught evading, the penalties imposed and the degree of risk aversion. An early model was suggested by Allingham and Sandmo (1972). There have been many refinements and extensions since and Sandmo (2005) provides an overview of some of the main themes.

Although this type of approach has some intuitive appeal, it does not seem to provide anything like a complete explanation of either compliance or non-compliance. For example, evidence from the USA suggests that reductions in the traditional enforcement activities in terms of auditing do not necessarily result in lower levels of compliance. Tax Notes (1988) reported that audit rates for individuals in the USA declined between the early 1960s and the late 1980s from around 6 per cent to 1 per cent. However, Long and Burnham (1990) found that, during this period, compliance levels in the USA remained relatively stable. There are explanations which are consistent with the narrowly defined economic utility approach. One is that taxpayers had not realised that audit rates had declined. Another is that the remaining audits had become much more effective in detecting evasion. However, it is also possible that taxpayers are not mainly motivated by some simple numerical calculation of the expected cash benefits of noncompliance in some sort of moral and social vacuum. This leads on to an alternative approach to tax compliance.

The responsible citizen approach

Looking outside economics, other academic disciplines have suggested factors which might be important in influencing taxpayers' behaviour. Sociology has offered a number of variables such as social support, social influence, attitudes and certain background characteristics such as age, gender, race and culture. Psychology reinforces this approach and has even created its own branch of 'fiscal psychology' (Schmölders, 1959; Lewis, 1982). The contribution from psychology includes the indication that attitudes towards the state and the revenue authorities are as important factors as perceptions of equity. The roles of individuals in society and the accepted norms of behaviour can also have a strong influence. The main theme of

this approach is that individuals are not simply independent, selfish, utility maximis-
ers (though this might be partly true). They also interact with other human beings in
ways which depend on different attitudes, beliefs, norms and roles.

The behavioural approach does have some empirical support. For example,
Milliron and Toy (1988) analysed the views of 152 public certified accountants
in small accounting firms in the USA and found support for the fiscal psychology
model. A similar conclusion was reached by Yankelovich, Skelly and White Inc.
(1984). They examined the data from 20 focus groups, led by a moderator and a
nationwide survey of 2,200 US taxpayers, using interviews in their homes. This
study found considerable concern over issues of fairness. There also seemed to be
a perceived norm of cheating - a majority of the sample said they thought over a
quarter of the population were evading taxes and nearly a quarter of the sample
thought that over half were evading.

If psychological and sociological factors are important then a major drawback
of the carrot and stick approach becomes apparent. While such an approach might
be considered by some as suitable for donkeys, human beings might not respond so
positively. The result might be a reduction in voluntary compliance. For instance,
Striimpel (1969) and Schmölders (1970) reported that the German tax system was
very rigid in its assessment procedures, which led to an effective but expensive and
confrontational system. The result was a high degree of alienation and resistance
among taxpayers.

The conclusion would seem to be that a successful compliance policy should take
account of a much wider range of motivations than simply rewards and punish-
ments. One example is Japan, where the purpose of the tax administration in the
self-assessment system is to ensure that all taxpayers understand the importance of
taxation and comply with the tax system voluntarily. To achieve this, the Japanese tax
administration aims to establish a consistent and sound environment for voluntary
compliance and sets out its policy in two main areas (National Tax Administration,
1992). The first is to encourage compliance through communications with taxpayers and to use the opportunity of audits to improve taxpayers' understanding and
facilitate voluntary compliance. The other is to 'develop self-disciplined and efficient
offices with good human relations ... with the right attitudes, taxpayers find it easier
to approach the tax authorities'.

The Internal Revenue Service in the USA has been developing a complex strategy
for compliance, as outlined in its document Compliance 2000 (Internal Revenue
Service, 1991). The policy was to approach compliance across a broad front consisting of 12 areas. This included customer service training, better public relations,
simplification and fairness and a more organised approach to influence legislation
in this direction. Also included were taxpayer service and education, attempts to
inculcate in citizens a sense of responsibility towards taxation and to devise ways to
reward compliant behaviour (not necessarily monetarily).

It would seem, therefore, that a successful compliance policy should include more
than just a set of rewards and penalties. Attention should also be paid to ways of

securing positive taxpayer motivation and encouraging and supporting taxpayers in their assessment tasks. Taxes are, or should be, raised for the benefit of society. It is in everyone's interests that the process should work well, because if participation is only achieved under the threat of severe penalties and enforcement action, this necessarily reduces the benefits of the whole exercise. Such considerations are particularly important as the United Kingdom moves towards greater self-assessment in its tax administration.

7.4 Tax ethics

The importance of ethics is being increasingly appreciated in the related areas of law and business. As Ross (1992) reminded us, in the 1974 Watergate scandal in the United States, almost all of those involved in the break-in and later prosecuted were lawyers. As a result the American Bar Association required instruction in 'the duties and responsibilities of the legal profession' as part of the accreditation for law schools.

The USA has also seen developments in tax ethics as part of the more general topic of legal ethics. Indeed some of the aspects, such as those relating to confidentiality and conflict of interest, would appear to apply in the same way to both taxation and law more generally. However there has been a significant increase in the literature relating specifically to tax ethics and this includes a student text (Wolfman and Holden, 1985) and a two-volume set on tax ethics for practitioners (Wolfman *et al.*, 1991).

This subject has a number of implications. One is that the tax practitioners' goal of minimising their clients' tax liabilities might not always be fully compatible with following a code of professional conduct and moral ethics (Hansen *et al.*, 1992). Another implication is that ethical attitudes may affect the willingness of individuals to comply with the tax system as described above. For example, in the USA, Reckers *et al.* (1994) examined ethical beliefs on tax compliance decisions. They found that individual moral beliefs were very significant in decisions about tax evasion. The importance of tax ethics is likely to grow in the future, particularly as the United Kingdom has now adopted a significant degree of self-assessment.

7.5 Tax harmonisation

A particular ongoing reform is European tax harmonisation. This can be analysed in terms of the principles outlined in Part I, in particular with respect to the effects of taxation on economic efficiency. The Treaty establishing the European Community (the EC Treaty) stated that its task was the creation of a common market, and Article 3 made it clear that the internal market was to be 'characterised by the abolition, as between Member States, of obstacles to the free movement of goods, persons, services and capital'. Abolishing tariffs is insufficient to achieve this aim. If the tax treatment of economic activities is different in different Member States, it is likely to generate economic distortions and increase the excess burden of taxation. If countries maintain independent tax systems, there might be discrimination against goods and services provided by other countries. The European Court of Justice has in fact intervened in a range of such cases, for instance in the so-called 'spirits cases'. Several countries were found to have discriminatory taxes in breach of Article 95 of the EC Treaty - France for having favourable tax rates for cognac over whisky, Italy grappa over rum and Denmark aquavit compared with other spirits (Weatherill and Beaumont, 1995).

The main provisions of the EC Treaty regarding taxation are Articles 95 to 99, and they are concerned almost entirely with indirect taxation. However, the European Court has been supportive of the development of an integrated system of taxation and included direct taxation in its decisions. Tax harmonisation is an important aspect of the development of the European Union, but progress towards its achievement has been uncertain and increasingly controversial.

Part of the reason for the difficulties in achieving tax harmonisation might be that there is insufficient agreement about the meaning of the term and about the degree of harmonisation that is desirable. These issues will be discussed in turn.

The meaning of tax harmonisation

Although the term 'tax harmonisation' is often used, it is not always clear what is meant and different writers have offered different definitions. At one extreme, for example, Dosser (1973) saw tax harmonisation as merely 'tax co-ordination among nations in the process of integration in a customs union or economic union', but this definition is no longer adequate to cover the full current use of the term. In particular 'tax co-ordination' might mean no more than operating tax systems in a similar sort of way. Rounds (1992) suggests that harmonisation 'refers to any situation where differences in taxation between the states (or provinces) are reduced either by co-operation among the states or by a federal government policy'. Hitiris (1994) takes a wider view of the term and describes two approaches to tax harmonisation - the equalisations approach and the differentials or fiscal diversity approach. Essentially the equalisations approach is that each country operates the same tax system. The differentials approach allows each country to use its tax system as a tool of policy in achieving major economic aims. Other commentators seem to have taken the meaning of tax harmonisation to be the process of achieving a single tax system - in other words there would be complete standardisation of taxes across the European Union.

Tax harmonisation has therefore been used to mean almost anything from tax systems somehow operating in harmony with each other to complete integration. It might clarity the discussion to identify possible dimensions of harmonisation.

These include the taxes levied, the tax bases, the rates of tax and the ways in which taxes are administered. Figure 7.1 offers a possible classification. At one extreme is the complete standardisation of taxes mentioned above. This means that each country has the same taxes, levied on the same tax bases at the same rates, and this is shown following the right-hand branch of Figure 7.1 At the other extreme is no harmonisation. Following the left branch of Figure 7.1 this implies different taxes in each country. It also implies no double taxation agreements. Administration considerations might also be important - for example involving co-ordination between the tax authorities in different countries over matters such as tax evasion. No harmonisation would also seem to imply no move towards greater administrative co-operation either.

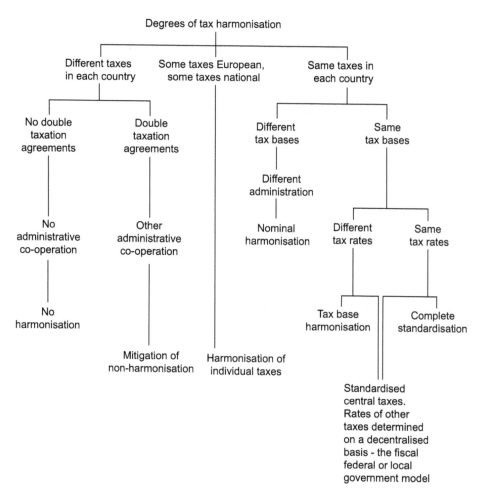

Figure 7.1 Classification of degrees of tax harmonisation

Between these extreme situations of no harmonisation at all or complete standardisation, it is then possible to develop the idea of degrees of harmonisation. One step forward might be some administrative co-operation between tax authorities regarding taxpayers with tax affairs falling within more than one tax jurisdiction. The next stage might be the development of formal double taxation agreements so that the same income is not taxed twice by two different tax jurisdictions. Although these might be described as forms of tax harmonisation, the term is normally used in a wider sense. In Figure 7.1 this situation is described as the 'mitigation of non-harmonisation'.

The middle solution would be to have some taxes levied in the same way across all countries in the European Union, but with Member States also free to impose other taxes of their choice. In other words, some individual taxes would be harmonised but not others. If this approach were preferred, there is much to be said on the relative merits of different taxes with respect to their suitability as taxes at the European or the Member State level.

The first major step towards a more comprehensive form of harmonisation is for countries to have the same taxes more generally. This applies already to the main taxes in the European Union - income tax, value added tax and corporation tax. However, there are considerable differences in their application in different countries, and the result falls far short of full harmonisation. For example the tax base is not usually the same. Each of the Member States has an income tax but the scope of the tax is different in different countries. The way the taxes are operated also varies. For instance, each of the Member States has a form of corporation tax but they use different forms of the classical system and the imputation system. This is described in Chapter 14, and the particular case of corporate tax harmonisation is discussed further in Section 14.5.

Differences in administration may be significant. The United Kingdom has its unique cumulative Pay-As-You-Earn system, discussed in the following chapter, whereas other countries have different methods of withholding tax from wages and salaries. As a result, in Figure 7.1 the situation where countries have the same taxes, but they are not levied on the same tax base, or by the same administrative methods, is described as 'nominal harmonisation'.

The next stage becomes a little more complicated. It is relevant to note that even within countries the tax system is not normally standard across all local areas.

In the United States the different levels of fiscal jurisdiction include the federal government, state governments, the District of Columbia and about 80,000 local jurisdictions and, for example, a federal income tax exists alongside state income taxes. In the United Kingdom, there is central and local government. Taxes are levied on the same base and in most cases at the same rates nationally. Within that framework there is the major local tax, now council tax but before that the community charge and before that local authority rates (see Section 11.4). Council tax is assessed on the same property tax base throughout the country, but local tax jurisdictions have the power to vary the rate at which it is levied. Property is used in many countries as a tax base for local tax jurisdictions, partly because it cannot be moved to areas with lower taxes. However, some countries use a local income tax, sales tax or other taxes on a decentralised basis. Some countries have more than one local tax. This topic is referred to as fiscal federalism or local government finance and has been the subject of significant research - see for example Gates (1991).

In Figure 7.1 this multiple-tier arrangement is therefore referred to as the 'fiscal federal' or 'local government model'. It might give an indication of a desirable level of tax harmonisation in the future of the European Union, with perhaps some taxes levied on a standardised basis throughout the union and others levied at different rates and perhaps bases in different Member States. To explore this further, it is necessary to examine the argument for tax harmonisation.

The desired degree of harmonisation

To make progress in establishing the desired degree of tax harmonisation, it is helpful to return to the need for taxation summarised in Chapter 2. Musgrave's (1959) classification of economic justifications for intervention in a market economy included resource allocation - that is, the efficient production of the right amounts of different goods and services. Markets left to themselves may fail in certain ways, particularly in relation to 'public goods' such as national defence, 'external effects' such as pollution and 'green issues', and 'merit goods' which, for various possible reasons, might be under-produced if markets were left to themselves.

The point here is that the demand for public sector provision arising from the issues mentioned in the previous sentence might not be the same in all areas of a political entity. For instance, an area with a large proportion of retired inhabitants or one with a large proportion of children might have very different demands on the public sector than one with a more even distribution of age groups. There may be considerable differences in public sector needs in poor areas compared with wealthier areas. It is just as possible for varying demands for public goods to exist between groups with different national and cultural traditions. The seminal work analysing how economic welfare might increase with different local tax and public spending regimes was that of Tiebout (1956), and this approach has been developed further.

However, the basic economic argument is that communities might be better served if there is an element of choice as regards the nature and extent of public sector activity in different areas (Member States in this case).

The fiscal federal or local government model would appear to be a fruitful line of approach to European tax harmonisation. Some of the opposition to tax harmonisation might be caused by fears that an ill-defined concept of harmonisation could lead to complete integration and standardisation across Europe. If the different needs and choices of Member States were to be explicitly recognised within the overall concept of harmonisation, progress might be easier to achieve.

Table 7.1 Some important taxes, receipts (£ million)

	Income tax*	Corporation tax	Inheritance tax	Petroleum revenue tax	Stamp duties
2006/07	147,134	44,308	3,545	2,155	13,393
2008/09	155,704	43,077	2,837	2,567	8,002
2010/11	151,604	42,016	2,717	1,465	9,008

	Alcohol	Tobacco	Betting and gaming	Hydrocarbon oils	Customs duties**	VAT
2006/07	7,913	8,149	1,391	23,585	2,325	77,360
2008/09	8,470	8,219	1,474	24,615	2,659	78,439
2010/11	9,400	9,144	1,533	27,256	2,998	83,486

Other taxes

	Motor duties		GDP (market prices) (for comparison)
2008/09	5,582	2008	1,449,861
2010/11	5,773	2010	1,395,312

Source: Financial Statistics, Office for National Statistics. June 2011, Tables 2.1C, 2.1D, 2.1E
* Including capital gains tax.
** Including agricultural levies.

7.6 The relative importance of United Kingdom taxes

This section provides a broad summary of the importance in terms of receipts of the main United Kingdom taxes. Table 7.1 provides information on this subject. In some cases, two similar taxes have been added together, as the table shows. Greater detail is provided in later chapters, for example in Table 11.1, for indirect taxes.

It can be seen that income tax is by far the largest source of revenue. Consequently, it is described in considerable detail in Chapters 8 and 9, with substantial attention being paid to possibilities of reform. Corporation tax and value added tax are also important sources of revenue, and are studied in some detail. It is interesting to note that, despite the volume of discussion and complaint that one hears about inheritance tax and capital gains tax, these taxes each raise less than 4 per cent of the revenue of income tax.

7.7 Taxation in different countries

According to popular mythology, the United Kingdom used to have one of the highest levels of taxation in the world. Although the UK tax system has unusual features, it is easy to show that the level of taxation is not exceptionally high.

The level of taxation

One of the conventional ways of comparing taxation in different countries is to compare their total tax revenue as a percentage of GDP. This method has its limitations, some of which are discussed in Messere and Owens (1987). For example, if a country changes from a policy of giving financial assistance to its citizens in the form of tax relief, to a policy of giving cash payments, its tax/GDP ratio will rise. This happened in the United Kingdom when payments of child benefit replaced the old income tax allowances.

Table 7.2 Total tax revenue as a percentage of GDP in 2006

	Including social security contributions		Excluding social security contributions	
Denmark	49.1	(1=)	48.1	(1)
Sweden	49.1	(1=)	46.6	(2)
Belgium	44.5	(3)	31.0	(7)
France	44.2	(4)	27.8	(12)
Norway	43.7	(5)	35.2	(5)
Finland	43.5	(6)	31.3	(6)
Italy	42.1	(7)	29.6	(10)
Austria	41.7	(8)	27.3	(14)
Iceland	41.6	(9)	38.2	(3)
Netherlands	39.3	(10)	25.1	(17)
United Kingdom	37.1	(11)	30.3	(9)
Hungary	37.1	(12)	25.2	(16)
Czech Republic	36.9	(13)	20.8	(25)
New Zealand	36.7	(14)	36.7	(4)
Spain	36.6	(15)	24.4	(18)
Luxembourg	35.9	(16)	26.0	(15)
Portugal	35.7	(17)	24.3	(19)
Germany	35.6	(18)	21.9	(21)
Poland	33.5	(19)	21.4	(22)
Canada	33.3	(20)	28.4	(11)
Ireland	31.9	(21)	27.6	(13)
Greece	31.3	(22)	20.2	(26)
Australia	30.6	(23)	30.6	(8)
Slovak Republic	29.8	(24)	17.9	(28)
Switzerland	29.6	(25)	22.7	(20)
United States	25.0	(26)	21.3	(23)
Japan	27.9	(27)	17.7	(29)
Korea	26.8	(28)	21.1	(24)
Turkey	24.5	(29)	19.0	(27)
Mexico	20.6	(30)	17.5	(30)

Note: Figures in brackets indicate country ranks.
Source: OECD (2008), Tables 1 and 2, p. 93.

Nevertheless, such a comparison does provide a rough picture of the tax position in different countries. Table 7.2 presents the figures for total tax revenue as a percentage of GDP in the 30 member countries of the Organisation for Economic Cooperation and Development (OECD). If social security contributions are included, it can be seen that the United Kingdom had the eleventh highest tax/GDP ratio in 2006 (up from seventeenth in 2002).

Table 7.3 Revenue from different taxes as a percentage of GDP in 2006

	Income and profits	Social Security	Payroll taxes	Property	Goods and services	Other
Australia	18.1	–	1.4	2.8	8.3	–
Austria	12.0	14.4	2.7	0.6	11.5	0.5
Belgium	16.8	13.6	–	2.3	11.4	0.0
Canada	16.2	4.9	0.7	3.4	8.1	0.1
Czech Republic	9.0	16.1	–	0.4	11.1	0.0
Denmark	29.5	1.0	0.2	1.9	16.3	0.0
Finland	16.6	12.1	–	1.1	13.5	0.0
France	10.7	16.3	1.1	3.5	10.9	1.5
Germany	10.8	13.7	–	0.9	10.1	0.0
Greece	7.5	11.1	–	1.4	11.3	-
Hungary	9.1	11.9	0.6	0.8	14.2	0.3
Iceland	18.3	3.3	0.0	2.2	17.6	0.1
Ireland	12.7	4.3	0.2	2.9	11.6	–
Italy	14.0	12.6	–	2.1	10.8	2.5
Japan	9.9	10.2	–	2.5	5.2	0.1
Korea	7.9	5.6	0.1	3.5	8.7	0.9
Luxembourg	12.5	9.9	–	3.3	10.0	0.0
Mexico	5.2	3.1	0.3	0.3	11.6	0.2
Netherlands	10.7	14.2	–	1.9	12.0	0.2
New Zealand	22.8	–	-	1.9	12.0	0.0
Norway	22.0	8.7	–	1.2	12.0	–
Poland	7.0	12.2	0.3	1.2	12.8	-
Portugal	8.5	11.4	–	1.1	14.5	0.1
Slovak Republic	5.8	11.9	–	0.5	11.5	-
Spain	11.4	12.2	–	3.3	9.9	0.2
Sweden	19.4	12.5	2.7	1.4	12.8	0.0
Switzerland	13.5	6.9	–	2.4	6.8	-
Turkey	5.3	5.5	–	0.9	11.9	0.9
United Kingdom	14.7	6.9	–	4.6	10.8	–
United States	13.5	6.7	–	3.1	4.7	–

Source: OECD (2008), p. 70.

There are several reasons why social security contributions should be included. Australia and New Zealand finance their social security systems entirely from general taxation revenue, and the social security systems in many other countries, such as Denmark and Ireland, are mainly financed in this way. On the other hand, several countries, such as France, Germany and the Netherlands, largely finance their systems from social security contributions. Such contributions are usually compulsory and have much in common with more conventional forms of taxation. (The position in the United Kingdom is discussed in Section 8.3.)

Depending on whether social security contributions are included, the picture (as in Table 7.2) can change significantly. For example, after inclusion, France increases its position from 12th to 4th, and Australia drops from 8th place to 23rd. The United Kingdom moves from 9th to 11th place – well into the top half of the table. With a tax/GDP ratio of 37.1 per cent, the United Kingdom is considerably lower than countries such as Denmark and Sweden (both at 49.1) and France (44.2). It seems reasonable to conclude that in terms of total tax revenue, the United Kingdom is not among the more highly taxed countries.

The sources of taxation

The United Kingdom is not particularly unusual in the sources of its revenue either. Table 7.3 shows that in 2006 United Kingdom tax revenue from taxes on income and profits amounted to 14.7 per cent of GDP. This is a significantly higher percentage than for countries such as Greece (7.5) and France (10.7). On the other hand, the figure is much lower than in countries such as Denmark (29.5), New Zealand (22.8) and Australia (18.1).

So, once more, the United Kingdom does not appear to have any special claim to fame in the fiscal league. However, in the structure of particular taxes, most especially income tax, the United Kingdom has some very unusual characteristics indeed. Detailed discussion of these features is presented in Chapters 8 and 9.

Further reading

A strategic approach to income tax reform may be found in James and Edwards (2007) and some of the difficulties of developing tax policy in James and Edwards (2008). Sandford's series on tax reform also provide a practical examination of tax reform (Sandford 1993, 1995, 1998). Sandmo (2005) provides an overview of some of the main themes in tax evasion and Congdon et al. (2009), James (2006) and Kirchler (2007) examine behavioural aspects of taxpayer compliance. A survey of issues in tax policy is given by Kay (1990), and a wide range of issues concerning tax policy in developing countries can be found in Bird and Oldman (1990). An interesting account of tax policy in OECD countries is to be found in Messere (1993) and a discussion of recent tax developments and some policy implications in Messere (2004). Globalisation and international trends in taxation are examined by James and Sawyer (2004) and Hines and Summers (2009). Many other aspects of taxation are included in James (2012).

References

Allingham. M.G. and Sandmo A . (1972), 'Income tax evasion: a theoretical analysis, *Journal of Public Economics,* Vol. 1. pp 323-38.

Armstrong Lord W. (1980), *Budgetary Reform in the United Kingdom,* Oxford University Press.

Beighton, L. (1987), 'Tax policy and management: the role of the Inland Revenue', *Fiscal Studies,* Vol. 8, No. 1.

Bilodeau, M. (1994), 'Tax-earmarking and separate school financing', *Journal of Public Economics,* Vol. 54, pp. 51-63.

Bird, R.M. and Oldman, O. (1990), *Taxation in Developing Countries,* 4th edn, Johns Hopkins University Press.

Bracewell-Milnes, B. (1976), *The Camel's Back,* Centre for Policy Studies, p. 11.

Buchanan, J.M. (1963), 'The economics of earmarked taxes', *Journal of Political Economy,* Vol. 71, pp. 457-69.

Congdon, W. J., Kling, J,R, and Mullainathan, S. (2009), 'Behavioral economics and tax policy', *National Tax Journal,* Vol 62. pp. 375–86.

Dosser, D. (1973), *British Taxation and the Common Market,* Charles Knight.

Gravelle, J. and Zimmerman, D. (1994), 'Cigarette taxes to fund health care reform', *National Tax Journal,* Vol. XLVII, pp. 575-90.

Hagemann, R.P., Jones, B.R. and Montador, R.B. (1988), 'Tax reform in OECD countries: motives, constraints and practice', *OECD Economic Studies,* No. 10, Spring.

Hansen, D.R., Crosser, R.L. and Laufer, D. (1992), 'Moral ethics v. tax ethics - the case of transfer pricing among multinational corporations', *Journal of Business Ethics,* Vol. 11, pp. 679-86.

Hicks, U.K. (1968), *Public Finance,* Cambridge University Press.

Hines, J.R. Jr. and Summers, L.H. (2009), 'How globalization affects tax design', *Tax Policy and the Economy,* Vol. 23, No.1, pp 123–158.

Hitiris, T. (1994), *European Community Economics,* 3rd edn, Harvester Wheatsheaf.

Internal Revenue Service (1991), *Compliance 2000: Report to the Commissioner of Internal Revenues,* IRS, Washington DC.

James, S. (2006), 'Taxation and the Contribution of Behavioural Economics' in *Foundations and Extensions of Behavioral Economics: A Handbook,* edited by Morris Altman, M.E. Sharpe, New York, pp.589-601.

James, S. (2012), *A Dictionary of Taxation,* 2nd ed., Edward Elgar, Cheltenham.

James S., and Edwards, A. (2007), 'A strategic approach to personal income tax reform', *Australian Tax Forum,* Vol. 22, No.2 pp. 105-126.

James, S. and Edwards, A. (2008), 'Developing tax policy in a complex and changing world', *Economic Analysis and Policy,* Vol. 38. No. 1, pp 35-53.

James, S. and Sawyer, A. (2004), 'Globalisation and international trends in taxation', *Asia-Pacific Journal of Taxation,* Vol. 8, No. 2, pp. 49-67.

Kay, J.A. (1990), 'Tax policy: a survey', *Economic Journal,* Vol. 100, March.

Lewis, A. (1982), *The Psychology of Taxation,* Blackwell.

Kirchler, E. (2007), *The Economic Psychology of Tax Behaviour,* Cambridge University Press.

Long, S.B. and Burnham, D. (1990), 'That number game: changes in tax compliance during the last 25 years', *Tax Notes,* 5 March.

Meade Committee (1978), *The Structure and Reform of Direct Taxation,* Allen and Unwin for the Institute for Fiscal Studies.

Messere, K. (1993), *Tax Policy in OECD Countries: Choices and Conflicts,* IBFD Publications.

Messere, K. (2004) 'Recent tax revenue developments in OECD countries and some policy implications (revisited)' *Bulletin for International Documentation,* Vol. 58, pp. 165-174.

Messere, K.C. and Owens, J.P. (1987), 'International comparisons of tax levels', *OECD Economic Studies,* Spring, pp. 93-119.

Milliron, V.C. and Toy, D.R (1988), 'Tax compliance: an investigation of the key features', *Journal of the American Taxation Association,* pp. 84-104.

Mueller, D.C. (1979), *Public Choice,* Cambridge University Press.

Musgrave, R.A. (1959), *The Theory of Public Finance,* McGraw-Hill.

National Tax Administration (1992), *An Outline of Japanese Tax Administration, 1992,* Japan.

Oates, W.E. (1991), *Studies in Fiscal Federalism,* Edward Elgar.

OECD (2008), *Revenue Statistics: 1965-2007.* OECD.

Owens, J. (2006), 'Fundamental tax reform: An international perspective' *National Tax Journal,* Vol. LIX, No.1 pp. 131-164.

Reckers, P.M.J., Sanders, D.L. and Roark, S.J. (1994), 'The influence of ethical attitudes on taxpayer compliance', *National Tax Journal,* Vol. XLVII, pp. 825-36.

Robinson, A. and Sandford, C. (1983), *Tax Policy-Making in the United Kingdom: A Study of Rationality, Ideology and Politics,* Heinemann.

Ross, S. (1992), 'Tax ethics education in the United States and Australia', *Australian Tax Forum,* pp. 27–49.

Rounds, T.A. (1992), 'Tax harmonisation and tax competition - contrasting views and policy issues in 3 federal countries', *Publius - the Journal of Federalism.*

Sandford, C. (ed.) (1993) *Key Issues in Tax Reform,* Fiscal Publications.

Sandford, C. (ed.) (1995) *More Key Issues in Tax Reform,* Fiscal Publications.

Sandford, C. (ed.) (1998) *Further Key Issues in Tax Reform,* Fiscal Publications.

Sandmo, A. (2005), 'The theory of tax evasion: A retrospective view', *National Tax Journal,* Vol. LVIII, No. 4, pp. 643-663.

Schmölders, G. (1959), 'Fiscal psychology: a new branch of public finance', *National Tax Journal,* Vol. 15, pp. 184-93.

Schmölders, G. (1970), 'Survey research in public finance - a behavioural approach to fiscal theory', *Public Finance,* Vol. 25.

Strümpel, B. (1969), 'The contribution of survey research to public finance', in A.T. Peacock (ed.), *Quantitative Analysis in Public Finance,* Praeger.

Tax Notes (1988), 11 April, pp. 109-112.

Teja, R.S. and Bracewell-Milnes, B. (1991), *The Case for Earmarked Taxes: Government Spending and Public Choice,* Institute of Economic Affairs.

Tiebout, C.M. (1956), 'A pure theory of local expenditures', *Journal of Political Economy,* Vol. 64, No. 3, pp. 416-24.

HM Treasury (1986), *The Government's Spending Plans* 1986-87 to 1988-89, HMSO, Cmnd. 9702-II.

US Treasury (1977), *Blueprints for Basic Tax Reform,* Washington DC.

Wallschutzky, I.G. (1993), 'Achieving compliance', *Proceedings of the Australasian Tax Teachers' Association,* January, Christchurch, New Zealand.

Weatherill, S. and Beaumont, P. (1995), *EC Law,* 2nd edn, Penguin.

Wilkinson, M. (1994), 'Paying for public spending: is there a role for earmarked taxes?', *Fiscal Studies,* Vol. 15, No. 4, pp. 119-35.

Wolfman, B. and Holden, J.P. (1985), *Ethical Problems in Federal Tax Practice,* 2nd edn, Michie Bobbs-Merrill Law Publishers, Charlottesville.

Wolfman, B., Holden, J.P. and Harris, K.L. (1991), *Standards of Tax Practice,* CCH, Chicago.

Yankelovich, Skelly and White Inc. (1984), *Taxpayer attitudes study,* Final Report for the Internal Revenue Service, Internal Revenue Service, Public Affairs Division, Washington DC.

SELF ASSESSMENT QUESTIONS

Suggested answers to self-assessment questions are given at the back of the book.

7.1   What are the advantages claimed for earmarked taxes?

7.2   Define tax compliance.

7.3   Which two UK taxes (excluding National Insurance contributions) raise the most revenue?

DISCUSSION QUESTIONS

1.   Why is successful tax policy-making so difficult?

2.   Should earmarked taxes be used more extensively?

3.   How might tax compliance be improved?

4.   How important are tax ethics?

CHAPTER EIGHT

Personal income tax

After reading this chapter, you should be able to:

- Describe the main features of the UK income tax.
- Explain the economic reasons for having a capital gains tax.
- Understand how the UK capital gains tax works.
- Describe the cumulative basis for withholding tax from employment income and its advantages and disadvantages.
- Outline the taxation of the self-employed.

8.1 Introduction

'It is a vile, Jacobin, jumped up Jack-in-office piece of impertinence - is a true Briton to have no privacy? Are the fruits of his labour and toil to be picked over, farthing by farthing, by the pimply minions of Bureaucracy?' (quoted in Sabine, 1965, p. 31). Income tax has never been popular in the United Kingdom, as illustrated by the above reaction from a member of the Navy to its introduction in 1799. Yet, as the coverage of the tax has grown wider and wider, the British seem to have learned to live with it.

However, the British income tax has many curious characteristics. Indeed, with the exception of the Irish system, there is nothing else quite like it in the world. In this chapter we shall try to describe the system. This will involve looking in turn at the development of the system, the current tax structure, the Pay-As-You-Earn machinery and the treatment of business income. In the following chapter we shall look at some of the proposals for reforming the British system.

8.2 Historical aspects of income tax

Like many other taxes, income tax began as a war tax. It was first introduced in 1799 to finance the war with Napoleon. When peace came in 1802 the tax was withdrawn, but re-imposed when hostilities recommenced in 1803. It was abolished once more when peace was achieved in 1815. The tax was reintroduced in 1842 and has remained in force ever since.

In its development the British tax system shares a number of characteristics with overseas systems. This includes its transformation from a primitive tax imposed at low rates on the few citizens who had relatively high incomes, to a modern sophisticated tax which is imposed at rather higher rates on the many citizens, including those who have relatively low incomes. As with many other taxes, it has also become a complicated tax.

However, as we shall see, the British tax system differs from its overseas equivalents in that it has developed the art of withholding tax at source to a very sophisticated degree.

Complexity

One of the common features of tax systems is complexity and there have been many calls for simplification. However, it is clear that tax systems often have to be complex and simplification is more difficult to achieve than is commonly thought – as indicated by James and Wallschutzky (1997) and James and Edwards (2008).

Certainly income tax and its administration have always been complicated. In 1799, income in excess of £60 a year was subject to a graduated scale of rates rising to a maximum of 10 per cent on income over £200. In calculating taxable income there was a wide range of deductions for dependants, life assurance premiums, debt interest and so on. The original Act (an amending Act was passed only three months later) was a complex document of some 152 pages in length, and the government felt it necessary to produce a guide entitled 'A Plain, Short and Easy Description of the Different Clauses of the Income Tax so as to render it Familiar to the Meanest Capacity' (Farnsworth, 1951, p. 15).

Nevertheless, compared to the modern income tax, the original version was simplicity itself. It could afford to be, as tax rates were comparatively low and were applied to only a small proportion of the population. The present tax is more complicated for a number of reasons.

First, taxes have to be acceptable to taxpayers, even if this sometimes involves the introduction of considerable distortions to the tax system. Examples include the introduction of the old system of schedules and of the cumulative Pay-As-You-Earn scheme which are described below.

Second, again because of high rates of tax, evasion and avoidance become very much more rewarding pursuits. If an individual is suffering tax at 40 pence in his or her marginal pound of income, it is clearly worth his or her while to spend up to 40 pence to save that pound from tax. And it is not simply the prerogative of the rich. With a basic rate of 20 per cent in 2012/13 (plus the National Insurance contributions discussed below), the incentive to reduce liability is widespread. There is also a similar incentive for the revenue authorities and the government to spend resources on preventing such evasion and avoidance.

Third, much of the complexity of a tax system arises, inevitably, from its legal basis. Tax law, unlike other branches of law, is 'purely the creature of statute' and there is no common law of taxation (Hepker, 1975; Mayson, 1980). Nevertheless, there is still a large body of statute. Nor is this new. For instance, the Income Tax Bill introduced in 1806 'contained 300 yards of parchment and if the operation is to be judged by the length, the public may dread its effect' (quoted in Hope-Jones, 1939, p. 26).

The point is that the law has to be precise and all-embracing. As Sir Ernest Gowers, a former Chairman of the Board of Inland Revenue, wrote in his *Complete Plain Words* in respect of a particular example of legal language (Gowers, 1954, Ch. 7):

[The] sentence is constructed with that mathematical arrangement of words which lawyers adopt to make their meaning unambiguous. Worked out as one would work out an equation, the sentence serves its purpose: as literature it is balderdash.

However, there has also been a growing concern that tax legislation is more complex and less comprehensible than it needs to be. Prebble (1994) quotes Professor David Walker, editor of *The Oxford Companion to English Law*:

More than any other branch of municipal law, tax law is open to the reproach of being utterly incomprehensible by the individuals afflicted, and even frequently by their legal advisers. The enormous complexity of the rules of law on each kind of tax gives rise to an enormous volume of dispute and argument and a great deal of litigation by way of appeal from assessments. Neither justice nor reason has any place in tax law, and many decisions of the superior courts are in plain conflict with all sense.

Prebble's view is that in taxation the difficulty arises from the attempt to fit the law around 'natural facts of economic life'. The law therefore attempts to solve insoluable problems and ends up as incomprehensible.

Other commentators such as Sabine (1991, 1993) and Williams (1993) have discussed other difficulties. One is the whole process of drafting tax legislation. It has been suggested that this has not always been done in the most appropriate way through factors such as a lack of pre-legislative consultation. The tax policymaking process discussed in Chapter 7 can also lead to difficulties, in particular as a result of the apparent lack of consistent policies. As Sabine (1993, p. 515) puts it: 'What policies? One common factor in all the Budgets covered is the *ad hoc* nature of the majority of measures: expediency, it would seem has been elevated to the status of a fiscal programme'.

Fourth, as the tax system has affected more and more people in more ways, there has been a temptation for governments to use it for purposes other than raising revenue. This inevitably means complexity. We have already seen in Section 3.8 that there is a good reason for lobby groups to believe that they may be better off if they demand government aid in the form of a tax concession rather than a direct cash subsidy.

A fifth factor is well described by Sabine (1965) at the end of his fascinating account of the history of British income tax:

One consistent feature of direct taxation has been its extraordinary sensitivity to criticism and its extreme flexibility and adaptability to accommodating such criticism.

This feature is not, of course, consistent with simplicity. The reasons for the complexity of modern tax systems are discussed further in James *et al.* (1987).

Nevertheless the UK tax system presents a striking paradox. Despite the underlying complexity of taxation, for most UK taxpayers for most of the time the system is remarkably simple. As we shall see, the system of allowances and tax rates has been simplified: most employees are not entitled to claim many, if any, expenses, and the UK PAYE system takes the process of assessment and collection largely out of the hands of most taxpayers.

The system of schedules

An early complication, introduced in 1803, was the division of the tax into five schedules - A, B, C, D and E. Under the previous system, a return of total income had been required and this proved highly unpopular, being considered as a serious infringement of privacy. With the 1803 system, taxpayers would declare income received under each schedule separately and so avoid the need for any official to know their total income. In fact, from 1803, returns of total income were not required on a wide scale until the introduction of super-tax in 1909.

With some modifications, the system of schedules survived until recently as one of the particular characteristics of the British income tax. The two most important schedules were Schedule E which covered income from employment, and Schedule D which included income from trades, professions, businesses, property and other annual profits. However in the process of consolidation and the re-writing of the legislation in plain English the schedules for income tax disappeared in 2005 though the substance of the legislation did not change.

Withholding at source

A further feature contributing to complexity, and one very much pioneered in the United Kingdom, is the extensive withholding of tax from incomes at their source. The principle of withholding tax in fact preceded income tax by many years. In an interesting investigation of the subject, Soos (1995) found that the principle of withholding tax at source was established in England during the sixteenth century and the first instance appears to have been with the lay subsidy of 1512.

Withholding at source has since developed into a fine art, and in the modern British income tax it takes three main forms. The first is withholding from wages and salaries through the sophisticated and uniquely British Pay-As-You-Earn system discussed in Section 8.5. The second is withholding from interest payments, which is also discussed below. The third concerns dividends and the imputation system of corporation tax, discussed in Section 12.5.

Withholding at source does not take place as such on dividends, but the effect of the imputation system is that there is no outstanding income tax liability except for higher rate taxpayers.

8.3 The income tax structure in 2012/13

One of the most noticeable characteristics of the British tax system is that it is subject to continual change. Writing about it is very much like trying to hit a moving target. This section describes the tax structure proposed in the Finance Bill 2012. It involves discussion of allowances and expenses, the rates of tax, National Insurance contributions and the treatment of married couples.

The principal Act concerning income tax is the Income and Corporation Taxes Act 1988, but certain amendments have been made in subsequent yearly Finance Acts, which are preceded by Budget statements and Finance Bills. These statutes are supplemented by case law which interprets some of the finer points. There are references to the sources at various points in this chapter.

Allowances and expenses

For the individual taxpayer, the process of income tax assessment begins with the calculation of his total income. The next stage is to calculate his taxable income, which is total income minus any allowances and expenses the individual is entitled to claim. For the purposes of our discussion it is useful to distinguish between allowances and expenses.

Allowances refer to income that is tax-free regardless of the individual's pattern of expenditure or the source of his income. They therefore include the personal allowances shown in Table 8.1.

Table 8.1   Allowances against gross income in 2012/13

	£
Personal allowance	8,105*
Personal allowance, age 65-74	10,500*
Personal allowance, age 75 and over	10,660*
Married couple's allowance (born before 6 April 1935)	7,705
Income limit for age-related allowances	25,400
Blind person's allowance	2,100

* From 2010/11 the personal allowance is reduced by £1 for every £2 income exceeds £100,000, irrespective of age.

These were originally granted in an attempt to reduce taxable income by the extent that an individual had his income pre-empted by responsibilities like a wife or children. It would appear to enhance equity if tax was thus based more closely on disposable income rather than total income. Also, the allowances act as a zero-rate band of income which takes large numbers of potential taxpayers out of the 'tax net' as well as contributing to the progressivity of the tax (see Sections 2.2 and 5.5).

The main personal allowances are required to be increased annually in line with the increase in the retail prices index for the previous year. Despite these provisions for indexation, lower increases can be made, of course, provided Parliament approves.

The personal allowance is available to taxpayers resident in the UK, though it is restricted or withdrawn altogether for those with 'adjusted net income' exceeding £100,000. The married couple's allowance survived the introduction of independent taxation for married couples in 1990. However, the rate of relief was restricted to 20 per cent for 1994/95, 15 per cent from 1995/96 and 10 per cent from 1999/2000. The married couple's allowance was abolished altogether from April 2000 for couples who were both aged less than 65 on that date and from April 2009 ceased to be available for couples unless at least one spouse was born before 6 April 1935. An age-related allowance is granted instead of the ordinary personal allowance to single people aged 65 years or more. If a person reaches 65 during a year of assessment he or she is entitled to the allowance for the whole year. A higher personal allowance is available for single people aged 75 or more. An age-related married couple's allowance remains for married couples or civil partners where at least one of the spouses or civil partners is aged 75 or over. However, the age-related allowances were intended to benefit only those on modest incomes and are restricted if income exceeds a certain amount. For 2012/13 they are reduced by £1 for every £2 by which the taxpayer's income exceeds £25,400 until they are worth the same as the personal allowance for those under 65 or a minimum of £2,960 for the married couple's allowance.

In addition to the allowances, there are also some expenses which are affected by income tax. Some types of expenses may be claimed only against specific sources of income. For example, the expenses incurred in running a business cannot be deducted from an individual's employment income. More details on allowable expenses are given in Section 8.6.

The rates of tax

A significant number of simplifications have been made to income tax rates.

Before 1973 income tax was levied at a single standard rate and surtax was levied at a series of more progressive rates on higher incomes. There was also an earned income relief so that two-ninths of earned income was exempt. From 6 April 1973 the standard rate income tax and surtax were formally unified, with the standard rate becoming known as the basic rate, and surtax as higher rates of tax. In addition, the two-ninths earned income relief was abolished.

Personal income tax: the discrimination between earned and unearned income was retained by the introduction of the investment income surcharge, but this too was abolished in 1984.

An additional lower rate of tax on the first £750 of taxable income was introduced in 1978 but abolished in 1980. Furthermore, the number of higher rates of tax was reduced from nine to five in 1979, and the range of income covered by each of the remaining bands widened considerably. Finally, all the higher rates except one were abolished in 1988, leaving the UK income tax with two rates: the basic rate on the first £23,700 (in 1991/92) and one higher rate of 40 per cent on the excess. An additional lower rate of 10 per cent was introduced again at the bottom of the scale in 1992 but abolished once more in 2008. For 2012/13 the basic rate of 20 per cent applies to the first £34,370, a rate of 40 per cent applies to taxable income between £34,370 and £150,000, and 50 per cent applies to the excess.

The very long basic rate band has for a long time provided another feature consistent with simplicity. It is the appropriate rate for the majority of taxpayers.

As will become clear later, the main reason for the long band has been that it allows tax to be deducted at source very accurately from the investment income and from any second and subsequent employments of most taxpayers. All that has to be done is to set the rate at which tax is deducted from these sources of income to that appropriate to basic rate taxpayers. The only adjustments then required after the end of the tax year are those for the relatively small proportion of individuals who do not pay tax at the basic rate. There is also an advantage in having the long basic rate band plus just one higher rate in that almost all taxpayers should be aware of the marginal rate of tax they pay. This would, of course, be much harder to establish if there were a more graduated rate scale.

However, the long basic rate band has some unfortunate implications for equity between taxpayers. It means that individuals on very low incomes pay tax at a high marginal rate (20 per cent in 2012/13). It also means, of course, that the same marginal rate applies to individuals over a very wide income range. For example, in 2012/13 an individual entitled only to the single person's allowance would pay the same marginal rate of tax whether he or she earned as little as £8,105 or as much as £42,475.

The effects that the long basic rate band have on work incentives are less clear cut. As we saw in Section 4.2, it depends on the reactions of taxpayers to the marginal and average rates of tax. It seems likely, however, that the individuals who are just over the threshold are subject to considerable disincentives. At this level the marginal rate is very high (discouraging work), while the average rate is low (also discouraging work). There might also be disincentive effects where the marginal rate increases from the basic to the higher rate (20 to 40 per cent in 2012/13). Nevertheless, this is insufficient evidence for us to conclude that the overall effects of the tax structure are adverse to work effort.

The taxation of investment income

Although, as already stated, the investment income surcharge was abolished in 1984, several arguments have been used to justify tax discrimination against unearned rather than earned income. One of the main reasons is that it is possible that income from employment is generally less reliable than income from investment. It might be argued that earnings arise from a 'wasting asset' - a human being - and will cease when that individual retires or dies. Furthermore, it has been argued that the wage or salary may fluctuate more than, say, an investment in gilt-edged security. The fluctuations may arise either from the individual falling ill, becoming pregnant or whatever, or from the nature of the job itself. The argument is, of course, limited by the fact that a proportion of investment income arises from risky ventures, or assets with values related to the rate of interest.

A second justification for the favourable treatment of earned income is that there are expenses incurred in obtaining it which are greater than those incurred in obtaining investment income. As we shall see shortly, this argument is especially relevant when National Insurance contributions are considered. A further aspect is that expenses incurred in acquiring the education and skills needed to carry out a particular occupation are not taken into account in assessing tax liability.

A third argument for an extra charge on investment income is that the ownership of the capital from which it is derived confers benefits over and above the pecuniary return. These benefits, such as added security, independence and the ability to 'dis-save', are discussed at greater length in Sections 5.3 and 10.7 and will not be repeated here. The justification for the additional levy is that these extra benefits indicate a greater taxable capacity than that measured by the investment income alone.

A fourth argument, perhaps the strongest politically, is that earnings represent the return to current toil, whereas investment income represents the return to either past toil or inherited wealth.

There are also arguments against a heavier levy on investment income. The most important is that it may discourage saving. Such discrimination would be in addition to any 'double taxation of saving' feature of an income tax such as was noted in Section 4.4.

However, the British income tax system has a number of built-in incentives for saving. These include various forms of tax relief for pensions, and specific savings arrangements such as individual savings accounts (ISAs).

As we shall see in Chapter 10, the tax systems in many other countries have been based on the conclusion that there are benefits from capital over and above the income derived from it. The difference is that, in these countries, the extra benefits have been taxed by a wealth tax imposed directly on the capital, rather than adding an extra charge to an investment income which, up to 1984, had been the policy pursued in the UK. It is argued in Chapter 10 that the same policy should be considered for the UK.

Taxation and marriage

The tax treatment of married couples is an aspect of the tax system which has received a great deal of attention in recent years. In 1980, the government published a Green Paper, The Taxation of Husband and Wife, which discussed a range of possible alternatives to the existing system. The subject was further discussed in the 1986 Green Paper *Reform of Personal Taxation*, and the current system was changed in 1990.

The tax treatment of married couples, as opposed to single people and those cohabiting, can be analysed in terms of the principles discussed in Chapters 3, 4 and 5. Clearly, within reasonable bounds, it is unlikely that the differential tax treatments have serious effects on efficiency, given the many other relevant considerations. As Frank McKinney Hubbard put it, 'nobody works so hard for his money as the man who marries it'. Nevertheless, Alm and Whittington (1995) found evidence that some individuals are influenced by taxation in their marriage decisions. Regarding incentives, we have already seen in Chapter 4 that, unlike the position for men, a change in the net wage has a large and positive effect on the number of hours of paid employment which married women undertake. Indeed the structure of allowances in the UK has in the past been used to try to influence the female labour supply. For instance, during the Second World War in 1942 the wife's earned income allowance was increased to the level of the single person's allowance, specifically to encourage married women to remain in employment in the public interest.

However, perhaps the area that has aroused most comment concerns equity. One approach might be that the tax system should not discriminate between taxpayers just because they are married. In other words, there should be no tax advantage or disadvantage to marriage. Another approach is that there should be no discrimination between married couples with the same income. These two approaches lead to two different possibilities - taxation on an individual basis and taxation on an aggregation basis.

On the individual basis everyone is taxed as if he or she were single. On the aggregation, or 'unit', basis the income of the family is added together and then subject to tax, after appropriate allowances, as if the family were one unit.

The advantage of the individual basis of taxation is that it would be neutral with respect to marriage, and there would be no tax advantages or disadvantages associated with getting married or, for that matter, with getting divorced. Such a system also allows complete privacy and independence for each spouse. Furthermore, as compared to a pure aggregation system, the individual basis might provide work incentives because any additional earnings of either spouse would not be subject to the marginal rates of tax which might apply to their combined incomes.

However, the arguments against the individual basis are obviously those which largely support some form of aggregation. It can easily be argued that marriage alters taxable capacity. It could be asserted that, if the wife (or husband) does not have paid employment, the remaining breadwinner has a dependant and therefore a lower taxable capacity. On the other hand, there may be economic benefits, inasmuch as a married couple living together can live more cheaply than two single adults can (though not if the latter cohabit!). In addition marriage will normally generate non-pecuniary income. For example, when a bachelor employs housekeeping and similar services, the transaction goes through the market and so is subject to tax. In marriage, the implicit income from a housewife's (and a husband's) services is not taxed. Therefore, so the argument runs, marriage confers a greater taxable capacity which, on equity grounds, should be taxed.

In principle one could extend the argument even further, though the practical implications are somewhat worrying. One of A.P. Herbert's famous cases (Herbert, 1966) comes to mind where marriage, as a popular commodity, might have the potential to raise considerable revenue if it were treated as a taxable luxury:

> Marriages, like intoxicating liquors, might be graded according to their strength; and the most passionate, happy, or fruitful couples could be made to pay more than the lukewarm or miserable!

However far this is taken, it seems reasonable to conclude that marriage changes taxpayers' circumstances, and the case for the individual basis of taxation is limited by the extent that it does.

The problem is that immediately the tax system is altered to take account of marriage, it necessarily ceases to be neutral with respect to marriage. For example, take an extreme form of the aggregation principle where husband and wife are treated as a single person. This would mean a tax penalty on marriage. The penalty would be greater the more progressive the tax system, since the couple's aggregated income would be pushed into higher rate bands. For the same reason, the penalty would be greater the more equal the partners' income.

The aggregation basis can, of course, be modified to reduce this penalty, or to provide some tax advantage to marriage. One method is the quotient system under which one-half of the aggregated income of the couple is allocated to each spouse, who is then taxed as a single person. One example is the French quotient familial system under which the incomes of the married couple, dependent children and certain close relatives are all aggregated - with children counting as a half for this purpose. The tax liability on a single part is then multiplied by the number of parts to give the total amount of tax due.

As an example of the effects of the quotient system, a couple with a combined income of £20,000 would be taxed as two individuals each receiving £10,000. If the two partners actually received the same income, suc h a system would be neutral with respect to marriage. However, if, as is more likely, they received different amounts, there might be a tax advantage to marriage. This advantage would be greater the greater the difference in income and the more progressive the tax system.

This result hardly seems equitable. For instance, take two couples whose joint incomes are both £20,000. With couple A, the total is earned by the husband while the wife remains at home. With couple B, both spouses earn £10,000. Couple A gain the imputed income from the wife's work around the home and avoid the costs of earning income (such as travel to and from work) that would arise if the wife did take paid employment. Yet both couples would pay the same amount of tax under the quotient system. Furthermore, there is an impediment for the wife in couple A to take paid employment, since she would face the couple's highest marginal tax rate from the beginning.

Further problems arise in other areas. For example, under a system of independent taxation, investment income can be transferred between spouses to reduce tax liability (although it has been suggested that British husbands are far too mean to consider such a possibility!). Other considerations include children, single parent families, other dependants and the treatment of the elderly. Nevertheless, even from this brief discussion, it can be seen that, whichever basis of taxation is employed, some anomalies will arise and the best arrangement depends on social preferences as to which anomalies are disliked the most.

As already indicated, the tax treatment of marriage in the UK has been reformed. When income tax was first introduced in the UK in 1799 a married man was responsible for declaring and accounting for his wife's income. In 1806 this arrangement was taken one stage further in that the 'profits' of a married woman were then deemed to be the 'profits' of her husband. The principle that the income of husband and wife should be aggregated has been reviewed on a number of occasions since that time. For instance, both the Royal Commission on the Income Tax in 1920 and the Royal Commission on the Taxation of Profits and Income in 1954 reported in favour of the aggregation rule. Furthermore the Green Paper The Taxation of Husband and Wife (1980, para. 26) concluded that the 'mere fact of antiquity does not mean that, taken as a whole, the system is necessarily out of date or incapable of catering for society as it is today'. It then went on to describe how the current arrangements gave the married woman 'a considerable degree of independence - at least as far as her earned income is concerned'. However this did not appear to be the general view in the 1980s, and a new system was finally introduced in 1990.

The new system is far closer to the independent basis of assessment. Since April 1990 both husband and wife have been taxed independently on all their income (and capital gains) and a married man is no longer responsible for his wife's tax affairs. There is a personal allowance available to everyone, male or female, married or single, which can be set against all forms of income.

A further change to reduce the tax penalties of marriage involved mortgage interest. Under the old system there was an anomaly in that two individuals buying their home together qualified for mortgage interest relief of up to £30,000 of loan if they were married, but up to £30,000 each if they were not. From 1988 the £30,000 limit applied to the residence rather than to the purchasers, however many of them there were. At the time it was suggested that the only remaining benefit of living in sin was the sin! However mortgage interest relief was withdrawn completely from April 2000.

National Insurance contributions

It is appropriate to treat National Insurance contributions under the general heading of taxation because most types are compulsory and are not always related to entitlement to National Insurance benefits. For example, Class 4 contributions do not attract any benefit at all. Another example was the extra levy imposed on employers' wage bills by the National Insurance Surcharge Act 1976. Although this levy has since been abolished, it was imposed under the name of National Insurance, and was a tax in every other sense (in this case a 'payroll tax') and not a contribution to the National Insurance Fund. The Meade Committee (1978, p. 373) had little doubt that 'National Insurance contributions are essentially a form of tax'. This is a view shared by many commentators; and Dilnot *et al.* (1984, p. 30) concluded that 'social insurance is not insurance, but it is inescapably social'.

The integration of income tax and National Insurance contributions

The integration of tax and National Insurance contributions has been discussed for many years and relatively recently by Adam and Loutzenhiser (2007). It has been suggested for several reasons. It is fairly easy to argue that National Insurance contributions are a tax by any other name. Taking the social security system as a whole the relationship between contributions paid and benefits received is often not a strong one since lack of entitlement to National Insurance benefits does not disqualify anyone from qualifying for other benefits such as Family Credit and Income Support. The 'National Insurance Fund' is not a reservoir of accumulated contributions from which future claims will be met. As Aneurin Bevan, principal architect of the National Health Service, apparently used to say: 'I'll let you into a secret. There ain't no Fund'. Rather the 'Fund' is run on a 'pay-as-you-go' basis and what tomorrow's claimants will get will depend on what tomorrow's taxpayers will let them have.

Even on more immediate considerations, the relationship between contributions and benefits is often not a direct one. For example, it has already been pointed out that Class 4 contributions do not attract any benefit at all.

There are also differences in the tax base. For example, some types of expenditure, such as employee contributions to approved pension schemes, may be deducted for the purposes of income tax but not National Insurance contributions. Other items, such as many benefits in kind, are subject to income tax but not National Insurance contributions. It has been suggested, for example by Atkinson *et al.* (1990), that the National Insurance tax base should be extended to include fringe benefits and that the employees' upper earnings limit be abolished, but full integration would appear a more logical step.

It has also been pointed out that National Insurance contributions are a tax on employment. Regardless of any arguments of the sort discussed above, that there may be a case for taxing investment income more heavily than earned income, it is earned income that has faced the higher rates since the abolition of the investment income surcharge in 1984.

The administration of the two levies also appears to have scope for some rationalisation. By far the largest type of contribution is Class 1, which relates to employees and is paid by both the employees and their employers. It is, however, withheld at source from salaries and wages and the Revenue is responsible for collecting it as well as income tax. In 2010/11 the Revenue collected £100 billion in contributions mainly from employees and employers on behalf of the Department of Social Security. In the same year the Revenue collected about £151 million in income tax, most of it from employees through the PAYE machinery. The two 'taxes' are normally paid by the same taxpayers, and collected by the same revenue service, yet they are administered on a completely different basis: income tax is subject to the cumulative PAYE machinery, National Insurance contributions to a non-cumulative arrangement. So far as administrative costs are concerned, about 10,000 civil servants are involved (Dilnot *et al.*, 1984, Ch. 1).

The integration of income tax and National Insurance contributions has also been supported on the grounds that it would encourage small businesses since the present 'administrative burden arising from the differing bases for income tax and National Insurance contributions seems . . . to be out of all proportion to any perceived benefits derived from separate taxation' (Institute of Chartered Accountants in England and Wales, 1986, para. 22).

Possibly it could be argued that taxpayers might be more willing to pay taxes which are called contributions than they are to pay taxes which are called taxes. Also the government believes that 'it is right to retain a link between contributions paid in and benefits received' (Reform of Social Security: Programme for Action, 1986). Yet it is clear that the link is a feeble one, and often no stronger for individuals than is the link between income tax and public expenditure generally. Perhaps income tax should be merged into National Insurance contributions and the result called the social contribution or national community charge!

Further developments

Possibly in response to such arguments, the 1999 Budget included significant changes to National Insurance contributions to bring the system into closer alignment with income tax. Such changes have continued from time to time, and a new initiative to consider further integration was announced in the 2011 Budget.

Currently there are four classes of National Insurance contribution. Class 1 relates to employees, Classes 2 and 4 to the self-employed, and Class 3 is voluntary. The Class 1 contribution is paid partly by the employee and partly by the employer. Employees pay a contribution based on their earnings between the 'lower earnings limit' and the 'upper earnings limit'. These limits were to be increased substantially but that proposal has been modified. The lower earnings limit is £107 from April 2012, and the upper earnings limit is £817 a week but 2 per cent is also levied on the excess. Also, the employer's National Insurance contributions on benefits in kind is being extended to cover not just cars and fuel but other benefits which are already subject to income tax. Class 2 contributions are levied at a flat rate of £2.65 per week on the self-employed earning more than £7,605 (in 2012/13). The self-employed are also liable to Class 4 contributions, which are related to the level of their profits. The rate of Class 3 (voluntary) contributions was £13.25 a week in 2012/13.

8.4 Capital gains tax

It is appropriate to deal with capital gains at this point because most forms of capital gains have much the same characteristics as income. Several types of capital gain are really income in disguise. For example, the value of National Savings Certificates is increased during their life as a method of paying interest. Similar forms of 'income' include the increase in value of bonds, arising from the approach of the date of redemption, and the capital appreciation of all kinds of securities resulting from ploughing back profits. To consider other types of capital gain, we should examine carefully what we mean by 'income'.

The precise definition of income has been the subject of considerable debate. Haig (1921), for example, gave the following definition: 'income is the money value of the net accretion to economic power between two points of time'. Another is the comprehensive definition of income by Henry Simons (1938): 'Personal income may be defined as the algebraic sum of (a) the market value of rights exercised in consumption and (b) the change in the value of the store of property rights between the beginning and end of the period in question'. Hicks' (1974) definition took income as the 'maximum amount of money which the individual can spend this week, and still be able to spend the same amount in real terms in each ensuing week'.

The definition that seems to be increasingly accepted is that of total accretion, that is the accrual of wealth. This includes as income an individual's spending in a given period, plus any changes in his net wealth. For example, if an individual spent £2,500 in one year, and the real value of his assets increased by £500, his income by this definition would be £3,000 in that year.

Many more types of capital gain may be considered as income. This definition includes inheritances, gifts, winnings from gambling and any 'windfall' gains. In principle, all these items might be considered as income for tax purposes.

The case for taxing capital gains can now be summarised under the twin headings of equity and efficiency. On equity grounds, if capital gains are equivalent to income, they should equally be subject to tax (see Chapter 5). The equity argument is reinforced as capital gains accrue unevenly among the population. Gains can only accrue to owners of assets and, as we shall see in Section 10.2, wealth is unevenly distributed in the United Kingdom.

The efficiency argument has two main aspects. The first is that, as many types of income can be converted into capital gains, to exempt the latter from tax would encourage such conversion. This might involve economic costs for the individuals taking such action and economic costs for the Revenue in trying to prevent them. The second, and perhaps more important aspect, is that a tax on capital gains reduces the attraction of investment in 'non-productive' assets such as antiques, coins, paintings, precious stones and stamps, which are bought because of anticipated increases in their value, rather than for any productive purpose.

So, in theory at least, there is a straightforward case for treating all capital gains as income. Needless to say, there are many practical difficulties.

Practical problems

The first and most obvious difficulty concerns capital gains, which arise only through increases in the price level. Such nominal gains do not, of course, increase an individual's real spending power and should not in principle be counted as income. However, there are other considerations which are discussed in Chapter 5, and there is also the practical problem of selecting an appropriate index number to take account of inflation.

A second problem is that, in principle, capital gains tax should be levied on an accruals basis. In practice this would involve the valuation of capital assets each year, so imposing a considerable administrative burden. It would also involve the risk that individuals might be forced to liquidate assets in order to pay the tax.

Capital gains tax in Britain avoids these problems because it is imposed on a realisation basis. But this in turn poses difficulties. First of all, asset-holders may be 'locked in', in the sense that they have an incentive to postpone payment of the tax by not realising the asset. Second, because assets are realised in uneven lumps, it is difficult to make the tax progressive. To do so would require complex averaging provisions, as otherwise there would be an incentive to realise assets in an even flow, which may be economically inefficient. This difficulty is aggravated because an individual's capital gains, whether realised or not, occur irregularly.

Administration is another major problem. Even with the realisation basis, a valuation is sometimes required both when an asset is bought, and when it is sold. For some types of assets, such as shares quoted on the Stock Exchange, valuation is relatively simple. For other types of assets, such as unquoted shares, it can be very much harder.

Capital gains tax in the UK

Although there had been previous attempts to tax certain types of capital gains, especially from land, the systematic taxation of gains did not begin until 1962. In that year a tax on short-term gains was introduced. In 1965 a more comprehensive capital gains tax came into operation. The tax is levied on a wide range of assets, but there are several exemptions, including a taxpayer's only or main residence, motor vehicles and gambling winnings. The justification for exempting the last of these was that, as there is no capital asset, there cannot be a capital gain. There is also an individual annual allowance (£10,600 in 2011/12 and in 2012/13).

In its early years, capital gains tax was subject to a separate rate of tax, which was 30 per cent from 1965 to 1988. However, the argument that capital gains are a form of income and should be taxed accordingly eventually prevailed. In his 1988 Budget speech (Hansard, 15 March 1988, col. 1005) the Chancellor of the Exchequer stated:

> In principle, there is little economic difference between income and capital gains, and many people effectively have the option of choosing to a significant extent which to receive. And in so far as there is a difference, it is by no means clear why one should be taxed more heavily than the other. Taxing them at different rates distorts investment decisions and inevitably creates a major tax avoidance industry. Moreover, at present, with capital gains taxed at 30 per cent for everybody, higher rate taxpayers face a lower – sometimes much lower – rate of tax on gains than on investment income, while basic rate taxpayers face a higher rate of tax on gains than on income. This contrast is hard to justify.

From 1988/89 onwards the rates of capital gains tax were brought into line with those of income tax so that capital gains tax was charged at the taxpayer's highest income tax rate. Nevertheless capital gains were still treated more favourably than other forms of income and only part of this can be attributed to the differences described earlier. As Robinson (1989) has pointed out, capital gains tax is payable in arrears, deferred on gifts, gives relief on retirement and exemptions on death. Furthermore after years of criticism of the inequitable affects of inflation on capital gains (see section 5.7) the government brought in a system of indexation based on the Retail Prices Index. This 'indexation allowance' gave relief for inflation between 1982 and 1998. From 1998 taper relief was introduced which reduced the amount of the gain according to the length of time the asset had been owned.

However in 2008 both taper relief and indexation allowance were withdrawn and the rate of capital gains tax was changed from a person's top rate of income tax to a flat rate of 18 per cent. There were both winners and losers as a result of this change and after strong lobbying an entrepreneurs' relief was also introduced in 2008. This applied where, subject to certain restrictions, all or part of a business is sold and can reduce the effective rate of tax on some gains to 10 per cent. In 2010 a new rate of 28 per cent was introduced for capital gains of individuals with total taxable gains and income exceeding the upper limit of the basic rate band. Capital gains accruing to companies are also taxed, though companies do not pay capital tax but corporation tax on their gains (see Section 12.4).

Although there have been several different ways of taxing a chargeable gain, the calculation of the gain itself has remained much the same. As one might expect, this is basically the sale proceeds less the purchase cost. One way in which the gain may work out to be smaller than at first expected is due to the sensible treatment of expenses. Those paid at acquisition are added to the original costs; those paid at disposal are deducted from the proceeds. This is illustrated below:

	2003 disposal price	2,000
	2003 cost of sale	200
	2003 net proceeds	1,800
1983 purchase price	1,500	
1983 costs of acquisition	150	
1983 total cost		1,650
	Gain	150

8.5 Wages, salaries and Pay-As-You-Earn

The United Kingdom's Pay-As-You-Earn (PAYE) mechanism for withholding tax from wages and salaries is unique, though a somewhat similar system was introduced in Ireland in 1960. The system is unique because it is capable of withholding tax extremely accurately. It is also unusual in that it requires very little co-operation on the part of taxpayers to work efficiently. This is because nearly all the work is done by employers and HM Revenue and Customs. However, before we examine the system in detail and discuss its advantages and disadvantages, we shall look at the reasons for its introduction.

PAYE was introduced in an attempt to overcome many of the difficulties of assessment and collection that arose during the Second World War. At that time the standard rate of income tax was raised to ten shillings in the pound (50 per cent) and the value of allowances reduced. The result was that large numbers of people were brought into the tax net who were unused to paying income tax especially at high rates. In fact, the number o f taxpayers rose from 4 million in 1938/39 to 12 million in 1943/44 (Inland Revenue, 1976, p. 21).

Up to 1940, most employees who paid tax did so in two equal instalments each year. This soon proved highly unsatisfactory, especially for those paid weekly. Therefore, in 1940 a new system was introduced which spread the payments of tax over periods of six months. For example, the tax to be charged on wages earned between 6 April and 5 October was withheld from the wages of the six months commencing the following February.

The collection of tax in arrears caused many difficulties. There were many cases of hardship, especially in industries where earnings fluctuated seasonally. This meant that tax due on high wages earned in favourable periods was frequently withheld from lower wages received in other periods. Similar hardship often arose when an individual moved to a lower paid job.

As the war progressed there was increasing pressure for a system in which the amount of tax withheld in any pay period was based on the income received in that period. The Inland Revenue said that it could not be done (Barr *et al.*, 1977, pp.

23 and 24). However, pressure continued to increase, much encouraged by the fact that both Canada and the United States had introduced 'Pay-as-you-go' methods of withholding. Finally, the Inland Revenue relented, and in 1944 the Pay-As-You-Earn mechanism (widely known at the time as Pay-All-You-Earn) was introduced.

The operation of PAYE

The difference between the British system and those introduced in North America is that the former is operated on a cumulative basis, while the latter are run on a non-cumulative basis. Cumulation simply means that a taxpayer's pay and allowances are accumulated throughout the tax year so that the amount withheld in any one period is dependent on the income received throughout the tax year up to and including the current period. On the other hand, a non-cumulative system treats each pay period separately. Consequently, a cumulative system is capable of withholding the correct amount of tax throughout the year and can payout a tax rebate when it falls due, rather than after the end of the tax year.

With a progressive income tax, a non-cumulative withholding system cannot achieve these results if taxpayers' incomes or allowances change or fluctuate during the tax year. The reason is that, since each pay period is treated in isolation, taxpayers are often pushed into higher tax brackets than would be appropriate if the position over the whole year were considered, and consequently too much tax is withheld.

The difference between the two systems is best illustrated by an example. Suppose that the basic rate of tax is 25 per cent. Suppose also that the individual in the example has total allowances of £2,080 for the year in question, and that his income varies from week to week. We shall now examine the workings of first a pure cumulative withholding system, and then a non-cumulative system using these figures.

Cumulative system

The effect of cumulation is to divide the taxpayer's allowances by the number of pay periods (say 52) and then cumulate them as the year progresses. In this example, the allowances of 'free pay' accumulate at the rate of £40 per week (illustrated by column 4 in Table 8.2). The cumulative free pay is then deducted from cumulative pay to date (column 3) to give cumulative taxable pay (column 5). Cumulative tax due is then calculated as 25 per cent of cumulative taxable pay, and the actual tax due is the difference between cumulative tax due and the tax already withheld.

Thus in week 1 of the tax year, the individual earns £160 and has free pay of £40, leaving £120 of taxable pay. The tax due on £120 is £30. Similarly in week 2, when the individual's pay rises to £200 and cumulative free pay rises to £80, the cumulative tax due becomes £70. However, £30 has already been withheld in the previous week so the final liability in week 2 is £40. Now suppose that in week 3 the individual's income falls to nothing. Free pay continues to accumulate and reaches

£120 in week 3, which means that cumulative tax due falls to £60. However, £70 has already been paid in tax, so the individual should, in principle, receive a rebate for the difference that week. However, this feature has been restricted in the UK system. From 5 July 1982 a taxpayer who becomes unemployed will not normally receive any rebate due until after either he ceases to claim unemployment benefit or Income Support, or the end of the tax year. In addition, from 1982, rebates cannot usually be paid while a person is on strike.

Table 8.2 An example of cumulation

(1) Week	(2) Gross pay	(3) Cumulative pay to date	(4) Cumulative free pay	(5) Cumulative taxable pay (col 3-col 4)	(6) Cumulative tax due (25% of col 5)	(7) Actual tax due
	£	£	£	£	£	£
1	160	160	40	120	30	30
2	200	360	80	280	70	40
3	0	360	120	240	60	-10

Table 8.3 An example of non-cumulative withholding

Week	Gross pay	Free pay	Taxable pay	Tax due
1	160	40	120	30
2	200	40	160	40
3	0	40	0	0

Non-cumulative system

It can be seen that with a cumulative system the correct amount of tax should be withheld each period. This is not the case with a non-cumulative system. If the same example is followed through in Table 8.3, the allowances are again divided between the number of pay periods, but are not accumulated. In the first two weeks the results are the same in both cases, but in week 3 the individual has not used up his full allowances.

There is no mechanism whereby the excess tax can be repaid during the tax year, and so by week 3 the non-cumulative system has withheld £10 too much. If, instead of using a single basic rate of tax in the example, a series of rates had been used, the withholding would have been even more excessive. The reason is that, in the high income weeks, the individual would be pushed into higher brackets than would be appropriate to his circumstances if the year were taken as a whole. It is true that with a non-cumulative system the excess tax withheld would eventually be repaid, but this would have to be after the taxpayer's final liability had been calculated. This could not be done before the end of the tax year, and might be done well after that date.

The PAYE code number

Having described the principle of cumulation, it is now worth describing how the system is operated in practice. The first stage of the assessment process is that the taxpayer provides details of his personal circumstances 'to the Revenue by completing a tax return. Most employees are not required to complete a return each year and, indeed, many go for several years without seeing one. As long as a taxpayer's circumstances do not change, the PAYE system makes an annual return unnecessary.

The allowances that the employee is entitled to claim are then translated into a code number. For example, a person entitled only to the personal allowance (£8,105 in 2012/13) would be given the code 810L. The numerical part of the code is calculated by adding up the taxpayer's entitlement to allowances and other allowable deductions and ignoring the last digit. The figure 810 therefore represents a band of allowances £10 wide. The result is that PAYE does not withhold tax with perfect precision but, as any advantage is given to the taxpayer, the system tends to withhold marginally too little. The suffix L represents the personal allowance and different suffixes apply to other circumstances.

The next stage is to send a 'Notice of Coding' to the taxpayer. This shows the code number and how it was calculated so that the taxpayer can check the Revenue's figures. If the taxpayer thinks they are wrong, he or she may appeal. The taxpayer is also warned to inform the tax office of any change in personal circumstances which may subsequently affect his or her code, and not to wait for a tax return.

The taxpayer's code number is then sent to the employer. Although the code is determined by the taxpayer's allowances, it does not disclose to the employer details of the employee's personal circumstances. The Revenue also supplies the employer with the tax tables needed to calculate the correct amount of tax to withhold.

At the end of the tax year (5 April) every employer is required to send to the tax office a list of his employees, together with details of their pay and tax withheld. The figures for each individual are then checked. Provided that the code number has been fixed correctly, and the PAYE system operated properly, no further adjustment should be necessary.

The advantages of PAYE

The most important advantage of a cumulative PAYE system is that tax is withheld very accurately from employment   income. This means that it is not necessary to make an end-of-year adjustment (involving either a further tax demand or a rebate) to most employees' tax payments. It also means that the majority of employees do not have to complete a tax return every year. In fact, about two-thirds of taxpayers are not sent a tax return in anyone year, and a large proportion of these taxpayers will not receive a return for periods of several years.

PAYE also has a number of other advantages. When a taxpayer's entitlement to allowances increases during the tax year, the code can be increased so that the benefit is received at once. (Note that an increase in the code number results in a decrease in the tax withheld.) If the taxpayer becomes entitled to a tax rebate, this also means that it can be paid during the current tax year, rather than after the end of the year.

However, it should be noted that, if the taxpayer's entitlement to allowances decreases, the code is not reduced in the same way. If it were, the extra tax (that should have been withheld week by week since the beginning of the tax year) would be withheld all in one go. This may mean hardship, and so the normal procedure is to reduce the code by the appropriate amount, but to operate it on the non-cumulative basis. This usually means that some tax liability is still outstanding at the end of the year, but less than would be the case if no action at all were taken.

Another advantage of PAYE is that it can be used to collect tax in respect of some forms of income not subject to withholding at source. Common examples are benefit from company cars and interest from some types of National Savings where the interest is taxable but the tax is not withheld at source. The method used, known as 'coding out', is to reduce the taxpayer's code number sufficiently to allow the tax liability on these other sources of income to be withheld from his employment income. It is usually not necessary to make a separate assessment on the non-PAYE sources of income if it is 'coded out' but clearly this method is unlikely to be accurate where large amounts of non-PAYE income are received, or where the income is unpredictable or fluctuating.

There is also a technique which is sometimes known as 'coding in'. This is used where a taxpayer has, for some reason, paid insufficient tax on his earnings at the end of the year. Instead of demanding immediate payment, Revenue and Customs may recover the outstanding tax slowly (and less painfully) over later years by reducing the taxpayer's code number by the appropriate amount.

The disadvantages of PAYE

Given that the essential advantage of cumulative withholding is accuracy, the essential disadvantages arise from the need to maintain that accuracy in different circumstances. The disadvantages themselves fall into two categories. The first covers the difficulties in maintaining the cumulative process. The second is the need to design other aspects of the system to avoid large numbers of end-of-year adjustments.

The difficulty in maintaining cumulation occurs when an employee changes his job. There are two aspects to this: first, it is necessary to ensure that the new employer has the information to continue the cumulative process; second, the employee's file must be transferred to a new tax district. This is necessary because a key feature of PAYE is that the employee's tax papers are filed with reference to the current employer, and so a new employer often means a new tax district.

The procedure for dealing with a change of employment is as follows. When an employee leaves his job, his employer issues a tripartite form (a P.45) which shows the employee's code number, gross pay, and tax paid to date. Part 1 of the P.45 is sent to the individual's original tax district, and parts 2 and 3 are given to the employee to pass on to the new employer. Part 2 of the form is retained by the new employer as an authorisation to withhold tax, and part 3 is sent to the new tax district. The second tax district then contacts the first, and the employee's file is forwarded on.

The P.45 procedure has a number of drawbacks. The first is the amount of work involved. In tax districts dealing with PAYE (which is most districts), at least 10 per cent of the districts' total staff resources can be employed on this work alone. A second drawback is that the complexity of the process means that parts of the P.45 are often lost or mislaid or issued well after the employee has left his original job. A third possible drawback (which may lead to employees suppressing their P.45s) is that the system may be considered to infringe on an individual's privacy, since the new employer can easily establish how much the new employee has earned in the previous job during the tax year.

In certain circumstances, it is not practical to operate the cumulative element of PAYE accurately. This occurs, for example, with higher rate taxpayers who have more than one job. The problem is that if each job were treated separately, PAYE would tend to withhold too little tax. The reason is that too much income would be subject to tax at the basic rate, and too little at higher rates. The problem is dealt with by setting the taxpayers' allowances against one job (or possibly more than one) and allocating a D code prefix to any further jobs. D codes are operated on a non-cumulative basis and, when a D code is issued, the employer must withhold tax at the appropriate rate on all payments to the employee.

Although the D code system improves the accuracy of PAYE in these circumstances, errors remain because of the non-cumulative element. For instance, if the taxpayer's income from his main job changes, the D code in force on second and subsequent jobs may cease to be appropriate and an end-of-year adjustment becomes necessary.

The D code system therefore provides an example of the difficulties involved in maintaining cumulation. It also shows why PAYE requires a long basic rate band to work efficiently. With such a band, straightforward withholding procedures can be used for many types of incomes; without it, withholding could not operate with the accuracy it does for most taxpayers, and many more end-of-year adjustments would be required.

We have seen that the cumulative element of PAYE avoids the need for most taxpayers to complete a return every year. This, however, has its disadvantages and can easily lead to the wrong amount of tax being paid. If an individual does not have to sign a statement of income each year, it is easy for him to 'forget' about casual earnings and occasional receipts. It is also possible that, without an annual return, taxpayers may not be aware of their entitlement to certain allowances and expenses, nor that it is up to them to claim.

There is a further concern with a system that takes tax administration largely out of the hands of most taxpayers, in that there is no pressing reason why they need to understand how the system works. For instance, a survey set up for the Royal Commission on the Taxation of Profits and Income (1954) found that: 'Only 3 to 5 per cent of the male sample (perhaps less for females) knew in any detail how they were affected by income tax' (Appendix 1, para. 5). It is possible that these figures have increased following the simplifications described above, but it is unlikely that they have changed dramatically because the basic system remains largely unchanged.

It could be argued that a system which demands little, if anything, from taxpayers (except, of course, their money) is the simplest possible for most individuals. However, it can lead to difficulties when something affecting a person's tax affairs changes and the taxpayer is then forced to deal with a system with which he or she is largely unfamiliar. It can also lead to extra administration and compliance costs arising from enquiries made of Revenue and Customs and others, not because of maladministration, but because taxpayers simply do not understand the system.

This point was examined by James *et al.* (1987) with particular reference to taxpaying pensioners. For instance, oh the basis of a survey carried out with the assistance of the Inland Revenue, as it was then, they found that of those pensioners who actually receive tax returns perhaps up to 80 or 90 per cent do not complete them correctly. As they put it:

> A more general picture seemed to emerge ... Without trying to be dramatic, a stylised description of many, if not most, taxpaying pensioners on receipt of a return might run something like the following. The taxpayer ignores the explanatory notes which are issued with each return, reads the return from beginning to end, needs to make entries on only two or three of the many sections, and still gets it wrong. (James *et al.*, 1987, p.9)

There may be a case for involving taxpayers a little more with their tax affairs, and we shall return to the issue in the discussion of self-assessment in the following chapter.

8.6 Self-employment income

The taxation of self-employment income differs from the taxation of employment income in a number of ways, of which one of the most important is the tax treatment of expenses.

For the self-employed, S74 of the Taxes Act 1988 provides that expenses are only deductible if they are incurred *wholly and exclusively* for the purposes of the trade, profession or vocation. In practice, the calculation of taxable income begins with the net profit for accounting purposes. Thus, the following would normally not have been deducted as expenses, nor should they be for tax purposes: capital items, taxation on profits and appropriations of profit (like drawings or partnership profit sharings). As far as the calculation of taxable income for the self-employed s concerned, the statutory and case rules are much the same as for companies. These can be found in Section 12.4. Here we will examine some other cases relating particularly to individual taxpayers, though some of them have relevance for corporations.

Case law has clarified what a 'trade' is. For example, *C.I.R. v. Rutledge* (14 TC 490) concerned a businessman who bought a million rolls of toilet paper in Berlin, and sold them in one lot on his return to England. Despite the fact that this was an isolated transaction, it was held that it was an adventure by nature of trade. This was partly because Rutledge was a businessman and partly because the goods were not normally associated with investment! As another example, in *Pickford v. Quirke* (13 TC 251) it was held that making gains from buying companies and 'asset-stripping' did constitute a trade because the taxpayer had done it four times, whereas it would not have been if done once only.

In another case, *Norman v. Golder* (26 TC 293), it was held that a sick person could not claim that doctors' bills were 'wholly and exclusively for the purposes of the trade', because they were also 'for the advantage and benefit of the taxpayer as a living human being.' Similarly, in *Bowden v. Russell and Russell* (42 TC 301) it was held that a solicitor travelling to America to attend a conference and to have a holiday could not charge his expenses against tax, because they were not exclusively for his profession. There was said to be 'duality' of purpose.

Travelling expenses on business, but not to business from one's home, are allowed. A number of cases have dealt with this (Pinson, 1986).

For employees, S198 of the Taxes Act 1988 provides that expenses are only deductible if they are incurred *wholly, exclusively and necessarily in the performance of* the duties of the employment. This makes it even clearer than for the self-employed that, for example, travelling to and from work is not allowable because it is not *in the performance of* duties. These words and the word 'necessarily' make the rules for employees much stricter than those for the self-employed.

Several expenses are not regarded by the Revenue as *necessarily* incurred. For example, in *Simpson v. Tate* (9 TC 314) it was held that a doctor could not claim subscriptions to medical societies, because keeping up to date was not necessary for the performance of duties, though it might be necessary for the *fit* performance of them. It is also clear that employees cannot in general claim expenses of tools, or clothing, unless these can be proved to be essential to the continuation of the employment. One case – *Ms Sian Williams v Revenue & Customs* [2010] UKFTT 86 (TC) – which clearly illustrates this situation and attracted considerable media attention, was that of the BBC newsreader who claimed expenses for professional clothing. It was argued on her behalf that she would be willing to read the news naked, but the BBC required her to wear clothes. Her claim failed because the clothes could be worn outside work and therefore the cost of them was not incurred wholly, necessarily and exclusively in the performance of employment duties.

However, the 1988 Taxes Act does allow deductions for certain subscriptions to professional bodies, which might be deemed to be necessary for some employees to join, e.g. architects or accountants. Furthermore, in practice, the Revenue allows academics to claim for books purchased for the purpose of teaching!

It is clearly useful for a taxpayer to try to establish that his or her income falls is treated as coming from self-employment rather than employment. The latter applies where there is a contract of service (whether written or verbal) and where the method of performance of duties is laid down by the employer. Even gifts which arise because of the employment are included; in *Cooper v. Blackiston* (5 TC 347) it was held that a vicar's receipts from an Easter offering were taxable because they arose from the vicar's job. On the other hand, it was held in *Hochstrasser v. Mayes* (38 TC 673) that compensation paid to an employee for loss on a house as a result of his being asked to move was not taxable, because it was not paid in respect of his services to the company.

Further, many benefits in kind received by employees are also taxable. For example, free or subsidised accommodation has been regarded as an emolument since S33 of the Finance Act 1977, unless the job requires the employee to live in the accommodation provided. Also, even clothing provided by an employer is an emolument; in *Wilkins v. Rogerson* (39 TC 344) it was held that the taxable benefit of a suit was its second-hand value.

As a final example, the benefit derived by an employee from the provision of a car by his employer is also taxable under a scale set out in the Finance Acts.

Having looked at the differences between the tax treatment of employment and self-employment income, it now seems appropriate to ask whether they are defensible. One strong argument for retaining the very strict rules regarding employment income, which disallow nearly all expenses, is that this is administratively efficient. Since there are so many employees, for the Revenue to have to enter into a process of checking all their claims and arguing against some of them would be very expensive. At present, many employees do not even have to fill in returns; this is partly because they would not be allowed to claim expenses and partly because the PAYE system copes with personal allowances and other complications.

In addition to this, it might be expected that employees would normally be provided with the necessary special clothing, tools of the trade, etc. In contrast, it is clearly necessary to allow expenses of various sorts to the self-employed, who provide their own workplaces, capital equipment, etc. In order to charge tax on *profit* which is the balance of revenues less expenses, it will always be necessary to have more complex returns for self-employment taxpayers. Fortunately, there are relatively few of them compared to employees. (For a more detailed statistical analysis of the differences in incomes and conditions of the employed and the self-employed, see Diamond Commission, 1979.)

Nevertheless, the Royal Commission on the Taxation of Profits and Income (*Final Report*, 1955) found that the administration of the rule regarding employment expenses 'is attended by rather wide-spread dissatisfaction' (para. 137). It recommended that the rule should be revised to the less restrictive 'all expenses reasonably incurred for the appropriate performance of the duties of the office or employment' (para. 140). This particular sentence was chosen in order to bring the arrangements for employment income closer to those for self-employed earnings.

Despite this recommendation, the difference in treatment of expenses for employees and the self-employed has not yet been reformed and the economic implications of the more generous treatment of the expenses of the self employed are analysed below.

The relative treatment of self-employed and employed taxpayers

The relatively favourable treatment of self-employed as compared to employed taxpayers for the purposes of income tax, and also National Insurance contributions, can be analysed in terms of the principles described in Part 1. In particular, there are implications for both economic efficiency and equity.

Economic efficiency suggests that it is normally inefficient for behaviour to be caused by tax considerations alone. In this case there is an artificial incentive for individuals to become self-employed even when it might be economically more efficient for them to work as employees. The Revenue, of course, also has the additional task of ensuring that taxpayers do not manipulate their employment status illegally.

In terms of equity, in so far as employees see the differential treatment as unfair, it may lead to a loss of 'tax-morale' and a reduction in the willingness of taxpayers to comply with the requirements of the tax system. An example of this was the reaction to the introduction of the community charge or 'poll tax' described in Chapter 11. Another, more related example, took place in Ireland in 1979, where 170,000 self-employed farmers faced a much lighter tax burden than that imposed on individuals in employment. The result was disturbances which led on 19 March 1979 to a one-day general strike by industrial and white collar workers which virtually closed all factories and offices and halted bus, train and airline services. The following day 150,000 workers took part in a demonstration in the centre of Dublin to protest against Irish tax policies.

Such an event is currently unlikely in the UK because, as noted in Section 8.5, many taxpayers in employment have relatively little knowledge of the UK tax system. This may be fortunate for those responsible for tax administration in the UK, but it is not a situation that will necessarily continue indefinitely.

Payment of tax

While employees are subject to withholding tax at source through the PAYE scheme described above, the self-employed pay tax directly to the Revenue. The tax is paid in two instalments on an estimated basis using the liability of the previous year. For example, for 2012/13 the instalments are payable on 31 January 2013 and 31 July 2013 and each instalment is normally half the liability for 2012/13. Any additional tax will be payable in 2014 but any overpaid tax will be refunded after the relevant calculations have been made.

Establishing employment status

Since there are advantages in being classified as self-employed rather than employed for the purposes of taxation it has been necessary to clarify the position. Essentially employment exists where there is a 'contract of service' and self-employment where there is a 'contract for services' but the issues can be complex. There has therefore been a great deal of case law, including the examples above, but areas of uncertainty remain. A number of tests have therefore been developed and HM Revenue and Customs has posted more detailed guidance on its website.

One test is the right of control or supervision. If there is a right to control how the work is done this is a feature of employment but it may not always be necessary – for example some employees such as a ship's captain may not be controlled in this way. Similarly if there is a right to control when and where the work is done this is an indication of employment. In contrast, a self-employed person is more likely to be free to decide how, when and where the work is done. A second test is personal service. If the worker has to provide the services personally that is an indication of employment. If the person can hire someone else to do the job instead that is an indication of self-employment. The provision of equipment is another test. An employee is likely to be supplied with the relevant resources to do the job, for example tools, computers and office space. A self-employed person generally provides his or her own equipment. A further test is financial risk – employees do not normally risk their own money, for example, in buying assets required for the work and meeting their running costs but self-employed people do. A similar pointer is the opportunity to profit – a person whose profit (or loss) depends on whether they can reduce overheads or improve the effectiveness of the work may well be self-employed. Employment status may also be indicated by benefits such as sick pay, holiday pay, membership of the employer's pension scheme and so on, which would not normally be available to the self-employed. A further factor is the basis of payment – an employee is likely to be paid a fixed wage or salary perhaps with additional payments such as overtime but a self-employed person is likely to be paid a fixed amount for a particular job. None of these tests (and there are some others) is conclusive. Nor can a decision be reached by simply adding up the number of factors indicating employment and the number indicating self-employment. However they can all be taken into account together with any other relevant information in establishing whether a person is working as self-employed or working as an employee in another person's business.

8.7 Administration and enforcement

Administration

Income tax administration has been subject to considerable change and this is likely to continue. One possibility is that following the shift to self assessment for taxpayers who are required to complete returns, self-assessment might be extended in the future and this issue is discussed in the following chapter. A related change has been the development of a system of tax rulings (James and Wallschutzky, 1995; Sandler, 1994). Self-assessment places the responsibility for producing accurate tax returns on the taxpayer rather than the Revenue. As the interpretation of tax law is sometimes open to dispute, a system of tax rulings becomes important. The Revenue therefore provides post-transaction rulings for non-business taxpayers where the tax treatment of a transaction is in doubt – such as in the case of an unusual transaction or one entered into in unusual circumstances.

Another important change is the move to electronic submission of tax returns. Known as 'electronic lodgement' such systems have been developed in Australia (where taxpayers lodge their returns rather than submit them) and in the United States. On the basis of overseas experience, it is clear that the potential gains of electronic lodgement are considerable for taxpayers, tax practitioners and the revenue service. These gains include much greater speed and accuracy in processing returns and lower administrative costs (James and Wallschutzky, 1993). Such computerisation also vastly increases the scope for checking taxpayers' returns with other information available (James and Wallschutzky, 1994) – a facility which might not always be welcome to taxpayers.

A related development consists of 'pre-populated' tax returns. These are tax returns produced by the revenue authority using information from third parties and other sources and are examined by Highfield (2006). Such arrangements have been used for some time – Denmark led the way by introducing such arrangements in 1988 though these originally were quite primitive since the amount of information that could be collected and processed was quite limited. However, the system was progressively enhanced during the 1990s and similar arrangements were introduced in Sweden in 1994 and Norway in 1998. As the application of technology to tax administration progressed other countries also followed. Pre-populated tax returns can contain details of most major sources of income together with the tax withheld, asset sales and purchases, specific deductions that are obtained from third party sources or calculated according to a formula, personal tax reliefs, tax credits and the calculations of tax payable or refundable. The role of the taxpayer in this process, of course, is to confirm that the information is correct and to supply any further information required.

Income tax

The administration of income tax was traditionally divided into two parts, assessment and collection. The assessment process was the responsibility of Inspectors of Taxes who are responsible for establishing each taxpayer's liability. The actual collection was then undertaken by Collectors of Taxes, who were quite separate from the Inspectors. The original reason for the separation was to prevent corruption. Indeed Johnston (1965, p. 135) reports that it was once thought 'essential to the maintenance of security that Inspectors were even forbidden to lodge in the same houses as Collectors'! However, the separation led to some confusion on the part of the public, and difficulties when the actions of a tax office and a collection office had been at variance. As a result, tax and collection offices were restructured to bring the two activities together. The general offices now consist of taxpayer services offices, also known as processing offices, which deal with the routine work relating to taxpayers' liabilities and tax district offices, which deal with the main technical and compliance work.

Enforcement

The Revenue has the power to inflict penalties for various offences and a new system of penalties was introduced in 2009. Penalties may be levied where a taxpayer does not pay enough tax as a result of an inaccurate tax return or other tax document or the taxpayer does not inform the Revenue that his or her tax assessment is too low. This system formalised a behavioural approach to penalties as the level of the penalty depends on the reason for the inaccuracy. No penalty will be levied where a mistake was made provided the taxpayer took 'reasonable care'. The definition of 'reasonable care' varies according to the person, their circumstances and abilities but normally includes keeping sufficient records to ensure tax returns are correct. The Revenue also takes the view that it is reasonable to expect a taxpayer who encounters something with which they are not familiar to establish the correct tax treatment and if they are still unsure to draw the Revenue's attention to the matter when the return or other document is submitted. The Revenue also expects to be informed promptly if the taxpayer discovers any error in a tax return or document after he or she has submitted it. For other errors there is an increasing range of penalties that may be applied as illustrated in Table 8.4. Thus the possible level of penalty depends on whether the error was considered to be careless, deliberate or both deliberate and concealed and can also vary according to whether the disclosure is unprompted or not. An unprompted disclosure occurs when a taxpayer informs the Revenue of the error when he or she has no reason to believe that the Revenue has already discovered it or is about to discover it. Any other disclosure is a prompted disclosure.

The Revenue also has other methods of encouraging compliance. For example in the case of a missing return the Revenue can simply to reduce the taxpayer's code number to the value of the personal allowance (or perhaps even less), so that the PAYE system withholds too much tax. As soon as the taxpayer conforms, his or her code is calculated accurately and the tax he or she has overpaid will be returned. The Revenue does not generally need to rely on penalties as much as some foreign administrations because, as we have seen, the PAYE system can extract tax from most individuals without any co-operation from the taxpayer. Even when penalties are imposed, the Revenue may accept a penalty below the maximum, depending on the circumstances of the case.

Table 8.4 The Calculation of Penalties

Reasons for the error	Penalty
Careless error	Between 0% and 30% of the extra tax due
Deliberate error	Between 20% and 70% of the extra tax
Deliberate and concealed error	Between 30% and 100% of the extra tax due

These penalties may also vary according to whether the taxpayer was prompted or not in disclosing the error.

When the Revenue has insufficient information to raise an accurate assessment, the Inspector may make an estimated assessment which, if it is excessive, will force the taxpayer to appeal and so reveal his or her circumstances. Furthermore, unpaid tax is subject to an interest charge from the date the tax should have been paid. Official efforts to counter evasion are given in the annual reports of the Revenue and Customs and take a variety of forms. Apart from checking that individuals are not unduly modest about their declared incomes, resources are devoted to chase those who have undeclared income from second jobs (known as 'moonlighters') and those for whom the Revenue has no records at all ('ghosts'). One technique is to compare a person's lifestyle with his or her declared income (if any) and another is to seek explanations for amounts paid into bank accounts. It has been rumoured that for this purpose the Revenue even keeps a record of all horse racing results!

Appeals

The appeals process for taxation was reformed in 2009 for a range of reasons including that the merger of previously separate appeals procedures logically followed the merger of the former Inland Revenue with Customs and Excise to form HM Revenue and Customs (Avery Jones, 2006 and Gething *et al.* 2009).

If a taxpayer disagrees with the Revenue he or she may appeal in writing, normally within 30 days. The Revenue will usually try to resolve the dispute directly with the taxpayer but if that fails the Revenue has an internal review procedure which is conducted separately from the original decision-making process. If that does not resolve the matter the appeal may proceed to a tribunal. The tax tribunals are part of the Ministry of Justice's Tribunal Service and consist of a First-tier tribunal and an Upper Tribunal as illustrated in Figure 8.1. Appeals are normally heard by the First-tier Tribunal. Appeals against decisions by the First-tier tribunal on a point of law may be permitted to proceed to the Upper Tribunal, though some particularly complex appeals may go directly to the Upper Tribunal. An appeal against an Upper Tribunal decision may be allowed on a point of law only to the Court of Appeal in England and Wales or Court of Session in Scotland. From there an appeal may go to the Supreme Court (before October 2009, the House of Lords) and then possibly to the European Court of Justice.

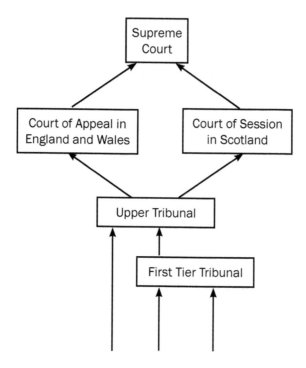

Figure 8.1 Appeals in the United Kingdom

Further reading

A comprehensive explanation of the UK's tax system can be found in Lymer and Oats (2009) and further numeric examples in Andrews *et al.* (2009). Age allowance is considered in Morris (1981). Taxation and marriage are considered in Barr (1980), *The Taxation of Husband and Wife* (1980), Morris and Warren (1981), Andic (1981), *The Reform of Personal Taxation* (1986), James (1987), and an international dimension is given by Pechman and Engelhardt (1990). National Insurance contributions are discussed in Adam and Loutzenhiser (2007), Creedy (1981), Dilnot and Webb (1989), Skinner and Robson (1992) and Williams (1978), and described in detail in Williams (1982). A history of the income tax is provided by Sabine (1965) and an account of the psychology of taxation is presented by Lewis (1982). The reform of direct taxation is discussed by Atkinson *et al.* (1990), Meade Committee (1978) and the Mirrlees Review (Mirrlees, 2010 and 2011). Kerridge (1990) examines the reform of capital gains tax and Stopforth (2005) discusses the introduction of capital gains tax in the UK. The whole area of the comprehensibility of taxation, and UK taxation in particular, appears in James *et al.* (1987). Other useful information appears in the Inland Revenue's annual *Reports* – which, after its amalgamation with Customs and Excise in 2005, are now the *Reports* of HM Revenue and Customs.

References

Adam, S. and Loutzenhiser, G. (2007), *Integrating Income Tax and National Insurance: An Interim Report*, Institute for Fiscal Studies, WP/21/07.

Alm, J. and Whittington, L.A. (1995), 'Income taxes and the marriage decision', *Applied Economics*, Vol. 27, pp. 25-31.

Andic, S. (1981), 'Does the personal income tax discriminate against women?', *Public Finance*, No. 1, pp. 1-15.

Andrews, R., Combs, A. and Rowes, P. (2009) *Taxation: incorporating the 2009 Finance Act*, Fiscal Publications

Atkinson, A.B. *et al.* (1990), *The Reform of Direct Taxation: Report of the Fabian Taxation Committee*, Fabian Society.

Avery Jones, J.F. (2006), 'The reform of the tax tribunals: A story of uncompleted business', *British Tax Review.*, Issue 3, pp. 282-293.

Barr, N.A. (1980), 'The taxation of married women's incomes', *British Tax Review*, I & II, pp. 398-412.

Barr, N.A., James, S.R. and Prest, A.R. (1977), *Self-Assessment for Income Tax*, Heinemann.

Beighton, L. (1987), 'Tax policy and management: the role of the Inland Revenue', *Fiscal Studies*, Vol. 8, No. 1, February, pp. 1-16.

Butterworths UK Tax Guide (1991-2), Butterworths.

Creedy, J. (1981), 'Taxation and national insurance contributions in Britain', *Journal of Public Economics*, Vol. 15, pp. 379-88.

Diamond Commission (1979), *Report No. 8*, Cmnd. 7679, HMSO.

Dilnot, A.W., Kay, J.A. and Morris, C.N. (1984), *The Reform of Social Security*, Oxford University Press.

Dilnot, A. and Webb, S. (1989), 'Reforming National Insurance contributions: a progress report', *Fiscal Studies*, Vol. 10, No. 2.

Farnsworth, A. (1951), *Addington, Author of the Modern Income Tax*, Stevens.

Gething, H., Paterson, S. and Barker, J. (2009) 'Transformation of the tax tribunal', *British Tax Review*, Issue 3, pp. 250-262.

Gowers, E. (1954), *The Complete Plain Words*, HMSO.

Haig, R.M. (1921), 'The concept of income', in R. M. Haig (ed.), *The Federal Income Tax*, Columbia University Press.

Hepker, M.Z. (1975), *A Modern Approach to Tax Law*, 2nd edn, Heinemann.

Herbert, A.P. (1966), *Wigs at Work*, Penguin, p. 100.

Hicks, J.R. (1974), *Value and Capital*, 2nd edn, Oxford University Press.

Highfield, R. (2006), 'Pre-populated income tax returns' in M. McKerchar and M. Walpole (eds.) *Further Global Challenges in Tax Administration*, Fiscal Publications, pp. 331-358.

Hope-Jones, A. (1939), *Income Tax in the Napoleonic Wars*, Cambridge University Press.

Inland Revenue (1976), *118th Report* (for the year ended 31 March 1975), Cmnd. 6302, HMSO.

Institute of Chartered Accountants in England and Wales (1986), *The Reform of Personal Taxation.*

James, S. (1987), 'The reform of personal taxation: a review article', *Accounting and Business Research,* No. 66, Spring, pp. 117-24.

James, S. and Edwards, A. (2008), 'Developing tax policy in a complex and changing world', *Economic Analysis and Policy,* Vol. 38. No. 1, pp. 35-53.

James, S.R., Lewis, A. and Allison, F. (1987), *The Comprehensibility of Taxation: A Study of Taxation and Communications,* Gower.

James, S. and Wallschutzky, I. (1993), 'Returns to the future: the case for electronically submitted tax returns', *British Tax Review,* pp. 401-5.

James, S. and Wallschutzky, I. (1994), 'Should we submit to electronic submission?', *Accountancy,* September.

James, S. and Wallschutzky, I. (1995), 'Considerations concerning the design of an appropriate system of tax rulings', *Revenue Law Journal,* Vol. 5, pp. 175-196.

James, S. and Wallschutzky, I. (1997), 'Tax law improvement in Australia and the UK: The need for a strategy for Simplification, *Fiscal Studies,* Vol. 18, No. 4, pp. 445-460.

Johnston, Sir Alexander (1965), *The Inland Revenue,* Allen & Unwin.

Kerridge, R. (1990), 'Capital gains tax - what next?', *British Tax Review,* No. 3.

Lewis, A. (1982), *The Psychology of Taxation,* Martin Robertson.

Lymer, A. and Oats, L. (2009) *Taxation: Policy and Practice,* (16th ed. 2009/10), Fiscal Publications

Mayson, S.W. (1980), *A Practical Approach to Revenue Law,* 3rd edn, Financial Training.

Meade Committee (1978), *The Structure and Reform of Direct Taxation,* Institute for Fiscal Studies.

Mirrlees, Sir James (Chair) (2010), *Dimensions of Tax Design: The Mirrlees Review,* Oxford University Press.

Mirrlees, Sir James (Chair) (2011), *Tax by Design: The Mirrlees Review,* Oxford University Press.

Morris, C.N. (1981), 'The age allowance', *Fiscal Studies,* November, pp. 29-36.

Morris, C.N. and Warren, N.A. (1981), 'Taxation of the family', *Fiscal Studies,* March, pp. 26-46.

Pechman, J.A. & Engelhardt, G.Y. (1990), 'The income tax treatment of the family: an international perspective', *National Tax Journal,* Vol. XLIII, No. 1.

Pinson, B. (1986), *Pinson on Revenue Law,* 17th edn, Sweet & Maxwell.

Prebble, J. (1994). 'Why is tax law incomprehensible?', *British Tax Review,* pp. 380-93.

Reform of Personal Taxation (1986), Cmnd. 9756, HMSO.

Reform of Social Security: Programme for Action (1986), Cmnd. 9691, HMSO.

Robinson, B. (1989), 'Reforming the taxation of capital gains, gifts and inheritances', *Fiscal Studies,* Vol. 10, No. 1.

Royal Commission on the Taxation of Profits and Income (1954), *Second Report,* Cmnd. 9105, HMSO.

Royal Commission on the Taxation of Profits and Income (1955), *Final Report,* Cmnd. 9474, HMSO.

Sabine, B.E.V. (1965), *A History of Income Tax,* Allen & Unwin.

Sabine, B. (1991), 'Further thinking on revenue law', *British Tax Review,* Nos. 5 and 6.

Sabine, B. (1993), 'Life and taxes 1932-1992. Part III 1965-1992: reform, Rossminster and reductions', *British Tax Review,* No. 6.

Sandler, D. (1994), *A Request For Rulings,* Institute of Taxation and the Institute for Fiscal Studies.

Simons, H.C. (1938), *Personal Income Taxation,* University of Chicago Press.

Skinner, D. and Robson, M. (1992), 'National insurance contributions: anomalies and reforms', *Fiscal Studies,* Vol. 13, No. 3, pp. 112-25.

Soos, P.E. (1995), 'Taxation at source and withholding in England 1512 to 1640', *British Tax Review,* pp. 49-91.

Stopforth, D. (2005), 'The birth of capital gains tax – The official view', *British Tax Review,* No. 6, pp. 584-608.

The Taxation of Husband and Wife (1980), Cmnd. 8093, HMSO.

Williams, D.W. (1978), 'National Insurance contributions - a second income tax', *British Tax Review,* No. 2.

Williams, D.W. (1982), *Social Security Taxation,* Sweet & Maxwell.

Williams, D.W. (1993), 'The Finance Act 1993: incredible drafting, extraordinary prose', *British Tax Review,* pp. 483-95.

SELF ASSESSMENT QUESTIONS

Suggested answers to self-assessment questions are given at the back of the book.

8.1 What is taxable income?

8.2 What arguments might be used for and against taxing income from investment at a higher rate than income from employment?

8.3 What is the difference between the individual basis of assessment and the aggregation basis?

8.4 Which classes of National Insurance contributions are levied on:
   (a) employees, and
   (b) individuals who are self-employed?

8.5 What are the main economic arguments for having a capital gains tax?

8.6 Why might a non-cumulative system of withholding income tax at source tend to collect too much money during the course of the tax year?

DISCUSSION QUESTIONS

1. Assess the current personal income tax in terms of efficiency and equity.

2. Is there a case for taxing income from investment at higher rates than income from employment?

3. Should married couples be taxed differently from single individuals or couples cohabiting?

4. How strong is the argument for integrating income tax and National Insurance contributions?

5. What are the advantages and disadvantages of replacing the British Pay-As-You-Earn scheme, which withholds tax on a cumulative basis, with a system that withholds on a non-cumulative basis?

CHAPTER NINE

Further aspects of income tax

LEARNING OBJECTIVES

After reading this chapter, you should be able to:

- Show how income taxes and social security systems can interact.
- Present the case for and against a system of negative income tax.
- Explain the arguments for and against a personal expenditure tax.
- Assess the case for extending self-assessment for income tax.

9.1 Introduction

Having examined the British system of income tax in Chapter 8, it is now appropriate to look at some possible reforms. As in Chapter 8, we are not concerned here with the overall level of income tax, but with the tax structure and methods of administration.

Given the extensive and complex nature of the present tax system, a general survey of potential reform would fill a much larger volume than this one. In order to keep our discussion within reasonable bounds, therefore, we shall confine ourselves to a discussion of negative income tax, to the arguments concerning a possible personal expenditure tax, and to self-assessment.

9.2 Negative income tax

One reform which has attracted a great deal of interest is negative income tax. Many different schemes have been suggested under names such as income maintenance, reverse income tax, social dividend and tax credits, as well as negative income tax.

Although the various schemes have many differences, the general aim is to provide an alternative method of taxing and redistributing income. The main characteristic of these schemes is that they combine the income tax and important elements of social security into a single co-ordinated system. The basic idea, therefore, is that the income of each person or family unit would be assessed. If the income exceeded a certain amount, then tax would be payable in the usual way. However, if the income fell below the relevant amount, then it would be supplemented with a cash payment. As income from other sources increased, the amount of benefit paid would steadily reduce until the person or family became a taxpayer in the usual way.

At present it is quite possible for some individuals and families to be liable to both income tax and National Insurance contributions at the same time as they are entitled to welfare benefits. With married couples counted as one, there were about 20 million income taxpayers in the mid-1980s and about 18 million receiving benefits. Some of these were both paying and receiving at the same time.

The difficulty is that the separate systems do not always result in a desirable outcome. The level of benefit payments is often related to the recipient's income (hence the term 'means-tested' benefits). They are therefore withdrawn as income rises, which creates an additional 'implicit' tax rate on extra earnings. It then becomes possible for someone who earns more, not only to pay more income tax and National Insurance contributions but also to lose income-related benefits. This can increase implicit marginal rates of tax considerably and so cause disincentive effects.

A further complication is that the main method of support can also give entitlement to related benefits such as free prescriptions on the NHS. If the claimant loses entitlement to the main benefit then the related ones are lost as well - producing a threshold where there could be quite severe disincentive effects.

Another problem is that the support system is subject to constant change. For example in recent years Family Credit, the main method of supporting working people on low incomes, was replaced by Working Families' Tax Credit in 1999. This new benefit did not last long as it was itself replaced by Child Tax Credit and Working Tax Credit in 2003. This might be a contributing factor to the number of people who do not manage to claim their full entitlement because they do not understand the system or they cannot navigate their way through it. Although, of course, the system is not a disincentive to people who do not receive their entitlement, it cannot be considered an advantageous feature in any other respect.

The situation where the tax and benefit systems interact so that a person earning more actually receives little or no extra money after deductions has become known as the 'the poverty trap'. Where it has meant that it was not financially worth taking a job at all, it has become known as the 'unemployment trap'. Going to work might involve considerable extra expense, for example in the form of childcare. This may be a particular disincentive for people on low incomes and therefore likely to come into the scope of income-related support schemes.

The changes in the social security system introduced in April 1988 were partly designed to reduce some of the worst of the disincentive effects, but problems remain. The question is whether the relationship could be more co-ordinated if the benefit system, on the one hand, and the tax system, on the other, were simply amalgamated.

Unclaimed benefits

A different problem with the present system is that many people do not claim the benefits to which they are entitled. For example, in March 1973 it was thought that 'only about half the total numbers eligible were actually receiving payments under Family Income Supplement' (Select Committee on Tax Credit, 1973, Volume 1, para. 30). It has also been estimated that for supplementary benefit (since replaced by Income Support), the take-up rate was around 84 per cent of eligible families but, for Family Income Supplement (which was replaced by Family Credit) it was thought only about 50 per cent of families received their entitlement (Barr, 1993, Ch. 10).

There are several reasons why individuals may not claim their full entitlement. In 1965 an enquiry was undertaken by the Ministry of Pensions and National Insurance (1966) into the financial and other circumstances of pensioners. The results suggested that there were two main reasons why pensioners did not claim their entitlement to National Assistance. The first was that many were unaware of their entitlement. The second was the stigma attached to claiming assistance. Between a quarter and a third of pensioners who did not claim gave their reasons as disliking charity or the National Assistance Board, or that their pride prevented them from applying for assistance. With a negative income tax scheme covering all or most adults, such problems should be minimised.

Benefit in cash or in kind

A separate aspect concerns the method of assisting poorer families. Many benefits take the form of either free goods and services (for example, free National Health Service prescriptions, and free dental treatment), or money related to particular forms of expenditure (for example, rent rebates).

It has often been argued that poorer families would be better off if the assistance they received were not tied to particular goods and services in this way. If poorer families had the cash, they could spend it on what they wanted most. In a proposal for a 'reverse income tax', for instance, it is argued that: 'Those who best understand the most urgent needs to which [social security] funds should be devoted are not the politicians and the bureaucrats, but the poor themselves' (Clark, 1977, p. 25).

There are, of course, limitations to this argument. Some individuals may be incapable of managing their own finances. Alternatively, the benefit of the payment may be intended for people other than the recipient. For example, the government may wish to ensure that children are adequately nourished.

Administration

A fourth aspect of the overlap between tax and benefits is administration. Some integration between the two systems is likely to reduce the costs of administration. The Green Paper Proposals for a Tax-Credit System (1972) stated that its proposals 'would enable an eventual saving of some 10,000 to 15,000 civil servants to be made' (para. 47). A better integrated system would also be easier for the public to understand.

For a number of reasons, therefore, various schemes for reform have been proposed. There are substantial differences between many of the schemes, and we shall look first at the social dividend scheme and then at aspects of some others.

The social dividend

A social dividend scheme was first proposed by Lady Rhys Williams in 1942 and has been much discussed and developed since. The basic idea is that all social security benefits and the income tax would be replaced by a single scheme. Everyone would be paid a social dividend. The size of the payment would depend on family circumstances and the scheme would be financed by a proportional tax on all income.

A simple social dividend system is described in Figure 9.1. At the pre-tax level of income (I_1) the individual would pay as much in tax as he or she received as a social dividend. Below I_1, the dividend would exceed tax liability, and above I_1 the reverse would be true. The level of the social dividend is then represented by OA, and the income tax is shown by the line AB. The rate of income tax is shown by the slope of AB.

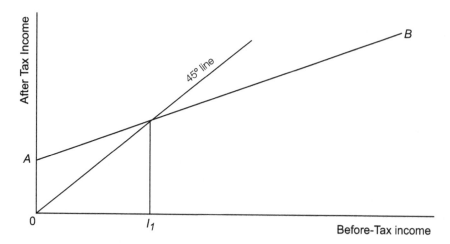

Figure 9.1 A simple social dividend scheme

The advantages of such a scheme are clear. The social security and tax systems would be co-ordinated, with a constant marginal rate of tax. As everyone would receive a payment, the take-up problem would disappear. Individuals would be given the cash to spend on what they wished, and there would also be a potential administrative saving.

The main problem with the scheme is raising sufficient revenue. If the level of the social dividend were to be sufficiently high to enable a family to meet certain minimum needs, the level of income tax would have to be raised considerably. For example, suppose that on average (allowing for differences in family status) the value of the social dividend was set at £60 per week and the proportional income tax at 33.3 per cent. On these assumptions, the break-even point would be a weekly income of £180, leaving vast amounts of revenue to be raised from higher incomes. A more realistic tax rate would be 50 per cent; the break-even point would then be £120. However, such a rate would appear to be politically unacceptable. Even with progressive tax rates, such a scheme provides formidable problems of financing.

A second problem involves the calculation of the social dividend. In practice, the circumstances of low-income families can vary considerably. For example, different families face different housing costs, and many families have dependants with particular disabilities or special needs. It is difficult to see how the size of the social dividend payment in each case can be tailored to such individual circumstances without involving at least some of the administrative complexities and difficulties that are to be found under existing arrangements.

Other schemes

The difficulties and the very high costs associated with a pure social dividend scheme have led to a number of less radical proposals. One involves higher rates of withdrawal of the subsidy. Another possibility is that much of the existing income tax and social security systems be retained. Many of the proposed schemes incorporate both of these modifications. Both would reduce the amount of revenue required to finance some form of negative income tax.

Schemes proposing higher rates of withdrawal include those by the Institute of Economic Affairs (1970), which proposed a withdrawal rate of 100 per cent, and Clark (1977), who proposed a rate of 70 per cent. Other suggestions have involved rates of 66j and 50 per cent. Among the schemes which have envisaged only a partial replacement of existing arrangements are the proposals of Tobin *et al.* (1967) and the *Proposals for a Tax-Credit System* (1972) put forward by a Conservative government. The main characteristic of the Conservative plans was that income tax allowances would have been replaced by a weekly tax credit. This would have assisted those who did not benefit fully from the personal allowances because they were below the tax threshold. It was intended that the scheme would come into effect by the end of the 1970s, but when the Labour Party was returned to office in 1974 it was shelved. It might be noted, however, that some progress has been made in this direction inasmuch as child tax allowances have been replaced by payments of child benefit.

One of the main reservations which has been voiced about a negative income tax, especially in the United States, has concerned the possible effects on incentives. Certainly in comparison with a system involving no redistribution of income, the introduction of a negative income tax would be very likely to involve both income and substitution effects which are adverse to work effort. Naturally, these effects would be less serious if comparison was between a negative income tax and the present arrangements in the UK.

Nevertheless, several experiments have been undertaken in the USA to try to discover the extent of these effects. Summaries of these studies appear in Ferber and Hirsch (1978) and in Brown (1983). It should be pointed out that the findings of these experiments must be treated with some caution. First of all, there is the celebrated 'Hawthorne effect' in which the very act of participating in a social experiment may affect behaviour. Incidentally, this refers to a series of experiments in the 1920s when it was observed that productivity increased each time the workers' environmental conditions were changed - even when they were eventually restored to their original state. It appeared that the workers thrived more on attention than on any particular environment. A second problem is that experiments which involve a tiny proportion of the population for a limited time will almost certainly have different results from a nationwide scheme which was considered to be permanent. Even so, these studies have provided a valuable contribution to the issue.

The first study was commissioned in 1967 and took place in urban areas in New Jersey and Pennsylvania. The actual experiment ran for three years. The results are presented in Kershaw and Fair (1976) and Watts and Rees (1977a; 1977b) and further discussion appears in Pechman and Timpane (1975). The analysis by Hall (1975) suggested that the experiment reduced the work of white husbands significantly, and another analysis by Cogan (1978) found more substantial disincentive effects. For black people, work actually increased (Watts and Rees, 1977a), though Hall suggested that the data for this group were unreliable on account of a high rate of attrition. It should also be pointed out that the experiment took place at the same time as the State of New Jersey improved its system of welfare payments. This must have affected behaviour. In addition there may well have been self-selection bias by the participants in what were anyway small sample sizes.

Another experiment was carried out in two rural areas in North Carolina and Iowa. Another, in Indiana, concentrated on urban black families, many of whom contained only one adult. Experiments in Seattle and Denver tried to assess the effects of a system in which the rate of tax declined as income rose. Also, in order to capture long-term effects, part of the sample was enrolled for 20 years, the others for five or three years. The results of these later experiments were similar to many of those of the original New Jersey survey. Negative income taxes appear to reduce work effort for most people and, in the case of married women, do so substantially - a result which is compatible with other evidence on taxation and the labour supply presented in Section 4.3.

9.3 A personal expenditure tax

The possibility of a tax based on consumption expenditure rather than on income has already been mentioned, and some of the arguments with respect to saving appear in Section 4.4, and with respect to equity in Section 5.3. However, the possibility of a personal expenditure tax merits further discussion in its own right, and it was one of the main proposals of the Meade Committee (1978). There has also been renewed interest in a direct consumption tax in the USA - see for example McLure (1992, 1993) and Sabelhaus (1993).

It should be stressed that a personal expenditure tax would not be the same as indirect taxes on expenditure. Instead, it would be a tax based on each individual's expenditure and, in principle at least, could be levied at progressive rates in the same way as income tax is levied on a person's income. There could also be personal allowances. A personal expenditure tax is an interesting idea in itself, but it is also a good example of a potential tax reform which can be analysed in terms of efficiency and equity and other economic considerations.

It should also be made clear that such a tax does not involve calculating each item of everyone's expenditure. An obvious starting point is a person's income since of course a person's income and expenditure are linked by changes in saving or borrowing. The calculation for a personal expenditure tax would involve adding income to any capital receipts plus any borrowing. This would show a person's potential spending power. The next stage is to deduct items such as spending on capital assets, lending, and repayment of debt. What is left is the individual's consumption expenditure. In principle, at least, the tax need not be horrendously complicated.

Furthermore some sort of pay-as-you-go system would be essential. This could be done fairly easily by continuing the present withholding of tax from incomes as a proxy for expenditure, followed by an assessment and appropriate adjustment at the end of the tax year, though this would involve a switch to self-assessment of some sort, and this is discussed in Section 9.4 below.

The idea of an expenditure tax is not a novelty. Its history can be traced back to Thomas Hobbes and it has been discussed by people such as John Stuart Mill, Alfred Marshall, Irving Fisher and Lord Kaldor. In fact, Kaldor (1955) deals with the arguments for an expenditure tax more fully than does the Meade Report. The implications of an expenditure tax have also been discussed overseas. Professor Sven-Olof Lodin designed an expenditure tax for the Swedish Royal Commission on Taxation (see Lodin, 1978) and Blueprints for Basic Tax Reform (US Treasury, 1977) discussed the tax in the context of the United States.

One of the reasons for introducing an expenditure tax is to have a tax system based on a set of clear principles. In the absence of such a basis, a whole range of anomalies of the sort already discussed will evolve over time. The Meade Committee considered the possibility of moving to a comprehensive income tax defined as a tax on the 'accretion of economic power'. However, the Committee (1978, p. 500) were convinced that:

> it would be extremely difficult, if not impossible, to introduce all the features of a comprehensive tax. In particular, we think that many of the measures which would theoretically be necessary to index the system for proper capital-income adjustments against inflation would not be practicable.

Therefore the Committee favoured a move towards an expenditure basis. They thought this would be feasible provided a system of self-assessment were first introduced for direct taxation.

A further argument concerns saving. The Committee argued that, 'a progressive expenditure tax is a tax which, by exempting savings and investment from tax, gives a maximum opportunity for economic growth and development in a mixed economy' (pp. 5 and 6). As they also pointed out (p. 33):

> with a progressive income tax a wealthy man with a high marginal rate of income tax of 83 per cent [which was the maximum rate on earned income at that time] will be able to use only £17 out of £100 of profit for the development of his business, whereas with a progressive tax on expenditure he could use all his profit to develop his business.

The argument assumes, of course, that more saving will mean more investment which in turn will mean a higher rate of economic growth.

Nevertheless, whether or not the overall level of saving would be affected by a change to an expenditure tax, it has been argued that such a change would radically improve the taxation of different types of saving and investment. The present system, as the Meade Committee showed, is highly arbitrary. The yield on different types of saving is affected by the interaction between income tax, capital gains tax and corporation tax. In addition, the yield is affected by such considerations as whether the investment is made through an incorporated or unincorporated business; the particular tax rules governing the depreciation of different assets; and whether the savings are channelled through loan or equity capital. The combined effects of all these factors mean that the treatment of saving ranges from the generous to the extremely severe. An expenditure tax, it is argued, would avoid such arbitrary effects.

Another major argument is that the proper basis of taxation is the amount an individual takes out of society's pool of resources (in other words the individual's consumption) rather than the amount he puts into it (as represented by his income). A particular aspect of this is consumption out of inherited capital. Such expenditure avoids income tax, but would be caught by an expenditure tax.

The Meade Committee's proposals

The Committee presented four possible ways by which the principle of an expenditure tax could be operated in practice. The one which found most favour with the Committee would require a taxpayer's consumption expenditure to be calculated in each period as follows:

1. The taxpayer's total realised income would be established.
2. Any capital receipts, such as the proceeds from the sale of capital assets and sums borrowed, would be added on.
3. All expenditure for purposes other than consumption would be deducted. This would include expenditure on capital assets, and sums lent out or repaid.
4. The final figure would be the amount spent on consumption.

The main advantage of this method over others is that, by providing a figure for each taxpayer's total consumption, it would permit an expenditure tax to be levied at a series of progressive rates.

The second method of taxing spending rather than saving would be a tax on value added. The third would be an income tax which exempted investment expenditure with a system of 100 per cent capital allowances. The final method, again an income tax, would exempt investment income from tax.

After considering these various possibilities, the Committee came down firmly behind two particular forms of expenditure tax. The first was a 'universal expenditure tax' (UET) which would be based entirely on the first method described above. The second was a two-tier expenditure tax (TTET). The lower tier would consist of a single basic rate levied through a value added tax. The upper tier would be a restricted version of the UET and would allow tax to be levied at higher rates on taxpayers with higher levels of expenditure. It would work in a similar way to the pre-1973 income tax system, whereby most taxpayers were subject to tax at the standard rate, and more prosperous individuals to surtax as well. Indeed, it would also resemble the present income tax with its long basic rate band. A TTET could be introduced more gradually than a UET, and could also provide a transitional stage in a move to a fully-fledged UET.

The limitations of the arguments

There are several limitations to the arguments in favour of an expenditure tax. First, there does not appear to be a strong relationship between the level of saving and the return to saving. Therefore, although an expen diture tax would increase the return to saving, this would not necessarily increase the level of saving substantially.

Second, even if the relationship were a strong one, there is still no close link between an increase in saving and an increase in economic growth. An increase in the amount that people wish to save does not necessarily lead to an increase in the amount that people wish to invest. On the contrary, as Keynes demonstrated convincingly, it is quite possible that saving, if carried to excess, could lead to a lack of aggregate demand and to economic recession.

A third limitation is that an expenditure tax may have adverse effects on work incentives. It is likely that an expenditure tax would have to be levied at higher rates than an equivalent income tax, since savings would be treated more favourably for tax purposes. It is not certain whether higher rates of tax would increase or decrease the incentives to work. However, if people are mainly concerned with immediate consumption rather than saving, it is possible (but not certain) that an expenditure tax may discourage work effort. If it did, and incomes fell, then the absolute level of savings might also fall, even if the proportion of income saved rose.

A fourth factor is uncertainty. The rates of income tax on income currently received are fairly easy to establish. With an expenditure tax, things are more complicated. It is true that an expenditure tax allows a greater yield to savings. However, taxpayers cannot know what the rates of tax will be when the amounts saved come to be spent.

A fifth limitation is that an expenditure tax does not necessarily treat spending and saving equally. Wealth confers benefits on its owners over and above any pecuniary yield, these benefits taking the form of security, independence, influence and so on (see Section 10.7). Therefore a person who saves might be considered to have a greater taxable capacity than a similar person of equal income who does not save. An expenditure tax on its own would not cover such additional taxable capacity.

Sixth, if one takes a taxpayer's life cycle as a whole, the expenditure tax would be more likely to impose hardship than an income tax. The expenditure tax would weigh more heavily in those years when a family's financial commitments were high relative to its income. This is likely to be the case with young families and for those living off their savings in retirement.

Practical considerations

One of the main arguments for an expenditure tax is that it is designed from basic principles. It may therefore be preferable to introduce such a new tax than to continue to patch up the existing tax system in an ad hoc manner. It is true that many of the existing defects and anomalies have been generated by departures from a well-defined set of underlying principles. Nevertheless, there must be some concern that a new tax, however well designed, may not survive the transition from the fiscal drawing board into practice in a recognisable form. Many of the anomalies of the present system have arisen as a result of pressure from special interest groups. There is no guarantee that such pressure would not also mutilate any future expenditure tax. It might even eventually become as complex and unco-ordinated as the present system. Perhaps someone might then suggest another radical reform with the introduction of a simple income tax!

Some idea of the possible complexity of an expenditure tax in practice can be gained from looking at attempts to introduce such a tax in the past. Plans for a personal and progressive 'spendings' tax were submitted by the United States Treasury to the Senate Finance Committee in 1942. The proposed tax had the twin aims of controlling inflation by taxing private spending and providing funds for war finance. The tax was to have been administered within the existing arrangements for income tax, but was nevertheless rejected by Congress largely because of the novelty and complexity of the proposals. In what seems to have been a typical reaction at the time, Senator Harry Byrd described the proposed tax as, 'the most complicated and unworkable plan' the US Treasury had submitted in nine years (Paul, 1954). Some further work in the USA, however, has suggested that the problems associated with the introduction of a direct consumption tax might not be as great as widely thought (Sarkar and Zodrow, 1993).

In India, following a report to the Indian government by Kaldor (1956), an expenditure tax was introduced in 1958. Although the Indian government had accepted Kaldor's proposals in principle, the tax as enacted differed substantially from the original proposals. Certainly it could not be described as a simple tax, and its repeal in 1962 was apparently 'welcomed in all quarters' (Khanna, 1964). However, 'the joy was short-lived' when the tax was reintroduced in 1964. The revived expenditure tax also proved to be short-lived, and was repealed once more in 1966. Although the Finance Minister at the time felt that 'on purely economic grounds, it would be a very sound principle to replace the income tax increasingly with a tax on expenditure', he went on to say, 'given ... the administrative difficulties and inconvenience to assessees involved in the assessment of expenditure, it is, however, not possible to attempt this substitution on any significant scale at the present stage' (*Bulletin for International Fiscal Documentation*, 1966, p. 201). A further relevant and interesting comment was made by B.K. Nehru (1977, p. 70), former Indian Ambassador to the USA and Indian High Commissioner in London:

> My distinguished contemporary Nicky Kaldor, whose theoretically perfect system of direct taxation was modified by us in practice - as I warned him it would be - into an absurd monstrosity which has had the most disastrous effect on our economic development and in the dismantling of which we have not yet fully succeeded ...

In Ceylon (now Sri Lanka) an expenditure tax was introduced in 1959, also following proposals made by Kaldor to the government. The tax was repealed in 1963, though it was reintroduced on a limited basis in 1976 and then withdrawn once more. Taking these three experiences together, therefore, it can be seen that previous attempts to introduce an expenditure tax have not been showered with success.

The introduction of an expenditure tax in the United Kingdom would also raise many practical administrative problems. First of all, there would be the transitional problems associated with any major change of the tax system - especially in relation to the re-education of taxpayers, tax advisers and tax administrators. Moreover, with a switch from an income to an expenditure tax base, existing savings require special consideration. When savings have been accumulated under an income tax regime, it is hardly fair to penalise them when they come to be spent under an expenditure tax regime. Like many other similar problems, it could be overcome, but only at the cost of greater administrative complexity and expense. A similar problem arises with emigration. Unless there were special provisions, individuals would be able to save under a favourable expenditure tax in the United Kingdom, and then emigrate to a country with an income tax system to dis-save. One possible answer might be some sophisticated form of emigration tax, but it is hard to see any satisfactory solution to this problem.

Finally, there are other ways of achieving the effects associated with an expenditure tax, which are based on the existing income tax system. We have already pointed out that an income tax that exempts investment income gives a similar result - though such an exemption may be unacceptable politically. Another possibility suggested by the Meade Committee (1978, Chapter 8) is an income tax with 100 per cent capital allowances (as explained in Section 12.4) against investment expenditure.

This list of limitations and difficulties suggests, therefore, that the case for an expenditure tax is not as strong as might appear at first sight. We now turn to the potential for a greater degree of self-assessment for direct taxation. Although this topic is highly relevant to any proposals for an expenditure tax, it will be discussed here in the context of income tax.

9.4 Self-assessment

In a press release issued on 16 March 1993, the Revenue stated that the Government's proposal to introduce the option of self-assessment from the 1996/97 tax year, together with the abolition of the preceding year basis of income tax, was 'the most fundamental reform of personal tax administration in about 50 years'. There had been many suggestions that the United Kingdom should move in the direction of self-assessment, for example by Johnson (1971) and Barr et al. (1977). The Meade Committee (1978, p. 483) seemed convinced by the arguments and supported the 'conclusions ... that self-assessment in the United Kingdom is both possible and desirable'. There had already been some moves in that direction. For instance, from 1990 individuals with a business turnover below a certain amount (£15,000 from 1992) have only been required to to provide three figures - gross earnings, business expenses and net profit. This was not, of course, full self assessment but it was a significant step in that direction.

Further indications that the arguments for self-assessment were attracting official notice came with the publication of two consultation documents (Inland Revenue, 1991, 1992). In the first of these, it was pointed out that Canada, Italy, Japan, Spain and the USA have full self-assessment, where the taxpayer is responsible for calculating the tax liability and paying the amount due. Australia and Ireland were currently introducing self-assessment. Other member countries of the Organisation for Economic Cooperation and Development have combinations of self-assessment and official assessment (Inland Revenue, 1991, pp. 54-5). It came as little surprise, therefore, that the Chancellor of the Exchequer in his Budget Statement of 16 March 1993 stated that 'self-assessment for income tax has operated successfully in many countries, including the United States, but none of [my] predecessors has found a way of introducing it here'. For those who are required to complete a return, the main elements of self-assessment were introduced in 1997/98. Although there were some initial difficulties, the Revenue claimed that 'Taxpayers and their agents coped well with the new system. We received fewer calls for help than planned and the standard of the tax return completion was higher than we expected' (Inland Revenue, 1998).

The main features of self-assessment

In essence, self-assessment means that the taxpayer rather than the revenue service is responsible for the following four calculations each year:
1.   the calculation of total income;
2.   the calculation of total tax-free income, i.e. the allowances and expenses to which the taxpayer is entitled;
3.   the calculation of total taxable income by subtracting (2) from (1);
4.   the calculation of the actual tax due.

Although self-assessment in other countries takes a variety of forms, there are some common features. Normally there is a system of withholding tax at source from employment income and also some form of advance payment of tax on other sources of income. Neither of these methods of collection is perfectly accurate but each individual's position is assessed on the basis of a tax return completed following the end of the tax year. Any over- or under-payments of tax are then rectified.

Self-assessment applies to taxpayers required to complete a tax return for income tax and capital gains tax. On the basis of the information contained in the return, taxpayers should include their own assessment of the amounts on which they are chargeable to income tax and capital gains tax. Taxpayers have to submit their returns and calculations to the Revenue by the 31 January following the end of the tax year. Individuals who are either unable or unwilling to work out their own tax liability will still be able to ask the Revenue to make the assessment on their behalf on the basis of the information contained in the return. However, they have to submit their returns earlier. In such cases the Revenue simply does the calculations and the assessment remains the taxpayer's rather than the Revenue's. In most cases the tax returns received by the Revenue are accepted without question, but the Revenue has broadly a year to raise any queries. In cases of suspected fraud, investigations can go back much further.

The advantages of self-assessment

Although self-assessment was introduced for the minority of UK taxpayers who complete returns, the question remains whether an extension to the rest of the tax-paying population is desirable. One of the main arguments for such a reform is almost circumstantial, whether the existing arrangements based around the UK's cumulative Pay-As-You-Earn system described in Chapter 8 will be suitable for the majority of taxpayers in the future. One way to tackle this question is to analyse the likely future tax environment. This has been done, for example, by James (1995) using a STEP analysis whereby the relevant factors in the social, technological, economic and political environments are examined in turn. The general conclusion is that taxpayers in the future will have increasingly complex financial circumstances. The stylised traditional family of two adults with children relying largely on a single employment income is likely to be replaced by a variety of more complicated arrangements. Increasingly taxpayers will have incomes from a range of sources. Some will have one or more employment incomes, partly from the increasing amount of casual and part-time employment. Others will have professional and self-employed income, sometimes in combination with employment income. As the population on average becomes older and wealthier, individuals will have a larger range of investment and pension incomes. There are also increasing numbers of higher rate taxpayers who cannot always be easily dealt with under existing arrangements. In general, taxpayers have higher levels of education than previously and many, particularly those in retirement, have the time and inclination to manage their financial and tax affairs more actively than they might otherwise have done. Issues of equity also appear to be important - as demonstrated by the rejection of the community charge by the community itself (see Section 11.4).

All of this suggests that the UK cumulative PAYE system - a simple, mass-produced arrangement which manages without the active participation of most taxpayers - will become increasingly unsuitable. In addition, the costs of the UK tax system are growing as the taxation environment grows increasingly complex. The main arguments for a more general introduction of self-assessment, therefore, would seem to revolve around the need for a tax system which is sufficiently flexible to take account of an increasing number of taxpayers who have more complicated financial circumstances. This will almost certainly mean that a more active role is required for UK taxpayers, and the most appropriate method for achieving this would seem to be an increasing element of self-assessment. Overall the arguments for extending self-assessment are convincing and it may well be that full self-assessment is inevitable.

The main public sector economies that would arise from the extension of self assessment in the United Kingdom would be associated with changes to PAYE. Because each taxpayer would assess his own liability, the constraint of having to avoid many assessments and end-of-year adjustments would disappear. So too, therefore, would the main reason for cumulation.

The disadvantages of cumulation have already been discussed in Section 8.5. The main problems are that it is both an expensive and difficult system to operate accurately. The Revenue itself has made a rather interesting comment on the situation. It suggested that 'it is not entirely light-hearted to compare the PAYE system to a vintage Rolls-Royce which the Revenue laboriously if not lovingly maintains' (Inland Revenue, 1978, p. 280). It might, of course, be the case that society would prefer a more economical administrative vehicle. Some savings should be made as computerisation proceeds, but without self-assessment a great deal of work would remain with the Revenue.

A further point which may be raised in this context concerns the future possibility of a local income tax. The Revenue, in its evidence to the Layfield enquiry into Local Government Finance (1976), stated that the administration of a tax such as that outlined by the Layfield Committee would necessitate the employment of an additional 12,000 staff. This could well be true if a local income tax were to be grafted on to the existing system. However, it would be unlikely to be the case if self-assessment were introduced. As the taxes operating in Canada, Sweden and the United States show, provided the national income tax is self-assessed, the administration of a local income tax does not impose a large additional burden on either the authorities or the taxpayers.

The second area to benefit from self-assessment would be the flexibility of the tax structure. For example, the need to have a long basic rate band to avoid end-of-year adjustments would disappear.

Finally, under self-assessment, the tax system would have to be designed and operated so that the average taxpayer could understand it. This in itself might lead to a number of economic benefits, such as a possible reduction in both administrative and compliance costs. Moreover, because taxpayers would be more involved with the assessment process, changes to the tax system might well attract greater public attention. This might result in taxpayers exercising greater influence over the ways in which they are taxed. It might also provide a constraint on the apparent propensity of the administration to complicate the system.

Arguments against self-assessment

There are also several arguments which have been used or might be used against the introduction of self-assessment in the United Kingdom. The first is that self-assessment would impose costs of its own. There would be the cost of changing over to a new system. Some of the savings of public sector expenditure might be replaced by an increase in compliance costs. Also, the increase in the number of returns and end-of-year adjustments, plus the problems associated with a peak load of activity when the returns were completed, would also impose costs on the public sector. This argument is not altogether convincing. To the extent that some taxpayers will be required to do things that they were not required to do before, compliance costs would rise if full self-assessment were introduced. How far they would rise would depend on a range of factors - most importantly on the form of self-assessment introduced. Also, the wider socio-economic trends described above make it likely that the compliance costs of taxation will drift upwards whatever the form of tax administration. In the United States, for example, Blumenthal and Slemrod (1992) found that there had been an upward drift in the compliance costs of individual income taxation. This was possibly due to the increase in the proportion of taxpayers who have high compliance cost characteristics in terms of both high income and sources of income such as self-employment, capital gains, pensions and annuity income and rental income. Similar trends are likely in the United Kingdom whether or not self-assessment is introduced, which make it even more important to adopt the most suitable form of tax administration.

A second argument, or rather assertion, against self-assessment is that it would be associated with a higher level of evasion. There is no reliable evidence to support this. Indeed, because returns are not sent to every taxpayer each year at present, there must be a much greater temptation not to disclose casual and other receipts in the United Kingdom than in other countries.

The third argument is that self-assessment would lead to a system of 'rough justice'. In other words, it might be suggested that self-assessment could lead to a greater variance of tax actually paid by taxpayers in identical circumstances. There are a number of responses to this argument. One is that the lack of a universal annual return may mean not only that some forms of income remain hidden, but that some taxpayers remain unaware of allowances to which they are entitled. A second response is that it ignores the present costs incurred in reducing 'rough justice', even supposing that it can be reduced by operating an expensive and complicated tax system. It may be that a complex tax system, even if designed to be equitable, benefits only those who have the ability or the resources to take advantage of its complications.

9.5 Broadening the tax base: the US experience

A further possible reform to the UK tax system would be a more radical widening of the income tax base. Although it might be difficult to carry through such a major reform, it is worth briefly describing the American experience of such a change.

As already mentioned, an expenditure tax has been seriously considered in the USA (US Treasury, 1977), but, rather than move in that direction, the USA has moved towards a more comprehensive income tax. Despite some early pessimism (in taxation a pessimist is someone who has studied the progress of other Good Ideas) and a great deal of opposition from lobby groups, this reform actually passed into law in 1986.

Before the US Tax Reform Act of 1986 (TRA86), the US income tax contained many tax expenditures (known as tax breaks or tax shelters) and different types of income were treated in different ways. As stated by Aaron (1987), the three aims of the reform were to produce a tax system which was 'more conducive to economic efficiency and growth, fairer, and simpler'.

Basically the reform involved broadening the tax base by abolishing a large number of special business deductions and reducing the tax concessions for various types of investment. Furthermore, the repeal of the investment tax credit, the revision of depreciation deductions and similar provisions reduced the differences in tax rates applying to different types of investment. Finally, before the reform, 60 per cent of long-term capital gains were excluded from taxation which provided an incentive to convert taxable income into long-term capital gains. This, too, was repealed.

These reforms improved economic efficiency since, for example, there were fewer (tax) incentives to channel investment money into wasteful uses. In addition, the broader tax base allowed statutory rates of tax to be reduced without any loss of revenue or of progressivity. It also became possible to increase personal exemptions (known as personal allowances in the UK) and make other changes so that about 6 million Americans on low incomes were taken out of tax altogether.

Auerbach and Slemrod (1997) undertook a comprehensive review of the effects of TRA86 a decade after its introduction. They reported that most analyses had concluded that TRA86 had improved the efficiency of the tax system. The US experience suggests that it is possible to broaden the tax base if the political leverage of the special interest groups can be outweighed by tax concessions for taxpayers as a whole. Since a single tax concession means a lot to the beneficiaries but very little to individual taxpayers, the former have more incentive to pursue their cause than the latter have to resist. But if more major reforms are considered which will mean a significant difference to individual taxpayers, it becomes possible to harness powerful pressure for change from the taxpaying population as a whole.

Further reading

For suggested reforms to the tax system, the best place to start is probably the Mirrlees Review (Mirrlees, 2010 and 2011). The arguments for and against an expenditure tax are discussed in Pechman (1980) and McLure (1992) and the introduction of a system of self-assessment into the United Kingdom is examined in Barr *et al.* (1977). US tax policy and reform are discussed in Aaron and Galper (1985), Aaron (1987), Bradford (1986), Pechman (1987), Pollack (1996) and Slemrod and Bakija (2008).

References

Aaron, H.J. (1987), 'The impossible dream comes true: the new Tax Reform Act', *The Brookings Review,* Winter.

Aaron, R.I. and Galper, H. (1985), *Assessing Tax Reform,* Brookings Institution.

Auerbach, A.J. and Slemrod, J. (1997), 'The Economic Effects of the Tax Reform Act of 1986', *Journal of Economic Literature,* Vol. 35, No. 2, pp.589-632.

Barr, N.A. (1993), *The Economics of the Welfare State*, 2nd edn, Weidenfeld and Nicolson.

Barr, N.A., James, S.R. and Prest, A.R. (1977), *Self-Assessment for Income Tax*, Heinemann Educational Books.

Blumenthal, M. and Slemrod, J. (1992), 'The compliance cost of the U.S. individual income tax system: a second look after tax reform', *National Tax Journal*, Vol. 45, No. 2, June.

Bradford, D.F. (1986), *Untangling the Income Tax*, Harvard University Press.

Brown, C.V. (1983), *Taxation and the Incentive to Work*, 2nd edn, Oxford University Press.

Clark, C. (1977), *Poverty Before Politics*, Institute of Economic Affairs, Hobart Paper No. 73.

Cogan, J. (1978), *Negative Income Taxation and Labour Supply: New Evidence from the New Jersey-Pennsylvania Experiment*, Santa Monica, Rand Corporation.

Ferber, Rand Hirsch, W.Z. (1978), 'Social experimentation and economic policy: a survey', *Journal of Economic Literature*, Vol. XVI, pp. 1379-1414.

Hall, RE. (1975), 'Effects of the experimental negative income tax on labour supply', in J.A. Pechman and P.M. Timpane (eds), *Work Incentives and Income Guarantees: The New Jersey Income Tax Experiment*, Brookings Institution.

Inland Revenue (1978), *Report* (for the year ended 31 March 1977), Cmnd. 7092, HMSO.

Inland Revenue (1991), *A Simpler System for Taxing the Self-Employed*, HMSO, London.

Inland Revenue (1992), *A Simpler System for Assessing Personal Tax*, HMSO, London.

Inland Revenue (1998) *Report* (for the year ending 31 March 1998), Cm. 4079, HMSO London

Institute of Economic Affairs (1970), *Policy for Poverty*.

James, S. (1995), *Self-Assessment and the UK Tax System*, Institute of Chartered Accountants in England and Wales.

Johnson, H.G. (1971), 'Self-assessment to personal income tax: the American experience', *British Tax Review*, No. 2.

Kaldor, N. (1955), *An Expenditure Tax*, Allen & Unwin.

Kaldor, N. (1956), *Indian Tax Reform*, Ministry of Finance, Government of India.

Kershaw, D. and Fair, J. (1976), *The New Jersey Income-Maintenance Experiment*, Volume 1, *Operations, Surveys and Administration*, Academic Press.

Khanna, K.C. (1964), 'An expenditure tax in India', *Bulletin for International Fiscal Documentation*, p. 361.

Local Government Finance (1976), Report of the Committee of Enquiry, Chairman F. Layfield, Cmnd. 6453, HMSO.

Lodin, S.-O. (1978), *Progressive Expenditure Tax: An Alternative*, Liber Forlag, Stockholm.

McLure, C.E., Jr. (1992), 'Substituting consumption-based direct taxation for income taxes as the international norm', *National Tax Journal*, Vol. XLV, pp. 145-54.

McLure, C.E., Jr. (1993), 'Economic, administrative and political factors in choosing a general consumption tax', *National Tax Journal*, Vol. XLVI, pp. 345-58.

Meade Committee (1978), *The Structure and Reform of Direct Taxation*, Institute for Fiscal Studies.

Ministry of Pensions and National Insurance (1966), *Financial and Other Circumstances of Retirement Pensioners*, HMSO.

Mirrlees, Sir James (Chair) (2010), *Dimensions of Tax Design: The Mirrlees Review*, Oxford University Press.

Mirrlees, Sir James (Chair) (2011), *Tax by Design: The Mirrlees Review*, Oxford University Press.

Nehru, B.K. (1977), 'B.K. Nehru' in J. Abse (ed.), *My LSE*, Robson Books

Paul, R.E. (1954), *Taxation in the United States*, Little Brown, p. 312.

Pechman, J.A. (1980), *What Should be Taxed: Income or Expenditure?*, Brookings Institution.

Pechman, J.A. (ed.) (1987), *Tax Reform and the US Economy*, Brookings Institution

Pechman, J.A. and Timpane, P.M. (eds) (1975), *Work Incentives and Income Guarantees: The New Jersey Negative Income Tax Experiment*, Brookings Institution.

Pollack, S.D. (1996), *The Failure of U.S. Tax Policy: Revenue and Politics*, Penn State University Press.

Proposals for a Tax-Credit System (1972), Cmnd. 5116, HMSO.

Sabelhaus, J. (1993), 'What is the distributional burden of taxing consumption?', *National Tax Journal*, Vol. XLVI, pp. 331-44.

Sarkar, S. and Zodrow, G.R. (1993), 'Transitional issues in moving to a direct consumption tax', *National Tax Journal*, Vol. XLVI, pp. 359-76.

Select Committee on Tax Credit (1973), *Volume I*, HC 341-1, HMSO. Select Committee on a Wealth Tax (1975), *Volume I*, HC 696-1, HMSO.

Slemrod, J. and Bakija, J. (2008), *Taxing Ourselves: A Citizen's Guide to the Great Debate Over Tax Reform*, 4th ed., MIT Press.

Tobin, J., Pechman, J.A. and Mieszkowski, P. (1967), 'Is a negative income tax practical?', *Yale Law Journal*, Vol. 77, No. 1, pp. 1-27.

US Treasury (1977), *Blueprints for Basic Tax Reform*, Washington DC.

Watts, H.W. and Rees, A. (eds) (1977a), *The New Jersey Income-Maintenance Experiment*, Volume n, *Labour Supply Responses*, Academic Press.

Watts, H.W. and Rees, A. (1977b), *The New Jersey Income-Maintenance Experiment*, Volume III, *Expenditures, Health and Social Behaviour; and the Quality of the Evidence*, Academic Press.

SELF ASSESSMENT QUESTIONS

Suggested answers to self-assessment questions are given at the back of the book.

9.1 What is an 'implicit' tax rate?

9.2 Why has it been argued that it is better to assist poorer families through cash rather than through free goods and services of equal value?

9.3 Is it true that there is no real difference between an income tax and an expenditure tax, it is just that the former takes the money when the taxpayer receives it and the latter when it is spent?

DISCUSSION QUESTIONS

1. What effects might a negative income tax have on work incentives?

2. Should the personal income tax be replaced with a personal expenditure tax?

3. How strong is the case for extending self-assessment to the majority of taxpayers in the United Kingdom?

CHAPTER TEN

The taxation of wealth

LEARNING OBJECTIVES

After reading this chapter, you should be able to:

- Give a definition of wealth.
- Identify the difference between an estate duty or capital transfer tax and an accessions tax.
- Describe the UK system of inheritance tax.
- Present the arguments for and against a personal net wealth tax.

10.1 Introduction

'Wealth is not without its advantages, and the case to the contrary, although it has often been made, has never proved widely persuasive' (Galbraith, 1962, p. 13). It is the taxation of these advantages with which we are concerned in this chapter. Initially we shall examine the definition of wealth and its distribution in the United Kingdom. Then we shall look at some historical attempts to tax items of wealth and at the operation of the modern inheritance tax. We discuss the pros and cons of net wealth taxes and consider the wealth taxes currently in operation overseas. Finally, we shall examine some of the proposals for introducing a wealth tax in the United Kingdom.

10.2 The definition and distribution of wealth

When considering the taxation of wealth, the first task clearly is to define what is meant by wealth, and then to attempt to discover how that wealth is distributed.

Wealth, like income, represents the command a person has over economic resources. The difference between wealth and income is that wealth represents a stock of resources at anyone point in time, whereas income is a flow of resources over time. For example, a person may own a government bond worth £100 which yields £10 per year. The £100 is clearly part of the person's wealth, while the £10 may be considered part of his or her income.

In practice, of course, deciding which assets to include in a person's wealth is a more complex problem. So, too, is deciding how much various assets are worth. Some assets, like the government bond mentioned above, have unambiguous market prices, but many other assets do not. As we are concerned here with personal wealth, perhaps the best way to examine these difficulties is to look at the wealth of a specimen household.

The most valuable asset that many people possess is their house. The value of a house is relatively easy to ascertain as reasonable estimates can be made on the basis of prices paid for similar houses in the same area. However, the total value of the house can be included as a net asset only if the person owns it outright. If the house is mortgaged to a building society, then clearly a liability is also involved. Only the net worth of the house, that is the value of the house less the mortgage, should be counted. For illustrative purposes the list of a specimen household's assets in Table 10.1 includes a gross figure of £180,000 for a house, minus a liability of £33,000 which represents a debt to a building society.

Table 10.1 The net wealth of a specimen household

	£	£
Assets		
House	180,000	
Furniture and other contents	7,000	
Car	3,400	
Pension rights	3,000	
Life assurance policy	1,000	
Building society deposit	500	
Cash	100	
		195,000
Liabilities		
Mortgage	-33,000	
Bank loan	-800	
HP loan	-1,200	
		-35,000
Net wealth		£160,000

Similarly, the contents of the home and any other personal belongings such as jewellery should be counted as wealth. If the family has a car, then it ought to be included as well. Any loans incurred to buy these items, whether from a hire purchase company, a bank, or an individual, should be deducted. Financial claims against other people or institutions, such as deposits in a bank or building society, must be treated as assets.

Presenting rather more difficulty are those items which are not immediately recognisable as wealth, such as life assurance policies and pension rights. Clearly, they represent command over economic resources as both life assurance policies and pensions are bought and sold for capital sums. As might be expected, there are considerable difficulties in valuing assets such as pension rights, and some of these problems are discussed in Section 10.8. However, there is no reason in principle why these items should not be included as wealth, and illustrative figures have been included in Table 10.1. In fact, the argument can be carried further to include National Insurance pension rights, and even rights to sickness and unemployment benefit.

The wealth tied up in human beings, 'human capital', might also be mentioned at this stage. It is possible to invest in human beings, for example, by teaching them new skills, just as it is possible to invest in machines. Industrial investment yields a return and so does investment in human capital, though in the latter case it may be a non-pecuniary return. The topic is discussed in more detail by Schultz (1961). Including human capital as wealth raises some fairly obvious difficulties. It is therefore excluded from this example, but will be discussed further in Section 10.7.

To complete the list of assets of the specimen household, any deposits in financial institutions such as building societies must be included, and any cash. Similarly, any further debts must be included with liabilities. The difference between the two is the net wealth of the household, and this is the figure that would be relevant for a wealth tax. Although the figures in Table 10.1 ignore the problems of valuation and are only for illustration, they do show that quite ordinary households have 'wealth' by the definition used here. We can now go on to see how wealth is distributed in the wider community.

The distribution of wealth in Britain

There are a number of ways by which the distribution of wealth in Britain may be measured. One method would be to derive estimates based on a sample survey of wealth holding. Another is to begin with the Revenue figures for the estates of deceased individuals. Each method has its drawbacks. A sample survey, for example, would encounter difficulties in obtaining an accurate and unbiased response. Two particular problems are the valuation of non-marketable assets, and the estimation of the wealth of individuals who are not covered by the Revenue's statistics. These issues are dealt with in more detail by Atkinson (1983).

Table 10.2 The distribution of personal wealth in the UK in 1994

Percentage of wealth owned by:	Column 1 Marketable wealth	Column 2 Wealth including occupational pension rights	Column 3 Wealth including occupational and state pension rights
Top 1 % of adults	19	14	11
Top 2% of adults	27	20	16
Top 5% of adults	39	31	25
Top 10% of adults	52	43	36
Top 25% of adults	74	66	58
Top 50% of adults	93	89	83

Source: Inland Revenue Statistics (1998), Tables 13.5, 13.6 and 13.7.
The figures for columns 2 and 3 are not available beyond 1994.

The figures used in Table 10.2 are those provided by the Inland Revenue (1998) and are based on information about the estates of deceased persons. The way this is done has been improved, and further details are given by Good (1990) and Stewart (1991). Column 1 covers marketable wealth only, Column 2 includes an estimate of the value of occupational pensions, and Column 3 also adds in a value for state pension rights.

We can see at once from Table 10.2 that the figures of the distribution of wealth depend largely on what is included as wealth. If the definition of wealth is confined to marketable assets (column 1) 19 per cent of personal wealth was owned by the top 1 per cent of the adult population in 1994; 39 per cent was in the hands of the top 5 per cent of the population, and 52 per cent was owned by the top 10 per cent. Although not shown in Table 10.2, Inland Revenue Statistics (1998) also revealed that 8 per cent of the adult population, or over 3,600,000 individuals, had marketable wealth in excess of £100,000 in 1995.

If, however, the definition of wealth is widened to include certain non-marketable assets, the picture changes. The figures provided by the Revenue are confined to the value of pension rights, partly because pension rights are one of the most valuable non-marketable assets an individual possesses, and partly because of the difficulty involved in obtaining reliable values for other assets. The result of including figures for pensions is to make the distribution of wealth look more equitable. If occupational pension rights are included then, for example, the share of the top 5 per cent of the adult population of personal wealth falls from 39 per cent to 31 per cent. If the value of rights to state pensions is included as well, the share of the top 5 per cent falls to 25 per cent of wealth. Unless more reliable figures become available, we can only speculate on what the distribution of wealth would look like if estimates of the value of other non-marketable assets were to be included.

10.3 Historical aspects of capital taxation

Taxes on items of wealth have a long history. The earliest forms consisted of the straightforward requisitioning of men and materials when needed. More formal arrangements were introduced in ancient Rome in the form of a tax known as the *tributum* which was levied when necessary. The assessment of this tax was undertaken by a local magistrate who kept a register known as the *census* which recorded the property of each citizen. The rates at which the tax was levied varied between 0.1 and 0.3 per cent of an individual's property, though the normal rate was 0.1 per cent (i.e. one-thousandth part). The *tributum* was abolished in 167 BC when the spoils of war made it no longer necessary to raise large sums from Roman citizens.

However, a 5 per cent inheritance tax was introduced in Rome in AD 6 on the estates of deceased persons and on legacies but it was levied only on Roman citizens. The extension of Roman citizenship to all the inhabitants of the Empire by Caracalla (AD 198-217) may well have been influenced by an early desire to expand the inheritance tax base. The Emperor and the poor were exempt from the tax. So, too, were near relatives on the grounds that an inheritance tax is likely to be more of a burden for closer heirs than for more distant beneficiaries. In fact, this last exemption did not lead to as much avoidance as one might at first suppose, as a result of the Roman habit of leaving property to friends rather than to children. Deductions were allowed for the costs of the funeral and a single monument provided it was not too expensive!

A problem that faced the old estate duty in the United Kingdom and, to some extent, still faces its successor, inheritance tax, is the potential delay in tax collection as a result of a contested will. In Roman days the problem was overcome by Emperor Hadrian who directed that the heir be put in immediate possession of the property, provided the will appeared valid. So long as the tax was paid, any arguments over the remaining spoils could then continue.

Various other taxes on types of property have existed from time to time. In Britain in the thirteenth century, a tax system of fifteenths and tenths developed, which was imposed on movable goods. An individual was taxed on movables such as coin, plate, household goods and debts owed to him (less debts owed by him), though there were some exemptions for certain personal goods such as clothes and armour. The tax was not levied on a regular basis, but only in times of particular financial need.

In more recent times, taxes on capital slowly became more systematic and widespread. In several European countries, for example, annual wealth taxes were introduced many years ago. For instance, a wealth tax was introduced in the Netherlands in 1892, in Denmark in 1904, in Sweden in 1910 and in Norway in 1911. A wealth tax was also introduced in Germany in 1922, though this was based on an earlier Prussian tax of 1893. However, such taxes have not always survived. A wealth tax was introduced in Ireland in 1975 but abolished in 1978. In France, a net wealth tax was introduced in 1982, repealed in 1986 and reintroduced in 1988. Wealth taxes were abolished in Austria in 1994 in Denmark and Germany in 1997, and in the Netherlands in 2001.

In the United Kingdom the two approaches to capital taxation in the twentieth century up to 1975 have been to tax wealth at death and to tax the income from wealth (that is, investment income) at a higher rate than income from employment. It was proposed as early as 1803 to incorporate an element of tax relief for earned incomes of less than £150 per year, the main argument for such a relief being that incomes from employment are less reliable and, since they have to be earned by personal effort, involve more 'pain' than incomes from investment. In fact, such a relief was not introduced in the United Kingdom until 1907. It is interesting to note that this was during the same period that a number of European countries were introducing taxes on wealth itself, rather than discriminating against the income from wealth.

Although the evidence suggests that the first death duties were levied in Egypt in the second century BC, they do not appear to have been used in Britain until the introduction of Probate Duty in 1694. The modern estate duty was enacted in 1894. It was introduced partially to pay for an expanding Navy, and particularly to reform the taxation of the existing death duties which numbered five by 1894. The Chancellor at that time, Sir William Harcourt, particularly felt it to be correct that the state should have the first claim on the estate of a deceased person. However, estate duty was abolished entirely for deaths occurring on or after 13 March 1975, and replaced by capital transfer tax.

At first sight, a tax such as estate duty would appear to be difficult to avoid. It is hard to imagine avoidance along the lines described by Will Rogers (1962): 'you won't catch those old boys dying so promiscuously like they did'! However, in practice, estate duty was thought to have a number of limitations. It is not clear that it contributed in any major way to the redistribution of wealth. More specifically, it appeared to be easy to avoid by the transfer of wealth at least seven years before death, though there is some evidence (Whalley, 1974) that the rich did not find this a good reason to give their wealth away - perhaps understandably. In any case, the tax could be reduced by investing in assets which were subject to low rates of duty (agricultural land and private business assets); by the manipulation of legal trusts; or by emigration (for example, see Atkinson, 1974, Chapter 7). The tax never formed a very large part of total revenue and its yield rose to a maximum of £458.6 million or only 3 per cent of total tax revenue in 1972/73 (Inland Revenue, 1977).

To reform the taxation of wealth, the government of the time, in a White Paper of August 1974, proposed the introduction of capital transfer tax to property passing in life as well as at death. In the same month, it produced a Green Paper containing plans for an annual tax on personal net worth. The wealth tax proposals have not been put into effect, but capital transfer tax was introduced by the Finance Act 1975 and operated until 1986.

10.4 Capital transfer tax

The original intention behind the introduction of capital transfer tax, in the words of the then Chancellor of the Exchequer, Denis Healey, was to form part of 'a determined attack on the mal distribution of wealth in Britain'. Capital transfer tax was to cover gifts made during life as well as transfers occurring at death or within a few years before death. The tax was to be levied on the cumulative total of transfers being made during life, with the final stage to include the property passing at death.

Although capital transfer tax was a major extension of estate duty, it never raised as much revenue, as a percentage of GDP, as estate duty had. Furthermore, its scope was soon greatly reduced. In fact, significant concessions were made to taxpayers in most of the years it was in force. In 1976, only a year after its introduction, several important reliefs were introduced. In particular, the tax on businesses was substantially reduced and the annual exemption for gifts doubled from £1,000 to £2,000. In 1978 the threshold was increased from £15,000 to £25,000. Only two years later, in 1980, the threshold was doubled to £50,000, which exempted about two-thirds of estates which would otherwise have been liable to tax.

In 1981 the period of cumulation was limited to ten years instead of extending over the full lifetime of the taxpayer. This was a costless concession in the short term since the tax had, of course, only been operating for six years. In addition, a more favourable scale for lifetime transfers was introduced and the annual exemption was increased from £2,000 to £3,000. In 1982 the thresholds for the different rates of capital transfer tax were indexed to changes in prices, and in 1984 the highest rate was reduced from 75 to 60 per cent and the scale for lifetime gifts was reformed so that it was always one half of that applicable on death.

This continual stream of concessions, and in particular the changes made in 1981, caused Sutherland (1981) to suggest that 'even without sophisticated tax avoidance, over 99 per cent of wealth owners will now be able to pay zero CTT when they hand on their assets. The burden to be borne by most of the remaining one per cent has been greatly reduced.' He also documented the continued erosion of the tax (Sutherland, 1984). It is not surprising that the number of people paying capital transfer tax fell from 48,000 in 1977/78 to an estimated 35,000 by 1985/86, its last year of operation. In comparison, in the same year there were some 23,700,000 individuals paying income tax (*Inland Revenue Statistics*, 1991).

10.5 Inheritance tax

Inheritance tax emerged from the remains of capital transfer tax in 1986 and has been subject to further modification. In 1987 its threshold was increased substantially and the number of rates of tax was reduced. In March 1988 the threshold was increased again, to £110,000, and the different rates of tax replaced by a single rate of 40 per cent. By April 2009 the threshold had reached £325,000. Furthermore, from

October 2007, if any part of this exemption is not used when a spouse or civil partner dies, it may be transferred to the surviving spouse or civil partner and used in the calculation of their liability to inheritance tax when they die.

The name 'inheritance tax' is somewhat misleading since, like its predecessors, the tax is based on how much the donor leaves on death (or gives in the years immediately before death), rather than on the amounts the recipients get. In the relevant literature an inheritance tax more usually refers to the latter, that is a tax on the inheritances a person receives. Indeed, capital transfer tax was not actually repealed but substantially amended, particularly by excluding most lifetime transfers, and retitled inheritance tax. We shall return to this point in the discussion of an accessions tax below. In a very real sense, the situation has now returned to the old pre-1975 position since basically inheritance tax, like the old estate duty, is levied on transfers between individuals made on the death of the donor, or up to seven years before his or her death. The value of the estate on death will be taxed as the top slice of cumulative transfers in the seven years before death (just three years less than the ten-year cumulation period for capital transfer tax). Liability arises as soon as the total amount of taxable transfers exceeds the threshold for tax (£325,000 from April 2009). Many of the rules relating to inheritance tax are a continuation of those applying to the previous capital transfer tax and estate duty.

Liability to inheritance tax

Individuals domiciled in the United Kingdom are liable to inheritance tax on property owned in the United Kingdom or overseas. Individuals who are not domiciled in the United Kingdom are subject to tax on their property located in the United Kingdom. For the purposes of inheritance tax, a person is treated as being domiciled in the United Kingdom if he or she was resident in the United Kingdom for at least 17 of the 20 years up to and including the relevant tax year. Married couples are taxed independently - in other words they can make separate claims for any allowable exemptions and can each make transfers up to the threshold before becoming liable to inheritance tax.

Inheritance tax may be charged on certain transfers of wealth made during a person's lifetime, on the value of a person's estate on death and on certain transfers in or out of trusts. Some transfers made during life are not considered to be transfers of value and are not included in the inheritance tax net. These include transfers for the maintenance of dependants such as a spouse, former spouse, children and relatives dependent by reason of age or infirmity.

In practice, few transfers made during life are subject to inheritance tax. Part of the reason is that there are important exemptions. All transfers between spouses and, from December 2005, civil partners, are exempt, though there may be a restriction if the transfers are made to a spouse domiciled overseas. As an aside, it might be mentioned that this exemption originally led to some speculation that wealth could pass between generations and avoid tax if the surviving spouse of the older generation married the future partner of an heir. This led to further speculation on the numbers of elderly gentlemen and gentlewomen either expiring with shock or perking up to live to ancient age. On the other hand, it was Richard Brinsley Sheridan who suggested that the marriage of an old man to a young wife was a crime that carried its own punishment along with it.

There are other important exemptions. The first £3,000 of transfers in a tax year are exempt and any unused part of the £3,000 exemption may be carried forward for use in the following tax year only. A lifetime gift is exempt if it can be shown that the gift is part of the normal expenditure of the transferor and is paid out of income. An example might be where a person pays life assurance premiums for the benefit of another person. There is a small gifts exemption - any number of gifts can be made to any number of people, provided the total value to anyone person in one tax year does not exceed £250. Also exempt are gifts in consideration of marriage - up to £5,000 by a parent, £2,500 by a grandparent, £2,500 by the bride or groom and £1,000 by anyone else.

Transfers to charities established in the United Kingdom, whether they carry out their work in the United Kingdom or overseas, are exempt. Transfers may be made to a range of national bodies such as colleges and universities, the British Museum, the National Trust and the National Gallery. Donations to political parties are exempt, providing the party had at least two MPs elected at the last general election or if it had one MP and at least 150,000 votes were cast for its candidates.

Works of art and objects such as pictures, prints, books, manuscripts and scientific collections which are of national, artistic, historic or scientific interest may be granted conditional exemption from inheritance tax. If such exemption is granted, the owner has to preserve the object, keep it in the United Kingdom and allow the public reasonable access to it. If these conditions are not met, an inheritance tax charge based on the current market value of the object may then be imposed.

Potentially exempt transfers

If transfers are not exempt, they may nevertheless be potentially exempt if they are made to:

1.   An individual.
2.   An accumulation and maintenance trust.
3.   A trust for a disabled person.

Potentially exempt transfers are subject to tax if the donor dies within seven years, but are otherwise disregarded. Where the donor dies within seven years, the donee is liable for any tax. In these circumstances, the value of the transfer is that at the time it was made but the rates of tax used are those applying at the time of the donor's death.

Table 10.3 Relief for gifts made before death

Years between gift and death	Percentage of full charge
0-3	100
3-4	80
4-5	60
5-6	40
6-7	20
Over 7	0

However, if such a transfer is made more than three years before the death of the donor, the rate of tax is reduced, as shown by Table 10.3. There is also a quick succession relief which applies where a person's estate is increased by a chargeable transfer, but then he or she dies within the next five years. In such a case, the tax levied on the second transfer is reduced by 100, 80, 60, 40 or 20 per cent depending on whether the death follows the transfer by less than one, two, three, four or five years, respectively.

Where the donor continues to benefit from a gift even after it has been 'given away', there are special rules. An example would be where parents give their valuable home to the children but continue to live in it without paying a market rent. The transfer can be considered as a potentially exempt transfer only from the date such a reserved benefit is given up.

Business property and agricultural property

Subject to certain conditions, there is special relief for business property. The property must have been owned by the donor during the previous two years. The relief is not normally available where the business is concerned mainly in dealing in securities, land or buildings, or in holding investments. In qualifying businesses, a sole proprietor or a partner's interest attracts a 100 per cent deduction, as do transfers from shares in an unquoted company, provided the transferor had more than 25 per cent of the voting rights before the transfer. A 50 per cent deduction is given for transfers from unquoted shareholdings of less than 25 per cent. Transfers from a controlling shareholding in a quoted company qualify for 50 per cent relief. Where the donor had control of the company or was a partner, an asset owned by the donor but used by his firm would attract relief of 50 per cent. Before March 1992, these reliefs were given at lower rates.

Similarly, subject to certain conditions, there is relief from inheritance tax for agricultural property.

Chargeable lifetime transfers

Inheritance tax is likely to be paid during life only on certain lifetime transfers. The most likely category is transfers to a discretionary trust, that is one where the trustees can decide how much of the income they distribute. The rate of tax chargeable on lifetime transfers is 20 per cent - half the rate applying to transfers on death.

Tax chargeable on death

For the purposes of inheritance tax, at death a person is deemed to have made a transfer equal to the net value of his or her estate. This is the value of all assets, less liabilities. Some parts of the estate might be exempt - for example, transfers to a surviving spouse or to recognised charities. Potentially exempt transfers made within seven years before death are included in the total and there may be further liability on chargeable lifetime transfers made in the same period.

The impact of inheritance tax

As a result of the various concessions, inheritance tax involved only some 27,000 taxpayers in 2008/09, compared with around 31 million income tax payers (HM Revenue and Customs, *National Statistics,* 2008). Also it raises an estimated £3.2 billion, which is only a fraction of 1 per cent of total government revenues.

All in all, it seems reasonable to suggest that inheritance tax, like its predecessors, estate duty and capital transfer tax, is largely voluntary and paid by those who are either overoptimistic about the timing of their demise or who consider leaving money to their relatives worse than leaving it to the government!

10.6 An accession tax

An accessions tax is based on the capital transfers that a person receives. This includes both inheritances and gifts made during the donor's lifetime. The receipt of these transfers would be cumulated over the recipient's lifetime and the tax levied on the total. The case for an accessions tax and how it might be operated is discussed further in Sandford *et al.* (1973).

In contrast, and as already mentioned, the UK 'inheritance tax' retains the principle incorporated in both capital transfer tax and estate duty, that tax liability is based on the amount given rather than on the amount received. This means that, with progressive rates of tax, the more a donor gives away, the higher the rate of tax. The circumstances of the receiver do not affect the rate of tax at all. This situation conflicts with the principle of horizontal equity and provides no incentive for inherited wealth to be distributed more evenly.

The principle of horizontal equity is that similar people in similar circumstances should be treated similarly. Certainly the estates of two individuals with the same wealth would be treated in the same way at death. However, two individuals with the same financial circumstances who each inherit would not be equally taxed. This is because a progressive donor-based 'inheritance tax' is based on the amount each donor has given rather than the amount each donee has received. So, for example, when a very rich person leaves money to a poor one it is likely that a high rate of tax would apply because it is related to the value of the estate and not to the amount of other receipts received by the poor person. Similarly, should a poor person leave money to a rich one, no tax would be payable.

Secondly, the UK 'inheritance tax' does not provide much of an incentive for a more even distribution of wealth. Consider a rich individual who is drawing up a will and is deciding how much to leave to two distant relatives. One of these has already inherited a large amount but the other has so far inherited nothing. Under the donor-based 'inheritance tax', the same amount of tax would be payable whichever way the donor decides to leave his money. However with an accessions tax the amount of tax payable will be lower the more is left to the one who has so far received nothing. It might be argued, therefore, that inherited wealth might be spread more evenly under a donee-based tax than under the present inheritance tax. It would depend on how far donors' choices are affected by tax considerations.

There is a minor qualification to this second point, where the donor is concerned not only with how much he or she leaves to immediate beneficiaries, but also with how much they in turn leave to the next generation. For example, suppose a rich uncle is considering whether to leave his money to nephew A or to nephew B. Suppose that A has already received a substantial inheritance but that B has not. It is true that, under a donor-based tax, the initial liability would be the same whether the money were left to A or B. But when the wealth came to be passed on again, liability would depend on the wealth of A and B. In these circumstances therefore, even with the present inheritance tax, the rich uncle would minimise overall eventual liability by leaving his money to the poorer individual.

This qualification is unlikely to be very important in practice. Donors may not be very concerned with such long-term considerations. In addition, the future is uncertain and so benefactors cannot know which of the potential recipients will have the higher liability to inheritance tax when the time comes to pass on their wealth.

Thirdly, an accessions tax would tend to reduce inequality for a further, similar, related reason. It is large inheritances rather than large estates as such which perpetuate inequality. By taxing in relation to the size of the receipt, an accessions tax goes directly to the source of inequality. Comparing taxes of equal revenue, an accessions tax would tax estates left to one or two people more heavily than would estate duty, while estates more widely dispersed would be taxed less heavily. An accessions tax reinforces this process by taking account of all legacies and gifts from whatever source.

Of course, the importance of these issues may not be considered to be enormous but, other things being equal, they point to the superiority of a donee-based accessions tax.

However, even with a donee-based transfer tax, there is a further aspect to the taxation of wealth. A simple accessions tax still taxes wealth only when it moves. It would not take account of the benefits of holding wealth, nor of the length of time wealth is held. It is true that the inheritance tax has a provision for 'quick succession relief' but obviously this does not transform inheritance tax into a wealth tax, and it is to this issue that we now turn.

10.7 The arguments in favour of a wealth tax

The main arguments put forward in favour of an annual wealth tax usually centre around the concepts of equity and efficiency analysed in Part I of the book, and the extent to which a wealth tax could be used as a method of redistribution and administrative control.

Horizontal equity

As discussed in Chapter 5, the principle of horizontal equity is that people of a similar taxable capacity should b e taxed similarly. It will be shown that the possession of wealth confers advantages over and above the pecuniary income derived from that wealth. It may be argued, therefore, that an income tax on its own is insufficient to achieve horizontal equity. A striking illustration is Kaldor's (1956, p. 20) example of a beggar and a rich man who keeps all his wealth in the form of gold and jewels. Neither individual has any income; yet the latter, despite his lack of money income, clearly has the greater taxable capacity.

Leaving aside any direct pecuniary income, the benefits of wealth include the ability to dis-save, the control of economic resources, non-pecuniary income and status.

The ability to dis-save has two important advantages. First of all it provides security. An individual with wealth is less dependent on earned income than someone without wealth. To some extent the need for economic security, narrowly defined, has diminished since 1945 with the growth of public welfare provisions. Nevertheless, the possession of capital makes it easier for an individual to maintain his standard of living if his earnings should fall. Even if his earnings do not fall, a wealthy individual is secure in the knowledge that unforeseen expenditure can be met from capital. Such economic security is particularly desirable in old age. People are notoriously nicer to rich old men and women than to poor ones!

Secondly, wealth allows its owner greater power to take advantage of any economic opportunities that may arise. Given imperfect capital markets it is not always possible for individuals without capital to undertake promising ventures, however profitable they may seem. For example, a particular course of full-time education or training may lead to increases in earnings that would more than cover its cost, including the earnings forgone during training. A person without capital may not be able to borrow the necessary money, whereas a person with wealth can always borrow from himself, as it were, and pay for the course out of his capital.

Wealth can also confer control over economic resources. Clearly, the amount of control can vary a great deal. The small saver has little more power than the ability to withdraw his savings from a particular institution, and sometimes, as in the case of National Insurance pension rights, even this power does not exist. In other circumstances, however, the situation may be quite different. For instance, after an examination of the subject, Atkinson (1974, p. 44) concluded that:

> despite the separation of ownership and control in the modern corporation, the wealthy shareholder may well be in a position to exercise considerable influence over a company's policy, and in a substantial number of cases the owners retain full control.

In addition to these advantages, wealth usually yields benefits which we would classify as income under the definitions in Section 8.4 but which are not considered to be so for income tax purposes. The two most important are capital gains and the implicit income derived from wealth. A capital gain in real (as opposed to money) terms may be considered a form of income as it can be spent without reducing the owner's original wealth. Suppose, for example, a person owned £100 worth of gold and the price of gold suddenly doubled. Clearly the lucky owner could sell half his gold, spend the proceeds, and still own £100 worth of gold. Although there is a capital gains tax in the United Kingdom, it is levied at rates lower than the tax on many other incomes when National Insurance contributions are taken into account. Capital gains tax also has a considerably higher threshold than either income tax or National Insurance contributions (see Chapter 8). Further, capital gains tax may be deferred until the value of the asset is realised, and there are several important exemptions such as gains from owner-occupied houses. It would seem, therefore, that even some of the explicit income from wealth is not fully taxed.

Perhaps more important in this context is the value of implicit income from wealth. What is meant by 'implicit income' here is the value of the services an owner receives from his property. For example, a person living in his own home enjoys the benefit of accommodation for which a tenant would have to pay rent. Similar benefits are received by owners of works of art and suchlike. Clearly, a comprehensive tax on income could in principle cover such non-pecuniary income and indeed until 1963 the imputed benefit received by owner-occupiers was included in the United Kingdom income tax base.

A final advantage of wealth is the status it confers. Scientific evidence is somewhat light on this particular aspect, and it is tempting to retire behind anecdotal evidence concerning conspicuous consumption. Perhaps we can leave the description to Galbraith (1962, Chapter 7): 'Wealth has never been a sufficient source of honour in itself. It must be advertised, and the normal medium is obtrusively expensive goods'. Similarly with the other incidental benefits associated with wealth; perhaps these are best described by the immortal words of Zsa Zsa Gabor: 'No rich man is ugly'.

So, for all these reasons wealth provides benefits for the owner, over and above current pecuniary income. It may be argued, therefore, that on the grounds of horizontal equity an income tax alone is not sufficient to cover the full benefits derived from the ownership of wealth. The argument is the same as the ability-to pay approach discussed in Section 5.3.

Benefit approach

A case for a wealth tax may also be made on the lines of the benefit approach to taxation (Section 5.3). In its most basic form it is derived from Locke's theory of the state as a protector of property. The argument suggests that those who require the state to protect their wealth should pay more in tax than those who do not require such protection. However, we have seen in Section 5.3 that there are limitations to the benefit approach. In addition, it seems reasonable to think that some types of property require more protection than others. Therefore, the benefit approach suggests a differential tax on particular items of property, rather than the more global net wealth tax with which we are concerned.

Efficiency arguments

The main efficiency argument rests on a comparison between a wealth tax and an income tax of equal yield. The two areas normally considered are the effects on the supply of labour and enterprise, and the effects on the use of existing assets.

It may be argued that a wealth tax would have a less adverse effect on work incentives than an income tax of equal yield, on the grounds that the former would apply to past rather than present effort. In other words, people are less likely to be discouraged from working harder or applying for more productive and highly paid jobs if they are taxed on their *past* efforts (i.e. their wealth) rather than on their present efforts (i.e. their current income). However, this line of argument is limited by the extent to which income taxes encourage people to work harder or less hard (see Sections 4.2 and 4.3) and the extent to which the object of work is saving (i.e. future consumption) rather than current consumption.

The second point is that a tax on income from wealth rather than on wealth itself provides an incentive for people to invest in assets with low pecuniary yields, or in assets with non-pecuniary yields that cannot be captured by an income tax. At the extreme, an income tax could be avoided altogether by investing in an asset which has no pecuniary yield at all, such as a painting for a private collection. In contrast, a wealth tax would be levied on various assets at the same rate, and so would not discriminate against assets with a high yield. For example, suppose an investor had a choice between two assets: a small business or a country house to be used as a weekend retreat. The small business yields a pecuniary income of £10,000 profit a year but has no non-pecuniary benefits. The country cottage produces no money income but yields other benefits which may be valued at £6,000 a year. To keep the example simple, suppose that the private benefits received by the owner are the same as the benefits to society, that is there are no effects external to the market. Secondly, suppose that the price of the two assets is the same (£100,000) and is not affected by different income or wealth taxes. Finally, suppose that the choice of tax is either a 50 per cent income tax or a 5 per cent wealth tax. We can then see that, without either a wealth tax or an income tax, the investor would be better off with the small business as this gives the highest overall benefit.

	Pecuniary income	Non-pecuniary income	Total income	Net income with 50% income tax	Net income with 5% wealth tax
	£	£	£	£	£
Small business	10,000	0	10,000	5,000	5,000
Country cottage	0	6,000	6,000	6,000	1,000

An income tax, however, captures the pecuniary income of the business and so makes it more profitable to invest in the cottage, even though the private and social benefits of the cottage are less than those of the business. In contrast, a wealth tax does not discriminate between assets of different pecuniary yields and so would restore the incentive for our investor to choose the small business. A similar result applies where the owner can control the yield of an asset. A farmer with a field, for example, may be said to have an incentive to use it productively under a wealth tax - even if for no other reason than to pay the tax. No such incentive exists with an income tax.

Redistribution

A wealth tax could be a powerful instrument for the redistribution of wealth. If the community has a preference for a more equal distribution of wealth than currently exists, it would be difficult to redistribute wealth if the only taxes that could be used were levied on the income from, or the movement of, wealth. Taxes on the income from wealth are limited by the pecuniary yield of that wealth. Inheritance tax is limited by the degree of movement of capital. Death duties also have a number of problems, not least of which is that they are imposed on a near-random basis, that is death. Only an annual wealth tax would cover wealth as it stands.

The incidence of a tax and its resultant expenditure is a complex matter (Chapter 5). If a wealth tax were to redistribute resources, it would have to be implemented with that specific purpose in mind. Otherwise, the equalising effect of the wealth tax might be offset either because the revenue was used for the benefit of the wealthy, or because the expenditure had the effect of increasing the return to factors of production owned more by the rich than the poor.

Administrative control

The argument here is that a wealth tax would generate information which could be used by the administration to tighten up the control of evasion and avoidance of income tax. Any apparent inconsistency between an individual's wealth and his income could be followed up by the revenue authorities. This was one of the reasons behind the introduction of the French wealth tax in 1982, and such crosschecking takes place, for example, in Sweden. A further incidental benefit would be the availability of more reliable data on the distribution of wealth, at least in so far as it is measured for tax purposes!

Wealth tax and human capital

For administrative reasons that are discussed below, if for no other reason, it is highly unlikely that a wealth tax could be levied on the capital tied up in human beings. We include in this concept of human capital the investment in time and money spent to allow individuals to acquire education, training and skills. It might be asserted, therefore, that a wealth tax would discriminate between different forms of investment: that there would be a tendency to invest in human capital even in cases where it might be socially more productive to invest in non-human capital. Any distributive aims of tax policy might also be frustrated. The rich might still be able to transmit their wealth to their offspring in the form of human capital and so avoid both wealth and inheritance taxes by making sure that their children are highly educated.

There are two things that may be said about this sort of argument. First, there is some reason to suppose that the market, if left to itself, will result in under investment in education (for example, see Blaug, 1970); and that education is something valuable and requires public encouragement. Second, income taxes can discriminate against investment in human capital relative to investment in physical capital (Nerlove et al., 1993; Trostel, 1993). In the United Kingdom, the income tax system discriminates against investment in human capital, partly for administrative reasons. While any increase in income resulting from an increase in skill is subject to income tax, most of the costs involved in the acquisition of such skill are not deductible against taxable income. It is not generally recognised in income tax law that human capital can depreciate in the same way as non-human capital. The reasons for this are perhaps understandable. As the 1955 Royal Commission in its *Final Report* pointed out, 'the practical difficulties of producing any system that would give verifiable figures for expenditure on the acquisition of personal capital are overwhelming'.

While some of the distortions against investment in education may be partly offset by state subsidy of education, a further offset would be provided by a wealth tax which discriminated in favour of such investment. It is not possible to say whether this is an advantage or a disadvantage of a wealth tax. Offsetting one distortion with another is almost certain to introduce a further set of anomalies. So we can only conclude that the fact that a wealth tax in practice normally discriminates in favour of investment in human capital is, on efficiency criteria, not necessarily a disadvantage, and could be an advantage.

10.8 The arguments against a wealth tax

As we have seen, one of the main arguments in favour of a wealth tax is that a man with more wealth has a greater taxable capacity than a man with less wealth. However, it has been suggested that the validity of this argument is not as obvious as might appear at first sight (see Prest, 1976).

The suggestion is that taxable capacity can be covered adequately by a perfect income tax: that is a tax on all accretions, including capital gains as they accrue, gifts and bequests. Suppose that such an income tax existed. Suppose also there are two individuals who have the same wage income and, to begin with, have no wealth. One of the individuals then accumulates a capital sum through saving while the other does not, and the first individual as a result pays income tax on the interest from that saving. The argument then suggests, on equity grounds, that he should not be subject to an additional tax, as both individuals had the same opportunity to accumulate wealth.

There are difficulties with this line of argument because clearly we do not have a comprehensive income tax as described above. So we turn back to the more orthodox arguments which centre around the effects of saving and the practical difficulties associated with the operation of a wealth tax.

The effects on saving

Wealth is accumulated saving. Therefore it might be asserted that a tax on wealth would discourage saving. However, this is not necessarily true. As we have seen in Section 4.4, we cannot say, *a priori*, that an increase in taxation will lead to either an increase or a decrease in saving. Given that income taxes involve the 'double taxation of saving' (Section 4.4) it is possible that the introduction of a wealth tax, accompanied by a reduction in income tax, might encourage saving. It could certainly shift the burden from those who are accumulating wealth to those who already have it.

Practical difficulties

The main practical difficulty that emerged from the evidence presented to the Select Committee on a Wealth Tax (1975) concerned the valuation of assets. The valuation of pension rights and life assurance policies poses particular difficulties. A memorandum by the Government Actuary's Department demonstrated the very wide range of values that would result from relatively modest changes in the assumptions underlying the calculations. An example was based on a 30-year-old man entitled at age 60 to a pension of £1,000 a year plus a lump sum payment of £3,000, both assumed to rise in line with the cost of living. Depending on a limited number of assumptions, the capital value of these pension rights varied from £580 to £60,190!

Other problems would be associated with the valuation of items such as stamps, books, coins, antiques and the like. One way round these difficulties, commonly used abroad, is simply to exempt these assets. The disadvantage of this solution is that one of the arguments for a wealth tax is that such assets should be included in the tax base. More generally, many of the other practical considerations, such as the methods of administration and the treatment of the 'national heritage', have not caused the problems in overseas wealth taxes that the more fervent opponents of a wealth tax have suggested they might in the United Kingdom.

10.9 Wealth taxes overseas

Wealth taxes are now employed in about 20 countries. The tax is largely confined to Europe, the Indian sub-continent, and Central and South America and, as already seen, a number of these taxes are well established. As we are concerned with the implications of existing taxes for the potential introduction of a wealth tax in the United Kingdom, we shall confine our attention here almost entirely to those of the above countries with a similar socio-economic background, that is European countries. It should be noted again that the details of foreign tax systems can change rapidly, and that the operation of wealth tax in different countries often takes place in different circumstances. The main areas of interest are the structure and the rates of the taxes, and how the practical problems of operating a wealth tax have (or have not) been overcome.

The structure and rates of wealth taxes

In Europe, at the time of writing, net wealth taxes are levied in Finland, France, Iceland, Luxembourg, Norway, Spain, Sweden and Switzerland. As noted earlier, a number of others have been abolished in recent years. European wealth taxes are imposed in addition to national (and often local) income taxes, but are levied in place of higher rates of tax on investment income. Many of the continental taxes were introduced at about the time that the United Kingdom income tax was reformed to discriminate against investment income (see Section 8.3).

Except for the Swiss cantons, European wealth taxes are administered centrally, though Norway has both a national and a local wealth tax. In some countries the practice is to confine the tax to individual persons. This is in line with a general principle that the net wealth of corporations should be imputed to their owners.

However, in some countries wealth tax has been levied on companies in their own right.

The tax unit normally includes the combined net wealth of husband and wife. Up to the age of majority, children's assets are also usually included with their parents'. This is the case in Norway and Sweden and was proposed for the United Kingdom in the 1974 Green Paper, *Wealth Tax*.

The annual rates of wealth tax vary significantly, but usually within the range of 0.5 to 2 per cent of net wealth per year, levels which hardly contribute to large scale redistribution and certainly not to the serious erosion of existing fortunes. The tax is levied at a flat rate in some countries, such as Luxembourg. In other countries the rates are more progressive, for instance in Finland and Sweden. Norway has gone a step further and has both a national wealth tax levied at progressive rates and a flat rate local wealth tax.

Wealth taxes are not normally deductible against income taxes. However, there may be a possibility that combined income, net wealth and other income-related taxes may consume a very large part of, or even exceed, an individual's income. Consequently, several countries have an upper limit to the percentage of a taxpayer's income that may be paid in tax.

Practical problems

On a number of occasions, particularly before the Select Committee (1975), it has been asserted that the introduction of a wealth tax in the United Kingdom would present a whole range of practical difficulties. These difficulties include decisions regarding the scope of the tax, that is which assets to tax and which (if any) to exempt; the problems of valuation; the treatment of agriculture and the national heritage; and which methods of administration to employ. From the studies that have been made of foreign taxes, especially the study by Sandford *et al.* (1975), it would appear that these potential problems do not cause a great deal of difficulty in practice, normally being dealt with by a judicious combination of principle and pragmatism.

Starting with the scope of the tax, in principle all types of assets should be included in a wealth tax. However, in practice this may be considered excessive, either because some assets are exceptionally difficult to value, or because society may regard certain possessions as 'necessities' and therefore not the proper subject for taxation. Thus, every wealth tax in operation seems to have some form of exemption for household and personal effects, though this may be limited if their value exceeds a certain sum.

The valuation of the assets that are taxed should, in principle, be based on their open market value. Yet in practice this may lead to a number of difficulties. For example, if the market prices of some assets are relatively volatile, conscientious valuation may lead either to high administrative and compliance costs, or to a lack of certainty about current tax liability until a valuation is made. However, it would appear that the valuation of assets overseas is neither expensive nor the basis of much argument, perhaps because the methods are well established and generally produce conservative values. For example, in Sweden land is valued every five years at the open market price, but that figure is then reduced by 25 per cent.

For various reasons, agriculture is a sector that receives a number of fiscal favours. Apart from the political power historically associated with land ownership, farmers have attracted sympathy for reasons such as the volatile price and output of agricultural products, the low rate of return to farming, and an apparent national desire towards self-sufficiency in food. Further factors are the unstable, and generally high price of land, and that the farm itself often forms the vast bulk of the wealth of its owner; about half of all agricultural land in the United Kingdom is owner-occupied.

These problems may be less serious on the Continent, as the average size of farm is smaller than in the United Kingdom. However, while many countries such as Norway and Sweden do not give explicit relief for farming, agricultural land is still usually treated favourably in comparison with other assets. If the rate of return on agricultural land is very low, either in a particular year or in general, there may be limits to the amount of wealth tax payable. In addition, the methods used to value land for the purposes of wealth tax normally produce a figure below the open market price. This benefits farming, sometimes deliberately.

The 'national heritage', in the form of works of art, is completely exempt from wealth tax in countries such as Sweden, not only to preserve the heritage, but also because of the difficulties of ensuring their disclosure and valuation. In other countries, works of art may be granted exemption if they conform to certain requirements regarding artistic, historical or scientific interest. Historic buildings do not generally receive the generous concessions often afforded works of art, but may still be treated leniently in comparison with other assets.

The administration of wealth taxes abroad is usually at least partially integrated with the administration of income taxes. In Norway and Sweden, both taxes are dealt with in the same office, and taxpayers make a combined annual return of income and wealth. The combined returns can be relatively simple. In Sweden, a straight-forward return covers both national and local income taxes, as well as the wealth tax; and the space for the details of net wealth is only about half a page. Some form of joint administration can have a number of benefits, such as the cross-checking of wealth and income information. In addition, valuations made for a wealth tax can also be used for other taxes, such as gift or inheritance taxes. In those countries that have been studied in detail, it appears that the administrative and compliance costs are not remarkably high (Sandford *et al.*, 1975, pp. 250-3).

So, in considering these various potential problems of operating a wealth tax in the United Kingdom, our brief survey of taxes operating overseas seems to suggest that, once a wealth tax is established, the practical difficulties are unlikely to be as great as might at first be thought. However, as pointed out in the discussion of a personal expenditure tax in Chapter 9, it is not always easy to introduce a new tax without it suffering considerable amendment on the way. Certainly the experience of the Irish wealth tax provides a further example of the problems of implementing a tax unscathed by the pressures of particular interests. In their study of the Irish wealth tax, Sandford and Morrissey (1985) doubted that it added 'one jot to the horizontal equity of the tax system' (p. 143). They continued:

> Had the proposals of the [Irish] White Paper been implemented, the verdict might well have been different, for the White Paper envisaged thresholds at roughly half of the level of those which actually came into force, no exemption of the owner-occupied house and a minimum of other exemptions and reliefs.

They also considered that it would have had hardly any effect on the distribution of wealth.

10.10 Proposals for a wealth tax in the United Kingdom

The preliminary proposals of a former Labour government's Green Paper, *Wealth Tax* (1974) were based on two rate scales, one rising from 1 to 2 ½ per cent, the other from 1 to 5 per cent. In both cases the first £100,000 of net wealth was exempt and the maximum rate was applied to wealth in excess of £5 million. The investment income surcharge, which was then in force, was to remain. The reason given for not proposing a lower wealth tax threshold, combined with the abolition of the investment income surcharge, was the administrative difficulties that a lower threshold would imply for both taxpayers and the Revenue. It was also proposed to operate the tax on the basis of self-assessment with sample checks.

The Green Paper proposals were subsequently examined by the Select Committee on a Wealth Tax (1975). The Report of the Select Committee states, somewhat briefly, that the Committee was unable to agree on a report. There then follow five minority reports, and three volumes of evidence submitted to the Committee. The five reports consist of a draft report proposed by the Chairman, a draft report proposed by the Conservative group, the Chairman's report as amended by the Committee but not adopted, and two other minority reports.

There is insufficient space here to discuss each report in detail. Suffice it to say that, perhaps as expected, the main areas of disagreement and concern were the threshold and rates of a wealth tax, and issues such as whether children's wealth should be aggregated with that of their parents, and how far owner-occupied homes, chattels, productive assets and 'the national heritage' (e.g. historic homes) should be subject to the tax. The· reason for the rejection of the Chairman's amended report was essentially the absence abroad of two Labour MPs when the crucial vote was taken. Yet we might note that the reasons put forward by the Committee for rejecting the Chairman's amended report were as follows. First, it was felt that the report failed to ensure that the proposed wealth tax would be substitutive rather than additive: in other words, to ensure that the proposed tax would be met from income, after allowing for a reasonable level of consumption, rather than by running down the taxpayer's assets. Second, the Committee would not accept the amended report because it failed to ensure a protective ceiling on tax payments. Third, the Committee was concerned about the problems of introducing a wealth tax during 'a time of high inflation and economic crisis'. With the possible exception of the third reason we may conclude, from the reasons given in the brief agreed report, that the members of the Committee who were present at the time of the critical vote were by no means in favour of a powerful wealth tax.

Further reading

Wealth transfer taxes are assessed by Aaron and Munnell (1992). An accessions tax is discussed in detail in Sandford *et al.* (1973). The same authors also cover the pros and cons of wealth taxes and the operation of some wealth taxes overseas (Sandford *et al.*, 1975), and the Irish wealth tax is examined by Sandford and Morrissey (1985). The UK inheritance tax is discussed in Sandford (1987). Proposals for a wealth tax in the UK have been put forward by Flemming and Little (1974) and the Meade Committee (1978). Tiley (2007) describes some of the former taxes on death. Finally, evidence on the relative importance of inherited as opposed to 'self-made' wealth is provided in Harbury and Hitchens (1979).

References

Aaron, R.I. and Munnell, A.H. (1992), 'Reassessing the role for wealth transfer taxes', *National Tax Journal,* Vol. XLV, pp. 119-43.

Atkinson, A.B. (1974), *Unequal Shares,* Penguin.

Atkinson, A.B. (1983), *The Economics of Inequality,* 2nd edn, Oxford University Press.

Blaug, M. (1970), *An Introduction to the Economics of Education,* Penguin.

European Taxation (1981), Vol. 21, No. 10, pp. 307-18.

Flemming, J.S. and Little, I.M.D. (1974), *Why We Need a Wealth Tax,* Methuen.

Galbraith, J.K. (1962), *The Affluent Society,* Penguin.

Good, E.I. (1990), 'Estimates of the distribution of personal wealth', *Economic Trends,* October.

Harbury, C.D. and Hitchens, D.M.W.N. (1979), *Inheritance and Wealth Inequality in Britain,* Allen & Unwin.

Inland Revenue (1977), *119th Report,* Cmnd. 6734, HMSO.

Inland Revenue Statistics (1987), HMSO.

Inland Revenue Statistics (1991), HMSO.

Inland Revenue Statistics (1994), HMSO.

Kaldor, N. (1956), *Indian Tax Reform,* Ministry of Finance, Government of India.

Meade Committee (1978), *The Structure and Reform of Direct Taxation,* Institute for Fiscal Studies.

Nerlove, M., Razin, A., Sadka, E. and von Weizsacker, R.K. (1993), 'Comprehensive income taxation, investments in human and physical capital, and productivity', *Journal of Public Economics,* Vol. 50, pp. 397-406.

Prest, A.R. (1976), 'The select committee on a wealth tax', *The British Tax Review,* No. 1.

Rogers, Will (1962), 'A Roger's Thesaurus', *Saturday Review,* 25 August.

Royal Commission on the Taxation of Profits and Income (1955), *Final Report,* Cmnd. 9474, HMSO.

Sandford, C.T. (1987), 'Death duties: taxing estates or inheritances', *Fiscal Studies,* Vol. 8, No. 4, pp. 15-23.

Sandford, C.T. and Morrissey, O. (1985), *The Irish Wealth Tax: A Case Study in Economics and Politics,* Economic and Social Research Institute, Dublin.

Sandford, C.T., Willis, J.RM. and Ironside, D.J. (1973), *An Accessions Tax,* Institute for Fiscal Studies.

Sandford, C.T., Willis, J.RM. and Ironside, D. (1975), *An Annual Wealth Tax,* Heinemann Educational Books.

Schultz, T.W. (1961), 'Investment in human capital', *American Economic Review,* Vol. 51, pp. 1-17, reprinted in M. Blaug (ed.), *Economics of Education I,* Penguin, 1968.

Select Committee on a Wealth Tax, Session 1974-75 (1975), Volume I, *Report and Proceedings of the Committee,* HC 696-1, HMSO.

Stewart, I. (1991), 'Estimates of the distribution of personal wealth II: marketable wealth and pension rights of individuals 1976 to 1989', *Economic Trends,* November, pp. 99-110.

Sutherland, A. (1981), 'Capital transfer tax: an obituary', *Fiscal Studies,* Vol. 2, pp. 37-51.

Sutherland, A. (1984), 'Capital transfer tax: adieu', *Fiscal Studies,* Vol. 5, No. 3, pp. 68-83.

Tiley, J. (2007), 'Death and taxes' *British Tax Review,* No.3. pp. 300-319.

Trostel, P.A. (1993) 'The effect of taxation on human capital', *Journal of Political Economy,* Vol. 101, No. 2, pp. 327-50.

Wealth Tax (1974), Cmnd. 5704, HMSO.

Whalley, J. (1974), 'Estate duty as a "voluntary tax"; Evidence from the stamp duty statistics', *Economic Journal,* Vol. 84, September.

SELF ASSESSMENT QUESTIONS

Suggested answers to self-assessment questions are given at the back of the book.

10.1   What is wealth?

10.2   What is human capital?

10.3   In what sense might the current UK inheritance tax not be considered an inheritance tax at all?

10.4   What are the main exemptions from inheritance tax?

10.5   A rich old miser, who has never given anything away, suddenly gives £6,000 to his housekeeper and dies the following year. Is the £6,000 chargeable to inheritance tax?

10.6   What is the key feature of an accessions tax?

I 0.7   A rich old lady wishes to leave her money to either or both of her two nephews with the intention that they in turn pass it on to the next, as yet unborn, generation. Suppose one nephew had already inherited a very large amount of money but the other had so far received nothing. If the rich old lady wanted to maximise the amount left to the unborn generation and nothing else mattered to her, to which nephew would she leave her money if an accessions tax were in force? Which one would she choose in the face of a capital transfer tax or the so-called UK 'inheritance tax'?

DISCUSSION QUESTIONS

1.   How important a role does the UK inheritance tax have?

2.   What advantages might an accessions tax have over a tax based on the amount a person leaves or gives away?

3.   How strong are the arguments for a wealth tax?

CHAPTER ELEVEN

Indirect and other taxes

LEARNING OBJECTIVES

After reading this chapter, you should be able to:

- Appreciate the advantages and disadvantages of indirect taxes.
- Understand the basic workings of indirect taxes, particularly VAT.
- Explain why there has been such controversy over local taxation.

11.1 Introduction

It was pointed out in Chapter 2 that the word 'indirect' when applied to a tax may be somewhat misleading. In this chapter, the word will be used in its common loose sense.

There are many 'indirect' taxes in operation in the UK. This chapter opens with a brief background to the arguments which might justify the use of indirect taxes, the types there may be, and the past and present taxes in use in the UK. Consideration is given in turn to excise and customs duties, purchase tax and selective employment tax (both of which have been discontinued), value added tax and to local authority taxation. Finally, there are sections about the overall regressiveness of the present system and possible future developments.

Arguments for indirect taxation

Before looking at particular taxes, some of the reasons for using indirect taxes should be briefly mentioned. We saw in Chapter 5 that indirect taxes may assist in the redistribution of income, though various unfortunate side-effects were examined in Chapter 3. Also, indirect taxes may be able to correct for market imperfections, such as the effects of monopoly on the supply of particular goods and the existence of externalities ignored by producers.

In addition, where people are thought to under-estimate the dangers or disadvantages of particular products, a paternalistic government may use indirect taxes to guide them. There may also be the advantage that some indirect taxes have only minor disincentive effects on the supply of effort (see Chapter 4).

From the point of view of governments, some indirect taxes, such as VAT, are appealing because they are related to prices and, hence, are buoyant. The tax take increases without the need for action by a government because, as prices rise, the proportional tax on sales also rises. The tax is index-linked, given that sales volume does not decline. However, other indirect taxes are not so attractive, as will be explained.

Types of indirect tax

A large variety of indirect taxes is possible. There may be overall sales taxes, which can include capital goods in their coverage. These overall taxes could use different rates for different goods. Alternatively, a sales tax could be selective in coverage. In each case, the stage of imposition is open to choice. The tax can be levied on the manufacturer, the wholesaler or the retailer. Indeed, it may be levied on all of them, as for VAT.

If the taxes are selective on particular goods, it is much simpler to tax at the manufacturing stage. This means that the number of taxpayers is smaller and that they are mostly large companies which are capable of efficient book-keeping. The UK purchase tax system was like this (see below). On the other hand, if a uniform ad valorem tax is required, it is necessary to tax at the retail level because the ratio of retail prices to manufacturers' prices differs by industry and by product within an industry.

Within multi-stage taxes there is yet another pair of possibilities. There may be either a system (as for VAT) under which the total tax bill is related to the final price, because at each stage there are credits for the previous tax borne, or a 'cascade' system (like that which once existed in some continental countries) under which the tax added at each level is based on the gross price up to that stage, including tax paid so far. The cascade system means that there will be a higher total rate of tax on products which involve a larger number of stages in their production. This encourages vertical integration of industries and is clearly economically inefficient. It has been replaced by a VAT in most countries.

Another possibility for any degree of comprehensiveness and any stage of imposition is to have a unit (or specific) tax rather than an ad valorem tax. However, although this has the merit of a certain simplicity, especially when one is not dealing with a large number of small items, it is clearly not suitable if a uniform rate of taxation is required. This is because taxation will represent a different proportion of the final value, depending on the value of the unit. A tax of £1 per bottle of wine will be a larger proportion of the price of a cheap wine than of an expensive wine.

Also, unit taxation may produce socially inefficient changes, such as larger sizes of product or larger packets, merely in order to reduce the proportion of the gross price which is paid in tax. This is not possible, however, for unit taxes per gallon of petrol or per pint of whisky, for example. There will also be a reduction in buoyancy because the tax revenue will not automatically increase with prices. Consequently, unit taxes have become less popular. We will see later that there has been a move away from various unit-based excise taxes.

History and present yields

Certain types of expenditure taxation on important goods (such as slaves) can be traced back as far as ancient Rome. Usually taxation has been associated with the need to raise funds for fighting wars. Recent British tax history begins with the introduction of expenditure taxes on alcoholic drinks, tea and coffee in the 1660s. At the time, efforts were made to exclude the expenditure of 'cottagers and paupers'. However, by the end of the seventeenth century, one half of the burden of excise taxes fell on beer, which was the drink of the labourers. During the nineteenth century, the real essentials of life, such as food, were generally free of tax. It was in 1940, in order to help pay for the war, that purchase tax was introduced. By 1947 the rates of tax were very high, including 100 per cent and 125 per cent rates. However, the tax base was fairly narrow, excluding food, fuel and services. By 1958 there were three different rates of purchase tax: 10 per cent, 15 per cent and a luxury rate of 25 per cent.

The importance of purchase tax gradually declined. One way of broadening the base of taxation was to tax employment in service industries which did not bear purchase tax. This was achieved with the introduction of selective employment tax (SET) in 1966. Both these taxes were replaced by VAT in 1973. VAT in the UK has seen a variety of changes since 1973, particularly to the number and level of its rates.

The importance of the various indirect taxes over the last few years can be seen from Table 11.1.

11.2 Excise and custom duties

The first four columns of Table 11.1 show that excise duties have generally been rising with inflation. In the period covered by the table, there were increases in rates of duty for specific taxes, though these did not always keep up with inflation. In volume terms, demand fell in the period for beer, spirits and tobacco and rose for wine (e.g. CSO, 1987). These shifts seem to be more connected with the state of the economy and changes in tastes than with the level of duty.

Tables 7.1 and 11.1 show how important excise taxes are as a source of revenue. However, it is clear that they are unattractive in some ways. First, although the government relies heavily on excise revenue, it nevertheless indulges in advertising campaigns and introduces controls against smoking and drinking.

Table 11.1 Important indirect taxes (£ million)

	Beer	Wine	Spirits	Tobacco	Hydro-carbons	Road licences	VAT	Customs duties
1982/83	1,525	453	965	3,447	5,239	1,864	13,815	1,028
1984/85	1,826	600	1,240	4,140	6,201	2,168	18,534	1,326
1986/87	1,975	661	1,469	4,769	7, 507	2,563	21,428	1,306
1988/89	2,105	784	1,576	4,990	8,679	2,785	27,328	1,673
1990/91	2,229	855	1,703	5,636	9,628	2,965	31,006	1,684
1992/93	2,378	981	1,661	6,041	11,442	3,306	37,340	1,801
1994/95	2,534	1,138	1,776	7,388	14,250	3,836	41,814	2,010
1997/98	2,696	1,363	1,546	8,356	19,454	4,704	50,585	2,263

Source: Financial Statistics HMSO, July 1987, Tables 3.14 and 3.15; November 1991, Tables 3.15 and 3.16; and July 1995 and March 1999, Tables 2.1 D and 2.1 E.

These campaigns would have disastrous effects on the budget if they were more successful. Fortunately for the government, it may reasonably be said that both its control activities and its fiscal activities are designed to fight smoking and drinking. A more serious problem is that some excise taxes might be regressive (see Section 11.6). In these cases, households with smaller incomes would spend a larger proportion on goods subject to these taxes and thus suffer proportionally more from the taxation. A contributory factor would be the low elasticity of demand for some of these goods. If the percentages of disposable income taken by excise duties on drink and tobacco are added together as in Table 11.2, we can see that a general charge of regressiveness has some foundation. An overall view of regressiveness is taken in Section 11.6.

Table 11.2 Drink and tobacco taxes as percentages of disposable income 1993 (non-retired households)

			Quintile groups			
	Bottom	2nd	3rd	4th	Top	Average
Original income (£)	3,040	10,530	17,950	25,300	43,420	20,050
Disposable income* (I)	8,820	12,110	15,330	19,270	30,570	17,220
Percentage of drink and tobacco	7.3	4.9	3.8	2.7	1.7	3.1
Percentage of IT and NIC	5.1	11.5	15.9	18.5	21.8	17.5

Note: *After tax and subsidies.
Source: Economic Trends. CSO, December 1994, Tables D, F and G, pp. 40-2.

Similar selective imposts will now be briefly discussed. The taxes on hydrocarbon oils are imposed partly to reduce demand for these goods and are no doubt successful because of the availability of alternatives. Some uses for hydrocarbon oils are exempted, such as fuel for fishing boats. The revenue raised by this taxation is also extremely useful. Road licences are a second example of duties applied to goods which are not in highly inelastic demand. There is some application of the benefit approach here, although the split of costs and benefits between private and commercial vehicles, and between stationary and moving vehicles - is open to manipulation. There may also be an element of expenditure-directing towards the railways.

Customs duties are levied on imported goods and some goods manufactured from them. They may also be levied on some exported goods. As well as raising revenue, these duties have included some which are designed to give protection to certain industries, or preference to imports from certain countries. As a result of entry into the EU and the resulting objective of removing customs barriers, protective duties have been absorbed into the other customs duties, which in turn have been adjusted to the EU Common Customs Tariff or converted into internal excise duties.

11.3 Sales taxes

As was mentioned in Section 11.1, purchase tax was introduced in 1940 and by the late 1950s was operated with three rates up to 25 per cent. Therefore, there was an element of progressiveness in the tax because the higher rates applied to the sort of goods which form a small proportion of the budgets of low-income families. As the ownership of televisions, record players, and so on became more widespread, the progressivity of purchase tax declined. Nevertheless, since food and fuel were untaxed, it never became regressive.

This tax on these relatively few types of goods was simple to collect from the manufacturers. There were between 60,000 and 80,000 collection points, and only about 1,500 civil servants involved in the collection. Nevertheless, purchase tax was a considerable revenue earner (£1,429m in 1971/72, about the same as hydrocarbons).

Partly because services were outside the scope of purchase tax, a further tax called selective employment tax (SET) was introduced in September 1966 as a tax on all payrolls which was then refunded to manufacturing industry, in some cases with a bonus. Its purpose was to encourage labour to move from service industries, which were allegedly 'unproductive', towards manufacturing industry (for analysis, see Reddaway, 1970).

It was always very unpopular with small traders, and its abolition became an aim of the Conservative Party in opposition. It was removed with purchase tax when VAT was introduced in 1973. However, those service industries which had complained about the effect of SET on their margins and administration costs were in for a unpleasant shock when they exchanged SET for VAT.

VAT was introduced in the UK in 1973, partly in order to satisfy the requirements of the EU. Harmonisation of indirect tax systems is called for by Article 99 of the Treaty of Rome; it should eventually extend to excise taxes, and it includes rates of tax as well as the tax base and the system. The harmonisation of indirect taxes is discussed further in Crosser (1983).

In the UK, VAT began with a single rate of 10 per cent covering about 55 per cent of expenditures. Other goods were either exempt or (more favourably, as explained below) zero-rated. Later a 'luxury' rate was temporarily introduced. In 1977-79 the rates were 8 per cent and 12.5 per cent. There were some problems in defining luxuries, of course. For example: ironing boards and films were taxed at the lower rate, whereas irons and cameras were taxed as luxuries.

The Conservative Party was returned to office in 1979 pledged to shift the balance of taxation from income tax to indirect tax. The argument concerned incentives, as discussed in Chapter 4, where it was pointed out that both theory and empirical evidence are inconclusive about the effects of lowering income tax (both marginal and average rates). Further, as the compensation for lower income tax is higher VAT, it should not take the average taxpayer/consumer too long to work out that extra disposable income has become less attractive because the average price of goods has risen.

Nevertheless, almost immediately after taking office, the Conservative government unveiled a Budget in which income tax rates were significantly lowered and VAT was raised to 15 per cent. This had a considerable effect on the inflation rate and brought cries of outrage from the Labour benches. However, one tangential advantage was a considerable step towards the harmonisation of rates of VAT in the EU (Dosser, 1981). For an analysis of the switch from direct to indirect taxes, see Atkinson (1981) and Kay and Morris (1979). VAT was further raised in 1991 to 17.5 per cent. A rate of 5 per cent applies to heating fuel.

In the context of the financial crisis of 2008/9, the rate of VAT was lowered to 15 per cent until the end of 2009. This prompted much international political argument about whether the effects would justify the loss of revenue. The Conservative party opposed it and President Sarkozy of France criticised it. There was also much academic debate (Crossley *et al.*, 2009; Barrell and Weale, 2009; Blundell, 2009). The rate is 20% from 4 January 2011.

VAT is a multi-stage tax which involves credits at each stage. Suppose that there is a manufacturer (M), a wholesaler (W) and a retailer (R) involved in supplying a good to a customer. Let us further suppose that there is a 10 per cent VAT rate and that the manufacturer extracts his own raw materials and pays no VAT for any purposes.

Table 11.3 VAT example

	VAT paid on inputs	Net price	VAT charged	Gross price	VAT to Customs and Excise
Goods leaving M	0.00	4.00	0.40	4.40	0.40
Goods leaving W	0.40	6.00	0.60	6.60	0.20
Goods leaving R	0.60	9.00	0.90	9.90	<u>0.30</u>
					<u>0.90</u>

Table 11.3 shows that, assuming the net prices are not adjusted as a result of the effect of VAT on demand, the traders do not directly bear any of the VAT. The customer bears the full 0.90, which is 10 per cent of the retail price and which is fully received by the Revenue and Customs. It should be pointed out, however, that the *effective incidence* of VAT may rest partly on the suppliers because demand for their goods may fall.

The goods which are *exempt* from VAT include postage and services such as education and health. No VAT is to be charged on these goods, but no VAT can be reclaimed on inputs. On the other hand, there are *zero-rated* goods such as food, exports, construction, books, newspapers and medical prescriptions. For these, no VAT is charged on outputs and VAT suffered on inputs is reclaimable. So zero-rated goods escape entirely from VAT, whereas exempt goods do not suffer any tax on the value added at the final stage.

A further detail of administration which is of great importance to many businesses is that there is a lower turnover limit below which traders need not register for VAT purposes. For many small traders this saves much administration and means that VAT need not be charged and paid over on their outputs. However, it also means that any VAT borne on inputs cannot be reclaimed. This lower limit changes fairly often. From April 2012 it was £77,000.

Arguments for and against VAT

The Green Paper proposing VAT (NEDO, 1971) said that indirect taxation should become a 'more broadly based structure which, by discriminating less between different types of goods and services, would reduce the distortion of consumer choice'. Since there was a Conservative pledge to remove SET, and since it was difficult to extend purchase tax to include services, VAT was proposed. It was argued that this would reduce the misallocation of resources of selective taxes (see Chapter 3). VAT is neutral between all goods (and services) if it is levied at a single rate on everything; it is neutral between vertically integrated companies and other (unlike the cascade system mentioned earlier); it is also neutral between companies with different ratios of labour costs to profit (unlike SET) (Johnstone, 1975).

However, although VAT is theoretically an overall tax with some exceptions, its actual coverage (according to Field *et al.*, 1977, p.102) was only 55 per cent of expenditures. In addition, there are still excise taxes at higher rates and VAT itself involves three percentage rates (0, 5 and 20). Therefore, although the neutrality argument was reasonably used for the introduction of a wide-based single-rate VAT system, it would be misleading to use it in defence of our present VAT. Extension of the VAT base is discussed by Davis and Kay (1985).

There is some effect on the encouragement of exports. This is because exports are zero-rated for VAT which can, therefore, be completely recovered. Previously, purchase tax and SET were charged on some inputs to exports, like stationery and office equipment. However, adjustments could have been made to the former taxes to achieve the same effect. It is additionally argued that it is easier to exempt capital formation under VAT.

VAT was also said to be more difficult to evade because, if a trader does not issue an invoice, then another trader is not receiving one. Therefore, the net effect should be less evasion. However, invoices to final customers can be omitted. In addition, since there are now around two million collection points rather than about 70,000, there are more opportunities for evasion and overdue payment.

A disadvantage that also follows from the increased number of collection points is the high cost of administration (Sandford *et al.*, 1981). This does not include the great amount of extra work created for industry and commerce in recording and processing VAT information. The present system of VAT assessment based on invoices could be greatly simplified if an alternative system based on accounts were used. Here there might be approximate self-assessment by companies each quarter using their sales and purchases figures. These could be checked more thoroughly and agreed by chief accountants, auditors and excise officials once every year.

Proposals for reform of VAT in the EU were being discussed in the mid-1990s (Lockwood *et al.*, 1995).

11.4 Local authority taxation

Like other taxes, those raised by local government may be assessed in terms of the criteria laid down in Part I of the book. Thus they should be designed to score well in terms of low excess burdens, administrative and compliance costs, and should not interfere unduly with incentives or be thought unfair. However, suitable local taxes should have some additional characteristics and the need for these lies in the nature of local government itself.

In economic terms at least, one justification for local government is that different parts of the country may have different preferences for different public services. For example, the inhabitants of a particular area may wish to have a higher level of, say, education or parks than that provided by the central government. If these inhabitants wish to pay higher (local) taxes in order to increase the provision of such services locally they should be free to do so.

While such services may attract some central funding, there is a strong case for at least part of the money being raised locally. One argument is that local funding facilitates local autonomy because if central government pays the piper it may also be tempted to call the tune. Another major issue is that of accountability. Local politicians may exercise more care if the money they spend comes directly from local voters rather than being seen as a free gift from central government. Equally, voters may be more vigilant in observing the behaviour of their local authority if there is a direct link between local spending and local taxation. To ensure such local accountability it has also been argued that local taxes should be perceptible to local taxpayers to ensure that they are fully aware of the costs of local government.

These considerations imply that a good local tax must meet some additional criteria. One is that it must be possible for local authorities to vary the level of the tax in line with local preferences. A tax which could only be raised at the same rate throughout the country would not allow much local autonomy. A second is that the tax base must be spread reasonably evenly throughout the country. A tax with a geographically uneven base might be very suitable as a national tax, but of little use as a local one. A third criterion is that the yield of the tax has to be substantial if local authorities are to continue to play a significant economic role

Local authority rates

Local authority rates on occupiers of land and buildings have a long ancestry and can be traced back to the compulsory poor rate raised under the Elizabethan Poor Relief Act of 1601 and indirectly to even earlier levies. In their modern manifestation local rates (until 1989/90) were a property tax levied on the 'rateable value' of property. Domestic ratepayers were charged at a lower rate than non-domestic taxpayers and there were also rebates for individuals on low incomes. The present council tax is an adjusted form of rates (see below).

In terms of the criteria described above, local authority rates scored quite highly. Excess burdens were lower than for many other taxes since, of course, existing property cannot normally be moved to low tax areas. The administrative and compliance costs were also low and rates were not considered to provide serious disincentives to work, save or invest. In terms of equity it has been argued that the amount spent on housing is (at least loosely) linked to income and wealth, and rate rebates were available for the less well-off. It has also been argued that a tax system may be progressive overall without every tax individually also having to be progressive. Finally, in so far as rates were levied on housing, their impact might have been partly offset by income tax and capital gains tax concessions to owner-occupiers.

Nevertheless, local authority rates were subject to considerable criticism over the years. The issue of fairness was frequently raised and it was said that rates did not take an individual's ability to pay into account and were regressive. Other criticisms came from the local authorities themselves, who complained that the rates were not a buoyant source of revenue and that they were too unpopular to raise the increasing income needed. Such criticisms are recorded in the reports of successive government enquiries into local government finance, for example Layfield (1976, pp. 12, 155-65).

The Layfield Report suggested that a change to a capital value basis for rates was necessary for greater comprehensibility and fairness and that other sources of local revenue should be developed. The most appropriate was seen to be a local income tax (Layfield, 1976, pp. 168-72, 196-208). However, there were serious obstacles to these alternative taxes in terms of administrative difficulties, particularly in operating a local income tax alongside the existing PAYE system (Section 8.5). There is also the aversion of the Chancellor to losing control of taxes on income or expenditure.

Nevertheless two government Green Papers on the subject followed (Department of the Environment, 1977; 1981), and there is discussion in Prest (1982) and Crawford and Dawson (1982).

There was a further consideration. From the time of its original election in 1979 the Conservative government had struggled to control the level of public expenditure of which, of course, local government expenditure is a large part. Although rates were acknowledged as a highly perceptible tax, they were actually paid by only a proportion of the local electorate. There was the possibility, therefore, of a majority of non-ratepayers voting for extra local expenditure without concern for who might end up paying.

The government therefore looked for a tax which promoted local accountability more effectively. The argument was that 'a substantial proportion of electors [should] have a direct interest in the decisions of their authority' and 'there should be a clear link between changes in [local] expenditure and changes in the local tax bill' (Department of the Environment, 1986, para 3.12). On this basis the possibility of a local sales tax was rejected, among other reasons, because it would not be perceived directly by those able to vote in local elections. Similarly the government rejected the possibility of a local income tax on the basis that, while there were over 35 million voters, there were only 20 million income taxpayers (though this counted married couples as one unit: at the time there were nearly 24 million individuals paying income tax). However, to try to ensure that as far as possible all voters contributed something to the cost of local spending, the government decided to introduce a community charge. A review of the arguments can be found in Smith (1988).

The community charge or poll tax

Although the experience of the operation of a poll tax in Britain had taken place many years before, the precedent was not encouraging. The Rising of 1381 originated from hatred of the poll tax (Trevelyan, 1946). The Archbishop of Canterbury who, as Chancellor of the realm, represented the government was beheaded by Wat Tyler's men on Tower Hill and, quite remarkably, the rebels captured London itself. Clearly the poll tax scored highly on the criterion of perceptibility.

The modern version of the poll tax, the 'community charge', was introduced in place of domestic rates in Scotland in 1989 and in England and Wales in 1990. To promote perceptibility, the tax was levied at a flat rate, payable by all adults at the level set by the local authority area. Assistance was available to individuals on low incomes but everyone was required to make a minimum payment of 20 per cent of the tax.

In many ways the poll tax scored very well in terms of the criteria listed above. Since the tax did not vary with any form of economic activity, there should in principle have been no excess burden or disincentive effects (except to the extent that for those on low incomes the proportion of the community charge payable rose from 20 per cent as income rose).

The disadvantage was that, for most people, the tax was entirely unrelated to any concept of ability to pay. One of the main lessons of the poll tax is that a tax which is considered to be unfair becomes difficult to administer and therefore expensive to collect. Although the experience of 1381 was not repeated in quite the same way, the country faced a considerable anti-tax campaign which included civil disobedience and a major riot in London. Finally, the unpopularity of the tax was such that it was undoubtedly a contributory factor in the events leading to the resignation of Mrs Margaret Thatcher as Prime Minister (Gibson, 1990).

Alternative forms of local taxation were quickly reviewed and proposals for the replacement of the community charge with a new council tax were rapidly advanced.

11.5 The council tax and the local business rate

The council tax (introduced in 1993) is based on property but there is also a personal element. The property element is assessed using a system of banding constructed around average property values. Every home in Britain is allocated to one of eight bands according to its value. Properties in the same band in a local authority area are assessed to tax on the same basis.

The assessment to tax begins with the assumption that each home contains two adults, but households of three or more adults are not charged extra. However, a personal element remains in that single-adult households receive a discount of 25 per cent of the basic charge. Unlike the community charge there is to be no minimum contribution. Individuals or couples on income support or equivalent levels of income, are entitled to 100 per cent rebates.

The result of all of this is that the council tax is partly a property tax, partly a household tax and, because of the rebates linked to income, partly an income tax. The structure of the tax and some of its effects are examined in Hills and Sutherland (1991) and Giles and Ridge (1993). The impact of potential reforms is discussed by Jones *et al*. (2006).

Local business rates

When domestic rates were replaced by the community charge, non-domestic rates were also reformed. The result is that the level of 'business rates' is now set by central government as a single rate and the proceeds distributed to local authorities as a common amount per adult.

11.6 Regression

The definition of a 'regressive' tax was considered in Section 2.2. It has been used in this chapter in its normal context, that is, in relation to income or disposable income. At its simplest, the reason why indirect taxes may be regressive is that there is no equivalent in indirect taxation of the zero-rate band due to personal allowances in income tax. A tax on beer is paid by poor consumers and rich consumers alike. To the extent that poor consumers spend a greater proportion of their incomes on beer, the tax on beer will be regressive. To the extent that the poor consume a greater proportion of their incomes (on goods that are taxed), the whole indirect tax system may be regressive.

In total, the system does in fact seem to be regressive, as Table 11.4 shows. The most regressive form of taxation can be seen to be tobacco tax, but this is something to do with absolutely higher consumption by lower earners. The regressiveness is a development of the 1980s onwards (Giles and Johnson, 1994).

Another regressive form of taxation was local rates. This regressiveness remained despite a tempering due to charging much higher poundages on commercial and industrial property than on domestic property, and by allowing rate rebates for low-income sections of society. This was one of the arguments for their abolition. However, it cannot reasonably be said that the local poll tax was an improvement on this count.

A note of caution must be sounded about the remarks in this section, however. It has been pointed out that the re distributive effects of indirect taxes are usually measured using nominal income rather than real purchasing power. In times of inflation this can be misleading (Levitt, 1976).

Table 11.4 Indirect taxes as percentages of disposable income 1993 non-retired households)

| | Quintile groups | | | | | |
	Bottom	2nd	3rd	4th	Top	All
VAT	11.2	9.9	9.5	8.6	7.1	8.6
Beer and cider	1.0	0.9	0.9	0.8	0.5	0.7
Wines and spirits	0.8	0.7	0.7	0.6	0.7	0.7
Tobacco	5.5	3.3	2.2	1.3	0.5	1.7
Oils	2.4	2.2	2.1	1.9	1.2	1.8
Car taxes	0.8	0.7	0.7	0.6	0.4	0.6
Other final goods	2.3	1.8	1.7	1.2	0.9	1.4
Intermediate taxes	7.1	5.8	5.3	4.8	3.9	4.9
Total indirect	31.2	25.4	23.0	19.9	15.3	20.2

Source: Economic Trends, HMSO, December 1994, Table G, p. 42.

Further reading

Value added tax is discussed in detail in Prest (1980) and Chown (1973) relating to the UK, and in Aaron (1981) for other European countries. More general coverage of indirect taxation may be found in Kay and King (1990), Musgrave and Musgrave (1989), Prest and Barr (1985) and in a special edition of *Fiscal Studies* (Symposium, 1982). More recent changes are discussed in Giles and Johnson (1994). A comparative review of VAT, sales taxes and other means of indirect taxation can be found in Sandford (2000).

References

Aaron, H.J. (ed.) (1981), *The Value-added Tax: Lessons from Europe*, Brookings Institution.

Atkinson, A.B. (1981), 'On the switch to indirect taxation', *Fiscal Studies,* July.

Blundell, R. (2009), 'Assessing the temporary VAT cut policy in the UK', *Fiscal Studies*, Vol. 30, No. 1.

Barrell, R. and Weale, M. (2009), 'The economics of a reduction in VAT', *Fiscal Studies*, Vol. 30, No. 1.

Chown, J. (1973), *VAT Explained,* 2nd edn, Kogan Page.

Crawford, M. and Dawson, D. (1982), 'Are rates the right tax for local government?', *Lloyds Bank Review,* July.

Crosser, S. (1983), 'Harmonisation of indirect taxes in the EEC', *British Tax Review,* pp. 232-53.

Crossley, T.F., Low, H. and Wakefield, M. (2009), 'The economics of a temporary VAT cut', *Fiscal Studies*, Vol.30, No.1.

CSO (Central Statistical Office) (1987), *Monthly Digest of Statistics,* HMSO, June, Tables 6.13, 6.14.

Davis, E. and Kay, J. (1985), 'Extending the VAT base: problems and possibilities', *Fiscal Studies,* February.

Department of the Environment (1977), *Local Government Finance,* Cmnd. 6813, HMSO.

Department of the Environment (1981), *Alternatives to Domestic Rates,* Cmnd. 8449, HMSO.

Department of the Environment (1986), *Paying for Local Government,* Cmnd. 9714, HMSO.

Dosser, D. (1981), 'The value added tax in the UK and the EEC', in A. Peacock and F. Forte (eds), *The Political Economy of Taxation,* Basil Blackwell.

Field, F., Meacher, M. and Pond, C. (1977), *To Him Who Hath,* Penguin.

Gibson, J. (1990), *The Politics and Economics of the Poll Tax: Mrs Thatcher's Downfall,* EMAS.

Giles, C. and Johnson, P. (1994), 'Tax reform in the UK and changes in the progressivity of the tax system, 1985-95', *Fiscal Studies,* August.

Giles, C. and Ridge, M. (1993), 'The impact on households of the 1993 Budget and the Council Tax', *Fiscal Studies,* August.

Hills, J. and Sutherland, H. (1991), 'The proposed Council Tax', *Fiscal Studies,* November.

Johnstone, D. (1975), *A Tax Shall be Charged,* HMSO.

Jones, C., Leishman, C. and Orr, A. M. (2006), 'The potential impact of reforms to the essential parameters of the Council Tax', *Fiscal Studies,* Vol.27, No.2.

Kay, J.A. and King, M.A. (1990), *The British Tax System,* Oxford University Press, Chs 9 and 10.

Kay, J.A. and Morris, C.N. (1979), 'Direct and indirect taxes: some effects of the 1979 budget', *Fiscal Studies,* November.

Layfield, F. (1976), *Local Government Finance,* Cmnd. 6453, HMSO.

Levitt, M.S. (1976), 'The redistributive effects of taxation', *Economic Journal,* September, p. 582.

Lockwood, B., de Meza, D. and Myles, G .. (1995), 'On the European Union VAT proposals: the superiority of origin over destination taxation', *Fiscal Studies;* February.

Musgrave, R.A. and Musgrave, P.B. (1989), *Public Finance in Theory and Practice,* 5th edn, McGraw-Hill, Ch. 20.

NEDO (National Economic Development Office) (1971), *Value Added Tax,* HMSO, para. 5.56.

Prest, A.R (1980), *Value Added Tax: The Experiences of the United Kingdom,* American Enterprise Institution.

Prest, A.R. (1982), 'On charging for local government services', *The Three Banks Review,* March 1982.

Prest, A.R. and Barr, N.A. (1985), *Public Finance,* 7th edn, Weidenfeld and Nicolson, Ch. 19.

Reddaway, W.B. (1970), *Effects of the Selective Employment Tax,* First Report, HMSO; Final Report, Cambridge University Press, 1973.

Sandford, C. *et al.* (1981), *Costs and Benefits of VAT,* Heinemann.

Sandford, C. (2000) *Why Tax Systems Differ: a comparative study of the political economy of taxation,* Fiscal Publications.

Smith, S. (1988), 'Should UK local government be financed by a poll tax?', *Fiscal Studies,* February.

'Symposium on Local Government Finance' (1982), *Fiscal Studies,* March.

Trevelyan, G.M. (1946), *English Social History,* 2nd edn, Longmans, Green and Co.

SELF ASSESSMENT QUESTIONS

Suggested answers to self-assessment questions are given at the back of the book.

11.1 What advantages and disadvantages do indirect taxes have, compared to direct taxes?

11.2 What is a 'cascade' system of sales tax, and what are its disadvantages?

11.3 What arguments are there for and against rates as a local tax?

DISCUSSION QUESTIONS

1 Is it possible for the total indirect tax system to be progressive?

2 Can a poll tax be fair?

3 How far would you consider value added tax to be an efficient and equitable tax?

CHAPTER TWELVE

Corporation tax

LEARNING OBJECTIVES

After reading this chapter, you should be able to:

- Appreciate the reasons for the separate taxation of companies.
- Explain the basis of calculation of taxable income, and particularly the adjustments from accounting net profit.
- Compare the classical with the imputation systems of corporation tax in theory and in UK practice.
- Understand some basic numerical applications of the above.

12.1 Introduction

This chapter is the first of three on the subject of corporation tax. It looks at the general purpose of such a tax, and at its scope and administration in the United Kingdom. The definition of taxable income is then discussed. Finally in this chapter, the 'system' of corporation tax is examined particularly with respect to the treatment of dividends.

In the next two chapters, attention is given to more complex aspects of the UK corporation tax and then to international aspects.

12.2 Special taxation for companies

It was only during the First World War that companies in the United Kingdom began to be treated differently from individuals for the purposes of taxation. Special taxes on companies were in force from 1915 to 1924, and then from 1937 onwards. However, the question whether a business is a separate entity from its owner or owners has a long history in the thought and practice of disciplines such as accounting, company law and economics. Italian accountants had decided by the thirteenth century that they wished to separate the business from its owners, so that the latter could see more clearly how the former was doing. Consequently, balance sheets of businesses show amounts called 'capital' that represent amounts contributed by the owners. During the nineteenth century, various laws were enacted in the United Kingdom to the effect that all companies have perpetual succession independently from their owners, that these companies may sue and be sued in their own names and that the owners are not liable for the debts of a company beyond their capital contributions. Economists have extended the separation of the owner from his business. When calculating the profit of the business to a sole trader, for example, its costs would include the opportunity costs of the amounts the owner could have earned with his time, property and money if they had not been invested in the business.

In this century, one aspect of the separation was that companies began to be taxed in a different way from individuals. As is frequently the case with taxation, the change was associated with the need to finance warfare. In particular, the rearmament before the Second World War imposed a heavy burden on the Exchequer, which was partly supported by the revenue from a new profits tax on companies. This was an additional tax to the existing income tax paid on the income of companies, partnerships, sole traders and other individuals. This profits tax was already providing 3 per cent of the total tax yield by 1938/39. By 1950/51 it provided 7 per cent, but by 1960/61 only 5 per cent, due to the substantial rises in the yields of income tax and indirect taxes.

This important step involving the taxation of companies at different rates from individuals and unincorporated businesses was followed during the Second World War by the introduction of a system of capital allowances for all businesses. The system has, from time to time, involved a number of different tax allowances and relief's aimed at encouraging investment by deferring or permanently reducing tax for those businesses which purchase capital equipment. In addition to this economic role of shifting the allocation of resources towards investment, the capital allowances system has been used to try to allocate resources to designated 'development areas' by making allowances more generous for companies operating in those areas.

We will look at capital allowances in more detail below. What should be noted here is that, for the purpose of capital allowances, partnerships and sole traders' businesses are included with companies. This seems reasonable, as the investment of unincorporated businesses probably needs even more encouragement than that of companies, because the former generally find it more difficult to raise finance for investment.

The next important change occurred in 1965 when the Finance Act of the Labour Chancellor, James Callaghan, introduced corporation tax to replace both income tax and profits tax on companies. The dividing line between businesses which pay corporation tax and those which do not remains the same as for profits tax. That is, partnerships and sole traders do not pay corporation tax. Their profits are split up amongst the owners, who add this to their other income and pay income tax on it. The dividing line is drawn in this way as part of the means of separating those businesses whose owners control and manage on their own account from those, typically larger, businesses whose owners are clearly separate from their businesses and who appoint directors to manage them. However, the separation is not as simple as this; see Section 13.3. So, the corporation tax was brought in partly to effect a greater separation of the taxation of incorporated business from that of individuals. This allows more flexibility for the Exchequer in fiscal policy. For example, the government might wish to reduce the taxation paid by companies, in order to encourage more investment. It would not be necessary to reduce personal taxation as well, now that the corporation tax rate is not tied to the income tax rate. The yield of corporation tax was discussed in Section 7.6. Devereux *et al.* (2004) examine the reasons for the surprisingly large yield of the tax in recent years.

Other arguments for the separate or additional taxation of companies include the benefit principle. It could be said that the tax that a company pays is the price for its legal privileges. However, the company also pays by having to disclose financial information. Anyway, it is not easy to measure the cost or benefit of the privileges, or to establish a relationship which justifies a tax proportional to profit; a licence would be more appropriate. This argument and others, which are all acknowledged to be weak, are mentioned by other writers (e.g. Prest and Barr, 1985). Kay and King (1990, p. 152) point out that limited liability is a voluntary agreement entered into by both sides, who can adjust the terms on which they are prepared to accept or contribute capital. Also, they note that, as companies are owned by individuals, there is no *separate* taxable capacity in a company. A corporation tax affects the owners, workers or customers of a company.

There is an argument that, since corporation tax exists, it should not be removed, because this would result in unexpected windfall gains for the existing shareholders, who have adapted to the existence of the tax (see Section 5.5 and Meade, 1978, p. 227). Incidentally, it is clear that corporations do need to be taxed, for otherwise there would be inequity with unincorporated entities. The need for a separate levy in order to tax the retained profits of companies is discussed in Section 12.5, where corporation tax systems are outlined.

A brief note on the incidence of corporation tax seems appropriate at this point. There is no theoretical conclusion about whether company employees, company owners or consumers bear a corporation tax in the last analysis. The initial incidence of the tax can be seen to depend upon exactly which system is adopted (Kay and King, 1990, Ch. 10). Much also depends on the degree of imperfection in the markets for products, labour and capital. Econometric studies are, unfortunately, equally indecisive about the incidence of corporation taxes (Musgrave and Musgrave, 1989).

12.3 Scope and administration

Corporate taxation in the United Kingdom is controlled, as with most other taxes, by statute, case law and the practice of the Revenue. The Income and Corporation Taxes Act 1988 contains many of the relevant provisions. This is supplemented by yearly Finance Acts, which are preceded by the related 'Budget' statements and

Finance Bills. In addition, a number of cases are relevant to the definition of income and to many other matters. Many of these statutory rules and cases apply to unincorporated businesses as well as to companies. This chapter includes some references to statute and case law.

Corporation tax is chargeable on resident UK companies and unincorporated associations (e.g. sports clubs or trade unions). It is not charged on partnerships, sole traders, charities or local authorities. Building societies and insurance companies are subject to special rules. As with income tax, there are different schedules and cases: for example, Schedule D Cases I and II are for trading profit. The tax is chargeable on a current year basis for a 'chargeable accounting period', which is normally the company's accounting year. The rate of tax relating to the fiscal year (1 April to 31 March for companies) is fixed in the Finance Act which is in process during that year. For example, the Finance Act 2012 sets the rate for the corporation tax year 2011: that from 1 April 2011 to 31 March 2012. However, rates are often announced in advance. If the accounting period straddles two fiscal years and if the corporation tax rate changes, an apportionment must be carried out. For clarity, this book refers, for example, to '2011/12' rather than to 'the tax year 2011'.

12.4 Taxable income

The determination of taxable income is broadly similar for companies and unincorporated businesses. It begins with net profit (that is, revenues less expenses) as calculated according to accounting conventions. This is a long-standing procedure which was made particularly clear by the Finance Act 1998 (S.42) (as amended in 2002) which refers to profit 'computed in accordance with generally accepted accounting practice'. The accounting profits referred to are those of individual legal entities, not groups. That is, the consolidated statements are not generally relevant for tax.

One important convention used by accountants is the realisation convention, which is that revenues will be recognised, for the purposes of calculating profit, not at the point of completion of a product ready for sale, nor necessarily at the point of collection of cash, but at the usually intermediate point when the sale is made, by the buyer and seller setting up legally enforceable obligations to each other. Consequently, a business will include sales on credit as part of its revenues, even though no cash has been received. The business has debtors instead of cash. Taxation is based on the profit calculated by using this realisation convention.

Accounting conventions are also followed for the treatment of interest and dividend payments. Interest is an expense of the business paid to outside lenders, and it is tax-deductible. Dividends are a share of post-tax profit paid to the owners, so they are not expenses for accounting and they are not deductible for taxation. The matter of whether the shareholders should be seen as totally separate from their corporation is discussed below (in Section 12.5), and there is a further examination of interest and dividends in Section 12.6.

However, there are several ways in which accounting profit, calculated using the above and other conventions, is different from taxable profit. These include capital allowances, unallowable expenses, untaxed incomes and special reliefs. These matters are discussed below. A numerical example which includes these points may be found in the appendix to this chapter.

Depreciation

One of the expenses that a business charges against its revenues is depreciation. Each year in which the asset is used, part of its cost is charged in the profit calculation. Before the Finance Act 2002, depreciation on intangible assets was not allowed for tax purposes, but now normal accounting rules (FRS 10 or IAS 38) are followed for some intangibles. In order to encourage research and development, deductions for such spending are 130% of costs for large companies and 175% for small companies.

Depreciation on tangible assets is one of the expenses which is still not allowed in the calculation of taxable profit. Instead, there is a scheme of accelerated depreciation called the *capital allowances* system. One of the reasons for this is that the estimation of depreciation is a fairly subjective matter. Many companies and many accountants come to many different answers to the questions of what rates and what methods of depreciation should be used. Consequently, it might be found that high depreciation charges were being used to calculate profit merely in order to reduce taxation. This occurs in many other European countries (e.g. see Nobes and Parker, 2012). Fortunately, it is not the case in the United Kingdom, so accountants can charge what they consider to be fair amounts of depreciation without affecting the tax bill.

As noted above, since tax works on unconsolidated statements, the above remarks should not apply, in principle, to consolidated statements prepared under IFRS in, for example, Germany. However, it might be possible for some tax-driven choices at the individual company level to find their way into an IFRS consolidation.

Another major reason for capital allowances is that they are a means of encouraging certain types of investment by postponing amounts of taxation paid by a company in proportion to the investment it carries out. Postponement of any payment is clearly useful to a company, because the money can be used for other purposes in the interim period. Postponement is particularly useful in times of inflation, when the real value of the eventual payment falls. From time to time, the government has given cash grants in addition to or instead of tax allowances. The incentive effects of capital allowances are examined by Bond *et al.* (1993).

The system (from 1970 onwards) is illustrated in Table 12.1. First-year allowances were a greatly accelerated form of tax depreciation. These were dismantled by the Finance Act 1984, partly on the argument that they warped the judgement of businessmen away from commercial good sense and partly because they might have unnecessarily encouraged the use of machines rather than labour, even in a period of high unemployment. The system from 1986 has been simple: most assets receive writing down allowances on a reducing balance basis; industrial buildings used to receive a 4 per cent writing down allowance on a straight-line basis; and commercial buildings continue to receive no allowances. The writing down allowance on plant and machinery is reduced to 20 percent for 2011/12 and 18 per cent for 2012/13 and the allowance for buildings was gradually abolished by 2011. Some more complicated issues (e.g. short-life assets) are dealt with in Appendix A.12.1.

Table 12.1 Capital allowances

(i)	Plant and machinery	
	27.10.70-19.7.71	60% first-year allowances
	20.7.71-21.3.72	80% first-year allowances
	22.3.72-13.3.84	100% first-year allowances
	14.3.84-31.3.85	75% first-year allowances
	1.4.86 onwards*	0% first-year allowances, except ...
	1.7.98 onwards	40% first-year allowances (e.g. for several years, for small and medium-sized companies, and in 2009/10 for all)

Writing down allowances of 25% per year on a reducing balance were also available (starting on an amount net of any first-year allowance). They fell to 20% for 2008/9 onwards, and then to 18% from 2012/13.

(ii)	Industrial buildings	
	5.4.70-21.3.72	30% initial allowance
	22.3.72-12.11.74	40% initial allowance
	13.1 1.74-9.3.81	50% initial allowance
	10.3.81-13.3.84	75% initial allowance
	14.3.84-31.3.85	50% initial allowance
	1985-86	25% initial allowance
	1.4.86 onwards*	0% initial allowance

A writing down allowance of 4% of cost is allowed each year until all the cost (net of any initial allowance) has been used up. However, this has been withdrawn; see text.

(iii)	Business cars	

Writing down allowances of 10% or 20% (depending on emissions) on the reducing balance. Lorries are considered to be plant.

*There was a temporary revival of initial and first year allowances in 1993

As part of the general process whereby the tax rules are made closer to accounting practice, from 2006 lessees rather than lessors receive capital allowances on 'long funding leases', which are similar to the 'finance leases' of the accounting standards (SSAP 21 or IAS 17).

When an asset is sold, it may be found that the capital allowances have exceeded or fallen short of the actual loss in value. This gives rise to 'balancing charges' or 'balancing allowances' to correct the difference. In the case of buildings, for example, it may also be that an asset is sold for more than its purchase cost; in which case there is a capital gain as well as a balancing charge. These problems are examined in the appendix to this chapter.

In order to illustrate the advantage given by capital allowances, suppose that a company has taxable profit of £5 million and has spent £4 million on machinery that is expected to have a useful life of ten years. For accounting purposes it might be depreciated at 10 per cent of cost per year. For tax purposes there is a writing down allowance of 20 per cent in the first year. Assuming a tax rate of 30%, this leads to a tax reduction for the year of £240,000 (i.e. £1,500,000 – £1,260,000) as follows:

	Non-spending company (£000)	Spending company (£000)
Taxable profit before allowances	5,000	5,000
Capital allowance (20% of £4m)	-	800
Taxable profit after allowances	5,000	4,200
Taxation (30%)	1,500	1,260
	3,500	2,940

The reason for saying earlier that capital allowances 'postpone' tax rather than permanently reduce it rests on a comparison between this scheme of accelerated depreciation allowances and the smaller depreciation charges used by accountants, which could be taken to be the alternative to capital allowances. Assuming that, under either system, the maximum eventual allowances against profit sum to the asset's cost, the system of capital allowances allows a higher charge against taxable profit in the first year, but lowers the charge in later years. In the extreme case of 100 per cent capital allowances in the first year, the following might result:

	Accounting treatment	Tax treatment
Purchase of asset (expected to last 5 years)	1,000	1,000
Depreciation or capital allowance, year 1	200	1,000
	800	0
Depreciation charge, year 2	200	
	600	
Depreciation charge, year 3	200	
	400	
Depreciation charge, year 4	200	
	200	
Depreciation charge, year 5	200	
	0	

In periods of high inflation combined with high capital allowances, the effect of the allowances is very large. For example, the estimated reduction in corporation tax receipts due to capital allowances was £6,700 million in 1980/81. The tax receipts after this and other reliefs were £4,650 million (Treasury, 1982, pp. 134, 136).

Suggestions for the reform of capital allowances include extending them to commercial buildings, such as offices and shops, and basing them on current cost accounting depreciation. The government regarded the former as expensive and a reduction in the bias towards investment in manufacturing industry (Treasury, 1982, Ch. 15). The latter became less relevant as inflation fell in the mid-1980s.

Because it is possible to see capital allowances as 'postponing' taxation, it is arguable that the implied outstanding liability should be recognised in the financial statements. This is called 'accounting for deferred tax', and is discussed in Chapter 13.

As noted earlier, a special tax regime for intangible assets was introduced in 2002 for intangibles created or acquired from 1 April 2002. Approximately speaking, amortisation for accounting purposes is allowed for tax. Expenditure on research and development is encouraged by receiving 130% capital allowances (or 200% for smaller companies).

Unallowable expenses

In addition to the disallowance of depreciation because of the alternative granting of capital allowances, all other forms of capital expenditure are also disallowed because they are not used up to earn the year's profit. Also, some other payments are disallowed because they are deemed to be unconnected with trading. These include taxes paid on profits, fines and legal costs related to illegal activities, the cost of tax appeals (a wry piece of humour) and political donations that cannot be clearly shown to be spent in order to preserve or enhance the trading of the business.

These disallowances follow from 8.74 of the Taxes Act 1988 which disallows expenses which are not 'wholly and exclusively laid out for the purposes of the trade'. This matter was considered in Chapter 8 with respect to the words 'wholly and exclusively'. It might be noted here that case law has further defined 'the purposes of the trade'. In Strong and Co Ltd v. Woodfield (5 TC 215) it was held that 'It is not enough that the disbursement is made in the course of, or arises out of, or is connected with the trade ... it must be made for the purpose of earning profits'. In this case the cost of damages paid to a customer who was hurt by a chimney falling from the taxpayer's premises was disallowed. As another example, in the case of Smith Potato Estates Ltd v. Bolland (30 TC 267) it was held that tax appeal expenses were not allowable.

In practice, the Revenue allows apportionment of expenses such as rates or car running expenses when they do not exclusively relate to a business. However, it is clear that any private benefit gained from the business's assets or current expenditure should lead to a reduction in the amounts allowable against profit of the business. This provides the ground for many a skirmish between the Revenue and the taxpayer; for example, there is the case of ShQ1*ey v. Wernher (36 TC 275). Lady Wernher transferred horses from her (taxable) stud farm to her (untaxed) racing stables. It was held that the stud farm should be deemed to profit from the market value of the horses, not their cost. This also applies to the private use of business stocks: for example, the use by a grocer of his business's lettuces for his own lunch.

The cost of entertaining customers, the cost of any gifts (unless they are under £50 each and constitute advertising) and part of the cost of hiring expensive cars (i.e. over £12,000 in 2010/11) are all unallowable for tax purposes, presumably on the grounds that the government does not wish to subsidise extravagance or provide easy ways in which tax can be avoided. From 2009, a new system based on emissions is introduced. Various legal charges which should properly be added to capital expenditure (such as legal fees for negotiating long leases or buying a factory) are not allowable as charges against current profit. However, since they increase capital expenditure, they will increase capital allowances.

Another area in which some expenses are not allowed for tax purposes concerns the bad debts which a business may suffer after having included the related credit sales in revenues. Any debt which is certain to be uncollectible is charged against accounting profit and is allowable for tax purposes. Any identified debts which are considered likely to be uncollectible are dealt with by creating a specific provision for doubtful debts. The creation or increase of such a provision is also charged against accounting profit and is allowable for tax purposes. This implies that any 'bad' debts which are later recovered and any specific provision which turns out to have been unnecessary will cause an increase in taxable profit. In addition, accountants often charge an extra amount against profit as a general provision for possible bad debts. This will be based on experience; it might be 5 per cent of debtors at the end of the accounting year. This is not allowed as a charge for the calculation of taxable profit, because it is subjective and therefore too easy to manipulate, rather like depreciation expenses.

A further point which may need clarification is that the splitting up of profit between shareholders (dividends) and internal uses (transfers to reserves) are not expenses, but appropriations of profit. Consequently, the payment of dividends or the transfer of amounts to reserves are not deductible in the calculation of taxable profit.

Without going into further detail (of which there is a great deal) this section has outlined several principles which cause payments to be disallowed. For example, non-trading expenses or expenses for private benefit cannot be allowed against the trading revenues of the business; distributions of profit cannot be treated as expenses; any form of capital expenditure must be allowed under the capital allowances system or not at all; and expenditure which is too subjective is disallowed, to avoid manipulation. Some of these adjustments cause permanent changes in tax, unlike capital allowances which might be said to cause a postponement.

The complex inter-linkage of tax and accounting varies over time and from country to country. For the UK, Freedman (1987 and 1993) provides an analysis. An international comparison for the UK, USA, France and Germany is provided by Lamb *et al.* (1998). This is updated, for Germany and the UK in Gee *et al.* (2010).

Financial income

Some revenues of the company are not taxable for corporation tax purposes. First, incoming dividends from UK companies are not taxed, because they will have been paid out of profit which has already borne corporation tax in the paying company.

For this reason, such income (when grossed up by the tax credit) is called 'franked' investment income. Income which has not borne corporation tax in the paying company, such as gross interest receipts, is called 'unfranked' investment income. Second, proceeds or profits from the sale of fixed assets are not taxable, although some part may be treated as a chargeable gain and there may be an immediate or eventual adjustment to capital allowances. There are more details in the appendix to this chapter.

In addition, companies are not subject to personal income tax. Therefore, any receipt (such as interest or patent income) that has suffered an income tax deduction at source will give rise to a reclaim by the company. Similarly, companies deduct income tax at source, on behalf of the Inland Revenue, when they pay interest, patent royalties or annuities. This tax then becomes due to the Revenue, but may be set off against the reclaims mentioned above.

For example, suppose that a company receives debenture interest of £5,000 and pays out interest of £2,000 to its own lenders. When it receives the interest, it can make a claim to the Inland Revenue for £1,000, which will have been deducted at source as income tax by the paying company. When it pays out its own interest, it must similarly deduct income tax at the basic rate on savings (e.g. 20% x £2,000 = £400). Thus, on balance, it reclaims £1,000 - £400 = £600. In practice, this paying or reclaiming is done using a quarterly system, as illustrated in the appendix. For both corporation tax and financial accounting purposes, the interest receipts and payments are treated gross of income tax.

A further point relating to financial income and expense (such as interest and rent) is that the tax system uses a cash basis rather than an accruals basis. That is, for example, interest income is treated on a cash receipts basis for the calculation of taxable income, whereas financial reporting recognises the interest income that relates to the accounting period, whichever period the cash is received in.

Capital gains

Capital gains of companies as well as those of individuals and unincorporated businesses are taxed. In all cases, there is no tax to be assessed until the gain is realised. The rules relating to the calculation of the gain are the same for all taxpayers. However, for businesses of all sorts, the tax on capital gains can be postponed indefinitely because of 'roll-over' relief. When a business replaces an asset, it may deduct any gain on the old asset from the cost of the new asset. This increases the eventual gain on the new asset, but then this cumulative gain may once more be rolled over into the next replacement. Assuming that assets are always going to be replaced, the tax on the capital gains will never be paid, particularly in times of inflation when replacement costs are rising. Let us look at a simple example where there have been no capital allowances because the asset is a commercial building:

		£	
Asset A sold in 2013 for		10,000	
Less costs of sale		600	
		9,400	
Purchase of A in 1994	5,000		
Plus costs	500		
Realised gain on A		5,500	
Purchase of replacement B in 2013		3,900	untaxed (see below)
Costs		15,000	
		1,500	
		16,500	
Less realised gain on A		3,900	rolled over
Purchase price used for eventual			
calculation of gain on B		12,600	

Companies do not pay capital gains tax as such. They pay corporation tax on their chargeable gains. The indexation of capital gains applies for companies as discussed in Chapter 8. However, the exemption or zero-rated band which applies to capital gains of individuals is not available for corporate capital gains.

12.5 Systems of corporation tax

Once taxable income has been determined, its interaction with a tax system can vary, in particular with respect to the treatment of dividends. Corporations, unlike partnerships, whose business income in most countries is taxed as though it were all distributed at the end of each year, may have both retained and distributed income for tax purposes. If business income is taxed only at the corporate level and only when it is earned, then different shareholders will not pay different rates of personal income tax. If income is taxed only on distribution, taxation may be postponed indefinitely. On the other hand, if income is taxed both when it is earned and when it is distributed, this creates 'economic double taxation' which could be said to be inequitable and inefficient (see below).

Systems of corporation tax are often divided into three types: classical, imputation and split-rate (OECD, 1974; van den Tempel, 1974). This is discussed further on an international basis in Section 14.5 in Chapter 14. In the United Kingdom, corporation tax was introduced in 1965, as noted earlier. Both classical and imputation systems have been tried.

Classical systems

There are two main criticisms of classical systems; both rest upon what has been called the 'economic double taxation of dividends', where distributed income is subject both to corporation tax and then to personal income tax. First, this double taxation is said to be inequitable when compared to the treatment of the distributed income of unincorporated businesses (e.g. partnerships). The income of such businesses, whether physically distributed or not, bears no corporation tax but bears current income tax in the hands of the owners of the businesses. Such single taxation would not be so easy to arrange for corporations. This is because retained profit does exist, both in reality and for tax purposes, and so, if there were no separate corporation tax, taxation could be indefinitely postponed if companies delayed distribution. As has been mentioned, the alternative of taxing income at the corporate level only would mean that all individual recipients would have borne the same rate of tax. This would be unacceptable as part of an otherwise progressive income tax system. Thus, double taxation of the distributed income of corporations results from a desire by governments to ensure proper taxation of retained income.

The second case against economic double taxation is that it introduces a bias against the distribution of dividends. Since both total income and then distributed income are fully taxed, the larger the distribution, the larger the total tax born by a company and its shareholders. It might be thought that such an encouragement to retain profits would promote investment. However, more subtle economic thinking might suggest that profitable and efficient investment would be more likely to occur if companies distributed their profits and then shareholders allocated these funds through the new-issue market to the most profitable companies. Unfortunately it is not proven that companies with a good earnings record will remain the most profitable (Whittington, 1971).

It should also be noted with regard to this second argument that, even if there were no effective corporation tax on distributed income (i.e. no double taxation), there would still be a bias against distribution if there were an income tax which had to be paid only when dividends were distributed. Arguments have also been raised that the burden of double taxation is less serious that it might seem (Partington and Chenhall, 1983).

The two cases against the economic double taxation of dividends have given rise to other systems of taxation which are designed to mitigate these effects of classical systems. Because of these arguments, the United Kingdom moved in 1973 to an imputation system. Such systems achieve the mitigation of double taxation by imputing to the shareholders some or all of the tax paid by companies. For example, taxpayers in the United Kingdom are deemed to have paid tax at the basic rate of income tax on their dividends grossed up at the basic rate.

Imputation systems

A frequently used way of mitigating the effects of economic double taxation is to impute to the recipients of dividends some of the tax paid by a corporation on the income out of which the dividends are paid. Tables 12.2 and 12.3 illustrate the contrast between the UK's pre-1973 classical system and its imputation system in 1979-83. The rates of corporation tax and tax credit have moved frequently since then, as will be explained below.

In the United Kingdom there is a 'basic rate' of income tax (see Chapter 8), which is the marginal rate for a majority of taxpayers; it has been assumed for this illustration that the basic rate is 30 per cent (see below), that the classical corporate tax rate is 40 per cent, and that the imputation rate is 52 per cent (as it was from 1973 to 1984). The rate of classical corporation tax in the United Kingdom between 1965 and 1973 was between 40 and 45 per cent. Such rates raise about the same revenue as a 52 per cent imputation rate. This is because, under the latter system, some of the corporation tax is imputed to the recipients of dividends as an income tax credit. In the United Kingdom, the tax credit is linked to income tax rates for administrative reasons, as will be explained later. For example, from 1979/80 to 1985/86, when the basic rate was 30 per cent, the tax credit was 30/70 or 3/7. Under the pre-1973 classical system, there was a withholding of standard rate income tax at source.

Let us look at the figures in Tables 12.2 and 12.3 in more detail. They assume that the taxable and accounting incomes are the same, and £1,000 in each case. Under the classical system shown on the left, corporation tax at 40 per cent is borne, and then income tax at 30 per cent is deducted at source. Thus, for basic rate taxpayers there is no further income tax to pay.

As the first column of Table 12.2 shows, the tax liability is £60 (i.e. 30 per cent of the gross dividend of £200). The tax already deducted by the company and paid to the Inland Revenue is also £60. Thus, there is no net liability.

Table 12.2 Classical and imputation systems (Low payout)

		Classical £		Imputation £
Company				
Income		1,000		1,000
Corporation tax[a]	(40%)	400	(52%)	520
Distributable income		600		480
Distribution (say) gross		200		
Less income tax deduction (30%)	60			
	Net 140		Cash	140
Retained income		400		340
Shareholders (basic rate)				
Dividend: cash received		140		140
Income tax deducted at source		60		0
Tax credit received (3/7)		0		60
Gross dividend		200	'Grossed-up' dividend	200
Income tax liability (30%)		60		60
Less tax already deducted		60		0
Less tax credit		0		60
Tax due		0		0
Total tax	(400 + 60)	460		520

Notes: [a] Ignoring the 'small companies' rate, see Section 13.2.

Table 12.3 Classical and imputation systems (high payout)

		Classical £		Imputation £
Company				
Income		1,000		1,000
Corporation tax[a]	(40%)	400	(52%)	520
Distributable income		600		480
Distribution (say) gross		500		
Less income tax deduction (30%)	150			
	Net 350		Cash	350
Retained income		100		130
Shareholders (basic rate)				
Dividend: cash received		350		350
Income tax deducted at source		150		0
Tax credit received (3/7)		0		60
Gross dividend		500	'Grossed-up' dividend	500
Income tax liability (30%)		150		150
Less tax already deducted		150		0
Less tax credit		0		150
Tax due		0		0
Total tax	(400 + 150)	550		520

The imputation system illustrated on the right in Table 12.2 is based on the UK system from 1979 to 1983. Corporation tax of 52 per cent is borne, and a tax credit of 3/7 the size of the dividend is given to shareholders. No further tax is deducted, so the dividend received by shareholders cannot sensibly be called 'net'. The tax liability is worked out on the cash dividend which is grossed up to include the tax credit. In this case, the example has been chosen to keep the 'grossed-up' (and post-tax) dividends the same for the two systems. Thus, the tax liability on the 'grossed-up' dividend of £200 is £60, but this may be settled with the tax credit of £60, leaving no net liability.

It should now be clear how useful it is administratively to set the tax credit (and the former tax deduction at source) at a rate related to the basic rate of income tax. It means that many taxpayers have no net liability to tax on dividends. In most other countries, where there is an absence of a long basic-rate band, such an advantage cannot be gained because there is no particular predominant marginal rate.

Table 12.3 shows a similar example, but one where the company pays out a high proportion of its post-tax profits. A comparison of Tables 12.2 and 12.3 shows that, for shareholders who pay only basic rate tax, the UK imputation system fully removes the double taxation of dividends. The total tax of £520 under the imputation system does not alter as the level of dividends rises; under the classical system, the total tax rises.

However, the case is different when there are shareholders who pay a higher rate of personal income tax. Then there is still a double taxation under the imputation system, and the bias against distribution remains. Examination of the top right-hand quarter of Table 12.4 shows that, where a taxpayer has a marginal rate of 50 per cent, the £60 tax credit is insufficient to cover the liability on the £200 'grossed-up' dividend. Table 12.4 also shows that total taxation is higher for higher rate taxpayers when there is a larger payout, not only under the classical system but also under the imputation system.

In 1993/94, the lower rate (20 per cent) of income tax was introduced, followed by a new starting rate of 10 per cent, as explained in Chapter 8. From that time, the size of tax credits has been tied to 10 per cent, not to the basic rate. Dividends are now taxed under Dividend Rate at a marginal rate of 10 per cent for basic rate taxpayers. For 40 per cent taxpayers, there is a balance of income tax to pay at 32.5% in 2012/13 (or 42.5% for 50 per cent taxpayers). The tax credit rate is 10/90.

Table 12.4 Classical and imputation systems (higher rate taxpayers)

		Classical £		Imputation £
Low payout				
Company (as Table 12.2)				
Shareholders (50% marginal rate)				
Dividend: cash received		140		140
Income tax deducted at source		60		0
Tax credit received		0		60
Gross dividend		200	'Grossed-up' dividend	200
Income tax liability (50%)		100		100
Less tax already deducted		60		0
Less tax credit		0		60
Tax due		40		40
Total tax	(400 + 60 + 40)	500	(520 + 40)	560
High payout				
Company (as Table 12.3)				
Shareholders (50% marginal rate)				
Dividend: cash received		350		350
Income tax deducted at source		150		0
Tax credit received		0		150
Gross dividend		500	'Grossed-up' dividend	500
Income tax liability (50%)		50		250
Less tax already deducted		150		0
Less tax credit		0		150
Tax due		100		100
Total tax	(400 + 1,500 + 100)	650	(520 + 100)	620

Table 12.5 Imputation system in 2012/13

	£
Company	
Income	1,000
Corporation tax (24%)	240
Distributable income	760
Distribution (cash)	180
	580
Shareholders (40% higher rate)	
Dividend, cash received	180
Tax credit (10/90)	20
Grossed-up dividend	200
Income tax liability (32.5%)	65
Less tax credit	20
Tax due	45

Table 12.5 provides an example similar to that of the right-hand columns of Tables 12.2 to 12.4 for a 40 per cent taxpayer, using the rates of 2012/13. If the shareholder paid basic rate tax or lower, the income tax liability under Dividend Rate would be calculated at 10 per cent, so it would be '20', and the tax due '0'.

The UK system, like most existing imputation systems, involves partial imputation. That is, only part of the corporation tax paid by companies is imputed to shareholders, In 2012/13 with a 24 per cent corporation tax rate, the part imputed is 35.2 per cent, as Table 12.6 shows.

Table 12.6 UK partial imputation 2012/13

Company	£	
Income		1,000
Corporation tax		240
		760
Dividend		760
		0
Shareholders		
Cash receipt		760
Tax credit (10/90)		84
'Grossed-up' dividend		844

$$\text{Partial imputation} = \frac{84}{240} = 35.2\%$$

It should be noted, in summary, that even a partial imputation system can totally remove double taxation and the bias against distribution in circumstances where the tax credit cancels the personal liability. Alternatively, the double taxation can be removed by fully imputing the corporation tax to shareholders. However, in this case, even if there is no double taxation because there is no effective liability to corporation tax, there could still be some bias against distribution if personal income tax is larger than the underlying corporation tax and if it operates only when dividends are paid.

Advance corporation tax

A further complication was introduced with the UK's imputation system, partly in order to maintain the government's cash flow. Under the classical system of 1965-73, the income tax deducted at source from dividends was payable to the Revenue soon after distribution. Since there is now no tax deducted from dividends, there would have been no tax payments until the corporation tax was paid (in those days, from 9 to 21 months after the company's year end). In order to obtain some revenue before this, advance corporation tax (ACT) was invented as part of the imputation system.

ACT was originally linked to the basic rate of income tax, and then to the lower rate of 20 per cent, in the same way as the tax credit is. ACT was not a separate tax but an advance payment of corporation tax liability. The remaining amount was called 'mainstream corporation tax'. ACT was abolished from 6 April 1999, although companies with unrelieved amounts were allowed to carry them forward under certain conditions.

In the financial statements of a company, dividends paid are shown as the cash amount paid out. However, until early 2000, dividends received were shown 'grossed up' by the amount of tax credits, with a corresponding increase in the tax expense shown. This was despite the fact that the tax credits relate to income tax (which is not paid by the company) and that franked investment income does not bear corporation tax. The fiction was required by Statement of Standard Accounting Practice (SSAP) No. 8. Under its replacement (FRS 16), dividends are shown at the cash amount. The same applies under IAS 12.

12.6 Interest

At this stage, it is probably sensible to recap on the subject of interest compared to dividends. As noted earlier, whereas dividends are not treated as expenses for the purposes of calculating taxable profit under most tax systems, interest payments nearly always are. Consequently, under most types of system, paying out £2,000 in interest is less expensive for the company in post-tax terms than paying £2,000 cash dividends, because the former payments reduce tax by £600 (assuming a corporation tax rate of 30 per cent). On the other hand, cash dividends are worth more to an individual than gross interest. This is because, although they are both investment income, the dividends are treated as though some tax had already been paid. The following example assumes a basic rate of income tax of 20 per cent, a lower rate of 10 per cent (which determines the rate of tax credits) and a corporation tax rate of 30 per cent.

	Dividend payment £	Interest payment £
Net profit before interest and tax	10,000	10,000
Less Interest (£1,600 net, £400 income tax deducted at source)	-	2,000
Net profit before tax	10,000	8,000
Less Tax at 30%	3,000	2,400
Net profit after tax	7,000	5,600
Dividend (equivalent to grossed-up income of £2,000)	1,600	-
Retained profit	5,400	5,600

The recipient of dividends, in this example, gets £1,600, which is the equivalent of £1,778 gross dividend with tax paid. For a basic rate taxpayer, this is exactly what the recipient of £2,000 in interest gets, because the company deducts £400 basic rate tax at source and pays it to the Revenue. The net effect is still that the interest payment is still cheaper, leaving a greater retained profit. The company will consider this and many other relevant factors when choosing between alternative ways of raising external long-term finance. One of the criticisms of the UK and other tax systems is that they are not 'neutral' in this respect, as they introduce a bias in favour of debt finance.

12.7 Tax rates, receipts and payment dates

The discussion earlier in this chapter has used various rates of corporation tax, and the rate can change each year. There is also a lower rate for companies with small profits, as examined in the next chapter.

As mentioned earlier, the rates used in the UK classical system (from 1965 to 1973) were between 40 and 45 per cent. The imputation system had a rate of 52 per cent from 1973 to 1984. However, the Finance Act 1984 dramatically reduced the level by stages, down to 35 per cent in 1986. At the same time, generous capital allowances and stock relief were abolished. The effects of this and a dramatic rise in corporate profitability led to a great increase in corporate tax revenues in the 1980s, as shown in Table 12.7 (see Devereux, 1987).

Table 12.7 Corporation tax receipts

	Total corporation tax	
	£ million	Percentage increase
1981/82	4,930	6.1
1982/83	5,677	15.2
1983/84	6,184	8.9
1984/85	8,341	34.9
1985/86	10,708	28.4
1986/87	13,495	26.0
1987/88	15,734	16.6
1988/89	18,537	17.8
1989/90	21,495	16.0
1990/91	21,495	0.0
1991/92	18,263	(14.9)
1992/93	15,783	13.6)
1993/94	14,887	(5.7)
1994/95	19,390	30.2
1995/96	23,570	21.6
1996/97	27,778	17.9
1997/98	30,437	9.6

The rate was reduced again to 33 per cent for 1991/92 onwards, then to 31 per cent for 1997/98, 30 per cent for 1999/2000 and 28 per cent for 2008/9. It fell again to 26 per cent for 2011/12, 24 per cent for 2012/13, then gradually to 22 per cent by 2014/15.

The due date for payment of corporation tax is nine months after the accounting year end. For large companies, payments have moved to a quarterly system.

Further reading

For a general treatment of corporate taxation, see Musgrave and Musgrave (1989). The technical details of the UK tax system are discussed in Carmichael; Harvey and Young; and Pritchard (latest editions in each case). More general coverage may be found in Brown and Jackson (1990), Kay and King (1990), Prest and Barr (1985) and White (1981). For the accounting treatment of taxation, see Scrimgeour (1984).

References

Bond, S., Denny, K. and Devereux, M. (1993), 'Capital allowances and the impact of corporation tax on investment in the UK', *Fiscal Studies,* May.

Brown, C.Y. and Jackson, P.M. (1990), *Public Sector Economics,* 4th edn, Blackwell.

Carmichael, K.S., *Corporation Tax,* HFL, latest edition.

Devereux, M. (1987), 'On the growth of corporation tax revenues', *Fiscal Studies,* May.

Devereux, M.P., Griffith, R. and Klemm, A. (2004) 'Why has the UK Corporation Tax raised so much money?', *Fiscal Studies,* Vol. 25, No. 4, pp.367-388.

Freedman, J. (1987), 'Profit and prophets – law and accountancy practice on the timing of receipts – recognition under the earnings basis (Schedule D, Cases I and II)', *British Tax Review,* Vol. 2, pp. 61-79; Vol. 3, pp. 104-33.

Freedman, J. (1993), 'Ordinary principles of commercial accounting - clear guidance or a mystery tour?', *British Tax Review,* Vol. 6, pp. 468-78.

Gee, M., Haller, A. and Nobes, C. (2010) 'The influence of tax on IFRS consolidated statements: the convergence of Germany and the UK', *Accounting in Europe,* Vol.7, No.1, pp 97–122.

Harvey, E.L. and Young, D.G., *Tolley's Corporation Tax,* latest edition.

Kay, J.A. and King, M.A. (1990), *The British Tax System,* 5th edn, Oxford University Press.

Lamb, M., Nobes, C.W. and Roberts, A.D. (1998) 'International variations in the connections between tax and financial reporting', *Accounting and Business Research,* Summer.

Meade, J.E. (1978), *The Structure and Reform of Direct Taxation.* IFS/Allen & Unwin.

Musgrave, R.A. and Musgrave, P.B. (1989), *Public Finance in Theory and Practice,* Chapters 21 and 22, McGraw-Hill.

Nobes, C.W. and Parker, R.H. (2012), *Comparative International Accounting,* Chapter 2, Prentice Hall.

OECD (1974), *Theoretical and Empirical Aspects of Corporate Taxation,* Paris.

Partington, G.H. and Chenhall, R.H. (1983), 'Dividends, distortion and double taxation', *Abacus,* June.

Prest, A.R. and Barr, N.A. (1985), *Public Finance,* 7th edn, Chapter 17, Weidenfeld and Nicolson.

Pritchard, W.E., *Corporation Tax,* Polytech Publishers, latest edition.

Scrimgeour, J.L. (1984), *Accounting for UK Company Taxation,* Longman.

Treasury (1982), *Corporation Tax,* Cmnd. 8456, HMSO.

van den Temple (1974), *Corporation Tax and Individual Income Tax in the EEC,* EEC Commission, Brussels.

White, R. (1981), 'The changing face of taxation - corporation tax', *British Tax Review,* No. 6.

Whittington, G. (1971), *The Prediction of Profitability,* Chapters 4 and 5, Cambridge University Press.

SELF ASSESSMENT QUESTIONS

Suggested answers to self-assessment questions are given at the back of the book.

12.1 What reasons are there for taxing companies separately from other businesses?

12.2 Where are the rules governing the calculation of taxable income?

12.3 What rates of capital allowance are available for investment in various assets?

12.4 How are corporate capital gains taxed?

12.5 What is the essential difference between classical and imputation systems of corporation tax?

12.6 How are dividends taxed for basic rate taxpayers?

12.7 What were the purposes of ACT?

DISCUSSION QUESTIONS

1. Why might 'economic double taxation' of corporate income be a bad thing?

2. What general categories of expenditure are unallowable for tax purposes? 'Categories' means groupings at a more general level than an item of expense such as depreciation.

Appendix to Chapter 12

This appendix provides numerical illustrations and some more detail on various issues covered in the chapter. These issues are covered here in the order in which they appear in the chapter.

A.12.1. Capital Allowances

Capital allowances were introduced in Section 12.4. Here, there are some illustrations and further complications.

Any capital costs unrelieved by allowances will be kept in a 'pool'. The pool is reduced by the 18 per cent annual allowances and by the sale price (up to the original cost) of any asset sold by the business. When the pool is exhausted, 'balancing charges' will arise and are added to taxable income.

There is a complication connected with 'expensive' cars: those over £12,000 in 2011/12. In order to discourage extravagance, capital allowances are restricted to £2,160 per year. So, if a car is bought for £14,000, the following occurs:

Cost	14,000
WDA Year 1 (Restricted)	2,160
Written down value	11,840
WDA Year 2	2,131
Written down value	9,709
WDA Year 3	1,848
Written down value	7,961
	etc.

Short-life assets

The 18 per cent writing down allowance (from 2012) on the reducing balance means that assets with a short working life are not fully allowed for tax until some years after their useful lives. For example, on this basis, it takes eight years to write off 80 per cent of the cost.

However, there are special provisions for 'short-life' assets. These allow traders to elect to have any asset designated as a short life asset, in which event that asset is not pooled with other plant and machinery, but is treated as a separate individual pool of its own. The writing down allowance is still 18 per cent but if the asset is sold or scrapped within eight years, the sale proceeds are used to calculate a balancing charge or allowance as the case may be. If the asset is still owned after eight years, the unallowed residual balance of expenditure is transferred to the main pool.

	Column I £	Column II £
Cost in 2012	1,000	1,000
Writing down allowance	180	180
	820	820
2012 Writing down allowance 18%	148	148
	672	672
2014 Writing down allowance 18%	121	121
	551	551
Sold for £100	100	
Balancing allowance	451	
2015 Writing down allowance		99
		452
2016 Writing down allowance		81
Eventually transferred to main pool		371

For example, suppose that an asset was acquired for £1,000 in 2012, and an election was made for the asset to be treated separately on the 'short-life' basis. In the following table, column I presents the relevant calculation where the asset is sold in 2015 and column II the relevant calculation where the asset is not sold until after eight years.

Capital allowances and capital gains

When a fixed asset is sold, capital gains and capital allowances will interact. Let us suppose the following case, where there is no roll-over relief. An asset is bought for £10,000; it has been depreciated by 30 per cent, but capital allowances have been claimed to the extent of 60 per cent; it is then sold for £11,000. Thus, we have:

	£	
Cost	10,000	
Book value	7,000	
Tax book value	4,000	
Sale	11,000	
Accounting gain	4,000	(i.e. £11,000 - £7,000)

For tax purposes, the accounting gain of £4,000 will be deducted from the accounting net profit. Then, since all the capital allowances are now found to have been 'unnecessary', there will be a balancing charge of £6,000 added to taxable income (assuming for simplicity that this is the company's only fixed asset with capital allowances). On top of this, £1,000 will be treated as a capital gain.

A.12.2 Calculation of taxable income

Section 12.4 discusses the various adjustments that are necessary to arrive at taxable income from accounting net profit. It may be useful here to add some detail under several headings.

Expenditure disallowed

1. Capital expenditure for the purchase of capital assets and related legal and other fees. Depreciation of capital expenditure is also disallowed.
2. Fines and legal costs for contravening the law.
3. Tax appeals.
4. Corporation tax.
5. Political donations.

6. Dividends and other appropriations, and transfers to reserves.
7. Some preliminary and formation expenses, and premiums and some expenses on the issue or redemption of shares and securities.
8. Entertaining customers or agents.
9. Providing gifts which either do not bear an advertisement or are over £10 in value.
10. General allowances for bad debts.
11. Part of the expenditure of hiring cars costing £12,000 or more. The amount *allowed* is given by:

$$\text{Hire charge} \times \frac{£12,000 + \tfrac{1}{2} \text{ excess cost over } £12,000}{\text{cost}}$$

The amount disallowed = hire charge − amount allowed

Income not taxable as trading profit

1. Profit on sale of capital assets.
2. Franked investment income (or group income).
3. Certain government and local authority grants.

Example

Let us now examine a simple illustration. Suppose that the accountants of Ganymede Ltd have calculated the company's profit in this way for the year ended 31 March 2012:

	£000s
Sales	12,000
Cost of goods sold	7,600
Gross profit	4,400
Dividends received (grossed up)	400
Bank interest (gross)	200
	5000
Expenses:	
Salaries	500
Rent	170
Rates and insurance	165
Depreciation	400
Office expenses	140

Travelling	190
Directors' fees	120
Auditors' fees	30
Legal fees (Note 1)	30
Miscellaneous (Note 2)	15
Bad debts (Note 3)	10

Net profit	1,770
	3,230

Note 1

£000s

Legal fees:		
	Defending the company in a tax case	7
	Work connected with new factory	12
	Debt collecting work	11
		30

Note 2

Miscellaneous:		
	Donation to Liberal Democrat Party	10
	Subscription to local Chamber of Commerce	5
		15

Note 3

Bad debts:		
	Specific debts written off	3
	Specific allowances for bad debts	3
	General allowance for 4 % of debtors	4
		10

Note 4
Capital expenditure for the year (£000s):

	Costs	Capital allowances	
Machinery	200	40	(20% writing down allowance)
Factory	200	-	(none for buildings)
Shop	39	-	(none for buildings)
Cars (4 at £5,000)	20	4	(20% WDA)
		44	

The adjustment of net profit to get taxable profit proceeds like this:

Net profits as in the accounts	3,230

Untaxable income:	
Franked dividends	400
	2,830

Unallowable expenses:

Depreciation	400	
Legal expenses	19	
Miscellaneous	10	
Bad debts	4	
		433
		3,263
Less capital allowances		44
		3,219 × 26% = 837

CHAPTER THIRTEEN

Further aspects of corporation tax

LEARNING OBJECTIVES

After reading this chapter, you should be able to:

- Appreciate the need for and the workings of the small companies rate.
- Identify criteria for deciding on incorporation.
- Understand the basics of the various reliefs available in the corporate tax system.
- Explain the causes of deferred tax and how it is calculated.
- Realise the sort of effects of inflation on the working of taxes.
- Describe the basics of petroleum revenue tax.

13.1 Introduction

This chapter examines further aspects of the UK corporation tax. First, there is the reduced rate of tax for 'small' corporations. The reduced rate affects most British companies, so it is of great importance in practice. This naturally leads on to a comparison of the taxation of partnerships and small companies. Then, there is an examination of various reliefs from tax due to losses or to the permission to create a group of companies for certain tax purposes.

The accounting treatment of corporation tax, particularly the issue of deferred tax, is the next topic. This is followed by an examination of the behaviour of corporation tax under inflationary conditions and then a brief look at another major British corporate tax, the petroleum revenue tax. Finally, there is a section on possible reforms of corporation tax. An appendix provides some numerical illustrations.

13.2 Small companies relief

In 1973, with the imputation system, a reduced rate of corporation tax was brought in, designed for small companies. Because it is difficult to define a small company, it actually applies to those companies with small taxable incomes. The reason for the lower rate is that small companies are particularly dependent on retained profits as a source of finance, since, for example, they are not able to afford an issue of shares or debentures to the public. Also, these companies are the most like partnerships, and a lower rate may reduce the differences in taxation between one form of business and the other. From 1999 to 2005, there were also even lower rates for companies with very small profits.

The definition of small profits changes from time to time. For 2012/13, the lower rate of 20 per cent applies to 'profits' up to £300,000. The profits are specially defined to be net taxable income after trading losses and annual charges, but including grossed-up FII. See the appendix to this chapter for a numerical example. The 24 per cent rate applies fully to profits above £1,500,000. In between these two levels, there is a tapering relief which gradually raises the average rate from 20 to 24 per cent. This tapering relief is necessary to avoid the very high marginal rates that there would otherwise be if the average rate suddenly rose from 20 to 24 per cent as soon as profits exceeded £300,000.

Thus, the lower rate does not apply to a band of income for all taxpayers, as occurs in income tax. The relief is specifically designed to benefit small profits only. To give such small profits a similar advantage using a true lower-rate band would involve the loss of much more tax revenue, because all corporation taxpayers would benefit.

In 1980/81 it was estimated that a remarkable 95 per cent of all companies either took advantage of the small companies relief or paid no tax at all (Treasury, 19S2, p. 119), and still a large majority of companies are affected.

Returning to the tapering relief, it should be clear that the maximum benefit of 4 per cent occurs at £300,000. This reduces to nil by £1,500,000. Thus the tapering proportion may be shown for 2012/13 to be:

$$\frac{0.04 \times 300,000}{1,500,000 - 300,000} = \frac{1}{100}$$

or 1.0 per cent of each pound that the profit is below £1,500,000.

The marginal rate of tax is therefore above 24 per cent for profits between the two threshold levels. Since so many companies are within the scope of the relief, the existence of higher marginal rates may act as a disincentive (Mayer and Morris, 19S2). The application of this to a specific example is shown in Appendix A.13.1.

As a way of stopping the manipulation of the small companies rate by the splitting up of companies, the limits for the lower rate and tapering relief are divided by the number of companies in the group. Companies are in the same group for this purpose if one is controlled by the other, or if both are controlled by the same persons.

13.3 Companies and partnerships

There are many factors, relating to taxation and other matters, which a business should take into account when deciding whether to operate as a company or as a partnership. Before discussing these, we should briefly examine a few distinctions between types of company.

Companies must obey a large number of rules, to be found in the Companies Acts. These include compulsory disclosure of substantial amounts of financial and other information in companies' annual reports and accounts. These accounts must (for companies above a certain size) be audited by independent qualified accountants. Other rules about disclosure and behaviour are made by the independent Accounting Standards Board and, if the company is listed, by the Stock Exchange.

Private companies are those which may not offer their securities for sale to the public. Some requirements, particularly those relating to disclosure and audit, are less onerous for some private than for public companies. No distinction is made for tax purposes between public and private companies. However, a special category for tax purposes comprises companies controlled by their directors or by five or fewer persons or families. These are called 'close' companies and can include public companies, but not if 35 per cent or more of the shares are publicly held. 'Controlled' means that either the majority of the capital or of the voting rights or of profit rights is held by the five or fewer associates or by the directors. Close companies constitute, for the purposes of taxation, the border area between individuals operating in business and corporations with a separate identity from their owners. On one side of the border, individuals operating as sole traders or partners pay personal income tax on the whole taxable profit of the business. On the other side, corporations pay tax on taxable profits, without reference to the owners' tax situations. Any of the profits of the corporation which are distributed may cause a recipient's tax bill to be adjusted. Consequently, for corporations whose owners pay higher rates of tax, there is a saving of immediate tax if profit is retained.

Since close companies are similar to partnerships in their ownership and control, it would seem unfair to tax the whole of partnership profits as though they had been distributed, yet not to tax the profits of close companies in a similar way. So, from the introduction of corporation tax, close company shareholders have had to pay personal income tax as though some proportion of the profits had been distributed. Up until the Finance Act 1980, this was a serious problem for many close companies. However, that Finance Act did away with 'apportionment' of trading profits to shareholders. It now only applies to part of estate and investment incomes.

Close companies versus partnerships

The question whether to run a small business as a partnership or a close company may well be decided by tax matters. The decision will depend upon the detailed circumstances of each case and, in real situations, professional advice should be sought. We can look at some main points here (using 2012/13 rates).

Partnerships: All profit is treated as distributed for tax purposes. Therefore the partners pay up to 50 per cent income tax on marginal trading income and on capital gains (after roll-over relief, exemptions, etc.).

Companies: All profit (including capital gain) is taxed at average rates from 20 to 24 per cent, depending on the size of profit. Any distributed profit is treated as though basic rate tax had been paid, but must be grossed up for possible taxation at higher rates as investment income (see Section 12.5). A way for the owners to extract some money tax efficiently might be to sell shares and use the capital gains tax exemption. A way to reduce corporation tax is to arrange for the company to pay directors' salaries and fees. This reduces the company's taxable income and gives the owners earned income. This is clearly better than receiving dividends after corporation tax and then paying higher rates of tax on them. However, the earned income is obviously subject to income tax.

Although the tax rates on profit may be lower for companies than for partnerships once profit reaches a certain level, the owners of the business must consider the additional eventual tax rates to be paid when the benefit is taken from the business: that is, they must remember the possibility of 'double taxation'. The combined corporate and eventual personal taxation on income or capital gains may be higher for companies than for partnerships. Note that, in either case, interest paid to outsiders is deductible from profit for tax purposes, and capital allowances are claimable. Also, the personal tax allowances of the owners can be used against their income from the partnership or from the company.

One particular advantage for companies is their ability to fund large pension schemes for their employees (e.g. directors). Payments into tax-exempt pension schemes for present and past years are tax deductible for corporation tax purposes. This is greatly more advantageous than the limited contributions (17.5 per cent of relevant income for many taxpayers) which partners can use as deductions for income tax purposes. A company may also have rather more advantageous ways of using up losses against the past, present and future profits; and it is able to smooth out fluctuations in the personal income of its owners, which will be of advantage under a progressive tax system.

There are also several important factors unconnected with tax which must be considered. First, many professional bodies do not allow their members to form limited companies. Consequently, solicitors, architects and some other professionals operate as partnerships or sole practitioners. Solicitors may become directors of companies not engaged in professional practice, but architects may not even do this. The reason for this ban is that the professional bodies wish to preserve reputations for high standards of practice and conduct, which might be damaged by some of their members if they had limited liability for the result of their firms' actions. The law allows such professional partnerships to exceed the normal limit of 20 partners. Accountancy firms were also restricted to unincorporated forms until the 1990s.

Second, disclosure requirements do not apply to partnerships. This may be important to a business in a competitive or sensitive area. Other legal requirements are also less onerous for partnerships. On the other hand, as we have noted, a company's owners have limited liability for the debts of the company, whereas partners are jointly and severally liable for all the debts of the business. Flowing from this is the important consequence that some owners of companies need not be managers, because they are reassured by limited liability. Therefore, even if a business needs to turn only to family and friends for share finance, it will be a great advantage to both sides if becoming an owner does not have to imply becoming a manager in order to safeguard one's personal assets. This becomes particularly important for public companies, of course, whose size is only feasible because their many owners are prepared to delegate management to directors. Another factor which may weigh in favour of the formation of a company is that it is easier to fragment a company, because the ownership shares are precisely defined and easier to transfer. For retirement or estate problems, this may be a considerable advantage.

13.4 Loss reliefs and group reliefs

There are many ways in which the losses of a company may be used to reduce taxation by absorbing taxable income of various sorts. Unfortunately, the rules relating to different types of losses are different. This section will briefly outline these reliefs, leaving more detailed consideration and example to the appendix for readers who require it.

Trading losses

Trading losses of a fiscal year may be set against any other income of the same year, or carried back against income of the preceding year (or in some cases up to three years). Income includes chargeable gains. If there are still unrelieved trading losses, these can be carried forward against trading profits only of future years. Rules for this are in Section 393 of the Income and Corporation Taxes Act 1988.

Charges on income, such as interest or patent royalties, can create or increase a loss that can be carried forward against future trading profits.

Non-trading losses

Examples of non-trading losses are capital losses or losses on property rental. These may be relieved against present or future profits or gains of the same type but may not be carried back.

Group relief for losses

This applies to members of the same group of companies. A group for this purpose contains UK companies which are at least 75 per cent owned by another company in the group or by a consortium of owners of at least 5 per cent each. The trading loss of one member of the group (the surrenderer) may be set against current taxable profits of another member (the claimer). The trading loss may be surrendered to several members of the group. Any payment for the loss to the surrendering company by the claiming company is neither taxable in the former nor tax deductible in the latter. Group relief must be claimed with the agreement of all the companies involved within two years of the end of the surrendering company's relevant accounting period.

As a result of an appeal by Marks & Spencer plc to the European Court of Justice, group relief was extended in 2006 to EU subsidiaries under certain conditions.

Transfer of assets

Using a similar definition of a group to that above, transfers of assets between members of a group are not subjected to tax on the capital gains. When the asset leaves the group, the purchase price paid by the original owner within the group is used for calculating the chargeable gain. In order to control manipulation of this concession, if the transferee leaves the group within six years of the transfer, a taxable gain is deemed to arise. Also, all companies and all trades in a group are treated as one for 'roll-over relief', which normally only applies to replacement assets for the same trade.

Group income

A 'group' for this purpose contains subsidiaries which are over 50 per cent held by a parent company or over 75 per cent held by a consortium of owners of at least 5 per cent each. Group income does not bear corporation tax in the receiving company, just as if it had been treated normally as franked investment income. This provision may also be claimed in order to avoid accounting for income tax on annual charges, like interest.

Unincorporated businesses

Loss reliefs for partnerships and sole traders bear similarities to the above reliefs for companies. The rules are to be found in SS 380-392 of the Taxes Act 1988. S380 gives a relief of losses against other income of the same or preceding year. S385 allows losses not relieved under S380 to be carried forward against profits from the same trade.

13.5 Accounting treatment of tax and deferred tax

The accounting treatment of the tax aspects of dividends paid and received is examined in Section 12.5.

A further accounting problem is whether to account (and then how to account) for the tax implications of various accounting practices. For example, when a building is revalued in a balance sheet, should one account for the implied eventual tax on the currently unrealised gain? If a company makes a taxable loss which cannot be used by carrying it back but can be carried forward, should this be treated as an asset? If accounting depreciation charges the cost of an asset more slowly than capital allowances do (which is frequently the case), should the accounts own up to the implied postponement of tax? These are all issues of 'deferred tax'.

Deferred tax is not amounts of tax bills which the tax authorities have allowed the taxpayer to postpone. It is amounts recognised as tax by accountants because they think the amounts relate to the current or previous accounting periods although the tax system does not yet recognise them. That is, deferred tax is caused by accounting for reversible timing differences between when expenses and revenues are included in the accounting calculations as opposed to when they are included in the tax calculations.

Let us look at a simple example of deferred tax in the context of the revaluation of fixed assets. Suppose that a company revalues a holding of land in the balance sheet from £3m to £9m. Suppose, also, that the corporate tax rate on capital gains is 30 per cent, but that the tax rules do not tax capital gains until disposal, which in this case is not intended by the company in the foreseeable future. No tax is payable as a result of revaluing, but it is possible to see how accountants (and users of accounts) might think that the potential liability to tax of £1.8m (i.e. £6m x 30 per cent) relates to the period up to the balance sheet date. If so, they might account for the implicitly deferred tax in the balance sheet, as in Figure 13.1. This is the case under IFRS.

In the United Kingdom, as will be examined further later, the accounting rule (FRS 19 of 2000) requires deferred tax to be recognised in such cases only when there is expected to be a liability. Consequently, UK companies would generally not account for the tax as in Figure 13.1, but would show a revaluation reserve of £6m.

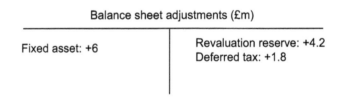

Balance sheet adjustments (£m)

Fixed asset: +6	Revaluation reserve: +4.2 Deferred tax: +1.8

Figure 13.1 Deferred tax on revaluation

Table 13.1 Depreciation and tax (£ million)

Accounting records		Tax calculations		
Year	Depreciation	Year	Expense	Tax reduction
I	2,000	I	10,000	5,000
2	2,000	2	0	0
3	2,000	3	0	0
4	2,000	4	0	0
5	2,000	5	0	0

The most frequently cited cause of substantial amounts of deferred tax is depreciation. Typically, depreciation is a large expense, and the tax rules can be substantially different from the accounting rules, as outlined in Chapter 12. Table 13.1 sets out a simple case, where there are 100 per cent tax depreciation allowances in the year of purchase of plant and machinery, a 50 per cent corporate income tax rate and the purchase for £10,000 of a machine which is expected to last for five years. The existence of 100 per cent tax depreciation is not fanciful. This applied for all plant and machinery in the United Kingdom from 1972 to 1984.

In Table 13.1, the accountants assume that the asset will have no residual value and will wear out evenly over time, irrespective of use. Consequently, for accounting purposes, they charge a depreciation expense of £2,000 per year. By contrast, the tax authorities allow an expense of £10,000 in the first year. So, there is a timing difference of £8,000. If the company takes the full allowance in the first year, there is a reduction in the tax bill of £5,000 in year one.

Suppose that the company uses the new asset very inefficiently or does not use it at all in the first year. In this case, depreciation may still be charged, because the asset is depreciating due to the passing of time. The net effect of the inefficient capital purchase on the post-tax accounting profit of year one is that the profit increases by £3,000 (i.e. depreciation expense of £2,000, and tax reduction of £5,000). Of course, if the company uses the asset effectively, profit will increase by more than this, as the company should at least be able to earn enough by using the asset to cover the depreciation on it.

This strange effect on profit is caused by deliberately charging the depreciation expense slowly but taking the tax reduction immediately. In order to correct for this, it would be possible, for accounting purposes, to record the benefit of the tax reduction more slowly, over the life of the related asset. That is, as in Table 13.2, one could express the tax reduction for accounting purposes as £1,000 per year, to fit with the depreciation expense. If this adjustment is made, it is called 'accounting for deferred tax'. In this example it would be necessary, at the end of year one, to increase the recorded tax expense by £4,000. The double entry would be:

Dr.   Tax expense   4,000

Cr.   Deferred tax   4,000

Table 13.2 Depreciation and deferred tax (£ million)

Accounting records			Tax calculations		
Year	Depreciation	Tax expense	Year	Expense	Tax reduction
I	2,000	1,000	I	10,000	5,000
2	2,000	1,000	2	0	0
3	2,000	1,000	3	0	0
4	2,000	1,000	4	0	0
5	2,000	1,000	5	0	0

The deferred tax credit balance would generally be recorded as a liability. Each year, the above double entry would be reversed by £1,000, so that no balance would be left by the end of the asset's life. An alternative way of expressing the above calculation at the end of year one is that the deferred tax balance would be:

(tax depreciation - accounting depreciation) x tax rate

= £(10,000 - 2,000) x 50% = £4,000

Permanent and reversible differences

It should be noted that the above examples of capital gain and depreciation are 'reversible timing differences' between accounting numbers and tax numbers. That is, in both cases, the financial statements record the revenues or expenses at a different time from the tax calculations. In these two examples, this gives rise to deferred tax liabilities. There can also be examples of deferred tax assets although, before recording these in financial statements, accountants need to be sure that they can be reclaimed against future tax payable.

There can also be examples of 'permanent differences', and these do not give rise to deferred tax. For example, entertaining expenses are not allowed for tax purposes. This adjustment to accounting profit is permanent, so it leads to an increase in taxable income, without a subsequent decrease.

Figure 13.2 provides a numerical illustration of tax adjustments to accounting profit: the tax exempt income might be dividends from subsidiaries, the tax depreciation is typically larger than the accounting depreciation and the general provisions for bad debts are not allowable. Assuming a corporate income tax rate of 30 per cent, the accounting and tax calculations would be:

Dr.	Tax expense (490,000 x 30%)	147,000
Cr.	Deferred tax (33,000 x 30%)	9,000
Cr.	Tax payable (457,000 x 30%)	137,000

Facts: (i) Pre-tax accounting profit £500,000
    (ii) Tax-exempt income included £10,000
    (iii) Depreciation expense already charged £80,000
    (iv) Tax depreciation to be claimed £120,000
    (v) Increase in general provisions for bad debts £7,000

Tax calculation (£m)

Pre-tax accounting profit	500,000
Permanent difference:	
Tax-exempt income	(10,000)
Accounting income subject to tax	490,000
Timing differences:	
Excess of tax over book depreciation	(40,000)
Increase in unallowable provision	7,000
Taxable income	457,000

Figure 13.2 Tax adjustments

Timing and temporary differences

As mentioned, the above differences between revenues/expenses for accounting and tax are called 'timing differences'. In contrast, the US accounting rules and those of the International Accounting Standards Board (IASB) operate on 'temporary differences' which are calculated by reference to assets/liabilities for accounting as opposed to those for tax. The rules are found in SFAS 109 and IAS 12, respectively.

In the above depreciation example (see Table 13.2), the accounting value of the asset at the end of the year is £8,000 whereas the tax value is zero. So there is a temporary difference of £8,000, which is the same as the timing difference.

Theoretical and practical problems

It is not entirely clear whether tax is an expense (and therefore potentially subject to allocation) as opposed to an appropriation of profit, or whether any deferred balance is a liability. The doubts about the latter become greater when a business has a continuing programme of investment in assets. In such a case, each year that the timing differences reverse, they will be replaced by new ones resulting from further purchases of assets. As a result, the 'deferred tax liability' may continually rise, especially in an expanding business or when prices are rising. In a sense, the balance then never has to be paid, so it might not be a liability. However, an overdraft may be expected to circulate continuously and to rise for the foreseeable future, but that does not mean that it is not a liability.

In the United Kingdom, deferred tax balances were very large by the late 1970s. Directors of companies did not like the effect of accounting for deferred tax because it made post-tax earnings look lower and liabilities higher. As a result of the doubts above, the standard-setters were persuaded to remove SSAP 11 's requirement to account fully for deferred tax (ASC, 1975), unless the 'liability' was expected to be settled in the foreseeable future. The resulting standard was SSAP 15 (ASC, 1978), which required 'partial accounting' for deferred tax. However, there was a return to fully accounting for deferred tax with FRS 19, with an exemption for revalued fixed assets.

Changes in tax rates

When corporate income tax rates change, should this affect the deferred tax balances that arose because of past transactions? The international consensus is 'yes'. The resulting method that uses current rates of tax (as a proxy for the future rates that will apply) is the 'liability method'. Under some previous accounting standards (e.g. APB, Opinion 11 of the USA), the 'deferral method', which uses tax rates at origination of the balances, was required.

Discounting

It would seem to make sense to take account of the time value of money when measuring deferred tax assets and liabilities. However, in order to do this, it is necessary to create a detailed schedule of the expected dates of the future removal of the timing differences. This is complicated and involves much estimation. FRS 19 allows discounting, but the US and IASB rules avoid creating a choice for companies by banning discounting.

13.6 Inflation

Between the early 1970s and the early 1980s, inflation was running at such high rates that traditional accounting became increasingly unrealistic, because it is based on historical cost figures. Profit figures may be seriously overstated for two main reasons. First, depreciation charges (the recognition of the using up of assets to produce profit) are based on the historical costs of assets, not on their current values to the business. Second, holding gains on stocks are included in profit. Many methods of adjusting accounts for the effects of inflation have been proposed and experimented with (Whittington, 1983).

The 'overstatement' of profit under historical cost accounting is important because it may give a false view of the operating success of the business, affecting different companies and industries by different amounts. Also it may lead to excessive distributions of profit to the shareholders, excessive claims against profit by employees and excessive demands by the Revenue. However, there were two important counteracting features in the tax system: capital allowances and stock appreciation relief.

Capital allowances, since they allowed 100 per cent first-year depreciation on many assets for tax purposes from 1972 to 1984, caused a full tax reduction at a time when an asset's historical cost was approximately its current value, i.e. in the year of purchase. Consequently, the corporation tax system was approximately index-linked (see the figures quoted in Section 12.4).

The other measure which afforded companies some protection from the effects of inflation on taxable income was stock appreciation relief, which operated from 1973 to 1984. It aimed to take out of taxable income that part of profit caused by unrealised gains on stocks. Consider this case in a simple retail organisation:

		£	£
	Sales		80,000
	Opening stock	10,000	
plus	Purchases	50,000	60,000
less	Closing stock	11,000	
equals	Cost of goods sold		49,000
	Gross profit		31,000

If the increase in stock of £1,000 does not represent a physical increase but has been caused by inflation, it is an unrealised nominal gain which is locked into the company. If it gave rise to a tax liability, the business might have to reduce its scale in order to pay the tax, and there would often be liquidity problems. The relief was substantial when inflation was high. In 1980/81, for example, the total corporation tax yield was £4,650 million, with the stock appreciation relief having been £2,050 million (Treasury, 1982, p. 136). In 1984, when inflation had fallen, the system was scrapped.

Because of these two main allowances the effective rate of corporation tax on companies (excluding financial companies) for the period 1976-80 averaged only 25 per cent (or 15 per cent excluding ACT) of historical cost profit (Treasury, 1982, p. 138). If the corporation tax had been levied on CCA profits for the same period, the yield would have represented a 65 per cent tax (or 40 per cent excluding ACT). For more discussion of these points, see Gibbs (1979), Meade (1980), Richardson (1980) and Bond et al. (1990).

As has been mentioned, since the 30 per cent rate is a flat rate of tax, indexation of bands is not necessary in the way that it is for income tax. However, the thresholds for small companies relief are raised from time to time.

13.7 Petroleum revenue tax

Petroleum revenue tax (PRT) is a system of taxation, set up by such regulations as the Oil Taxation Act 1965, which taxes profits arising from the extraction of oil and gas in British territory (land and sea). The tax is chargeable on each field separately, and the liability is apportioned among the participants. The tax has been amended several times by Finance Acts.

The tax is charged at a rate of 50 per cent on the net income from a field (at 75 per cent before 1993). The net income is the gross revenue less royalties, operating costs and some other taxes. The royalties include those to the government, which are really a separate tax. The operating costs exclude interest payments. The tax is assessed on a half-yearly basis but paid monthly. Fields approved for development after 15 March 1993 are exempt from PRT.

There are allowances in the PRT system. First, for most purchases of fixed assets there is a 'capital allowance' of 135 per cent, which may be spread over several years. The 35 per cent uplift ceases when cumulative income has exceeded cumulative outgoings. Nevertheless, this does mean that PRT needs not be paid until net income (as defined above) considerably exceeds capital expenditure on exploration and development.

Second, there is an 'oil allowance' (for example, from 1982 to 1993, of half a million tonnes per chargeable period, up to a maximum of 10 million tonnes). Unused allowances cannot be carried backwards or forwards.

There are a few implications for corporation tax. First, PRT and royalties are deductible in the calculation of profit for corporation tax purposes. Second, in order to stop manoeuvres that would reduce corporation tax, a company is prevented from setting losses and capital allowances from other activities against its net income from oil and gas extraction.

For a more detailed analysis of the system after the important changes in the Finance Act 1979, see Devereux and Morris (1983), Johnson (1979), and Kemp and Cohen (1980).

13.8 Reform

There have been many suggestions for the reform of corporation tax (see, for example, Alworth, 1980; Devereux and Freeman, 1991; Kay, 1986; Kay and King, 1990; Mayer, 1982; Meade, 1978). Despite, or perhaps because of, many tinkerings with the system to take some criticisms into account, it has still been argued that 'the system is in total disarray' (Kay and King, 1990). Some suggestions for reform will be considered below. However, it should be remembered that a strong argument against structural change is that companies have already had to cope with two major changes of system in the last two decades. Further, since the corporation tax is still a major source of revenue in the United Kingdom (see Table 7.1), the government has expressed an unwillingness to consider abolishing it or substantially reducing its total tax take (Treasury, 1982, p. 5).

The Meade Committee (Meade, 1978) devoted some attention to the major problem in corporate taxation which imputation is designed to solve, that is, the different taxation of retained and distributed profits. On the one hand, it might be argued that any double taxation of income (on the company and on the shareholder) is inequitable when comparisons are made with unincorporated businesses. This argument is used to justify imputation of corporation tax to the shareholders. On the other hand, it is argued that it is inequitable, again compared with unincorporated businesses, to allow companies to accumulate retained profits which have not borne tax at the shareholders' marginal rates. This argument may justify a separate corporation tax at a higher rate than basic rate income tax, if shareholders are assumed to pay higher rates of tax.

One approach to solving these problems is that of the split-rate systems, which have a lower rate of corporation tax for distributed income than for retained income. Other approaches seen in Chapter 12 are to tax corporate profits at fairly high rates and then to impute all or part of this tax to shareholders with their distributions. Also, a shift to expenditure tax rather than income tax was discussed by the Meade Committee.

The Committee reasonably proposed that one theoretically sound solution is for retained profit to be apportioned to shareholders just as if they were partners ploughing back profit. This apportionment would be taxed with the dividends at the shareholders' marginal tax rates. There would be a full imputation of corporation tax via a tax credit on both distributed and apportioned profit. In this way, the company would effectively bear no tax, and corporation tax would be a sort of withholding tax. This would solve the problems of double taxation and retained profits. Incidentally, it would be necessary to adjust capital gains tax in order to avoid a double taxation of the gains arising from retained profits.

Clearly, there would be some administrative problems with this system and some unfortunate implications for the cash flow of shareholders of companies which retain a higher proportion of profits. However, the idea is very attractive theoretically.

The government published a Green Paper called Corporation Tax in 1982 (Treasury, 1982). This provided a mass of fascinating statistics about corporation tax, and discussed various possible reforms. It looked at different tax bases (for example, using cash flows or current cost accounting profit for taxation), different tax systems (for example, split-rate) and less drastic changes (like changing loss reliefs or tax depreciation allowances). The Green Paper constituted a useful wide ranging discussion of possible reforms. However, it did not come to firm conclusions, and in many places seemed to be merely a marshalling of all the available arguments against a particular proposed reform. For a review of this Green Paper, see Edwards (1982). Further proposals for reform, in the context of the EU, are found in Cowie (1991).

Further reading

As for Chapter 12.

References

Alworth, J. (1980), 'Are there feasible reforms for corporation taxes?', *Fiscal Studies*, July.

ASB (1995), *Accounting for Tax*, Accounting Standards Board.

ASC (1975), *SSAP 11, Accounting for Deferred Taxation*, UK Accountancy Bodies.

ASC (1978), *SSAP 15, Accounting for Deferred Taxation*, UK Accountancy Bodies.

Bond, S., Devereux, M. and Freeman, H. (1990), 'Inflation non-neutralities in the UK corporation tax', *Fiscal Studies*, November.

Cowie, H. (1991), *The Future of Corporation Tax in the European Community*, Federal Trust and Ernst & Young.

Devereux, M. and Freeman, H. (1991), 'A general neutral profits tax', *Fiscal Studies*, August.

Devereux, M.P. and Morris, C.N. (1983), *North Sea Oil Taxation: The Development of the North Sea Tax System*, Report Series 6, Institute for Fiscal Studies.

Edwards, J. (1982), 'The Green Paper on corporation tax: a review article', *Fiscal Studies*, July.

Gibbs, M. (1979), 'Inflation accounting and company taxation', *Fiscal Studies*, November.

Johnson, C. (1979), 'The improvement of the North Sea tax system', *Fiscal Studies*, November.

Kay, J.A. (1986), 'Tax reform in context: a strategy for the 1990s', *Fiscal Studies*, November.

Kay, J.A. and King, M.A. (1990), *The British Tax System*, 5th edn, Oxford University Press.

Kemp, A.G. and Cohen, D. (1980), 'The new system of petroleum revenue tax', *Fiscal Studies*, March.

Mayer, C. (1982), 'The structure of corporation tax in the UK', *Fiscal Studies*, July.

Mayer, C. and Morris, C.N. (1982), 'Marginal rates of corporation tax: a disaggregated analysis', *Fiscal Studies*, July.

Meade, J.E. (1978), *The Structure and Reform of Direct Taxation*, IFS/ Allen & Unwin Meade, J.E. (1980), 'Companies, inflation and taxation - comment', *Fiscal Studies*, March.

Richardson, G. (1980), 'Companies, inflation and taxation', *Fiscal Studies*, March. Treasury (1982), *Corporation Tax*, Cmnd. 8456, HMSO.

Whittington, G. (1983), *Inflation Accounting: An Introduction to the Debate*, Cambridge University Press.

SELF ASSESSMENT QUESTIONS

Suggested answers to self-assessment questions are given at the back of the book.

13.1   What is the purpose of the 'small company rate' of corporation tax?

13.2   Is the corporation tax 'progressive' as a result of the small company rate?

13.3   What is the general cause of deferred tax? Give examples of partial causes.

DISCUSSION QUESTIONS

1.   What various factors should the owners of a business consider when deciding whether to incorporate?

2.   Discuss the effects of corporation tax on:

      (a) investment decisions (in any company).

      (b) investment (in total in the economy).

      (c) capital raising decisions.

      (d) liquidity.

Appendix to Chapter 13

This appendix provides numerical illustrations for two of the issues examined in Chapter 13: small companies relief and loss reliefs.

A.13.1 Small companies relief

This relief is discussed in Section 13.2, and numerically illustrated here. The relief is in the form of a lower rate of tax on small profits, designed to encourage small businesses. The various thresholds and limits change from time to time. For 2001/2002 onwards, profits under £300,000 are taxed to corporation tax at the lower rate. Profits above £1,500,000 are subject fully to the 26 per cent rate (in 2011/12). In between these figures, there is a tapering provision. Profits are defined as the company's net taxable income after trading losses and annual charges. This includes chargeable gains and franked investment income (FII) grossed up to include the tax credit. However, FII bears no corporation tax in the receiving company.

Suppose that the following facts relate to a company:

	£
Trading profit	20,000
Rent received	1,000
Chargeable gains (net of losses)	300
Dividends received (cash)	2,535
Loan interest paid (gross)	4,000
Dividends paid (cash)	5,000

'Profit' for small companies relief is:

	£
Schedule D Case I	20,000
Schedule A	1,000
Gains	300
Dividends $\dfrac{100}{90}$ × 2,535	2,817
	24,117
Less Interest	4,000
'Profit'	20,117

Therefore, the company is a 'small company'.

Corporation tax would be levied at 20 per cent on £17,300 (i.e. excluding FII) £3,633.

To illustrate tapering relief, let us suppose that all the figures are the same as those above, except that the trading profit was £420,000 not £20,000. In this case 'profit' would be £420,117 (i.e. £400,000 larger than the previous 'profit') and tapering provisions would apply. The tapering provisions mean that profits between £300,000 and £1,500,000 are taxed at 24 per cent, with a relief to reduce the effective rate to somewhere between 20 and 24 per cent. As explained in Section 13.2, the relevant fraction when the rates are as above is 1/100.

Another slight complication arises because the FII does not take part in the relief, as before. Consequently an apportionment is necessary, the formula for which is:

$$\text{Relief} = \frac{1}{100} \times (M - P) \times \frac{I}{P}$$

Where M = the upper limit, P = 'profit', I = taxable income excluding FII. In this case:

$$\frac{1}{100} \times (1,500,000 - 420,117) \times \frac{417,300}{420,117} = £10,726$$

Therefore corporation tax is given by:

417,300 × 24% = 100,152
    loss relief   <u>10,726</u>
               <u>89,426</u>

Where there are several companies under the same control, the profit limits are shared between them (see Section 13.2).

A.13.2 Loss reliefs

There are some details on loss reliefs in Section 13.4. Some numerical examples are given here.

Let us look at this simple example:

Year end	31.12.94	31.12.95	31.12.96
Trading profit/(loss)	18,800	(55,200)	25,400
Other income	1,000	1,200	1,400

The claims available for 1995 are, first, to set other income against the trading loss. This leaves a £54,000 loss. This can be carried back against the total income, i.e. £19,800 of the previous year. This now leaves £34,200 (i.e. £54,000 - £19,800) to be carried forward against trading profits, including the £25,400 of 1996.

The following situation remains:

Year end	31.12.94	31.12.95	31.12.96
Trading profit/(loss)	18,800	(55,200)	25,400
Other income	1,000	1,200	1,400
	19,800	(54,000)	26,800
Loss used	(19,800)	————	(25,400)
Adjusted income for tax	0	0	1,400

The loss has been used up in the following ways:

1995 loss	(55,200)
1995 other income	1,200
	(54,000)
1994 all income	19,800
	(34,200)
1996 trading profit	25,400
Carry forward against Future trading profit	(8,800)

In cases where there are excess charges on income (patents, annuities, interest), these augment a loss but can only be carried forward to set against future trading profits.

CHAPTER FOURTEEN

International aspects of corporate income taxes

LEARNING OBJECTIVES

After reading this chapter, you should be able to:

- Appreciate that there are major international differences in the calculation of taxable income.
- Outline how tax planning and transfer pricing affects this.
- Explain how tax systems differ across the world.
- Describe the process and progress of EU tax harmonisation.

14.1 Introduction

As examined in Chapters 12 and 13, the taxation of corporate income can differ substantially from year to year. It can, of course, also differ from country to country. There are three main categories into which these differences can be grouped: tax bases, tax systems and tax rates. The tax base (i.e. the amount that is being taxed) can be greatly affected by tax planning and by transfer pricing between parts of the group. All these issues are examined below, after which there is a discussion of harmonisation of corporate income taxes in the European Union.

14.2 Tax bases

International differences in tax bases (i.e. in the definitions of taxable income) are very large. In some countries, such as Germany and Italy, taxable income is very closely linked to accounting profit, and therefore varies with the particular countries' rules in this area. In other countries, such as the United Kingdom, the Netherlands and the United States, there are substantial differences between accounting and taxable incomes, and the nature of these differences varies by country. Even when concentrating on one country, such as the United Kingdom, the tax base changes from year to year, as explained in Chapter 12.

In all countries the calculation of taxable income starts with accounting net profit, but the size of adjustments from the latter to the former varies greatly, as noted above. To some extent this is seen in a negative way by studying the problem of deferred taxation, which is caused by timing differences between tax and accounting treatments (see Section 13.5 in Chapter 13). In the United Kingdom, the Netherlands and the United States, for example, the problem of deferred tax has caused much controversy and a considerable amount of accounting standard documentation.

Turning to France, Germany or Japan, it is found that the problem is minor; for in these countries, the tax rules are largely the accounting rules. In Germany, the tax accounts (Steuerbilanz) should be the same as the commercial accounts (Handelsbilanz). There is even a word for this idea: the Massgeblichkeitsprinzip. However, it is important to remember the point raised in Chapter 12, that tax works on unconsolidated statements. Therefore, IFRS consolidated statements in these countries might not be affected by tax considerations.

One obvious example of the areas affected by this difference is depreciation. In the United Kingdom, the amount of depreciation charged in the published financial statements is determined according to custom established over the last century and influenced by the accounting standard FRS 15 (or IAS 16). The amount of depreciation for tax purposes in the United Kingdom is quite independent of these accounting figures. As discussed in Chapter 12, it is determined by capital allowances, which are a formalised scheme of tax depreciation allowances designed to standardise the amounts allowed and to act as investment incentives. Because of the separation of the two schemes, there can be a complete lack of subjectivity in tax allowances, but full room for judgement in financial depreciation charges.

At the opposite extreme, in countries such as Germany, the tax regulations lay down maximum depreciation rates to be used for particular assets. These are generally based on the expected useful lives of assets. However, in some cases accelerated depreciation allowances are available, for example, for industries in Eastern Germany or those producing energy-saving or anti-pollution products or, in the past, for those operating in West Berlin or other areas bordering Eastern Germany. If these accelerated allowances are to be claimed for tax purposes (which would normally be sensible), they must be charged in the financial accounts. Thus, the charge against profit would be said by the UK accountant not to be 'fair', even though it could certainly be 'correct' or 'legal'. This influence is felt even in the details of the choice of method of depreciation, as shown by an extract from the 2008 Annual Report of BASF: 'Movable fixed assets are mostly depreciated by the declining balance method, with a change to straight-line depreciation when this results in higher depreciation amounts'.

A second example of linkage between the tax and accounting bases, leading to an overriding effect of taxation on accounting measurement, is the valuation of fixed assets in France. During the inflationary 1970s and before, French companies were allowed to revalue assets. However, this would have entailed extra taxation due to the increase in the post-revaluation balance sheet total compared to the previous year's. Consequently, except in the special case of merger by fusion, when tax-exempt revaluation is allowed, revaluation was not practised. However, the Finance Acts of 1978 and 1979 made revaluation obligatory for listed companies and for those which solicit funds from the public; it was optional for others. The purpose was to show balance sheets more realistically. The revaluation was performed by use of government indices relating to 31 December 1976. The credit went to an undistributable revaluation reserve. As a result of this, for depreciable assets, an amount equal to the extra depreciation due to revaluations is credited each year to profit and loss and debited to the revaluation account. Thus the effect of revaluation on profit (and tax) is neutralised. This move from no revaluations to compulsory revaluations was due to the change in tax rules. In Spain, Italy and Greece, government-induced revaluations have occurred several times (e.g. 1991 in Italy and 1996 in Spain).

Further examples are easy to find: bad-debt allowances (determined by tax laws in many continental countries) or various impairments for inventories or investments.

The effects of all this are to reduce the room for operation of the accruals convention (which is the driving force behind such practices as depreciation) and to reduce 'fairness'. Until the legislation following the EU's fourth Directive, the importance of this effect was not disclosed in published accounts. With some variations, this Massgeblichkeitsprinzip operates in Germany, France, Belgium, Italy and many other countries, such as Japan. It is perhaps due partly to the predominance of taxation authorities as users of accounting.

The alternative approach, exemplified above by the United Kingdom, the United States and the Netherlands, is found in countries with a greater interest in capital markets, where commercial rules can operate separately. There is a major exception to this in the use of LIFO inventory valuation in the United States, largely for tax reasons (Nobes and Parker, 2012, Ch. 8).

The degree of connection between accounting and tax has been examined in detail for the United States, the United Kingdom, France and Germany by Lamb *et al.* (1998). They suggest that there are many areas where tax has different rules from accounting in the United Kingdom and the United States (e.g. asset valuation, depreciation, pension expenses, bad-debt provisions, fines, development expenditure, long-term contracts). There are fewer areas in France, and very few in Germany. Similarly, there are no areas where tax rules override accounting rules for financial reporting purposes in the United Kingdom and the United States but there are several such areas in Germany. This suggests a strong influence of taxation on accounting in Germany but weaker influences in the United Kingdom and the United States.

14.3 International tax planning

International tax planning is exceptionally complex but can involve enormous rewards in terms of lower taxes for multinational companies (and in terms of fees for tax lawyers and tax accountants). Multinationals will be trying to:

- move profits from high-tax countries to low-tax countries;
- avoid the taxation of the same income in two countries (double taxation);
- get tax deductions twice for the same expenses;
- arrange for some income to be taxed nowhere.

The first of these issues is the field of transfer pricing, which is addressed in the Section 14.4. The second point (avoiding international double taxation) is partially achieved by bilateral tax treaties between countries. Generally, it is possible to get a credit in one country for tax paid on the same income in another.

The third point above (getting tax deductions twice) is sometimes called 'double dipping'. For example, suppose that a British company obtains machinery on a finance lease (see Section 12.4) from a French financial institution. In the UK, the tax system approximately follows the accounting system for this purpose and grants capital allowances to the lessee. However, in France, leases are not capitalized in individual financial statements or for tax. So, the French lessor gets tax depreciation. Consequently, the lessor is able to charge an attractively low lease payment, and the lessee benefits twice: low lease payments and tax depreciation deductions. As usual, there are other complications, such as the treatment of the UK lease rental payments. However, there is at least scope for tax advantage.

The fourth point (untaxed income) is sometimes referred to as 'white income'. As an example, suppose that a compound financial instrument (e.g. a convertible debenture) is treated as a debt in the country of the issuing company but mostly as a share in the country of the owner of the instrument. The issuer's payment of interest will be tax deductible, but the owner's receipt might be treated as a non-taxable dividend.

14.4 Transfer pricing

When transactions take place between units within a company, it is necessary (at least for management accounting purposes) to set a 'transfer price' for them. When the units are separate companies within a group, the transfer pricing is also necessary for financial reporting and for the calculation of taxable income. When the companies or units are in different tax jurisdictions, the issue becomes important because of different accounting rules, tax rates and so on. UNCTAD (1997) suggested that the value of goods and services being transferred within MNEs was greater than the value of all other exports from one country to another. The discussion below assumes the context of multinational enterprises (MNEs).

The way in which transfer prices are set depends upon the policies of the MNE, but it is quite common to use an approximation of arm's length market prices. Indeed, this is probably a good idea for the assessment of performance of units within the group, particularly to protect the interests of any non-controlling share-holders. Nevertheless, an MNE may choose artificial prices in order to move profits around the group, perhaps in order to move profits away from high-tax countries. The charging of royalties, interest or management fees is another mechanism for moving profits.

On the theoretical side, McAulay and Tomkins (1992) and Leitch and Barrett (1992) examine the variables that might affect transfer pricing behaviour. These include such issues as financial markets, government intervention and administrative procedures. Elliott and Emmanuel (2000) look at the organizational issues in an international context. Lin *et al.* (1993) examine the relationship between taxes and tariffs. They point out the importance of withholding taxes in the context of Asian Pacific countries. Emmanuel (1999) creates a model, using the institutional arrangements of the United States, Taiwan and Greece. He suggests that different rates of tax are the most important variables in enabling the minimization of post-tax group income.

Johnson (2006) examines three transfer pricing models for intangible assets. Gresik and Osmundsen (2008) discuss how tax officials can best approximate the prices that would apply in arm's length transactions, concluding that some version of 'cost-plus' is a good proxy.

Research differs about what MNEs actually do. Plasschaert (1985) suggested that manipulation of transfer prices is more common in developing countries, where governments are poorly equipped to monitor MNEs. Al-Eryani *et al.* (1990) found that, for US MNEs, there was strong compliance with laws and that larger companies were more likely to use a market-based approach. Harris (1993), Klassen *et al.* (1993) and Jacob (1996) all suggested that US-based multinational companies move income around the world in response to changes in tax rates. Oyelere and Emmanuel (1998) studied the practices of UK-based enterprises controlled from abroad. They also found evidence of significant shifting of income. Hung Chan and Lo (2004) find that the market-based approach is used where management believes that relationships with local partners and host governments need to be good. Wu and Sharp (2007) survey the transfer pricing practices of US MNEs.

Of course, tax authorities are alert to the problem of transfer pricing, which has become more important as globalization proceeds. Consequently, governments have empowered tax authorities to make adjustments to the calculation of taxable income to try to correct for transfers that are not at arm's length. The result of the adjustments may be that there is double taxation of some income of MNEs. The United States took the lead in regulations in this area. Section 482 of the Internal Revenue Code, which is the basic transfer pricing rule, has led to many regulations and tax cases. In 1992, extensive documentation requirements and penalties were introduced (US Treasury, 1992). In the United Kingdom, statutory requirements for detailed documentation on transfer prices were introduced in 1999/2000 (Rust and Graham, 2000). In some cases, governments have taken a different approach and have required apportionment of worldwide profits of the MNE (the 'unitary' or 'global' method). However, there is no international consensus on this rather broad-brush approach.

So as to add order in this area, governments have made tax treaties with each other on the subject of transfer prices. These are generally based on model tax treaties, such as those prepared by the Organisation for Economic Co-operation and Development (OECD, 1979 and 1995/6) and the United Nations. Deloitte (2002) summarizes the transfer pricing rules for several countries.

14.5 Tax systems

The classical and imputation systems as operated in the United Kingdom over more than the last three decades are outlined in Chapter 12. As may be seen from Table 14.1, both systems can currently be found in the European Union. Some countries, such as Belgium and Denmark, have moved from a classical system to an imputation system and back again. The United States also has a classical system, whereas Canada and Australia have imputation systems.

Table 14.1 shows the countries of the EU before the expansion of 2004. The table contains examples of other systems that mitigate double taxation, such as dividend-exempt or dividend-deductible.

Table 14.1 EU corporation tax systems in 2008/9

(1) Country	(2) System	(3) Corporation Tax rate %*
Austria	Classical (Split rate to 1989)	25
Belgium	Classical (Imputation 1963-89)	34[b]
Denmark	Classical (Imputation 1977-91)	25
Finland	Classical (Imputation 1990-2005)	26
France	Classical (Imputation 1965-2004)	33.33
Germany	Dividend partially exempt[c] (Imputation (1977-2000)	15.83[d]
Greece	Dividend exempt (Dividend deductible to 1992)	25
Ireland	Classical (Imputation 1976-99)	12.5
Italy	Classical (Imputation 1977-2003)	27.5
Luxembourg	Classical[e]	22.88[f]
Netherlands	Classical	25.5

Portugal	Classical (Imputation 1989-2001)	25
Spain	Classical (Imputation 1986-2007)	30
Sweden	Classical	26.3
UK	Imputation (1973+)	28

Notes:
[a] Withholding taxes have been ignored throughout.
[b] This includes austerity surcharge..
[c] 60% of dividends are taxable.
[d] Including a solidarity charge.
[e] 50% of dividends are not taxable for resident shareholders.
[f] Including employment surcharge.
Source: Compiled from various sources, including International Bureau of Fiscal Documentation

Split-rate systems

A second way to reduce the effects of double taxation is to charge a lower rate of tax on distributed income than on retained income. The West German system until the end of 1976 was a split-rate system, with a 51 per cent rate for retained income and a 15 per cent rate for distributed income. The Austrian and Portuguese systems were also split-rate until 1989. The German imputation system from 1977 to 2000 also had two rates.

It is possible to reorganise a partial imputation system into a split-rate system with identical tax liabilities and, therefore, unless they are perceived differently, identical economic effects (Nobes, 1980). Therefore it could be said that, for the purposes of classification, split-rate systems and partial imputation systems are in the same category.

Other ways to mitigate double taxation

There are many other ways to reduce double taxation. In the USA for example, the classical system was modified, until 1987, in that the first $100 of dividends (plus interest) received by an individual each year was exempted from personal income tax. Such a system operates in Luxembourg and the Netherlands. The German system from 2000 onwards exempts half of dividends, and the Greek system exempts them entirely. Alternatively, the 'primary dividend' system allows companies to deduct some proportion of dividends in the calculation of their taxable incomes. Such a system operated in Greece until 1992, where dividends were fully tax deductible, thus avoiding double taxation.

14.6 Tax rates

Another rather obvious way in which taxes may vary is by the level of the tax rate. Table 14.1 shows the rates for some EU countries. However, these rates may be misleading because of varying definitions of the tax base, as noted above. Also, some countries have additional local income taxes, and taxes on bases other than income (e.g. the size of capital or assets).

14.7 Harmonisation

The existing differences between effective taxation burdens in different countries give rise to great difficulties for the Revenue authorities who tax multinational companies. These companies themselves put considerable effort into reducing overall taxation by moving capital and profits around the world. However, these are matters of international business finance and management accounting, rather than the province of this chapter. The existence of these differences has not yet given rise to the same plethora of proposals and committees for international harmonisation as have the differences between accounting systems. However, within the EU, harmonisation of taxation is in progress. Many Directives on the harmonisation of VAT and other forms of indirect taxation have been passed. Direct corporate taxation, with which we are concerned here, has also been the subject of proposals for harmonisation. Progress in this area has been slow because of the reluctance of governments to lose any control over direct taxation, which is such an important source of revenue and regulator of the economy.

The Treaty of Rome of 1957 calls for the elimination of customs duties between member states, the introduction of common tariffs with third countries and the removal of barriers to the free movement of persons, capital, goods and services. The interest in taxation shown by the EU Commission, which is the guardian of the Treaty of Rome, stems from this desire to promote free movement. The free movement of goods and services implies particularly the harmonisation of indirect taxes. Similarly, the free movement of persons and capital implies the harmonisation of direct taxes. If there were no harmonisation of taxes and if barriers to movement were eliminated, there might then be encouragement or obstruction of flows of people, capital and so on to particular countries within the EU for purely fiscal reasons.

It is the aim of harmonisation (Burke, 1979; Dosser, 1973) that the conditions of competition and the returns to capital and effort should not be significantly affected by differences in effective tax burdens. So far, the EU Commission's published proposals have covered tax systems rather than tax bases. The Commission's activity in this area will now be outlined.

In 1962, the Neumark Committee (1963) recommended to the Commission that a split-rate system should be adopted. Later, the van den Tempel Report (1974) described the three types of corporation tax system, and recommended the classical system. However, the Commission's draft Directive (Commission, 1975; Nobes, 1979) on the harmonisation of corporate taxation proposes the imputation system. This must be partly due to the fact that a majority of EU countries were already using such a system or had plans to introduce one. In 1975, Belgium, France and the United Kingdom were using an imputation system. Since then, Germany, Denmark, Ireland, Italy, Spain and Portugal have introduced one (see Table 14.1, column 2). However, more recently, Belgium and Denmark have reverted to the classical system.

Some of the reasons for choosing an imputation system have been mentioned. They include the fact that the tax credit reduces the bias against distribution and favours small investors (lower-rate taxpayers). Also, the system should reduce the incentive for evasion by lowering the effective marginal rate of tax on dividends. In addition, since the corporation tax rate tends to be higher under an imputation system, there is a fairer comparison between the rates of tax borne on company retained profits and partnership profits (European Taxation, 1976; OECD, 1974).

Article 3 of the draft Directive proposes that there shall be imputation systems in operation with a single tax rate between 45 and 55 per cent. Also, Article 8 proposes that imputation credits shall be between 45 and 55 per cent of the corporation tax that would have to be paid on a sum equal to the taxable income out of which the dividend could be paid (i.e. on the dividend increased by the corporation tax; see Table 14.1). The rates in force in the EU in 1998/99 are shown in Table 14.1, which reveals that little notice has been taken of these proposals. Other proposals are that there should be a compensatory tax like an ACT or a *précompte* (Article 9); that there should be a withholding tax of 25 per cent unless shares are registered, as in the United Kingdom (Articles 14-17); and that tax credits should be available to shareholders irrespective of their member state (Article 4). This last requirement is clearly designed to promote the free movement of investors' capital. These various requirements would necessitate some important adjustments to the UK corporation tax system. The tax systems of some other EU countries would need even greater adjustments, as Table 14.1 suggests.

The draft Directive has been criticised on many grounds (see, for example, Lee *et al.*, 1988). The omission of a proposed treatment for capital gains is important. Unless their taxation is also harmonised, there will be much wasteful manoeuvring in order to create capital gains in favourable member states, rather than income in any state or capital gains in unfavourable states. Another criticism is that other corporate taxes, like net worth, turnover and local taxes, ought to be included in the harmonisation. More generally, the different rules relating to the calculation of taxable income need attention if total effective tax burdens are to be harmonised. A further criticism is that some countries in the EU are intrinsically less attractive to companies for economic, geographical and political reasons, and that these countries need advantageous corporate tax regimes if they are to encourage investment and employment. Therefore, to harmonise taxation without altering these other factors might give rise to undesirable regional side-effects.

The 'opinion' of the European Parliament (Official Journal, 1979) on the draft Directive stressed the need to include the problem of different tax bases as well as tax systems. Partly as a result of this and partly because member states are not enthusiastic about changing their tax systems or losing flexibility, the 1975 draft Directive - and that concerning the taxation of financial institutions (Commission, 1978) - were delayed. In the 1980s, the Commission had been preparing a Directive on the harmonisation of tax bases. However, in 1990, the Commission abandoned its plans for general harmonisation in order to concentrate on those details that particularly affect cross-border activity (Devereux and Pearson, 1990). These moves include the Parent-Subsidiary Directive (Council, 1990a), which is designed to reduce the taxation paid between companies resident in member states, where there is a holding of at least 25 per cent; and the Merger Directive (Council, 1990b) which allows the deferral of capital gains on certain cross-border reorganisations.

In 1992, the Ruding Committee reported to the EU on the reform of corporation tax (Commission, 1992). The report concerned two main issues: proposals to reduce tax discrimination against cross-border investment and proposals for the harmonisation of tax bases and tax rates. The harmonisation proposals did not recommend immediate action or a system to be adopted as a basis for harmonisation.

In 2001, the Commission established a policy to move towards a 'common consolidated tax base' in the EU. In 2003, the Commission proposed using IFRS accounting as the starting point for the tax base. However, the whole project has generated opposition from companies who fear an attack on the competitiveness of Europe and from particular member states (e.g. Ireland) that operate especially attractive tax regimes. So, progress on this will be slow.

Further reading

For an overview of transfer pricing, see Elliott (2005). For more details on overseas tax systems, see PricewaterhouseCoopers (2001). For a review of EU harmonisation, see Devereux and Pearson (1990).

References

Al-Eryani, M., Alam, P. and Akhter, S. (1990) 'Transfer pricing determinants of US multi-nationals', *Journal of International Business Studies*, 3rd Quarter.

Burke, R. (1979), 'Harmonization of corporation tax,' *Intertax*, June-July.

Commission (1975), Proposal for a Directive Concerning the Harmonization of Systems of Company Taxation and of Withholding Taxes on Dividends, COM(75) 392 final, Brussels.

Commission (1978), *Proposal for a Directive on the Application to Collective Investment Institutions* (of the 1975 draft Directive), COM(78) 340 final, Brussels.

Commission (1992), *Report of the Committee of Independent Experts* on *Company Taxation*.

Council (1990a), Directive 90/435/EEC.

Council (1990b), Directive 90/435/EEC.

Devereux, M. and Pearson, M. (1990), 'Harmonising corporate taxes in Europe', *Fiscal Studies,* February.

Deloitte (2002) *Strategy Matrix for Global Transfer Pricing: Comparison of Methods, Documentation, Penalties, and Other Issues*, Deloitte Touche Tohmatsu, New York.

Dosser, D. (1973), *British Taxation and the Common Market,* Charles Knight, Chapters 1, 4 and 6.

Elliott, J. (2005) 'International transfer pricing', Ch. 11 in Lamb, M., Lymer, A., Freedman, J. and James, S., *Taxation: An Interdisciplinary Approach to Research*, Oxford University Press, Oxford.

Elliott, J. and Emmanuel, C.R. (2000) *International Transfer Pricing: A Study of Cross- border Transactions*, Chartered Institute of Management Accountants, London.

Emmanuel, C.R. (1999) 'Income shifting and international transfer pricing: a three-country example', *Abacus*, Vol. 35, No. 3.

European Taxation (1976), International Bureau of Fiscal Documentation, Amsterdam, Vol. 16, Nos. 2, 3 and 4, pp. 41-51.

Gresik, T.A. and Osmundsen, P. (2008) 'Transfer pricing in vertically integrated industries', *International Tax and Public Finance*, Vol. 15, No. 3.

Harris, D.G. (1993) 'The impact of US tax law revision on multinational corporations' capital location and income shifting decisions', *Journal of Accounting Research*, Vol. 31, Supplement.

Hung Chan, K. and Lo, A.W.Y. (2004) 'The influence of management perception of fundamental variables on the choice of international transfer-pricing methods', *International Journal of Accounting*, Vol. 39, No. 1.

Jacob, J. (1996) 'Taxes and transfer pricing: income shifting and the volume of intrafirm transfers', *Journal of Accounting Research*, Vol. 34, No. 2, Fall.

Johnson, N.B. (2006) 'Divisional performance measurement and transfer pricing for intangible assets', *Review of Accounting Studies*, Vol. 11, Nos 2 and 3.

Klassen, K., Lang, M. and Wolfson, M. (1993) 'Geographic income shifting by multinational corporations in response to tax rate changes', *Journal of Accounting Research*, Vol. 31, Supplement.

Lamb, M., Nobes, C.W. and Roberts, A.D. (1998), 'International variations in the connections between tax and financial reporting', *Accounting and Business Research*, Summer.

Lee, C., Pearson, M. and Smith, S. (1988), *Fiscal Harmonisation: An Analysis of the European Commission's Proposals,* Institute for Fiscal Studies Report, R 28.

Leitch, R.A. and Barrett, K.S. (1992) 'Multinational transfer pricing: objectives and constraints', *Journal of Accounting Literature*, Vol. 11.

Lin, L., Lefebvre, C. and Kantor, J. (1993) 'Economic determinants of international transfer pricing and the related accounting issues, with particular references to Asian Pacific countries', *International Journal of Accounting*, Vol. 28, No. 1.

McAulay, L. and Tomkins, C.R. (1992) 'A review of the contemporary transfer pricing literature with recommendations for future research', *British Journal of Management*, Vol. 3, pp. 101–2.

Neumark Committee (1963), *EEC Reports* on *Tax Harmonization*, International Bureau of Fiscal Documentation, Amsterdam.

Nobes, C.W. (1979), 'Fiscal harmonization and European integration: a comment', *European Law Review*, August.

Nobes, C.W. (1980), 'Imputation systems of corporation tax in the EEC', *Accounting and Business Research*, Spring, Appendix.

Nobes, C.W. and Parker, R.H. (2012), *Comparative International Accounting*, Prentice Hall.

OECD (1974), *Theoretical and Empirical Aspects of Corporate Taxation*, Paris.

OECD (1979) *Transfer Pricing and Multinational Enterprises*, Paris.

OECD (1995/6) *Transfer Pricing Guidelines for Multinational Enterprises and Tax Administrations*, Paris.

Official Journal of the EC (1979), C140, see also report in *Intertax*, October.

Oyelere, P.B. and Emmanuel, C.R. (1998) 'International transfer pricing and income shifting: evidence from the UK', *European Accounting Review*, Vol. 7, No. 4.

Plasschaert, S.R.F. (1985) 'Transfer pricing problems in developing countries', in A.M. Rugman and L. Eden (eds), *Multinationals and Transfer Pricing*, St. Martin's Press, New York.

PricewaterhouseCoopers (2001), *International Tax Summaries*, Wiley, New York.

Rust, M. and Graham, P. (2000) 'Transfer pricing – is your house in order?' *Accounting and Business*, April.

UNCTAD (1997) 'Overview' in *World Investment Report – Transnational Corporations, Market Structure and Competition Policy*, United Nations, Geneva.

US Treasury (1992) *Regulation S.1.6662* of the Internal Revenue Code, Washington, DC.

van den Tempel, A.J. (1974), *Corporation Tax and Individual Income Tax in the EEC*, Brussels.

Wu, F.H. and Sharp, D. (2007) 'An empirical study of transfer pricing practice', *Institutional Executive*, Vol. 22, No. 2.

SELF ASSESSMENT QUESTIONS

Suggested answers to self-assessment questions are given at the back of the book.

14.1   Why would you expect there to be little problem with deferred tax in Germany?

14.2   Which is the most popular system of corporation tax in the EU?

14.3   Is the United Kingdom a high tax country for corporation tax?

DISCUSSION QUESTIONS

1.   In what various ways can the 'economic double taxation' of corporate income be mitigated or eliminated?

2.   How easy is it to harmonise corporate taxation in the EU?

Glossary of tax terms

In addition to the terms included in this glossary, further tax terms are explained in Simon James (2012), A Dictionary of Taxation, *2nd ed. Edward Elgar, Cheltenham.*

Ability-to-pay approach   The view that the amount of taxation individuals pay should be related to their means rather than to the benefits they may receive from public expenditure. See also *Benefit principle.*

Accessions tax   A tax imposed on the recipients of gifts and legacies (in contrast to an Estate duty or the UK *Inheritance tax* where the tax is levied on the amount given by the donor).

Administrative costs   The costs to the public sector of operating a tax.

Ad valorem taxes   Taxes based on the price or value of a good or service.

Advance corporation tax (ACT)   As its name suggests, this is usually not an extra tax on corporations but an early payment of part of the *Corporation tax* liability, triggered by the payment of dividends to a company's shareholders. ACT was introduced in 1973.

Age allowance   A personal allowance granted to elderly people on modest incomes. Allowances Income regarded as tax-free.

Assessment   The detailed calculation of a taxable amount, for example taxable income.

Average rate of tax   The amount of tax paid as a percentage of (usually) income related to a particular period.

Avoidance   The arrangement of one's affairs, within the law, to reduce one's tax liability.

Basic rate of tax   The main rate of income tax in the UK, which is the marginal rate paid by most taxpayers.

Benefit principle   The approach which holds that an equitable tax system is one in which the amount of tax a person pays is in line with the benefits he or she is thought to receive from the public sector. See also *Ability-to-pay approach.*

Benefits in kind   Benefits paid to employees in the form of goods and services, rather than as additional salary. Some of these benefits, such as the use of a company car, are subject to tax.

Black economy   Economic activity which is not declared for tax purposes.

Capital allowances   A system of depreciation charges specifically for the tax assessment of businesses.

Capital gains tax In the UK, a tax first introduced in 1965 on the 'income' due to increases in the value of assets.

Capitalisation Tax Capitalisation describes the effect on the market price of an asset when a tax influences the expected yield of that asset.

Capital transfer tax A tax on the inter-personal movement of wealth. It replaced Estate duty in 1975 and was itself replaced by Inheritance tax in 1986.

Close company A company controlled by five or fewer shareholders or their associates. Code Device used within the *PAYE* system to summarise the amount of allowances due to a taxpayer in order to determine taxable income.

Community charge A form of *Poll tax* introduced to replace domestic local authority Rates in 1989 in Scotland and in 1990 in England and Wales. It was replaced in turn with a Council tax in 1993.

Compliance costs The costs to the private sector of complying with the requirements of a tax.

Corporation tax The equivalent of *Income tax* on UK corporations. This tax was introduced in 1965, amended to the *Imputation system* in 1973, and further reformed in 1984 when rates were lowered but allowances decreased.

Council tax A local tax based mainly on domestic property introduced to replace the *Community charge* in 1993.

Cumulation A system, used within PAYE, of withholding tax at source so that the amount of tax withheld in any week or month is based on the cumulated total of taxable income (gross income less allowances) since the beginning of the tax year. See also *Noncumulation*.

Current year basis of assessment Income is charged to tax in the assessment year in which it arises. See also the *Preceding year basis of assessment*.

Customs duties Taxes levied on imports. The term has also been used to include taxes on exports.

Deadweight loss see *Excess burden*.

Death duties see *Estate duty*.

Development land tax A tax on the gain due to changing the use of land. It was in force in the UK from 1976 to 1986.

Direct tax A tax which is assessed and collected from the individuals who are intended to bear it. See also *Indirect tax*.

Domicile The concept of domicile is complicated and there is no single definition. However, it may be thought of as the country to which a person 'belongs' (though this is not necessarily the one in which that person was born) and it has been said that while 'residence' is where you live, domicile is where you think you live.

Double taxation The situation where the same income is taxed twice. This can happen either because income earned in a foreign country may be subject to tax by both home and foreign governments, or income might be subject to two taxes, for example where income paid out as dividends is subject to both corporation tax and personal income tax.

Earmarked taxes Taxes which are used to pay for specific public expenditures.

Effective rate of tax The *Average rate of tax*.

Emoluments The remuneration of employees for tax purposes, defined by legislation as including 'all salaries, fees, wages, perquisites and profits whatsoever'.

Estate duty A tax on property left on death. In the UK estate duty was replaced by *Capital transfer tax* in 1975, and then *Inheritance tax* in 1986.

Evasion The illegal manipulation of one's affairs to reduce one's tax payments.

Excess burden The loss of economic welfare which results from economic behaviour caused by a tax rather than by consumers' and producers' preferences. The excess burden is a cost to the community over and above the revenue raised.

Excise duties Taxes levied on goods produced for home consumption. See also *Customs duties*.

Exemptions see *Allowances*.

Finance Act The annual Act of Parliament that amends the tax system, fixes tax rates, etc. It follows a Finance Bill, based on a Budget.

Fiscal drag The loss of spending power in the economy which can occur when rising prices and incomes cause a progressive tax system to take an increasing proportion of national income. The effect can be counteracted by indexing personal taxation and the use of indirect taxes based on value (*Ad valorem taxes*).

Fiscal policy The government's use of taxation and public expenditure to influence the aggregate level of economic activity.

Franked investment income Income, received by a company, that has already borne *Corporation tax*; for example, dividends from other UK companies.

GAAR General Anti-Avoidance Rule.

Gross income Total income before the deduction of Allowances and allowable expenses to give taxable income.

Head tax see *Poll tax*.

Higher rate of tax A marginal rate of income tax higher than the Basic rate of tax, which is paid by taxpayers above a certain level of income.

HMRC HM Revenue and Customs

Horizontal equity The similar treatment of individuals in similar economic circumstances. See also *Vertical equity*.

Imputation system The system of *Corporation tax* introduced in the UK in 1973, and used in many other EU countries. It imputes to a company's shareholders all or part of the corporation tax paid by their company. The imputation is carried out by means of a *Tax credit*, which may be used towards payment of the income tax liability on dividend receipts.

Imputed income Income which is not received in money form, such as the benefit that owner-occupiers receive from living in their own homes and, if they were not the owners, for which they would have to pay rent.

Incidence of taxation The eventual distribution of the burden of a tax following any changes in prices, etc., caused by the imposition of the tax.

Income effect The effect on behaviour which is caused by the changes a tax makes to a person's net income. See also *Substitution effect*.

Income tax A tax on the income of individuals that dates back in the UK to the Napoleonic Wars. It was reformed substantially in 1973, with the incorporation of Surtax into the system and the removal of earned income relief.

Independent taxation An arrangement, introduced in the UK in 1990, whereby husbands and wives are taxed independently on their own incomes.

Indirect tax A tax which is levied on a taxpayer with the intention that it should be passed on. For example, value added tax is imposed on, and paid by, businesses but, to the extent that it causes prices to rise, is passed on to the final consumers.

Inflation tax Inflation tax describes the fall in the value of government debt, including money, caused by inflation. In this way wealth is transferred from the holders of that debt to the government.

Inheritance tax A tax on the passing of wealth on death, introduced to replace *Capital transfer tax* in 1986.

Investment income Income such as interest, dividends and rent.

Investment income surcharge An extra part of *Income tax* specifically related to *Investment income*. It was introduced in the UK on the abolition of earned income relief in 1973 but was abolished in turn in 1984.

Laffer curve Named after the American economist Arthur Laffer, an illustration of the idea that increasing the rates of tax leads to an increase but then a decrease in total tax revenues, and that there is some rate at which tax revenue is maximised.

Mainstream corporation tax That part of a company's *Corporation tax* liability that remains to be paid (normally nine months after the company's year-end) in excess of *Advance corporation tax*.

Marginal rate of tax The rate of tax applicable to a small increase in a person's income. National Insurance contributions A form of taxation levied as four 'classes', of which the most important are Class 1 paid by employees and their employers, and Classes 2 and 4 which are paid by the self-employed.

National Insurance contributions A form of UK taxation which may give rise to certain state benefits.

Negative income tax An income maintenance scheme in which those whose income falls below a certain level receive a payment which is linked to their income. There is a minimum level of payment for those with no other source of income.

Neutrality Refers to taxes which do not affect economic behaviour. See also *Excess burden*.

NICs National Insurance contributions.

Non-cumulation A system of withholding tax at source in such a way that the amount of tax withheld in any week or month of the tax year is based on the income received in that period less the appropriate fraction of annual allowances and deductions, but without reference to the income received or tax paid in preceding periods. See also *Cumulation*.

Optimal taxation The design of tax systems to minimise the Excess burden of taxes while achieving a socially desirable distribution of income.

PAYE (Pay-As-You-Earn) The mechanism for withholding tax from wages and salaries. In the UK this is done on a cumulative basis (see *Cumulation*), but in nearly all other countries which operate an income tax, on a non-cumulative basis (see *Non-cumulation*).

Payroll tax A tax on the income from labour. In the UK *National Insurance contributions* (Classes 1, 2 and 4) may be described as a payroll tax.

Personal allowances see *Allowances*.

Poll tax Also known as a head tax: a lump sum tax levied on every person. 'Poll' refers to the part of the head on which hair grows, but baldness does not mean exemption from a poll tax!

Potentially exempt transfer (PET) A transfer of wealth which would become subject to *Inheritance tax* if the transferor died within seven years.

Poverty trap The situation where either all or most of any increase in earnings is lost through a combination of income tax, National Insurance contributions and the withdrawal of income-related social security benefits. See also *Unemployment trap*.

Preceding year basis of assessment Income is charged to tax in anyone year on the basis of the preceding year's taxable income. See also *Current year basis of assessment*.

Progressive tax A tax where the *Marginal rate* exceeds the *Average rate* so that the proportion of income (or wealth, etc.) taken in tax rises as income (or wealth, etc.) rises.

Proportional tax A tax where the *Marginal rate* and *Average rate* are equal so that the same proportion of tax is taken from all incomes, however large or small.

Rates A local property tax which can be traced back to the poor rate of Elizabethan times and even earlier forms of taxation. However, domestic rates were replaced by the *Community charge* and then by the *Council tax*. Business rates remain.

Regressive tax A tax where the *Marginal rate* is less than the *Average rate* so that the proportion of income taken in tax falls as income rises.

'Roll-over' relief This relief may be available where a business asset is sold and the proceeds used to buy a replacement asset.

Small companies relief A lower rate of *Corporation tax* applied to companies with income below a certain level.

Standard rate of tax Before 1973 income tax was levied at a single 'standard rate' and a separate *surtax* was levied on higher incomes. In April 1973 the two were unified with the standard rate becoming the *Basic rate of tax* and surtax the higher rates. However the term 'standard rate' is still widely and erroneously used to refer to the basic rate of tax.

Substitution effect The effect on economic behaviour caused by the changes a tax makes to relative prices, relative wages, etc. See also *Income effect*.

Surtax see *Standard rate of tax*.

Tariffs Taxes imposed on imports and (sometimes) exports. The term was originally used to describe an official list of *Customs duties* to be imposed on imports and exports.

Tax A compulsory levy made by a public authority for which nothing is received directly in return.

Taxable income Gross income less allowable expenses.

Tax base That which is liable to taxation, for example, income, wealth or expenditure. Tax breaks US term for tax concessions.

Tax credit 1. A credit against tax. For example, in the UK corporation tax system, dividends to shareholders are accompanied by a tax credit which is set against shareholders' tax liabilities.

    2. A tax credit system is a form of *Negative income tax*.

Tax expenditure A fiscal advantage conferred on a group of taxpayers, or in respect of a particular activity, by reducing tax liability rather than the payment of a cash subsidy.

Tax havens Countries or areas where tax rates are substantially lower than those to which a taxpayer would be subject elsewhere.

Tax planning The arrangement of one's affairs so as to maximise after-tax returns.

Unearned income see *Investment income*.

Unemployment trap Similar to the Poverty trap except that the disincentives are sufficient to discourage a person from taking a job at all.

Unitary tax A tax based on the proportion of a business's world-wide income and not just the income arising where the business is being taxed.

Value added tax (VAT) A tax levied on the value a business has added to its outputs. In other words, it is the value of the business's outputs less the value of its inputs.

Vertical equity The consideration of the extent to which individuals in different economic circumstances should be treated differently. See also *Horizontal equity*.

Answers to self-assessment questions

Chapter 2

2.1 (a) To overcome inefficiencies in the market system.
(b) Redistribution of income and wealth towards society's view of what is equitable.
(c) Economic stabilisation.

2.2 (a) In the provision of public goods.
(b) Merit goods.
(c) Where there are external effects.
(d) Imperfect competition.

2.3 One possible definition of a tax is: 'A tax is a compulsory levy made by a public authority for which nothing is received directly in return'. However, like many definitions, it may not always work with precision in practice.

2.4 Corporation tax is a direct tax.

2.5 The average rate of tax is the percentage of income paid in tax. The concept can also be
applied to other taxes.

2.6 The marginal rate of tax is that applying to a small increase in income (or other tax
base).

2.7 No. A tax which simply takes more from those on higher incomes than it does from those on lower incomes is not necessarily progressive. A progressive tax must take a higher proportion of income as income rises. In other words, the marginal rate of tax must exceed the average rate of tax. Also, of course, a rich person could have a smaller income than a poorer person, so we would need to ask: 'Progressive' with respect to what criterion?

2.8 The main criteria are:
Efficiency
Incentives
Equity
Macroeconomic considerations
Administrative aspects.

Chapter 3

3.1   The excess burden of a tax is the loss of economic welfare caused when a tax distorts the preferences of consumers or producers or both.

3.2   Excess burden will be influenced by a range of factors including:
(a) Whether or not the relevant part of the economy is operating efficiently.
(b) The elasticity of supply and demand of the goods and services subject to tax.
(c) The elasticity of factor inputs.
(d) The width of the tax base.

3.3   The individual would be likely to favour the unpleasant job.

3.4   A tax might be used to increase economic efficiency if it offset some other economic distortion. For example, the production of a good might involve external costs, such as pollution, on other people. Suppliers might not take account of such costs in a purely market system. However a tax on the pollution could simulate those costs to producers and encourage them to reduce output or to tackle the pollution problem directly.

3.5   The excess burden of a tax imposed on a good which has a zero elasticity of demand is zero.

3.6   Zero.

3.7   Administrative costs and compliance costs.

3.8   Tax expenditure occurs when some fiscal advantage is conferred on certain individuals, or in respect of a particular activity, by reducing tax liability rather than by a direct cash payment.

Chapter 4

4.1   The income effect of a tax is the effect on the taxpayer's economic behaviour as a result of the change a tax makes to a person's income.

4.2   The income effect is determined by the average rate of tax.

4.3   The substitution effect is the effect on a taxpayer's economic behaviour caused by the change a tax makes to relative prices, including wages as the price of labour.

4.4   The substitution effect is determined by the marginal rate of tax.

4.5   If taxes were increased, the income effect would be likely to encourage taxpayers to work more.

4.6   If the marginal rate of income tax were increased, the substitution effect would be likely to encourage taxpayers to work less.

4.7   The income effect.

4.8   This can be analysed by looking at each range of income. For those with incomes below £3,000, tax liability remains zero and there is no income effect. There is also no substitution effect unless individuals limited their work to stay under the £3,000 threshold. For such people the change would generate a substitution effect in favour of more work. For those between £3,000 and £4,000 the outcome is uncertain. The income effect means they are better off, which might be a disincentive to work, but the lower marginal rate produces a substitution effect favourable to work. For those with more than

£4,000 the marginal rate of tax and therefore the substitution effect is unchanged. However, the income effect means they are better off, which might be a disincentive.

4.9 The double taxation of savings is said to occur when the interest on money saved out of after-tax income is also subject to income tax.

4.10 A tax system with loss-offsets might encourage enterprise since the government through the tax system would share in both the profits (through the tax) and losses (through the loss-offsets). This would reduce both the return and the risk of investment for the entrepreneur. The income effect might then encourage the individual to increase income by investing more or by switching to higher return/higher risk projects.

Chapter 5

5.1 Horizontal equity requires that equal people in equal circumstances be taxed equally.
Vertical equity requires that relevant differences between people should lead to different taxation.

5.2 There is no clear answer to this question. It would be possible to use endowment-based criteria, utility-maximising criteria or equity-based criteria. There is no strong philosophical basis for concentrating on one of these to the exclusion of the others.

5.3 Ability-to-pay is of course affected by income and wealth. It might be measured by expenditure. It might also be affected by non-discretionary spending, e.g. basic living expenses. Some expenses are discretionary in the long-run but non-discretionary in the short-run, e.g. paying for children and for mortgage interest.

5.4 Expenditure taxes (e.g. VAT) are levied on producers and distributors but are to some extent borne by consumers. Selective taxes on particular goods will affect the owners and workers of businesses in that field, depending on the elasticity of supply and demand. In the end, all the tax is borne by individuals somewhere.

5.5 The value of an asset reflects its expected post-tax income. Obviously, this can change as taxes change.

5.6 Distribution and redistribution can be measured in various ways, including by Gini coefficients. It is clear that the UK system does redistribute income, but that the degree of effect varies over time. The degree of progressivity has reduced over the last decade.

5.7 Marginal rates exceed average rates in a progressive system.

Chapter 6

6.1 Fiscal policy is the use of taxation and public spending to influence the overall level of economic activity.

6.2 The tax multiplier is the relationship between changes in taxation and changes in national income. A simple formula is:

$$\frac{-b}{1-b}$$

where b is the marginal propensity to consume.

6.3 'Crowding-out' describes the possibility that the effectiveness of an expansionary fiscal policy through increased public expenditure might be reduced if it displaced some private expenditure.

6.4 Three types of lag are the recognition lag, the implementation lag and the response lag.

6.5 Criteria for judging taxes as instruments of stabilisation policy might include their appropriateness, that is whether they have a strong influence on aggregate demand, the speed with which they can be adjusted and the size of the tax base.

Chapter 7

7.1 It has been argued that earmarked taxes might keep government decisions closer to taxpayers' preferences and that individuals might be more willing to pay their taxes.

7.2 One definition of tax compliance is taxpayer behaviour which is consistent with the spirit as well as the letter of the law.

7.3 Income tax and value added tax.

Chapter 8

8.1 Total income less any allowances or expenses to which the taxpayer is entitled.

8.2 There are several arguments for taxing investment income at higher rates than employment income. They include that investment may be a more reliable and stable source of income than employment, that employment may involve more expenses than investment, that the ownership of capital provides benefits over and above the pecuniary return and that earnings represent a return to current work whereas investment income represents either past work or inherited wealth. Arguments against a higher rate of tax for investment income include the possibility of discouraging saving and investment.

8.3 The individual basis of taxation assesses individuals without reference to their family circumstances whereas the aggregation basis uses the family as the basis of assessment. 8.4 Class I National Insurance contributions are payable in respect of employees and Classes 2 and 4 are levied on the self-employed.

8.5 The basic argument for a capital gains tax is that capital gains are a form of income and, if income is taxed, so should capital gains be. On efficiency grounds, this is to remove the incentive for taxpayers to convert other forms of income into capital gains to avoid tax. On equity grounds, it would appear unfair to tax some forms of income and not others, given that capital gains are unequally distributed across the population.

8.6 A non-cumulative system might tend to over-withhold tax because it deals with each pay period separately. If a person's income changes, he or she might then face higher tax rates in the high income periods than would be appropriate given the lower income received in other periods.

Chapter 9

9.1 The loss of income-related benefits caused by an increase in income.

9.2 It has been argued that cash is the best form of material assistance because it can be used by the recipients to buy what they need the most.

9.3 No - income that is saved is treated more favourably by an expenditure tax than it is by an income tax. This is because the expenditure tax allows the tax to be deferred until the savings are spent - which means that interest can be received on the gross amount.

Chapter 10

10.1 There are several definitions of wealth. One is a stock of resources at a particular point in time. Another is any tangible or intangible possession which can be exchanged for money or goods. A basic feature of wealth is that it has the potential to generate income.

10.2 Human capital is wealth tied up in human beings. Investments can be made in increasing the productivity of people as well as that of other factors of production.

10.3 In the sense that the UK inheritance tax is levied on the amount the transferor leaves on death, or in the years just before death, rather than on the amounts that various individuals actually inherit.

10.4 The main exemptions from inheritance tax are:
Transfers between spouses £3,000 annual exemption
Normal expenditure out of income
Small gifts exemption (up to £250 per person) Gifts on marriage
Gifts to charities
Gifts to certain specified national bodies Gifts of national interest
Donations to qualifying political parties.

10.5 No. The £6,000 gift is exempt through the use of the £3,000 annual exemption and the £3,000 unused annual exemption of the immediately preceding year.

10.6 The main characteristic of an accessions tax is that the rate of tax is calculated on the basis of the amount of capital a person receives rather than the amount a person gives or bequeaths. These receipts would be cumulated over a person's lifetime and the accessions tax levied on the total.

10.7 If a donor-based accessions tax were in force, the rich old lady would minimise the tax payable if she left her money to the nephew who had not received an inheritance. Under a donor-based capital transfer tax, the tax would be the same whichever nephew received the money. However, when the money came to be passed on again, there would be a lower liability if it passed through the hands of the nephew who had not already inherited a large amount.

Chapter 11

11.1 Indirect taxes can assist in the redistribution of income, but they are generally not as effective as direct taxes for this purpose. However, indirect taxes can correct for market imperfections and can be used to encourage or discourage particular purchases or activities. Some indirect taxes are buoyant with respect to inflation.

11.2 A cascade system is a multi-stage sales tax where the tax at a stage is based on the gross price (including tax) up to that stage. Such a tax is inefficient because it encourages the removal of stages, Le. vertical integration.

11.3 The 'excess burden' of rates is fairly low because property cannot be moved. The administrative costs, compliance costs and disincentive effects are also fairly low. However, rates are not buoyant with respect to inflation and they are not closely related to ability-to-pay. Perhaps the main reason for the popularity of rates as a local tax is that all the alternatives seem worse.

Chapter 12

12.1 Companies might be seen as separate legal and accounting entities from their owners, and therefore as possessing separate taxable capacity. Certainly, the existence of retained earnings might suggest an argument for taxation. Companies might also be seen as taxable because of benefits that they gain from the state, in terms of legal rights or protection.

12.2 The rules are to be found in the Income and Corporation Taxes Act, supplemented by Finance Acts and tax cases. The Inland Revenue operates statements of practice, which could be challenged in a court. In principle, taxable income is accounting net profit with certain adjustments. So, many accounting rules are relevant.

12.3 There are no capital allowances for commercial buildings, but industrial buildings receive 2 per cent writing down allowances on cost. Plant and machinery receive a 20 per cent allowance on a reducing balance basis.

12.4 Corporate capital gains are calculated as for personal capital gains, although there is no personal allowance. The chargeable gains (relieved by indexation) are taxed as ordinary income.

12.5 The difference relates to the treatment of dividends paid by a company. Under the classical system, the dividends are fully taxed in the hands of the recipient shareholders. Under the imputation system, the shareholders receive a tax credit for some or all of the corporation tax paid by their company.

12.6 Dividends are taxed to Dividend Income which, for basic rate taxpayers, applies a rate of 10 per cent to dividends grossed up by the tax credit. In other words, no extra tax is payable.

12.7 ACT was designed to ensure that a company paid at least enough corporation tax to cover tax credits. It also gave a more regular flow of tax receipts to the government.

Chapter 13

13.1 The small companies rate is designed to reduce the burden of taxation on the companies that are most likely to need to rely on their retained profits for investment. Small companies have no access to certain capital markets, e.g. the Stock Exchange. Also, a lower rate for small companies may be fairer when compared to the same low rate for the income of small unincorporated businesses.

13.2 The corporation tax is not progressive in the sense that, for large companies, the marginal rate equals the average rate. This is also true for companies below the lower threshold of the relief. However, for the many companies receiving tapering relief, the marginal rate is above the average rate. Also, large companies pay a higher average (and marginal) rate than the smallest companies.

13.3 The general cause of deferred tax is reversing timing differences between taxable expenses/ revenues and accounting expenses/revenues. Another way of looking at this (e.g. in the United States) is that it relates to temporary differences between the tax basis and the accounting basis of an asset or liability. Some examples of causes are capital allowances (compared to depreciation) and, for temporary differences, the revaluation of assets for accounting purposes.

Chapter 14

14.1 Because of the Massgeblichkeitsprinzip, there are generally few differences between tax and accounting figures in Germany. Therefore, deferred tax is a minor problem.

14.2 At the end of 1994, of the then twelve member states of the EU, the imputation system was marginally the most common, even after Belgium and Denmark had moved back from this to the classical system. By 1999, with more countries having joined the EU, imputation was still the most common. At the end of 1994, of the then twelve member states of the EU, the imputation system was marginally the most common, even after Belgium and Denmark had moved back from this to the classical system. By 1999, with more countries having joined the EU, imputation was still the most common. However, most of the imputation systems have now been removed, and replaced once more with classical systems.

14.3 As may be seen in the text, the rates of corporation tax in the United Kingdom are among the highest in the EU. A decade ago, the UK's rates were the lowest. Of course, many companies benefit from the 'small companies' rate. In addition, there are no local income taxes, as there are in Germany or Italy, for example. However, concentration on rates ignores the fact that the calculation of taxable income varies internationally. For example, German companies seem generally to have lower accounting profits than UK companies. This affects their tax bills. Nevertheless, UK taxable profit is generally lower than accounting profit, partly because of capital allowances.

Index

ASTON UNIVERSITY
LIBRARY SERVICES

WITHDRAWN
FROM STOCK